basic research
methods

basic research methods

carol a. saslow
OREGON STATE UNIVERSITY

ADDISON-WESLEY PUBLISHING COMPANY

Reading, Massachusetts
Menlo Park, California · London · Amsterdam · Don Mills, Ontario · Sydney

Copyright © 1982 by Addison-Wesley Publishing Company, Inc. Philippines copyright 1982 by Addison-Wesley Publishing Company, Inc.

ISBN 0-201-06640-8
ABCDEFGHIJ-AL-8987654321

__preface__

For people interested in studying one of the social sciences or in working in the human services area, learning about scientific methodology and statistics may seem to be a major obstacle. Yet a career in a social science or in human services will be greatly hampered by a lack of expertise in basic research methodology. Even those of us who are not expecting to be directly involved in doing research will find that much of the information we need to understand must be deciphered from research literature. For people who do not have an extensive science background (or who may even have a definite allergy to science) simply reading a book about research methods and memorizing formulas and definitions doesn't help very much. What is needed is presentation of scientific concepts in everyday language and application of these concepts to real, intelligible social science problems. Research methodology is something you learn by doing rather than by just reading about it.

The structure of this book encourages you to interact with the text and to apply the information as you read. The content of the book is broken down into sections of a few pages each. At the end of each section is a list of *Behavioral Objectives* which tell you what you should be able to do with the information you have just been given. You don't have to guess about what your instructor wants you to get out of this book. If you can do the objectives, you've mastered the material; and if you can't, you should seek help from your instructor. Some of the objectives are also illustrated by more specific *Sample Test Questions* which test your knowledge. Many of these test questions reappear as examples in later sections so that you can apply new concepts to research situations with which you are already familiar.

Each section also has a *Recapitulation* which is a succinct summary of all the important points of the section. The Recapitulations have been written so that by themselves they form a much shorter and more sophisticated text on research methodology. Usually, reading the Recapitulation and checking yourself against the Behavioral Objectives will be all that is necessary to review for a test.

The book begins with simple concepts which are progressively elaborated. Often the same idea will reappear several times at increasing levels of complexity. The book starts by using everyday language, but by the time you have finished it, you should be comfortable using common research terms. You must master each part of the material as you read. In later sections, the Behavioral Objectives and Sample Test Questions will require that you display skills learned in earlier sections. If you fail to acquire one of the more basic concepts, you'll have trouble understanding some of those that come later.

This book has been successfully used in a variety of learning situations with both college students and professionals. In a personalized self-instruction course, the students worked on their own with the text and informed the instructors when they had finished a section. They were then tested on one or more of the Behavioral Objectives and proceeded to the next section only after demonstrating mastery. In a modular learning course, students attended lectures and discussions and took regularly scheduled weekly tests covering the Behavioral Objectives of several sections. If they did not meet the instructor's criterion for success, they tested on that module, or part, of the course at a later date. Finally, in more traditional lecture/midterm/final courses, the instructors lectured on research material from their own social science area while the students used the book to learn the basics as specified by the Behavioral Objectives. This approach both helped the students learn research methodology and exposed them to information in a specific social science field. For any of these course structures, a coordinated laboratory or a subsequent individual research project can help the student put the research methodology into practice.

By the time you finish this book, you'll be able to independently design a social science research project, carry it out, analyze its results, and report on them to your colleagues. Even if you don't actually do any research, you'll find the literature in your field a lot easier to evaluate and understand.

Corvallis, Oregon   C.A.S.
September 1981

acknowledgments

Many people other than the author are necessary to development of a book of the nature and scale of *Basic Research Methods*. Although they cannot be recognized individually, approximately 1000 students to date have patiently coped with the text in manuscript form and have given extensive feedback through personal comments, test performances, and attitude surveys. Since this was to be a text for the student, this input has shaped and reshaped the resulting book. Over the years several graduate teaching assistants have participated in teaching my research methods course, and in particular I would like to recognize the contributions of Jeff Le Roux, Mike Reed, and Dave Watkins. Since it is all too easy for an instructor to get used to teaching things her way, the other instructors who have used my materials for part or all of their course have made a substantial contribution to the book. In particular, I would like to thank Janice N. Yamodis of the Department of Nursing, Southern Oregon State College, who taught a class of nursing students from the manuscript, and my husband, Michael G. Saslow, who stepped back into a teaching role especially to try out my materials with graduate students and professionals in an Oregon State University summer program. Both Michael and my mother-in-law, Julia A. Saslow, took time from their busy professional lives to help with the arduous labor of editing and proofing the manuscript. Throughout the task, we all appreciated the fast and accurate typing, as well as the enduring good humor, of Donna Norvell-Race who plowed her way through several drafts. My neighbor and friend, Angela L. Phelps deserves recognition for sacrificing valuable time from her high school activities and horseback riding to help me with the job of indexing. Lastly, I want to acknowledge the contribution of the reviewers and editorial staff of Addison-Wesley in helping to bring to completion a project of five years duration.

contents

5 DESCRIBING WHAT YOU'VE FOUND

6 ANALYZING RESEARCH RESULTS

7 INTERPRETING THE RESULTS OF RESEARCH

8 COMMUNICATING ABOUT YOUR RESEARCH

9 PLANNING YOUR OWN RESEARCH PROJECT

chapter 1

what is research?

SECTION 1: WHY DO RESEARCH?

IN THE BEGINNING

We all have a great store of wisdom in our heads and rarely ask where it came from. By and large, the knowledge upon which we base our decisions comes from what we have been told rather than from direct experience. We usually are not too careful about the source of our information, even when it is the basis of very important decisions. Doing our own research and experimentation allows us to make direct examination of the information we already possess as well as providing us with new information.

In Mark Twain's story, "Eve's Autobiography," (1962), Eve examines the problem of being newborn in a world in which knowledge is not communicated:

> But studying, learning, inquiring into the cause and nature and purpose of everything we came across, were passions with us, and this research filled our days with brilliant and absorbing interest. . . . Each was ambitious to beat the other in scientific discovery, and this incentive added a spur to our friendly rivalry, and effectively protected us against falling into idle and unprofitable ways and frivolous pleasure seeking. (p. 71)

Some of Adam and Eve's experiments bear fruit:

> Our first memorable scientific discovery was the law that water and like fluids run downhill, not up. It was Adam that found this out. Days and days he conducted his experiments secretly, saying nothing to me about it; for he wanted to make perfectly sure before he spoke. . . . My astonishment was his triumph, his reward. He took me from rill to rill—dozens of them—saying always, "There—you see it runs downhill—in every case it runs downhill, never up. My theory was right; it is proven, it is established, nothing can controvert it."
>
> In the present day, no child wonders to see the water run down and not up, but it was an amazing thing then, and as hard to believe as any fact I have ever encountered. . . . (pp. 71–72)

1

In the story, Adam and Eve proceed from one discovery to another about their environment and themselves. However, the mere fact that they are engaged in "scientific research" does not always lead them to interpretations that are beyond challenge:

> I scored the next great triumph for science myself: to wit, how the milk gets into the cow. Both of us had marveled over that mystery a long time. We had followed the cows around for years—that is, in the daytime—but had never caught them drinking a fluid of that color. And so, at last we said they undoubtedly procured it at night. Then we took turns and watched them by night. The result was the same—the puzzle remained unsolved. . . . One night as I lay musing, and looking at the stars, a grand idea flashed through my head, and I saw my way! . . . deep in the woods I chose a small grassy spot and wattled it in, making a secure pen; then I enclosed a cow in it. I milked her dry, then left her there, a prisoner. There was nothing there to drink—she must get milk by her secret alchemy, or stay dry.
>
> All day I was in a fidget, and could not talk connectedly I was so preoccupied; but Adam was busy trying to invent the multiplication table, and did not notice. Toward sunset he had got as far as 6 times 9 are 27, and while he was drunk with the joy of his achievement and dead to my presence and all things else, I stole away to my cow. My hand shook so with excitement and with dread failure that for some moments I could not get a grip on a teat; then I succeeded, and the milk came! Two gallons. Two gallons, and nothing to make it out of. I knew at once the explanation: *The milk was not taken in by the mouth, it was condensed from the atmosphere through the cow's hair.* I ran and told Adam, and his happiness was as great as mine, and his pride in me inexpressible.
>
> Presently he said, "Do you know, you have not made merely one weighty and far-reaching contribution to science, but two!"
>
> And that was true. By a series of experiments we had long ago arrived at the conclusion that atmospheric air consisted of water in invisible suspension; also, that the components of water were hydrogen and oxygen, in the proportion of two parts of the former to one of the latter, and expressible by the symbol H_2O. My discovery revealed the fact that there was still another ingredient—milk. We enlarged the symbol to H_2O,M. (p. 73)

All the steps of scientific research are shown in Twain's story. Eve asks a question to which she wants an answer. When systematic observation fails to provide an answer, she then plans an experiment, devising a methodology and working out a way to collect data. After analyzing her data (determining that she has two gallons of milk) and, presumably, checking to see that her methods have not gone astray (namely, that the cow had not strayed over the fence), she reports the results and her conclusion to her colleague. Finally, she and Adam attempt to generalize her conclusion more widely and fit it in with other information they already possess.

Adam and Eve's conclusion may be open to challenge, as are the results and conclusions of any research. One of the greatest strengths of scientific method as a way of gaining knowledge is that this knowledge is always subject to further testing. Eve's experiment should be conducted on other cows; the cow she watched might be unique. The experiment also should be continued for a longer period of time; there might be distressing effects on milk production, not to mention the cow, if Eve continued to withhold fluids. If she thinks hair is important in the process, she might try shaving the cow. She might also try confining the cow to areas where no grass grows, which should not affect milk production if her air-suspension theory is correct. A single experiment or research project rarely provides final answers; it simply helps eliminate unlikely explanations. Scientists are not only interested in testing what they have been told, they also must be able to pinpoint weaknesses in applications of scientific method and weight the truth of any conclusions accordingly.

WHAT IS WRONG WITH BELIEVING WHAT WE ARE TOLD?

After all, we're not Adam and Eve. In fact, according to the anthropologists, what distinguishes us from monkeys is that we have culture which can be handed down from generation to generation. This culture consists of physical objects and knowledge communicated both orally and in writing. If we want to know how the milk gets into the cow, all we need do is ask someone or look it up in a book. Yet if you were to pursue this question with someone who "really knows," you would be likely to find out that this is an area of current research. The improvement of milk production through feeding, genetics, and milking practices is still going on. The answer you get this year may not be the same as the one you would get ten years from now, and it certainly won't be the same as the answer you would have got in 1900.

Is the solution, then, to believe nothing of what we are told and to discover everything through direct experience? The problems would be overwhelming. There simply isn't enough time to gather all information firsthand. Besides, a small portion of direct experience by itself can be misleading, as we saw with Eve's work. What we need is a means of estimating how much we should trust a particular piece of information. In addition, we need a process by which we can generate new information when we feel the need for a firmer base for our decisions.

Scientific method is a set of procedures that allows us to generate information of high quality and to check the worth of what we have been told by others. Scientific research does not provide final answers, but it increases the probability that the information obtained does reflect reality. One hallmark of scientific method is that it is self-correcting. Properly applied, scientific procedures will expose weaknesses in information gathered in earlier research and suggest new research to deal with these weaknesses. Scientists "believe" something only on a provisional basis. They are aware that any particular belief may have to be altered because of future research findings. Behaving like a scientist means fighting a continuing battle against the inclination to be dogmatic about what we "know." It is especially important for those of us hoping to work with other people to ride herd on our beliefs. Whether we are psychologists, sociologists, educators, anthropologists, health-service practitioners, politicians, or business managers, we are constantly making decisions that affect our fellow human beings. Our work often costs other people money, takes up their time, subjects them to discomfort, interferes with their family relationships, affects their health, changes their children, and, sometimes, may even endanger their lives. Considering this, it is our responsibility to base our decisions on the best possible information and not just on our unsubstantiated beliefs. We need to become proficient in testing our beliefs, in examining what we are told, and in improving the quality of information upon which we base decisions.

SURELY WE CAN BELIEVE KNOWLEDGE GAINED THROUGH OUR OWN EXPERIENCE

Let's consider the kind of information that most of us would expect to be sure of through our own personal knowledge. If you are one of the vast number of people who drink soda pop, you undoubtedly have a favorite brand. You would, of course, be very upset if an enterprising soda pop supplier hooked up all the buttons on the machine so that the brew supplied was the same no matter which cola you had selected. If you paid for Pepsi and your cup contained Royal Crown, you'd taste it at once and make a fuss. Or would you?

Research has revealed the surprising fact that most people would be unlikely to detect the switch (Pronko and Bowles, 1949). It seems that people in general are not very good at recognizing by taste alone the cola they say they prefer. Probably the most important factor in determining preference for particular colas is the money spent on advertising and not taste. Why isn't it generally known that we can be fooled this way? To get this kind of information you have to do more than rely on your own personal experience.

You need to set up a situation where you are sure that the only way people can identify the cola they say they prefer is by taste. You put out samples of the three most popular brands, ask a friend to tell you which of the three she prefers and then ask her to taste all of them and pick the one she said she preferred. Of course, you couldn't display the samples in their original bottles, because then your friend might be choosing by label rather than taste. It wouldn't be a fair test, either, if the colas differed in temperature or in how long the bottles had been opened. So you carefully open the bottles straight from the refrigerator and pour the colas into three identical cups. If you know which cola is in which cup, you should leave the room while your friend is making her selection. You'd be surprised how much you can convey by an involuntary movement, gasp, nod, or smile as you see your friend start to choose a cup you know is "wrong." You want to be absolutely sure that her choice is based on her taste and not on your unconscious hints.

Unfortunately, even if your friend makes the correct choice, it still doesn't mean that she picked the cola by taste. Since you put out only three kinds, she has a one-in-three chance of guessing correctly even if all the samples taste like dishwater. This means you would either have to run lots of tests on this friend to see whether her success rate is considerably better than what she could be expected to do by guessing, or you would have to test a large number of friends to see whether more than one-third of them are correct in their identifications. Running repeated tests on the same person or testing more than one person raises yet another problem. The order in which your friends taste the colas may affect their identifications. For example, there may be a preference for choosing the last one sampled, or one of the colas might be so potent that it kills the taste for anything following. To give each cola a fair chance, you would have to switch around the order in which they are tasted in the different tests.

Obviously, you would have to take many precautions before you could generate dependable information on even so simple a question as whether people can identify by taste the cola they say they prefer to drink. Personal experience, in the absence of such precautions, can yield misleading information. Even if you are able to establish with these precautions that something is true for yourself, you still don't know how true it is for other people. *You* might be able to identify your favorite cola by taste every time, but that doesn't mean everyone else can. Research allows you to organize and extend your personal experiences to gain firsthand information that is more in accord with reality.

WHY NOT ASK AN EXPERT?

Asking an expert is the way most of us seek to improve the quality of our information when making decisions. Being unable to research every issue for ourselves, we ask the opinion of someone more knowledgeable. There is nothing wrong with this, as long as we remember that experts too have to get their information from somewhere, so the quality of their advice will vary. Experts obtain some of their information from their own research, but a lot of it comes from other experts. And very often, when we chase down the origins of some widely-accepted piece of "expert advice," we find that it stems from a single rather shaky source. Even if you don't intend to do much research yourself, you need to be able to evaluate the research done by others so you can judge whether the information offered by experts is in fact worth anything.

THE CASE OF HANS THE CLEVER HORSE

Experts were certainly fooled in the case of "Hans the Clever Horse" (von Pfungst, 1911). In the early part of this century, several experts were asked to determine whether a mere animal could reason and "talk." Hans had been trained by a retired mathematics teacher, Mr. von Osten, using methods developed at the end of the nineteenth century for teaching severely handicapped deaf-mute children. These techniques had achieved some spectacular successes, most notably that of Helen Keller who within a few years progressed from "animallike" behavior to enrolment at Radcliffe College. Mr. von Osten suspected that animals might have great reasoning powers but, in the absence of language be, like the deaf-mute children, unable to demonstrate them.

Over several years, von Osten laboriously taught the horse to communicate by tapping its forefoot and moving its head. A nod of the head meant, "Yes"; a shake, "No." Numerical answers could be given by repeated taps. Mr. von Osten devised a code for verbal information in which each letter was represented by a pair of two numbers. The letter *A,* for example, was coded as "one tap, pause, one tap"; and the letter *I* could be given as "three taps, pause, two taps." After learning to tap his foot or move his head when questioned, Hans was presented with simple problems and given a piece of bread or a carrot for correct answers. At first von Osten had to ask the same question over and over again to get a correct answer. After several months of work, however, Hans began to answer correctly questions he had not been asked before. Von Osten borrowed equipment from a local school, made up daily lesson plans, spent several hours a day with his pupil, and took him through a series of increasingly complicated problems. Of course, the teacher always kept the bag of treats handy (even not-so-clever horses don't work for free).

At the end of his education, Hans could spell words spoken to him, written on a slate, or represented in pictures. He could locate objects requested verbally or in writing. He especially excelled in mathematics. He could solve complicated numerical problems in his head, tell time, make calculations based on the calendar, and handle money problems. He could correctly recognize musical tones and tell you what note should be eliminated to make a discordant chord sound more pleasing. He had a fabulous memory, readily naming from photographs people whom he had met only briefly months before. Most impressive of all, strangers who had never worked with him could ask him questions and he would answer correctly (provided they came supplied with goodies).

Hans became the toast of Germany. His image appeared on liquor labels and picture postcards. His name was immortalized in vaudeville songs. His ungainly form was duplicated in a line of children's toys. Fortunately Hans, who lacked beauty, had brains.

As well as arousing popular interest, Hans's abilities were important to educators and scientists. Not only did the results of his training have possible implications for human education, there was considerable theoretical debate at the time as to whether or not animals possessed reasoning power in any way similar to that of humans. It was considered so important to determine whether Hans was actually reasoning and communicating that an official commission of 13 scientists, educators, and public officials met to examine the horse in 1904. A circus manager, familiar with horse tricks, was included in the group because he would be especially alert to any signals being given to Hans. Hans passed this examination with flying colors. The experts were so impressed that they published a report stating that there was no evidence of any intentional influence or aid on the part of Hans's questioners. Moreover, they went on to say that "unintentional signs of the kind which are at present familiar are . . . excluded." Individual scientists went further and touted Hans's humanlike reasoning abilities. A few die-hards, who still thought he was being signaled, muttered about telepathy and "N-rays."

One scientist, however, was dissatisfied. Oskar von Pfungst had observed that Hans liked to face his questioner and suspected that this might be due to more than mere politeness. Pfungst first asked that Hans be tested with blinders positioned so that he could see only his questioner. He then tried a very simple experiment. He wrote numbers on a series of cards and held them up one by one. He asked Hans to tap out the number written on each card. Half of the cards Pfungst held so that only Hans, but not Pfungst, could see what was written on them. For the cards that Pfungst could see, Hans performed with his usual brilliance, scoring 92 percent correct. But for those that Pfungst could not see, Hans scored a miserable 8 percent. Pfungst repeated similar experiments on all Hans's abilities. Again and again, he got the same result: Hans answered correctly only when the questioner knew the correct answer.

Why hadn't this been discovered before? Many experts and ordinary people had "talked" with Hans. Nobody had tried systematic experiments, however; people had simply relied on their own experience. As Pfungst said, they had been misled by "looking for, in the horse, what should have been sought in the man." The issue had been further confused because horses have excellent distance vision. On the rare occasions that a speaker didn't know the correct answer, Hans had been able to see members of the audience who did.

Exactly what it was that people were unintentionally doing to control Hans's behavior remained to be discovered. Pfungst returned to watching Mr. von Osten and others when they were working with Hans. After much careful observation, he decided that most people made tiny involuntary movements of the head, shoulders, and eyebrows when asking questions and listening to answers. As soon as they stated a problem to Hans, most questioners would incline the head and upper body very slightly. When the correct number of hoof taps was reached, people would make a slight upward jerk of the head. After Hans had stopped tapping, questioners would raise the head to its normal position. If this were not done promptly, Hans would stamp with his other front foot, giving one more tap. Many questioners would also accompany each correct tap with a nod, all unconsciously. When Pfungst made use of these movements on purpose, he found that he could directly control the position of the horse's foot in the air. While Hans was not answering questions unassisted, he was an expert at reading faces and body movements. Pfungst continued his research on nonverbal communication in the laboratory, finding that humans also respond to the slight movements and gestures of other humans, mostly unaware.

Despite his years of close work with the horse, Mr. von Osten had never suspected that Hans had learned to "read" him and was not demonstrating reasoning powers. In fact, he said he felt "betrayed" by Hans and was quite angry at the horse for the deception. Personal experience and observation often cannot yield reliable information. Even experts can be fooled if they don't make proper use of research procedures to check their observations.

HANS RIDES AGAIN

The case of Hans is not a mere historical curiosity. Early in 1980 (Wade, 1980) the New York Academy of Sciences hosted a conference of several hundred people at which Hans was an important topic of discussion. The conference members were very interested in the question of whether or not chimpanzees can really be taught to use language. The Gardners' early work in teaching their chimpanzee Washoe sign language sparked several similar ventures, created a great deal of enthusiasm for the possibility of ape language, and generated much speculation about the origins and development of human language. For many, the ability of chimpanzees to use sign language for communication is an established fact. Other scientists, however, remembering Hans, wonder if what the apes are demonstrating is actually language. The work of Terrace and his colleagues (1979) with "Nim Chimpsky" convinced these researchers that the chimpanzee's use of sign language is more similar to Hans's ability to watch humans and give them what they seem to want. The debate continues vigorously to this day, and the issue can only be resolved by future research.

RECAPITULATION

for WHY DO RESEARCH?

Those of us who are in the social sciences are often called upon to make decisions that affect the lives of our fellow human beings, not to mention ourselves. It is our responsibility to base these decisions on the best quality of information available to us. Most of the things we "know" were told to us by someone else. Some of our knowledge comes through personal experience. In both cases, the information we have may be incorrect, misleading, incomplete, or affected by our own biases. It is unlikely that good decisions ever result from inaccurate information. We, like Eve in Twain's story, need a way to estimate the probability that any information we have is actually in agreement with reality. We need as well a way to generate new information when we find that what we "know" rests on a shaky or untraceable base. Doing research using the methods of science will help us improve our information. Knowledge of research procedures will also permit us to evaluate the quality of information provided by others. Scientific research does not give final answers; rather, it is a process of constantly improving and refining the information available to us.

BEHAVIORAL OBJECTIVES

for WHY DO RESEARCH?

1. Write down three things you know about human behavior. Then for each of these figure out the source of your information. Classify each one of them as a "fact" or an "opinion."
2. From either the "cola" example or the "Hans" story, describe a research precaution that had to be taken in order to generate better-quality information than could be generated by "personal experience" alone.
3. Given a description of a precaution taken in the cola experiment or in Pfungst's research on Hans, explain why that precaution was necessary to yield improved information.

4. Give an example of a piece of information from an "expert" that you feel may be misleading or inaccurate. Then describe the grounds for your suspicion.

5. Given a decision to make, specify the sources of information you would use to make the decision. Then describe how each source might be misleading.

SAMPLE TEST QUESTIONS

for WHY DO RESEARCH?

1. You are choosing a college to attend. Your grades are sufficiently good that it is likely you'll be accepted almost anywhere. Your finances are not unlimited, but you can manage most reasonably priced institutions.

    a. How would you go about selecting a college?

    b. What sources of information would you use?

    c. For each source, specify how it might be misleading.

2. A friend of yours is having problems with her roommate. The roommate is messy and sometimes says things that hurt your friend's feelings. Your friend feels she doesn't have enough money to move out and asks you for suggestions as to how she might improve the roommate's behavior.

    a. What suggestions would you make?

    b. What is your basis for making each suggestion?

    c. How might the sources of information upon which you based your suggestions be misleading?

3. As a nursing-home attendant you notice that several of the old people sit around all day doing nothing and seem depressed to you. You want to make a recommendation to your superior about the situation and feel that you'd better be able to back up what you say.

    a. What recommendation would you make?

    b. What sources of information would you use to back up your recommendation?

    c. For each source of information, specify how it might be misleading.

SECTION 2: GATHERING INFORMATION BY OBSERVING

Simply observing is one way of gathering information about what is going on in the world. This approach is the main one used in the fields of ethology, the study of animal behavior in its natural habitat, and anthropology, the study of humans in different cultural groups. Research by observation of ongoing behavior is also widely used in the other social sciences, resulting in the publication of case histories, longitudinal and cross-sectional surveys, and correlational studies.

"JUST OBSERVING" ISN'T ALL THAT EASY

We all observe things all the time, but we aren't necessarily doing research or even greatly improving our own private store of information. Unless we are trained as observers and practice our skills regularly, we are uncertain what to watch for, do not remember what we have seen, change what we are looking for from one moment to the next, are overly impressed by unique cases, and communicate our observations poorly. There have been many studies of "eye-witness" testimony which show that people observing the same event tell completely different stories. Other research on memory processes indicates that as time progresses our memories fade quickly and selectively. Studies in perception have established that we can't react to or process all the sensory information available to us at any one point in time. Even in the initial stage of sensing our environment we pick and choose what we react to.

If the information produced by observing is to be of any long-term or general use, it has to be repeatable information; in other words, it has to be information that would be obtained by any one else attempting to make the same observations. This means that the observing that is done in scientific research must be much more systematic than the undirected observations we make in daily life.

SYSTEMATIC OBSERVATION

When doing research, observers must answer some questions before making observations. *What* are they looking for? *Whom* are they going to observe? *When* and *where* is the observing to be done? *How* are the observations to be made? *In what form* are the observations to be recorded? In other words, for observational research to yield useful information, the observing has to be done according to a system.

What Is to Be Observed?

Mere contact with an animal or a person doesn't mean you know a lot about it. Mr. von Osten, after all, had years of close association with Hans and still never observed that the horse needed to see the face of at least one knowledgeable person in order to answer questions correctly. In addition, many other people had carefully watched Hans performing without noticing the unconscious facial expressions and small body movements of the horse's examiners. Pfungst "noticed" these things because he had previously decided to look to see if they were there. *Before* he began taking observations he had theorized that the horse was responding to unintended signals from human examiners. He then conducted his observations specifically to test this idea. By placing blinders on the horse to restrict its field of vision, Pfungst confirmed that the horse insisted on seeing at least one human when answering questions (Hans would break his rope, or, failing that, kick out if Pfungst inconsiderately asked a question while standing behind the horse's back). With this information, Pfungst knew that he must watch the human questioners and be alert to any small visual signals they might be giving. Having defined exactly what to look for, Pfungst then "noticed" small changes of facial expression and body position which had escaped more casual observers. To make systematic observations you must define the particular behaviors of interest in such a way that when they occur you will spot them.

Who Is to Do the Observing?

If observers have had training and practice in recognizing a particular behavior, they will be much more likely to notice it when it occurs. How much training and practice are needed depends in part on how well defined the behavior is. In Eve's study, what she wanted to observe was straightforward, the amount of milk produced by her cow. Even in this case, an untrained observer might have fouled things up. A person unskilled in milking may get almost no milk out of a full udder!

The observer's own beliefs may alter observations, especially when what is being looked for is poorly defined. For example, parents of problem children frequently observe the bad and ignore the good. An outside observer might record that about 60 percent of the time a mother asks her child to do something the child does it while the other 40 percent of the time the child either ignores the request or talks back. However, when the mother is asked to describe the child's behavior, she is likely to say that the child "*never* does what I ask." In this case, before much progress can be made with the child's problem, the mother needs some training as an observer. Her beliefs and frustrations are getting in the way of her seeing how the child is actually behaving.

Who Is to Be Observed?

If you're trying to get information that can be widely applied, then you must be concerned about who it is that you are observing. It would be just your luck to get an unusual case. Eve's one cow, for instance, might have had a severe case of mastitis (inflammation of the udder) and therefore would not produce much milk in Eve's test. Observing only one peculiar cow, Eve might mistakenly conclude that withholding water for one night prevents milk formation in all cows. If you observe only one person (or cow), you may be able to produce a good story about *that* person, but that doesn't mean that you've produced any information that will be true for others. When we are not being "scientists" we have a strong tendency to give other people advice about life based on our observations of only a single example. Doing research, however, requires either that we observe many people or that we make a good case that the single person we have observed is typical.

When and Where Are the Observations to Be Made?

In **systematic observation,** we have to establish when and where the observations are to be made. It would be unfair, for example, for a therapist to conclude that a child wasn't much of a problem to his or her parents on the basis of an office visit. The "sweetie" in society might be a thoroughgoing demon at home. Thus not only do we have to worry about whether the person being observed is typical of other people, we also have to worry about whether we are observing behavior that is typical for that person. Changing either the time or the location of observations may make a big difference in what we see. Therefore, we have to specify the conditions under which we plan to do our observing.

How Are the Observations to Be Recorded?

Unfortunately, we can't trust our memories very far, especially when we are trying to observe several things at once or trying to catch some small nuance of rapidly changing behavior. After all, what we want to know is what we observe, not what we remember. Even trained observers find that they can't trust their memories. Part of systematic observation is devising some kind of recording system, and this can become complicated at times. A naturalist chasing deer through the forest or a therapist who doesn't want to let keeping records interfere with a therapy session has to be pretty clever about coming up with a workable recording system. The most common technique is to write things down, often using symbols or shorthand to speed the process. Tape recorders, cameras, special record sheets, and one-way windows have all been employed in various studies to improve recording of observations. Whatever technique is used, it should permit immediate and accurate recording and should not interfere with what is being observed.

CASE STUDIES

A **case study** is a narrative description of an individual's history, symptoms, behavior, and response to treatment. Sometimes case studies are published in professional journals, but more often, they are expanded and published as books, such as psychoanalyst Dorothy Baruch's *One Little Boy* (1952) or anthropologist Oscar Lewis's *Pedro Martinez* (1967). The case-study technique is borrowed from medicine. A doctor may publish a report of a single interesting or unusual case that apparently has responded to some new treatment. This is to alert other doctors to watch for the phenomenon or to consider a change in treatment. Case-study information in medicine is considered to be suggestive rather than conclusive.

Case studies in the social sciences may be fascinating reading, but are not by themselves a dependable source of information. Frequently the authors present after-the-fact conclusions rather than summarize systematically done observations. Also they may present the case from a particular point of view without even including information that might make alternative interpretations possible. Even if systematic observation is done and the authors are careful about jumping to conclusions, a case study still presents information about a single individual who just possibly is a "law unto himself." Case studies can be valuable as suggestions for future more controlled research. Sometimes, they can be useful as illustrative examples if care is taken to establish that a particular case is typical of some group of people. Case studies, by themselves, are a weak support for scientific conclusions since they are based on such limited observation.

NATURALISTIC OBSERVATION

In **naturalistic observation** a number of animals or people are observed in their natural setting. The observer attempts to remain out of sight so as to avoid interfering with what is happening. Before beginning observation, the observer has carefully defined what to look for and has worked out a recording system. This differs from the case-study approach in that the observer collects the same information in the same way about a number of individuals. Observations of this sort allow for comparisons between individuals and for detection of behaviors that are common to different individuals.

Ethologists and anthropologists have made excellent use of naturalistic observation as a research technique. Social scientists in other fields who want to do naturalistic observational research should have some background in ethology or anthropology. Ethologists in particular have developed observational techniques that reduce or correct for the effect of observer preconceptions and interference. Good naturalistic observational research requires careful preparation and a great deal of time in the field. It is often a very slow way to get information since the non-interfering observer has to sit around (often in a puddle) and wait for things to happen naturally. Anyone considering a career as a naturalistic observer should read about E. F. Darling (1937) crawling on his belly after his herd of red deer, Jane Goodall (1963) living for months in the open with her chimps, or Margaret Mead (1928) waiting on a South Seas island for a year or more.

A limitation of naturalistic observational research is that while it may reveal *what* happens in a given set of circumstances it does not yield much information about *why* something happens. To find out why things happen it is often necessary to tamper with the natural course of events. Even ethologists sometimes supplement their naturalistic observations by making changes in the environment and seeing what happens. Having observed, for instance, that the male stickleback fish readily leads females to his carefully prepared nest but violently attacks and chases away other males, the curious ethologist may start to ask just what it is about other male fish that the stickleback doesn't like. Work done with sticklebacks in tanks indicates that attack behavior is elicited by the color of an approaching fish (Tinbergen, 1952). In mating season, the normally brown and silver male stickleback acquires a bright blue back and a red stomach. A piece of wood similarly colored is just as effective as a real fish in starting an attack even if it isn't shaped quite right and doesn't move like a fish! This information could not have been obtained by simply observing the fish under natural conditions. Researchers often try to repeat the results of naturalistic observation under more controlled laboratory conditions in an attempt to find out exactly why something happens.

SURVEY STUDIES

Survey studies are large-scale observational studies done on groups of humans. The instrument of observation is usually a questionnaire or structured interview. The results of surveys are used to summarize the characteristics of different groups of people or to estimate their feelings and attitudes about issues. Creating a survey instrument that will yield dependable information requires special training in questionnaire design and statistics. The exact way questions are worded determines whether you get meaningful and consistent answers from a survey. The way in which you require people to respond may influence their answers and may make it more or less difficult to compare the responses of different individuals. How you select the people you question is another factor affecting the use you can make of survey information. Just running around being unsystematically nosy doesn't produce much repeatable or usable information (no matter how much fun it may be).

Techniques of Surveying

Interviewing.   Survey information may be collected in person. The interviewer has a list of questions either written down or memorized. Depending on how the questions are worded, they may call for categorical responses or they may be **open-ended.** Asking "yes-no" or factual questions makes it easier to summarize the responses of large numbers of people and to make comparisons. However, imposing limits on the answers that can be given may cause you to miss what a person really thinks. Unlimited or open-ended questions may allow you to gather more information about an individual but make it harder to combine the responses of different people to arrive at an answer typical for a group. In addition to deciding what questions to ask and whether these questions should be categorical or open-ended, it is important to decide how structured the interview should appear. In some situations you may want to maintain a conversational atmosphere yet fit all the standard questions into the discussion. Doing this well requires not only a good memory for both questions and answers but also a lot of supervised practice.

Questionnaires.   Written questionnaires are frequently used to make surveying more efficient and standardized. The questions may occasionally be open-ended and require essays, but more often they are accompanied by a series of preprinted categorical answers. Some questions may require a person to mark "yes" or "no," while others allow checking a graduated answer ranging from total agreement to total disagreement. If you decide to use questions that can be answered categorically, you can summarize your survey information easily by counting how many people marked each category. Deciding how to word questions, which questions to include on a questionnaire, what answers should be allowed, and how to summarize the answers requires technical training in questionnaire design. Of course, if you decide to use written questionnaires you are limiting yourself to surveying people who are literate.

Problems in Surveying.   One problem in surveying is being sure you are asking the right questions. Sometimes in putting together questions or making use of the information gathered by a questionnaire, researchers lose sight of their original intention. For example, the results of student-evaluation questionnaires on college teaching are sometimes presented as if they measure "teacher performance." All that such a questionnaire can measure is the average student attitude at a particular time about their experience in a course. Other observations would have to be made to determine whether a course was actually effective in teaching students new information, concepts, or skills. Teacher performance involves a lot more than can be measured by using survey questionnaires to determine student attitudes.

Another problem in surveying is being sure you have asked the right people. One popular (and easy-to-do) form of surveying is to publish questions in a magazine or newspaper and invite people to send in their answers. These "surveys" may give some astonishing results. A survey on "Friendship in America" (Parlee, 1979), for instance, reveals such interesting tidbits as "29 percent of people have a close friendship with a homosexual," "92 percent feel that friendship is a form of love," and "77 percent would tell a friend they love him or her." But what can we make of this information? We can't even be sure it reflects the feelings of people who subscribe to or buy this particular magazine. Only people interested enough to take the time to fill out the questionnaire, address the envelope, and spend money on postage have their views represented. We can't be sure exactly whose opinions these answers reflect. A useful survey is much more careful about choosing the people who are asked questions.

Surveys rely on the accuracy of an individual's answers. Usually the researcher has no independent way of checking whether a person's answer is true. This can cause problems. Sometimes a person may answer in order to impress or astonish the surveyor. Other times, memories may be faulty when information about past events is sought. Anyone interpreting survey information has to remember that the information obtained is what people choose to reveal at any one moment.

Some Types of Surveys

Opinion Polls.   Politicians want to know who people are likely to vote for or what positions they support. Corporations want to know the effect of their advertising on the public's reaction to a product. Television companies want to know what shows are being watched. Large organizations exist just for the purpose of collecting such information for these people and institutions.

Attitude Questionnaires.   Sometimes a researcher wants to know how people feel about an idea, an issue, a social change, or a process being experienced. Since "feelings" can't be measured directly, people are asked to express how they feel on an attitude questionnaire. For example, there has been a great deal of research on people's attitudes concerning racial matters. Investigators have been interested in learning how expressed attitudes are reflected in actual behavior and what procedures are effective in changing attitudes. Developing a questionnaire that reveals consistent underlying attitudes rather than casual momentary reactions to a particular set of questions requires a good deal of expertise and time spent testing the questionnaire. To measure people's attitudes about something, it's better to use an already published questionnaire than to make up one of your own in the absence of training in questionnaire construction.

Questionnaires Assessing a Person's "State of Mind."   How anxious are you? How depressed are you? How self-confident are you? Do you have a good self-concept? How outgoing are you? How suggestible are you? How satisfied are you? One way of observing these "states of mind" is by asking people to describe themselves via a questionnaire. For example, many investigators have been interested in measuring the anxiety people feel either in general or in specific situations. The Alpert-Haber (1960) Achievement Anxiety Test uses 19 questions to estimate the anxiety that people report for testing situations. The State-Trait Anxiety Inventory (Spielberger, Gorsuch, and Luchene, 1970) asks people to indicate which of several statements about anxious feelings and behaviors best describes how they react in general or in some specific situation. Several other scales have also been developed to try to summarize reports of anxious feelings. As with measuring attitudes, it's a good idea to see what published and tested questionnaires are available before developing your own questionnaire about "states of mind" (try Shaw and Wright, 1967, or Robinson and Shaver, 1973).

Cross-Sectional Surveys.   A researcher may be interested in comparing groups of people to see in what ways they differ. In a **cross-sectional survey,** people from two or more different groups are asked the same questions or observed in the same way. For example, a classical study by Hollingshead and Redlich (1958) compared the occurrence, diagnosis, and treatment of mental illness in persons of a cross-section of social classes in New Haven, Connecticut. Hollingshead and his colleagues found that lower-class mentally ill patients were much more likely to be diagnosed "schizophrenic" and to be treated by institutionalization than were upper-class patients. These differences did not appear to be entirely explained by differences in actual recorded symptoms.

Longitudinal Surveys.   Sometimes researchers are interested in comparing changes in survey information that occur with the passage of time or as people switch their group membership. A **longitudinal study** of attitudes of persons of different ages would repeatedly observe the attitudes of the same group of people as they grow older. In contrast, a cross-sectional study of attitudes of persons of different ages would measure at the same time the difference between persons representing different coexisting age groups. Longitudinal studies are more difficult to do than cross-sectional studies since time has to be allowed to pass. Also, if the researcher wants to follow exactly the same individuals as they change, problems of keeping track of independent, mobile humans arise. In Myers and Bean's (1968) ten-year follow-up of the patients originally studied by Hollingshead *et al.,* they had to eliminate 359 private patients for whom longitudinal data was not available. In tracing patients they had to receive permission from 87 different agencies to review records, and they employed methods that stopped just short of hiring a detective agency to trace some of the people. Humans are under no obligation to stand still to be studied!

Retrospective or Historical Surveys.   As well as going forward in time with a longitudinal survey, researchers may want to look back in time to compare the situation in the past with present observations. This can be tricky, since the researcher either must depend on people's faulty memories or use records that may be incomplete or may not have been kept in a form suitable for present purposes. In medicine, for example, the increased rate of diagnosis of a disease may reflect an actual change in its occurrence or it may mean only that there has been improvement in the detection and recording of this disease. Similarly, a retrospective study on the success of different methods of dealing with juvenile delinquents might be hampered by changes in the definition of delinquency by the courts and alterations in what records it is permissible to keep on delinquents. Interpretation of historical surveys is limited because the way in which observations are made is not under the control of the researcher.

CORRELATIONAL RESEARCH

Correlational studies are a sophisticated type of observational research. In correlational research a number of different things are simultaneously observed about each person. Then statistical techniques are used to see whether certain things tend to occur together in people. If it is found that two things are associated in most persons, then it is possible to use one kind of observation to predict another. For example, observational **correlational research** has shown that high school grades, college-entrance tests, IQ measures, and college grades all tend to vary together. If one person scores high on three of these things, he or she is very likely to score high on the fourth. If you know a student's high school GPA (grade point average), IQ score, and scores on college boards, then you can make a very good prediction about his or her probable college GPA. This prediction won't be true in every case, since other factors, like special motivation to excel, are not considered. Nevertheless, in the vast majority of the cases, your prediction will be surprisingly accurate.

Correlational techniques take us one step beyond simple observation in that they attempt to make predictions about future events. They do not, however, do much to explain why the things we observe or predict happen. For example, doctors could predict who was likely to get throat cancer by knowing their patients' smoking habits long before there was any explanation of why the two things are associated. Arriving at explanations takes more than just observing.

RECAPITULATION

for GATHERING INFORMATION BY OBSERVATION

The casual observing we do in everyday life is not the same thing as doing observational research. Observational research requires that observations be made *systematically.* This means that before we can begin observational research we have to answer the following questions: What, exactly, is to be observed? Who is to do the observing? Who is to be observed? Where and when are the observations to be made? How are the observations to be recorded? Only when these questions are answered will it be possible to collect useful and repeatable information by observing. *Case studies* are a primitive form of observational research in which a narrative description is written about the history, symptoms, behavior, and treatment of a single individual. *Naturalistic observation* involves systematic observation of the behavior of a number of individuals in their natural habitat. In naturalistic observation observers try not to interfere in any way with ongoing behavior, waiting patiently until desired situations occur and they get a chance to observe what they are looking for. *Survey studies* limit themselves to relatively few behaviors in a very large number of individuals. With humans, surveys are usually done by questionnaires or short interviews. Constructing a questionnaire that asks the right questions and permits answers that will yield dependable and useful information requires special training. Conducting interviews that will obtain the same information about each of a number of persons also requires special training and supervised practice. Surveys can be used to assess such things as opinions, attitudes, and internal states, all of which are difficult to observe directly. Cross-sectional surveys compare different groups observed at the same time while longitudinal surveys follow individuals as they age or change group membership. Historical surveys attempt to go backward in time to assess how people have changed. *Correlational research* studies observe several things about each individual at the same time. Then statistical techniques are used to discover whether different observations are associated so that knowing one thing about people will allow you to predict something else. The techniques of observational research yield a good deal of information about what is happening and may even, as in the case of correlational research, allow you to predict with some accuracy what will happen in the future. However, observational research does not yield much information about why things happen.

BEHAVIORAL OBJECTIVES

for GATHERING INFORMATION BY OBSERVING

1. Write out the five questions that must be answered before beginning to do systematic observation of behavior.
2. Give an example of an observational study that might be done on humans, answering all the questions necessary for doing systematic observational research.
3. Given a description of an observational study, pick out the features that make the observations systematic and, therefore, likely to produce usable information.
4. Explain what is meant by a "case study." Discuss at least one limitation of case studies as a source of information about human behavior.
5. Describe "naturalistic observation" as an approach for studying human behavior. Discuss the role of the observer in such a study.

6. Describe two kinds of survey studies that might be done to gather information about human behavior.

7. Given a description of a survey study, decide whether it is a cross-sectional or a longitudinal study.

SAMPLE TEST QUESTIONS

for GATHERING INFORMATION BY OBSERVATION

1. There has been concern that student anxiety in a test situation may interfere with performance. Several different questionnaires have been developed to assess a person's feelings of anxiety. Students in a mid-western university were all given the State-Trait Anxiety Inventory (Spielberger, 1970) at the beginning of the 1978 academic year. It was decided that a score of 30 or above on the inventory could be considered as reflecting high levels of anxiety about testing. It was found that while 28 percent of the Freshman class and 25 percent of the Sophomore class scored higher than 30, only 16 percent of the Junior class and 14 percent of the Senior class scored this high. It was suggested that college students become less anxious about testing the more of it they have experienced.

   a. Answer the following questions:

      1) What was observed?

      2) Who did the observations?

      3) Who was observed?

      4) When and where were the observations done?

      5) How were the observations recorded?

   b. Was this a cross-sectional or a longitudinal study?

   c. Can you think of an interpretation of the results other than the one that was suggested?

2. It has been suggested that preventing a mother from cuddling or handling her infant in its first few days (such as is the case with some premature babies) may weaken the mother-child bond and be observable as an altered pattern of inter-action between the mother and child. Babies 12 months of age were brought by their mothers to a university child-care center in response to a letter asking for volunteers for a study on infant play behavior. Letters were sent both to mothers of normal-term babies and to those who had premature infants who had needed an incubator. Each mother was asked to play with her baby for an hour in a comfortable, homelike room provided with toys and a crib to put the baby in if it fell asleep. Graduate students behind a one-way window observed the sequence of behaviors between mother and child, noting when one touched the other, made facial expressions directed at the other, made sounds, or reached toward the other. These behaviors were recorded by symbols on a con-tinuously moving paper chart which kept track of when each behavior occurred and how long it lasted. The babies who had been premature made somewhat fewer gestures toward the mother to initiate action although there were no dif-ferences in the mother's response to the infant's overtures. These babies also

spent more of the hour sleeping than did the babies who had not been premature. The results suggested the possibility that lowered rates of interaction with premature babies might be due in part to the baby's behavior rather than to a change in how the mothers respond to the baby.

    a. Answer the following questions about this study:
       1) What was observed?
       2) Who did the observations?
       3) Who was observed?
       4) When and where were the observations taken?
       5) How were the observations recorded?

    b. Ethologists say that in naturalistic observation we must be concerned with the effects of the observer and the circumstances of observation. Do you see any possibility in this study of the situation itself or the way in which the observation was done creating behavior that would not be quite the same as might be observed in a more natural environment?

SECTION 3: GATHERING INFORMATION BY EXPERIMENTING

While research using only systematic observation has provided us with a great deal of information about animal and human behavior, this approach by itself has some limitations. Observational research allows us to find out what has happened in a given situation and even permits us to make predictions about what will happen in the future under similar circumstances. Pure observational research, however, gives us little information about *why* things are happening. If *explanation* is our goal, rather than just description and prediction, we need to do more than passively observe our world.

WHAT IS AN "EXPERIMENT"?

In an experiment researchers make changes in the environment and observe what effect these changes have on animal or human behavior. Instead of waiting for things to happen, the researcher attempts to establish a **cause-effect relationship.** Knowledge of such relationships allows us to improve our prediction of future events and to exert some control over their occurrence. Doing **experimental research** requires all the observational skills mentioned in the last section in addition to knowledge of how to introduce into the environment changes that are likely to expose cause-effect relationships clearly.

    Two general approaches are used in social-science experiments. One is to observe a group of people, make a change in their environment, and again observe the same people to see whether the change has altered their behavior. Another approach is to take two similar groups of people or animals, introduce an environmental change for only one of the groups, and then observe both groups to see if the change has produced any differences between them. Either approach requires special precautions to be sure that the changes you introduce are the only ones that might be affecting the observed behavior. The less control you have over possible causes, the weaker your claim to have established a cause-effect relationship. Much of what you need to know about research methods involves learning how to take the precautions that will enable you to make strong cause-effect statements.

CONTROLLED NATURALISTIC OBSERVATION

Eve's research on her cow was a primitive experiment. She interfered with the normal course of events by trapping the cow for a night without access to water or other fluids. Doing this provided information that Eve hadn't discovered from simple observation; namely, that milk is not just water flowing through a cow and tinged white in the process. Unfortunately, Eve stopped her investigations with one cow and one "experiment." Further experimentation might have revealed to her that while water does not turn directly into milk, milk production is nevertheless eventually dependent in part on overall water consumption. Since her day other researchers have extended her findings.

Ethologists have gathered a wealth of information about animal behavior by controlled naturalistic observation. Observing, for example, that ants seem able to find their way home from incredible distances, several investigators have wondered how they do it. Experiments with mirrors have shown that ants use the angle of sunlight to orient themselves. Sneaking up on a homeward-bound ant and using a mirror to reverse the direction of light falling on the ant from right to left results in the ant turning around and confidently marching off on a path directly away from home (Santschi, 1911). Work with other insects, such as bees, also has shown the importance of polarized light from the sun in helping insects stay oriented in their environment. This would not have been found out by just observing without experimenting.

Investigators interested in human behavior and functioning have done many controlled naturalistic observation studies of social behavior in primates. For example, Harlow and Suomi (1974) conducted experiments in which one or more customary associates of a monkey were suddenly removed from the monkey troop. This produced reactions to the loss that looked very similar to behaviors occurring in humans said to be suffering from "depression." Studying what produces such depressed behavior and what contributes to recovery from it yields information which may be useful in preventing and treating human depression.

LABORATORY EXPERIMENTS

To identify exactly what is causing what, researchers may retreat from the natural environment to a more artificial situation. Pfungst, for instance, created an artificial situation, or "laboratory," in which to study Hans. He removed Hans's trainer and audience and eliminated other features of the environment from view by screening an area in the courtyard around the horse. Since horses have a field of vision which extends to the side and behind them, Pfungst placed blinders on the horse to restrict its vision to the front. He took all these precautions so that he could be very sure at any moment exactly what Hans was seeing and hearing when responding to questions. Finally, he asked Hans questions in a very orderly way so that the only thing that changed from question to question was whether or not Pfungst knew the correct answer. In this controlled laboratory situation it became apparent that Hans had been getting visual hints from his questioners as to the correct answer. A more natural barnyard situation in which many things were allowed to vary uncontrollably at the same time would have made it impossible to discover such a cause-effect relationship.

Research questions are seldom completely answered by any single investigation. Often, naturalistic observation suggests a possible relationship which is then checked out more carefully in a laboratory setting. The results of the lab work, in turn, suggest further observations and experimentation in the natural environment. For example, in the 1960s observation of hearing capabilities of entering college Freshmen indicated a marked increase in hearing losses (Lipscomb, 1974, pp. 53 ff.). Young people, especially males, showed the type of hearing loss seen only in middle-aged and older people in our society. During this same decade it became popular to listen to rock-'n'-roll music at high amplification. These associated (correlated) observations led some people to suggest that the increase in young persons' hearing losses might be caused by exposure to extremely loud music.

It would be ethically questionable purposely to subject humans to loud music with the intent of damaging their hearing, so guinea pigs in the laboratory were pressed into service. The unfortunate creatures were forced to listen to rock-'n'-roll-like sounds for periods of time and at levels of amplification that were typical for devotees of this type of music. The guinea pigs showed hearing losses which became permanent on repeated exposures. Microscopic examination of the sensory portion of their inner ears showed destruction of nerve cells which was the probable basis for the hearing loss (high-intensity classical music produced the same results). This series of laboratory experiments (Lipscomb, 1974, pp. 60 ff.) established a cause-effect relationship between hearing loss and prolonged exposure to amplified high-intensity music, a relationship that originally had only been suspected. This and related work on hearing loss due to industrial noise suggested that some of the deafness experienced by older persons in our society was not, as previously believed, simply an inevitable effect of aging, but resulted partly from summated effects of exposure to moderate levels of environmental noise. Further field observations in a remote area of Africa (Lipscomb, 1974, pp. 252 ff.) established that isolated tribesmen do not show nearly as much hearing loss with age as do people in industrialized societies. Research on an interesting question never stops. One piece of information usually leads to curiosity about something else. Investigation shifts back and forth between pure naturalistic observational studies, controlled research in the natural environment, and laboratory experiments as scientists try to put together a complete explanation.

BUILDING THEORIES AND TESTING THEM WITH EXPERIMENTS

A **theory** is a tentative explanation of how something happens. Theories are tested by research. Starting from a theory, a researcher forms a prediction or **hypothesis** about what could be expected to happen in a specific situation. The researcher then designs an experiment to test this hypothesis. If the information gained from the experiment does not support the hypothesis, then the theory from which it was derived is weakened. Theories themselves are not proved or disproved, but if a number of hypotheses stemming from the same theory are not confirmed, then people begin to search for a better explanation. Even a theory that is discarded in the long run serves a purpose in scientific investigation. Such a theory can still inspire research which helps generate better theories.

For example, several theories have been successively proposed and discarded in the investigation of the development of human visual capacity. Some psychologists have theorized that processes in an infant's brain are so haphazard and random at birth that the newborn cannot make any sense out of the sensory information available to it. It was thought that the world must be a mass of "booming confusion" (James, 1890) to the newborn and that a good deal of experience with the world was necessary before the infant could begin to respond to things as separable objects. In one form or another, this idea has been put forth by philosophers for several centuries.

As knowledge was gained about the brain, one psychologist (Hebb, 1949) formulated the theory that repeated experience with visual stimuli in the environment was necessary to form the connections in the brain that allow the infant to start to respond to the visual world in an organized fashion. To another psychologist (Riesen, 1950) this suggested the hypothesis that if an infant in its first few months were prevented from seeing the world, it later would be unable to respond normally in tasks involving identification of objects by sight. Such an infant would have failed to "learn to see" and would not have formed the necessary brain connections for normal use of vision. To test this hypothesis, Riesen carried out a series of experiments on chimpanzees in which he raised the animals in complete darkness from birth. His results indicated that these chimps, when eventually given the opportunity to see, acted as if they could make no sense out of visual information and had to investigate all objects by touch.

However, other investigators who became interested in this research soon found out that the problems of Riesen's chimps were due not to a lack of opportunity to "learn to see" but to actual destruction of light-sensitive cells in the eye (Chow, Riesen and Newell, 1957). In other words, the infant chimpanzees really were blind. Although these findings didn't support the Hebb-Riesen hypothesis about the formation of new brain connections with visual stimulation, the information was gained that infant animals need light at least part of the day to keep their eyes from deteriorating. This has stimulated a great deal of research on the development and biochemistry of the eye.

With this knowledge, Riesen modified his approach. He next did experiments which allowed the infant animal diffuse (unpatterned) light, but restricted it from having any other experience with the visual world. These infants' eyes did not deteriorate. Nevertheless, animals reared in this manner were still found upon later testing to have problems in identifying and responding to objects using vision alone. Again, these findings appeared to support the theory that experience was necessary to create the connections that allow a person (or animal) to see order in their visual world.

But other investigators established that while diffuse light prevents deterioration of the eye itself, nerve cells were being destroyed in other places in the nervous system as a result of Riesen's rearing conditions (Wiesel and Hubel, 1963). Neurophysiological work with very young animals has confirmed this (Wiesel and Hubel, 1965). One current view is that young animals (and people) are born with a highly organized visual system ready to process visual information and do not need a period of visual experience to make sense of what they see. However, if they are not permitted to use these existing connections, the system deteriorates.

The Hebb-Riesen theory about the role of visual experience in establishing new connections in the nervous system has had many of its specific hypotheses disproved and new theories with more research support are now being offered. However, without the research stimulated by the Hebb-Riesen theory, the information that suggested the newer theories probably would not have been obtained. In science, even an incorrect explanation can produce much useful information as people set about disproving it. The only "bad" theory is one that generates no testable hypotheses. Sometimes an explanation offered for human behavior is so vague that it is impossible to make any reasonable predictions or hypotheses based on the theory. Other theories claim to "explain everything" so that the theory is said to be supported no matter whether reasonable hypotheses are proved or not. A *scientific* theory is one that is capable of having its hypotheses disproved if the theory is incorrect.

BASIC OR APPLIED RESEARCH?

The purpose of doing research varies from project to project. Sometimes research is done in a specific situation with the aim of finding an immediate solution to a practical problem. This is called **applied research.** In other cases, the researcher's goal is not to find out what happens in one specific situation but to explain how things happen in general, to develop or test a theory about how nature functions. This kind of research, intended to increase understanding rather than to solve specific problems, is called "theory-building" or **basic research.**

There has been much argument concerning which kind of research is "better" to do. In particular, should those of us who pay for research through taxes and donations concentrate on supporting basic or applied research projects? On the one hand, applied research with its narrow focus yields results applicable to only a limited number of situations. On the other hand, basic research, while it increases understanding, may seem to produce little that can be immediately put to use in any practical situation. When a quick answer is needed to a practical problem, applied research is more likely to result in an immediate solution. However, major breakthroughs in understanding how nature functions are much more likely to result from basic research. Such breakthroughs, when they do occur, often can solve a large number of practical problems at one time. For example, information from applied medical research has enabled us to prolong the life of cancer victims; however, the eventual control of this disease is more likely to result from basic research into cellular mechanisms that result in cancerous growth. Both kinds of research are necessary in working on this problem.

Research in any area of the natural or social sciences should include both basic and applied studies. Even if a major breakthrough in understanding some process, like cancer, results from basic research, applied-research studies may still be necessary to put the new findings into effect. It is often easier to find support for applied-research projects since the nonscientific community more readily understands and appreciates their practical aims. However, without the body of knowledge produced by basic research, society may find itself having answers to many minor technicalities, but lacking solutions for major problems.

EVALUATION OR EXPERIMENTAL RESEARCH?

The relatively new field of **evaluation** consists of a set of procedures for gathering information about the effects of social, clinical, or educational programs on human behavior. Evaluation is often confused with experimental research, especially with applied research. Whereas research is intended to improve our understanding of how nature functions, the purpose of evaluation is simply to determine whether an existing program has produced a product and whether that product is worthwhile. Evaluators use many of the techniques of research, but there are important differences between doing evaluation and doing research.

To begin with, the evaluator usually has no control over the program or process being studied. Unlike an experimenter doing applied research, the evaluator cannot set up the situation with the intent of gathering dependable information. The program being evaluated is, after all, created for other than research purposes. For example, an evaluator might be called in to study the effectiveness of a federally funded program for dealing with developmentally delayed children within a school district. The purpose of the program is to help the children, not to provide a tidy research situation. The evaluator might have difficulty with things like finding equivalent children for comparison purposes who have not been exposed to the program. A researcher certainly would avoid a situation like that, but an evaluator may have no choice.

Another difficulty experienced by evaluators is that they are unlikely to have much control over what observations are made before the program is begun or while it is in progress. Different schools, for instance, may have made different kinds of observations on their developmentally delayed children. Even if the observations are somewhat consistent across the schools within the program, they may not be the same as those made in other programs. Often, evaluators are not called in until a program is completed. The lack of a systematic observation procedure set up at the very beginning of a program is felt when the evaluator tries to make comparisons.

To make matters worse, evaluators may find little agreement about the goals or aims of the program. Even if they can get people to agree on a statement of goals, the goals may be so broadly worded that it is difficult to devise measures to demonstrate whether the program is meeting its goals. Evaluation of college teaching, for example, is difficult because different professors in different subject areas either have different goals or express them differently. Think of taking on the task of deciding whether professors in sociology, science, philosophy, and art courses are equally effective! The administration of a liberal arts college is faced with just such a problem when it tries to make promotion decisions or to change where it spends its money. Outside evaluators are sometimes called in to assess the relative effectiveness of very different educational approaches.

Finally, an evaluator, unlike a researcher, is called upon to make a judgment about whether the product of the program being studied was worthwhile. This kind of value judgment is not part of experimental research.

Evaluators certainly need training in research methods, but they need many other skills as well. They have to use diplomatic and political skills to convince people responsible for social, clinical, or educational programs to agree on goals. They have to be able to convert broad statements of goals into something that can be measured or else they have no hope of getting evidence that the goals are being met. They have to devise observational techniques that do not interfere with the purposes of the program. They may have to persuade people involved in the program to spend extra time taking observations, time the personnel may feel would be better spent in carrying out the program. Since people involved in any program usually have a good deal of attachment to it, evaluators have to be able to deal with suspicion and even hostility if it looks like their evaluation is going to come out negative. Learning research procedures is only a starting point for someone intent on a career as an evaluator.

RECAPITULATION

for GATHERING INFORMATION BY EXPERIMENTING

In an *experiment* researchers make changes in the environment and observe what effect these changes have on animal or human behavior. The researchers hope thereby to establish a *cause-effect relationship.* Pure observational research describes what happens in a given situation and permits some prediction of what will happen in similar circumstances. Experimental research aims at providing an explanation of how something happens, improving our capacity to predict and even to control future events. Experiments range from *controlled naturalistic observation,* in which the natural environment is altered only slightly, to *laboratory experiments,* in which all aspects of the environment are controlled. Laboratory experiments expose cause-effect relationships most clearly, but the artificial lab situation may also produce results not readily obtained under natural conditions. To answer fully any research question about human behavior usually requires studies done both in the lab and under natural conditions. The purpose of doing research can range from *applied research,* in which immediate answers are sought for particular practical problems, to *basic research,* which aims at providing explanations about how nature functions. Such proposed explanations are called *theories.* For any one research study, a *hypothesis* or prediction is derived from a more general theory and an experiment is designed to test that hypothesis. If the hypothesis is not supported, the theory is weakened. If other hypotheses stemming from the same theory also fail to be supported, then a new or modified explanation may be necessary. In trying to answer any particular question about human behavior, a balance of applied and basic research is usually needed. Experimental research should not be confused with *evaluation.* Evaluation is a relatively new set of information-gathering procedures aimed at determining whether an existing program is meeting its goals and whether these goals are worthwhile. Although evaluators adopt some research techniques, they have little control over the processes they are asked to study and, often, little say about what observations are made. Evaluators are expected to make value judgements, whereas researchers are not.

BEHAVIORAL OBJECTIVES

for GATHERING INFORMATION BY EXPERIMENTING

1. Describe how doing an experiment differs from doing naturalistic observation.
2. Give an example of a simple experiment, indicating what change you are making in the environment and what you expect to observe happen as a result.
3. Given examples of research situations, identify whether they represent pure observational research or experimental research.
4. Describe the purpose of doing experiments. What does the researcher hope to discover?
5. Define the terms *theory* and *hypothesis.* Discuss why a theory would be discarded or replaced by a new theory.
6. Compare "basic" and "applied" approaches to research. Discuss the strength(s) and weakness(es) of each type of approach.
7. Describe the purpose of *evaluation.* Describe two ways that doing evaluation differs from doing research.

SAMPLE TEST QUESTIONS

for GATHERING INFORMATION BY EXPERIMENTING

1. For the following research situations, decide which ones represent observational (O) and which represent experimental (E) research.
    a. A study done several years ago reported that 78 percent of high school female students carried their school books held in both arms while less than

20 percent of males did. Most male students carried their books under one arm against their hip. (One interpretation given for this is that women carry objects like they would babies.)

b. To see whether male-female differences in book-carrying behavior still oc-cur now that so many students are using backpacks for their books, a group of students who use backpacks regularly were compared to a group that does not. Men and women from both groups were invited to participate in an "interview study." While they were waiting for the interview to begin, the researcher casually asked them if they would help get the interview room ready by moving some piles of books to a room down the hall. Almost all the males and females from the backpack group used both arms as did the females from the nonbackpack group. The majority of nonbackpack males, however, used a one-armed technique.

c. Dogs were started in obedience classes at either six months or one year of age. The younger dogs were found to require more training sessions before they could qualify at "novice" level than did the older dogs.

d. A phone survey was done in a large metropolitan city to determine TV view-ing habits. It was found that the period of time between nine and eleven o'clock in the evening had the most viewers.

e. In a study done in a city in Canada it was found that people who watched a great deal of TV were more likely to be fearful of experiencing violence. The researchers suggested that violent programs on TV may result in people fearing that violence will happen to them.

f. In a study on "helping behavior," researchers placed a car with a flat tire and a helpless young woman next to a busy highway. For part of the time this "decoy" was present, there was a "model" situation also in existence one mile up the road. The "model" consisted of a similar disabled vehicle and women with a second car which apparently had stopped to help. The re-searchers found that many more passing motorists stopped to offer assis-tance to the "decoy" when they had recently passed the "model" situation. They concluded that helping behavior becomes more likely when people have recently seen someone else helping out.

2. For the research situations you identified above as "experimental," describe the way in which the experimenter interfered with the natural course of events.

chapter 2

speaking the language of science

Before beginning to do your own research, or even to read intelligently about research done by others, it is necessary to learn some of the language of scientific method. This language may seem dry at times, but it ensures that communication about research is clear and unambiguous. Once you can use it fluently, it will aid you both in planning your own research and in assessing the research efforts of others as possible sources of information for your own decisions. There are reports of three research studies at the end of this chapter. One concludes that an individualized way of teaching a college nutrition course is superior to the more usual lecture-discussion-lab method. Another suggests that if you want fat children to lose weight, the most effective procedure is one that both rewards the child for success and penalizes the parents for failure. A third study presents a treatment for nervousness when speaking in public that is more effective than several sessions with a psychotherapist. By the time you get to these reports you will be familiar enough with the language of science to evaluate the worth of each study as an information source.

SECTION 1: TAKING MEASURES

Measuring things about people and reporting these measurements is a customary part of daily life. Whenever you describe someone, you are reporting the results of a number of casual measurements you have taken on different aspects of the person. A young woman might come home and blithely report to her parents: "I've met the most wonderful young man. He's a handsome six-footer with an engaging smile, long brown hair, and a guitar." And on second thought, she hastily adds: "He works as a computer consultant and drives his own Porsche." This description includes the results of her measurement of the young man's age, sex, height, facial expression, hair length, hair color, hobby, occupation, and financial standing. Her conclusion from the result of her measurements is that he is "wonderful." Her parents might not jump to the same conclusion from her report; or, at the very least, they might want to take additional measurements, under more controlled conditions, and with a less biased observer.

Measurement in a research study differs somewhat from the casual measures we take in everyday life. When doing research, it is necessary to define our measurement process in such a way that other observers can use it and come up with the same measures. If the measurement of "handsomeness" were done in a research study, different observers would have to agree on how "handsome" a particular young man was. It is also essential in research that the measurement process be applicable to more than one individual; it must be possible to measure a number of people on the same basis. Just as in everyday life, measurements taken in research studies are used to permit researchers to "jump to conclusions." However, the greater care taken by researchers in the measurement process increases the likelihood that different people will come to the same conclusions from a set of measurements.

MEASURES VARY FROM CRUDE TO PRECISE

Measurements can vary from very crude to extremely precise. Describing a man as "handsome" is relatively crude. A listener might be interested in whether this measure meant simply "not ugly" or was one of a larger set of potential measurements sensitive to different degrees of attractive appearance. Classifying a man as a "six-footer" is potentially very precise, depending on the accuracy of the process used to arrive at the measurement. Saying that a man is "young" is a rather imprecise measurement of his age, but in this case one could potentially make a more precise measurement (the parents might demand to see his driver's license). Some aspects of a person, such as height or income, can potentially be measured in a very precise fashion. Other aspects, such as attractiveness of appearance and originality of personality, do not lend themselves to the same degree of precision of measurement.

EXAMPLE OF TAKING MEASURES: STUDY
OF A CLASS OF PRESCHOOLERS

A class of 24 preschoolers in a college-sponsored day-care program are available for study by members of your family life class. You are interested in what influences activity in children of this age group (you have a little cousin who is a "holy terror" and never sits still). To begin with, you decide you need some experience in determining children's activity levels, possibly by measuring "activity" in several different ways. First, you ask the preschool teacher to write down for each child whether she considers the child to be "hyperactive," "normal," or "withdrawn" based on her experience with children of this age group. Second, you ask two of your fellow students to observe the children at play on two different days and to agree between themselves on a rating of each child on a five-point scale as follows: 1-inactive, 2-slightly active, 3-moderately active, 4-very active, 5-extremely active. Finally, you yourself observe each child separately in a room for one-half hour. The room contains several interesting toys and games at fixed locations, but no people. You watch the child through a one-way window and record the number of times the child moves from one toy to another.

In this study you are taking three different and independent measures of the activity level of each child: the teacher's classification, the rating assigned by the college students, and the number of times each child switches toys in a half-hour period when playing alone. The results you might get for these measurements are given in Table 2.1.

Table 2.1 Activity Measures on Members of a Preschool class

Child	Teacher's Classification	Student's Rating	Number of Switches
1. John	Hyperactive	4	29
2. Mary	Normal	2	8
3. Susie	Normal	2	3
4. Jim	Normal	3	15
5. Carl	Withdrawn	2	8
6. June	Normal	2	7
7. Nora	Hyperactive	5	20
8. Tom	Normal	4	20
9. Paula	Withdrawn	2	5
10. Mark	Normal	4	20
11. Ben	Hyperactive	4	25
12. Pete	Normal	3	10
13. Joe	Normal	3	14
14. Rachel	Normal	3	11
15. Josie	Normal	2	12
16. Marilyn	Normal	3	13
17. Mike	Hyperactive	5	42
18. Jane	Withdrawn	2	4
19. Steve	Withdrawn	2	7
20. Martin	Normal	4	15
21. Amy	Normal	3	11
22. Dick	Withdrawn	3	11
23. Jessie	Normal	4	22
24. Pauline	Normal	2	6

DEFINING A SCALE OF MEASUREMENT

In order to measure anything, you first have to define your **scale of measurement.**
A scale of measurement specifies all the possible values a given measurement
could have. In the preschool study you defined three different scales of measurement that could be used to measure "activity." You instructed the teacher to use a
scale with only three potential measures: withdrawn, normal, and hyperactive.
You provided your fellow students with a measurement scale having five potential
values: the ratings 1 through 5. The scale used by you in determining how many
times a child switched toys in half an hour had a very large number of possible
measures on it: from 0 to infinity (some children seem to move at the speed of
light). Each of these different scales permitted you to assign a measure to each
and every child, to label each child according to the value of the measure taken on
him or her. John, for instance, is a "hyperactive child" on the teacher's scale, a
"#4" child according to student ratings, and a "29-switches" child according to
your own observation.

THE SCALE OF MEASUREMENT IS NOT AFFECTED BY THE RESULTS OF THE MEASUREMENT PROCESS

What defines a scale of measurement is the set of *potential* measurement categories,
not the categories your subjects actually fall into. Thus your scale can have potential
measures which never are assigned to any subject in any particular group you are
measuring. In fact, if you look at Table 2.1 you'll see that none of the children
received a "1" rating from the students. This doesn't mean that the measure doesn't
exist, it just means that none of these children were placed in that measurement category. Similarly, just because the measure "9 switches" was not assigned to any child
does not mean that this measure is not a part of the measurement scale.

A scale of measurement is defined before any observing is done or any measurements are taken by the experimenter. After the measurements are made, the experimenter can look at the measures taken on the different subjects and see how they
distribute themselves among the potential measurement categories. The experimenter can record the **frequency** of times each measure was assigned to one of the
subjects.

If we summarize the measurements assigned by the teacher to her preschoolers,
we find that she classified five children as withdrawn, four as hyperactive, and fifteen as normally active. This kind of summary is called a **frequency distribution.**
Looking at the results in this way tells us how frequently the subjects distributed
themselves into each measurement category on our scale. Such a frequency distribution would usually be presented as in Table 2.2.

A frequency distribution of the results of your fellow students' ratings could
also be made. Looking at Table 2.3 we can see that the measurement category "1"
has a frequency of zero for this particular class of preschoolers. Your student raters
felt that none of the children should be labeled as inactive (Category 1) although
they did label a fairly large number as slightly active (Category 2).

Although the number of potential measurement categories is very large on the scale used to measure switching between toys, we can still make up a frequency distribution of your results, such as is given in Table 2.4. We didn't finish Table 2.4 because it was becoming rather lengthy and wouldn't be of much use for communi-

Table 2.2 Teacher's Categorization of Activity Levels for 24 Preschoolers

Measurement-Scale Values	Frequency of Children Assigned Each Value
Withdrawn	5
Hyperactive	4
Normal	15

Table 2.3 Ratings of Activity Levels of 24 Preschoolers

Measurement-Scale Values	Frequency of Times a Child Was Assigned That Value
1	0
2	9
3	7
4	6
5	2

Table 2.4 Number of Switches between Toys Recorded for 24 Preschoolers

Measurement-Scale Values	Frequency of Children Assigned Each Value
0	0
1	0
2	0
3	1
4	1
5	1
6	1
7	2
8	2
etc.	etc.

cating these results. (Who would read through it to its end?) A common way to get around this problem is to combine adjacent measurement categories on the measurement scale when making up a frequency distribution of results. Table 2.5 sacrifices some detail, but it presents your results in a more readable manner.

If you complete the frequency distribution in Table 2.5, you will again find that some of the potential measurement categories were not assigned to any of the preschoolers (for example, the "45–49" category) and are given a frequency of 0. Nevertheless, those categories still remain part of your originally defined scale of measurement.

Table 2.5 Number of Switches between Toys Recorded for 24 Preschoolers

Measurement-Scale Values	Frequency of Children Assigned the Values	
0– 4	2	
5– 9	6	
10–14	7	
15–19	2	
20–24	4	
25–29	—	(reader fill in)
30–34	—	"
35–39	—	"
40–44	—	"
45–49	—	"
50–54	—	"
55–59	—	"
etc.		

RECAPITULATION

for TAKING MEASURES

Every time we describe a person, we are reporting the results of one or more measurements we have taken on that individual. The first step necessary in measuring anything is to define the scale of measurement we intend to use. This means we have to specify all the possible values our measure could have. Measures can be relatively crude, with the scale of measurement having only a few possible values; or they can be very precise, with a large number of potential values on the scale. After the scale is defined, we can use it to measure a number of different individuals. The result of our measurement process can be expressed by reporting the frequency with which we assigned each of our potential measurement categories to the individuals we observed. Measures that happen not to be assigned to any particular individual still remain as part of our measurement scale.

BEHAVIORAL OBJECTIVES

for TAKING MEASURES

1. Given a description of a measure that might be taken on a group of people, write out a possible measurement scale for that measure.

2. Given a summary of a research study, pick out the different types of measures used in the study and describe the scale of measurement used for each measure.

3. Given a description of the results of measurements taken in a study:
   a. specify what was measured.
   b. list the categories on the measurement scale.
   c. identify the frequencies with which each measurement was assigned.

4. Given measurements taken on individuals in a study, make up a table (complete with title and headings) expressing the results as a frequency distribution.

5. Given an example of a crude measurement scale, think of a way to measure the same thing more precisely.

6. Think up a measure that might be taken on people in a research study and define a scale of measurement for it.

7. Define both scale of measurement and frequency distribution. Give an example pointing out which is which.

SAMPLE TEST QUESTIONS

for TAKING MEASURES

1. In coming to a decision about which of several compact cars to buy, you feel that your major concerns are the purchase price, what kind of gas mileage you're going to get, and whether or not you can get an acceptable color. You decide to visit several car lots and collect information about possible cars. List the measures you want to take on each car. For each measure, define the measurement scale that you would use (be sure to indicate all the possible measurements on each scale).

2. The results of a poll taken in your precinct on 1000 voters indicate that 220 of them strongly agree with the president's energy program, 130 strongly oppose it, 319 are mildly in favor of it, 221 mildly oppose it, and the rest are neutral on the subject. Make up a frequency distribution of the results and present it as a table complete with title and labels.

3. In a study of the functioning of business organizations, you are particularly interested in the extent to which various individuals will participate in a group

discussion. You want to compare this with their status in the organization. You are allowed to observe and hear several conferences through a one-way window. What measure(s) might you take on the individuals you observe to indicate their degree of participation? Be specific as to the entire scale of potential measurements you would use for each measure you decide to take.

4. Horses in races are classified as first, second, third, etc. How might you measure their performance more precisely? Describe fully the scale of measurement you would use.

5. Distinguish between a *measure,* a *scale of measurement,* and a *frequency distribution.* (This might appear as a series of multiple-choice questions rather than a short-answer essay.)

6. Complete the frequency distribution in Table 2.5 (if you haven't already done so).

SECTION 2: CHARACTERISTICS OF DIFFERENT TYPES OF MEASUREMENT

Any scale of measurement that we use will have certain common characteristics, whether we are using **qualitative measures,** like classifying children as "good" or "bad," or **quantitative measures,** such as determining the number of minutes a child spends playing with a certain toy. First, *a measurement scale must consist of at least two different possible measurement categories or values.* A "scale" that has only one category or value to which everyone will be assigned isn't a scale at all. A measurement scale must have at least two possible measures, even if, as in the case of a simple qualitative measurement scale, one possible value is the possession of a trait (this child is a "brat") and the other possible value is not possessing it (these children are "not brats").

Also, to be a usable scale of measurement, the set of possible measures we intend to use should be *complete or exhaustive.* This means that when we use the scale to observe a group of people we must be able to assign an appropriate measure from the scale to each and every person. For example, if you are measuring the political-party identification of a group of voters, you are going to need more than the measures "Democratic" and "Republican" on your scale. Depending on what you intend to do with the measurements, it may be sufficient to include only a third measure, "Other," or you may want to be more specific as to membership in other political groups. This is something you have to decide ahead of time.

Finally, the measures we define along our scale of measurement should be *mutually exclusive.* As we measure each person we should not be in doubt as to what measure to assign him or her. We cannot simultaneously assign one and the same person to two different places on a single measurement scale. If you are measuring the behavior of a group of children, you can't place the same child in both the "brat" and the "not-brat" categories. If you keep feeling uncertain about which category the child belongs in, this would suggest that your original scale of measurement needs more measurement categories (suggestions: "perfect angel," "holy terror," and "sometimes a brat"). Again, you have to decide this ahead of time so all your subjects will be measured with the same scale.

INTERVAL SCALES OF MEASUREMENT

Characteristics of Interval Scales

In many ways, the most useful measurement scales are those whose measures possess what are called *interval characteristics*. This type of measurement is what most people think of when they identify a measure as quantitative.

First, an **interval scale** must have the basic measurement characteristic of *allowing you to categorize people.* In the preschool example (p. 31) you were able to classify each child according to the number of switches he or she made between the available toys in a given amount of time (Table 2.1). You found, for instance, that Rachel, Amy, and Dick were all "11-switch" children.

Next, an interval scale must consist of potential measurement categories that possess an *inherent order.* It must be possible to say that subjects classified into one measurement category have more or less of what is being measured than subjects classified into another. The "number-of-switches" measure meets this second criterion. The "11-switches" children identified above can be said to have switched toys more often than the "8-switches" children (Mary and Carl) but less often than the "20-switches" children (Nora, Tom, and Mark).

Finally, in addition to possessing the property of ordered measurement categories, the possible measures along an interval scale of measurement must have the property of being *equidistant,* of representing equal differences. Only when this is true can we make statements about the differences between measures assigned to different people in addition to saying simply that one person has more or less of something than another. The "number-of-switches" measure meets this third criterion. The measure "12-switches" is as far away from the measure "11-switches" as the latter is from "10-switches." We can say that Martin's activity (15 switches) exceeded Pete's (10 switches) by the same amount that Pete's exceeded Paula's (5 switches). We can also say that the difference in activity between the most active switcher, Mike (42 switches), and the next most active, John (29 switches), was considerably larger than the difference between John and his closest competitor, Ben (25 switches).

Advantages of Interval Scales

Interval scales of measurement are preferable, when it is possible to use them, because they permit the adding and subtracting of measurements and allow comparisons of the sizes of the differences between measurements. Since the "number-of-switches" measurement is interval, we can add all the children's measurements together and obtain a mean or average measurement for the group of 14.1 switches per child. Adding and subtracting measures and taking their average is permissible only when the potential measures on the measurement scale are both ordered *and* represent equal-sized increments.

Combining Interval-Scale Categories

Depending on how precisely we obtain the interval measurements, it may be convenient to lump several adjacent measurement categories together when presenting a frequency distribution of the persons who were placed in each category (see Table 2.5). We can do this and still have an interval scale of measurement as long as we make these new categories equidistant and of equal size. Actually, some kinds of interval measurement, such as determining the amount of time spent doing something, always represent such lumped categories. Although we may make our time measurements in minutes, there is the possibility of making them in seconds. If we make the measurements in seconds, we have lumped together potential measurements of fractions of seconds. When you define such a measurement scale, you must indicate how precisely you intend to measure and must keep your possible measurements equidistant.

ORDINAL SCALES OF MEASUREMENT

Characteristics of Ordinal Measures

Sometimes the scale of measurement that we use will possess ordered categories, but the possible measures along the scale will not be truly equidistant. Such an **ordinal scale** is shown in Fig. 2.1. This scale does have the characteristic of order. Category 7 does represent more agreement than Category 6. However, we do not know for a given person if the change in amount of agreement between Category 7 and Category 6 is the same as the change represented by going from, say, Category 4 to Category 3. In other words, we do not know whether the amount of agreement represented by each category is an equal increase in agreement from the category just below it. In fact, one truism in interpreting rating-scale questionnaires is that people

FIG. 2.1

A typical questionnaire rating scale.

Item: A woman's place is in the home.
(Please rate your agreement below)

1	2	3	4	5	6	7
Strongly disagree	Disagree	Mildly disagree	No opinion	Mildly agree	Agree	Strongly agree

tend to shy away from the extremes. It would take a very strong increase in agreement to make people switch from Category 6 to Category 7, quite possibly much more than it would take to make them switch from Category 5 to 6. If this is so, then the measurement categories cannot be said to be equidistant, even if "numbers" have been arbitrarily assigned to them. Since numbers assigned this way do not represent equidistant intervals, then adding them, subtracting them, or taking their average is a questionable procedure.

Another example of an ordinal **rating scale** is the one you had your student colleagues use in the preschool example. The student raters classified each child on a five-point scale from inactive (1) to extremely active (5). Again, even though you gave your raters numbers to indicate their classifications, there is no guarantee that these numbers represent equidistant measures. While it might have taken only a small increase in a child's activity to change the rating from slightly active (2) to moderately active (3), it might take a very large increase in activity to change the rating from very active (4) to extremely active (5). Therefore, while you can assume that your student raters used the ratings in an orderly fashion such that Category-5 children possess more of what they called "activity" than did Category-4 children, you cannot say exactly how much more of this quality the Category-5 children had.

Rank-Ordering Changes Interval to Ordinal Scales

Any situation that calls for **rank ordering** measures from first place on down is an application of ordinal measurement. Thus a horse show or a beauty contest in which the measures given the participants are first, second, third, etc., is an example of asking the judge to use ordinal measurement. The first- and second-place winners in a beauty contest might be very close in beauty in the opinion of the judges while the difference between the second- and third-place contestants in attractiveness might be very large. Again, such rankings do not represent equal distances, only order. In fact, we often use ordinal measures in situations where it would be very difficult for judges to assign and defend an interval measure because of the complexity of what we are asking them to judge. Quantifying the beauty of a Miss America or the performance of an English Pleasure horse would be a difficult process indeed; therefore, we are generally content to use ordinal measures in these situations.

NOMINAL SCALES OF MEASUREMENT

Sometimes the measures we want or can take in a given situation are very primitive. In nominal measurement, the set of possible measurement categories used does not have the equal step sizes necessary for interval measurement nor does it have the inherent order necessary for both interval and ordinal measurement. Measuring the sex of each of a group of preschoolers by labeling each child as "boy" or "girl" would be an example of a **nominal scale** with two possible measurement categories. Or, suppose that in a study of toy preference we offered a selection of toys (say: doll, truck, book, gun, hammer) and determined for each child which toy he or she selected. This, too, would be a nominal measure, for the toys (measurement categories) themselves have no inherent order. Frequency distributions can be obtained for nominal as for other types of measures, but in the case of nominal scales there is no necessary order in which the measures have to be listed when reporting your results. The ordering of the measures in Table 2.6, for example, is arbitrary. Any other ordering would do just as well.

Nominal categories may be represented by numbers as labels, but don't be fooled, they are still nominal measures with no necessary order. When numbers are used as labels (names), such as in assigning football numbers or giving participants in a horse show numbers, the scale is still nominal. Also, for convenience of scoring, nominal categories may be assigned numbers before feeding the information into a computer. Thus, in reporting the measure of "sex" you might designate boys with a "0" and girls with a "1" but you still would have a nominal measure since there is no necessary order of boy before girl or girl before boy.

Table 2.6   Toy Selection by 24 Preschoolers

Measures (Toys)	Frequency of Children Assigned Each Measure
Doll	8
Book	2
Hammer	3
Gun	8
Truck	3

Sometimes you will have a measurement scale that has a few qualitative categories, like the examples of nominal scales given above, but the categories do possess some rationale for ordering them. The measurement scale used by the teacher in the preschool study had only three qualitative categories (withdrawn, normal, and hyperactive) but we might argue that they represented an underlying order of increasing amounts of activity. If so, then this is really a type of ordinal scale. An ordinal scale with so few categories, however, is often treated in data analysis as if it were only a nominal scale. This sort of scale might best be called a **"weak-ordinal" scale of measurement.**

RECAPITULATION

for TYPES OF MEASUREMENT

Any scale of measurement must have two or more possible measures to assign to subjects. These measures must be so defined that each and every subject can be assigned a measure, making the scale exhaustive. Also, the measures must be mutually exclusive so that no subject can be assigned two different measures on the same scale at the same time. If the scale of measurement possesses only these properties of qualitative measurement, then it is *nominal* in type. If, in addition to these properties, the possible measures of the scale also have a natural order, then the scale is *ordinal*. If the set of possible measures not only possesses an order, but also represents equal-sized steps along an underlying quantitative dimension, then the scale is an *interval* scale. Only measures assigned according to an interval scale can legitimately be added and subtracted.

BEHAVIORAL OBJECTIVES

for TYPES OF MEASUREMENT

1. Name the three types of measurement scales presented in this section.
2. Given a characteristic of a measurement scale, indicate which of the three types of scales possess this characteristic.
3. Given a description of an actual measurement scale, recognize whether the scale is nominal, weak-ordinal, ordinal, or interval in type.
4. Describe a specific example of each of the three types of scales.
5. For each of the three types of measurement scales, list all of the characteristics it possesses.
6. Explain what is meant by saying that a measurement scale is:
   a. exhaustive.
   b. composed of mutually exclusive categories.
   c. ordered.
   d. composed of equidistant categories.
7. Describe the measurement processes of "rating" and "rank ordering." Identify which type of scale of measurement is used for each of these procedures.

SAMPLE TEST QUESTIONS

for TYPES OF MEASUREMENT

1. After each of the following statements, indicate to which type of scale or scales the statement applies:
   a. Measurement categories on the scale are so defined that each subject is placed in only one category at a time.
   b. The possible measurement categories on the scale represent equal-sized steps.
   c. It is possible to add measurements together and/or to calculate differences between measurements.
   d. The measurement categories can be placed in any order without destroying the scale.

2. For the following examples, indicate whether the measures taken are nominal (N), weak-ordinal (w-O), ordinal (O), or interval (I):

 a. In a study on the effects of nicotine, 12 rats are dosed and then run down a two-foot-long alley. The running time for each rat is recorded.

 b. At a grocery story display, volunteers are given four colas to taste (Coca Cola, Pepsi Cola, Diet Rite, and Royal Crown) without knowing which is which. They are asked to indicate which one they prefer of the four they have sampled.

 c. You determine for each person in a neighborhood whether or not he/she has cable TV.

 d. In a survey about nuclear power as a source of energy, you ask people to rate their agreement with each of ten statements about nuclear power on a scale of 1 to 7.

 e. During 15-minute job interviews for graduating college students, you measure GSR (Galvanic Skin Response, a physiological indicator of nervousness) and heart rate of the persons being interviewed. You compare these measures to the same measures taken for 15 minutes before and after the interview.

 f. You mentally classify the girls you know as thin, fat, or just right.

 g. Students are ranked according to their scores on a final test.

SECTION 3: THE EFFECTS OF TAKING MEASURES ON THE THINGS BEING MEASURED

Sometimes taking a measurement can change the thing being measured. When this happens, we say that the observer used a **reactive measure.** In some situations, reactive measures can completely distort conclusions based on the measurements. For example, if a police officer sitting in her car in full view of traffic concludes on the basis of her visual measurement of vehicular speeds that we are all law-abiding citizens, she is probably coming to a false conclusion based on having used a reactive measure. We react to the means by which she is taking the measure by slowing down to the speed limit. This means that the measure she gets of our speed does not reflect how rapidly we generally travel. If the police officer wants a nonreactive measure of our speed, she is going to have to hide.

In the preschool study we discussed earlier in this chapter, the different ways you measured the children's activity level are all potentially reactive. The presence of the two college-student raters, especially if having visitors to the classroom is an unusual event, may change the children's overall activity pattern. If the college students obviously must watch each child to reach their decision about the child's activity classification, this may alter the child's behavior. (Why are those creeps prowling around watching me?) If the teacher behaves naturally while making her observations, the children will probably be less reactive to her measure since they are used to her. Your own observation of the children's toy-switching behavior through a **one-**

way mirror should keep them from reacting to your presence, but the fact that you are placing them in a strange room to take the measurements may affect their behavior.

SOLUTIONS TO THE PROBLEM OF REACTIVE MEASURES

The Observer Can Hide

Obviously, one solution to the problem of human subjects reacting to being watched is the one suggested for the police officer: the observer can hide. The one-way mirror is a technique that has been developed to permit such inconspicuous observation, especially in clinical settings. However, it is likely that many adults are aware of the existence of such a thing as one-way mirrors and will assume that they are being observed even if no one is in the room. Secret tape recorders, movie cameras, and "peek-holes" are other possibilities, if it is indeed important to obtain a nonreactive measure. However, use of these devices may raise some ethical and legal questions.

The Observer Can Take on Protective Coloration

Sometimes, the observer can become part of the group being observed or at least an inconspicuous part of the group's environment. The teacher in the preschool study is likely to cause less disruption in her students' behavior than are outsiders since she is a standard part of the children's environment. Disguising the observer as a participant of a group being studied may be possible, although it is sometimes difficult to make detailed observations without giving yourself away (imagine dressing your college raters up as preschool children). When sampling public opinion or collecting information through interviews, it may be best to have your interviewer resemble the people being interviewed as much as possible. For instance, it was found in one study that when black children were tested individually they had higher IQ scores with black interviewers as opposed to white interviewers (Canady, 1936). In another study, which traced the genetics of albinism in an Indian tribe, an Indian interviwer acquired much more accurate information about the occurrence of births where the probable father was not a woman's legal husband than did white anthropologists (Woolf and Dukepoo, 1969). Again, as with hiding the observer, having the observer take on protective coloration may raise ethical or legal issues. After all, in other contexts, the labels "spy" or "agent provocateur" might be applied to a disguised observer.

The Purpose of the Measurement Can Be Disguised

Another approach to creating nonreactive measures is to disguise the purpose of the measurement from the subject. This is often done in experiments with humans, when knowledge of what is being measured is very likely to influence people's behavior. In the Milgram (1974) series of experiments on aggression, the participants were led to believe that they were giving real electric shocks to improve a student's learning performance. They were told that what was being measured was the rate at which the "student" was learning. Actually, the important measures being taken were the intensity and duration of the bogus "shocks" the participants were willing to administer to another human being just because an experimenter had told them to do so. Although such deception has been profitably used in many social-science research projects, concern about experimenter ethics may somewhat limit future use of the technique.

The Degree of Reaction to the Measure May Itself Be Measured

Sometimes, a study can be designed to combine a potentially reactive measure with some way of measuring the degree to which the subject is reacting. This is a technique often used in designing questionnaires. As a simple example, you might ask persons both their age, and, at another point in the questionnaire, their birthdate. Often people who react to a question about age by underestimating it do not alter their birthdate to be consistent. The MMPI (Minnesota Multi-Phasic Personality Inventory) contains a scale that estimates how truthfully the person is responding to the questionnaire by checking the consistency of certain answers. Sometimes, it is possible to "spot-check" for reactivity of a measure. In a study of the personalities of New Orleans blacks, a sample of subjects being interviewed in depth by white psychiatrists was also interviewed by a black psychiatrist. In this case, not much difference was reported in the two sets of interview results (Rohrer and Edmonson, 1960), making the investigators feel more secure about the information gained from the interview.

The Passage of Time May Make the Subject Less Reactive

In some cases, the solution may be simply to let time pass. Often, people become so engrossed in what they are doing that they stop reacting to being observed. While the initial measures of a person's behavior may be reactive, the later ones become much less so. In fact, there are situations in which it is probably better to be open with people about observing them rather than to leave nasty suspicions in their minds that they are being secretly spied upon.

Unobtrusive Measurement

It may be possible to make a measure nonreactive by measuring not the individuals themselves but their by-products. You might, for example, measure alcohol consumption in a family by unobtrusively checking their garbage pails and counting the number of bottles. This would most likely be a less reactive measure (unless they caught you in the garbage pail) than getting the family to agree to consume alcohol only from graduated bottles which you obviously checked periodically. To get back to our preschool class, if you wanted an **unobtrusive measure** of toy preference you might check on the wear and tear on the toys. Those toys more in demand should deteriorate at a faster rate than those left on the shelf. Webb *et al.* (1966) have written a book, *Unobtrusive Measures: Nonreactive Research in the Social Sciences,* which can be very helpful to those in search of creative nonreactive measures.

RECAPITULATION

for EFFECTS OF TAKING MEASURES

In summary, there are some measures that may result in changes in the thing they measure. These are said to be *reactive measures.* In any research, the observers will have to consider the possibility that their measure is reactive and will also have to estimate the extent to which its reactivity may distort conclusions. Many of the suggestions for making measures on people nonreactive hinge on disguising from people what is being measured or preventing them from knowing that measurement is even taking place. While these techniques have been useful in the past, the researcher of the future will have to consider more seriously possible ethical issues raised by their use.

BEHAVIORAL OBJECTIVES

for EFFECTS OF TAKING MEASURES

1. Define the term *reactive measure.* Give an example of a reactive measure, explaining how it might change what it is measuring.
2. Describe three of the different solutions suggested for reducing the reactive effects of a measure.
3. Given a description of a situation in which a measure is being taken:
   a. identify the measure.
   b. describe how it may be reactive.
   c. suggest a way to make the measure nonreactive.
4. Given a description of a situation in which steps have been taken to make a measure nonreactive, identify the technique used to decrease reactivity and discuss what problems may have been prevented by using this technique.

SAMPLE TEST QUESTIONS

for EFFECTS OF TAKING MEASURES

1. You are interested in determining the attitude toward abortion of mothers on welfare. Accordingly, you ask the social workers in the welfare office to interview all the mothers they come into contact with about how they feel toward abortion and then to judge whether overall each woman could be said to be favorable, unfavorable, or neutral. What measure is being taken in this study? In what ways could it be reactive? How might you take a better measure?

2. In a study of toy preferences of children in a kindergarten class, you station two student observers near where the toys are kept and ask them to write down which child takes which toy and how long he or she plays with it. What measures are you taking in this study? In what ways might they be reactive? How might you take less reactive measures?

3. You are interested in whether relaxation training can reduce students' anxiety while taking tests in school and help improve their test performances. You will be testing each student in your lab both before and after relaxation training on both a written test and a motor test. You tell them that the written test is an IQ test and that the motor test is a test of their manual dexterity. What measures are you taking in this study? Why are you trying to make the tests seem important to the subject? What problem might occur if the subjects didn't believe that the tests were very important to them?

4. Investigators wanted to determine how people in big cities as compared to those in small towns would respond to a strange child's request for help. One way suggested to do this was for the investigators to pick people on the street at random and interview them with several specific questions about what they would do if a child had approached them at that moment. This was rejected in favor of having an actual child approach selected people in the street and ask for help in a standard fashion. Two concealed observers would record what the person approached did and also rescue the "dummy" child if necessary. Why did the investigators favor the second measure? How might the first way of measuring have been reactive? Which method do you feel might raise some ethical issues and why?

SECTION 4: WHAT IS A VARIABLE?

Experiments and research studies are designed around **variables.** Variables are measured; variables are manipulated by the experimenter to see how they affect other variables; two or more variables are measured at the same time to see if there is any relationship among them. So what then is a variable? It is anything that can vary along some dimension, or, in other words, it is anything that can be measured.

DISTINGUISHING BETWEEN A VARIABLE AND A SINGLE VALUE OF A VARIABLE

For something to be called a variable, it must be capable of varying; that is, it must be able to take more than one **value** or **level.** For example, "sex of subject" is a variable, since it can take two values: male and female. "Female" by itself is not a variable, but rather a **single value of the variable** "sex of subject." "Femaleness," however, might be a variable if you could think of a way to measure it.

Application 1 of the Concept of a Variable

From the following list, identify those items that represent variables (V) and those items that represent only a single value (SV) of some variables.

male	Republican
political party	time spent talking
98	height
test score	67
sex	2 minutes
female	Democratic
63 inches	red
house	tree

You probably decided that the following items represent variables: political party, test score, sex, color, time spent talking, and height. In each case, you could think of two or more values these items could have.

The other items in the list are more likely to be single values of variables. "Male" and "female" are obviously two single values of the variable "sex." "Republican" and "Democratic" are two possible values of the variable "political party." The numbers "67" and "98" might be two single values of the variable "test score." "Sixty-three inches" could be a single value of the variable "height," and "2 minutes" might well be a single value of the variable "time spent talking." The items "tree" and "house" might both be single values of some such variable as "representational objects in children's drawings." If these items had been something like "size of house" or "type of tree," then they would have been variables.

Application 2 of the Concept of a Variable

In each of the following cases, come up with a variable name which would include the collection of single values listed:

1. housewife, secretary, nurse, teacher . . .
2. 10 years, 18 years, 2 years, 9 years . . .
3. 14 minutes, 2 minutes, 1 minute, 10 minutes . . .
4. new textbook, old textbook . . .
5. brick, asphalt, dirt, crushed rock, cement . . .

In order to figure out the possible variables to which these collections of single values belong, you have to use a bit of imagination. The first set of values might be from a variable called "women's occupations" or, perhaps better, "traditional women's occupations." It's hard to say since you were given only a partial list. The second set of values, varying on a dimension of years, might come from a variable called "age of subject," although it might also be from a variable such as "years of schooling." Without further information, the third variable might best be called "time" and left at that. The fourth variable looks as if someone wants to compare the effects of two textbooks in an educational setting. We might as well call the variable something like "type of textbook." The final set of values might come from a variable called "type of road surface."

WHAT DOES IT MEAN TO "OPERATIONALLY DEFINE" A VARIABLE?

Defining a variable completely so that another person interprets the variable in the same way is called "operationally defining the variable." In order for the results of an experiment or research study to be of any use to the rest of the world, the results must be repeatable. This means not only that the original researcher should get the same results when the research study is repeated, but also that any other person who repeats the same research should get the same results. It is pointless to try to make any theoretical or practical use of a research procedure that works one way for one person and another way for another person. To ensure that your research will be repeatable by other investigators it is necessary that you be perfectly clear as to how your variables are defined in terms of what you did to vary them or to measure them. Only if others can interpret your variables in the same way as you did originally will they be able to replicate your research.

Much of the confusion that exists about differing results of what appears to be the same research procedure can be traced to differing operational definitions of variables called by the same name. If Study 1 says that increased "anxiety" improves "learning" and Study 2 says that increased "anxiety" impairs "learning," don't throw up your hands in despair, chuck the studies in the wastebasket, and walk off muttering that you knew there was nothing to social science research. Stop and take a look first at how the variables were operationally defined in the two studies. Does "anxiety" mean the same thing in both studies? Was "learning" measured the same way in the two studies? The apparent difference in results may actually represent a difference in the **operational definitions** of the variables in the experiments. If you want to apply the research results of others to your own work, you have to look for the operational definition closest to your definition of the term.

Application 1 of Operational Definition of Variables

For each of the variables below, think of two different ways you might operationally define the variable. Be very specific in your definitions so that another person could not be confused about your meaning.

learning
hunger
political viewpoint

For the variable *learning,* you could probably come up with different operational definitions as long as you continued to think about it. An operational definition of "learning" for a particular experiment or research study must specify what is being learned, the conditions under which it is being learned, and how the learning is being measured. Thus for one experiment, an operational definition for learning might be a score on a particular test; for another, it might be the solution time for a puzzle; and for another, it might be the rate of learning a new task; and so on.

Hunger is another term that may be operationally defined in many ways. In animal experiments it is often operationally defined as "hours without food." Some animal researchers, however, believe that "percent of normal body weight after deprivation" is a better operational definition. Another possible definition of "hunger" may be expressed in terms of how much trouble the subject is willing to go to to get at food. To be precise, researchers might measure the intensity of electric shock the animal is willing to experience to gain access to the food. If you are dealing with humans, you might ask them either directly or indirectly how hungry they feel at a given moment. Or you might offer them some food and note whether or not they take any, and, if they do, how much they take. Obviously, with a little thought, you could come up with a vast number of operational definitions of "hunger."

Political viewpoint is yet another general term that would have to be operationalized for any particular research study. Political viewpoint might be defined for your purposes as the political party to which a person is registered. Or you might want to define it in terms of the person's response to a set of questions about current political situations. Maybe you might prefer to have the people rate themselves on a conservative-to-liberal scale. There are still other ways you could operationally define political viewpoint. You could ask people who they voted for in a recent election or determine their score on a standardized questionnaire (for example, the Radicalism-Conservatism Scale published by Comrey and Newmeyer, 1965). However you define the variable, it must be possible for someone else to read your operational definition and be able to take measures of political viewpoint in the same way.

Application 2 of Operational Definition of Variables

For each of the following definitions of variables, specify in what ways the operatioal definitions are not complete by writing down at least one further question you'd want to have answered before you could use the variable in your own research study.

1. *Amount of stimulant consumed:* Each subject will consume either no stimulant, a moderate dose, or a large dose.
2. *Activity level:* The children in the classroom will be classified as withdrawn, normal, or hyperactive.
3. *Toy preference:* The same set of six toys will be presented to each child and the one he or she prefers noted.

None of the three variable definitions given above is a good operational definition. For each of them, you would have to ask the researcher some questions before you could determine exactly what was meant. For the *amount-of-stimulant-consumed* variable, the first question that probably occurred to you is "what stimulant?" It would make a lot of difference if the researcher were talking about "amphetamine" rather than "caffeine." Another obvious question would be what is meant by "moderate" and "large" doses. It would be necessary to be much more specific about dosages before this would begin to be a usable operational definition that would allow someone else to repeat the research.

"Hyperactivity" is a word that is often used, but rarely well defined. When you use *activity level* as a variable in a research study, it is necessary to be very specific about the basis on which you will decide that a given child should be classified as withdrawn, normal, or hyperactive. In the preschool class example at the beginning of this chapter, you used three different possible operational definitions of activity level. In one case, you asked the teacher to sort the children into three word-labeled categories. For another measure, you asked two student raters who did not know the children to observe them and to agree on a rating of their activity. Your third operational definition concerned the frequency with which each child would switch among toys under set conditions. Probably this last operational definition is the most repeatable by a new researcher, but it might not be exactly what you feel is meant by "activity level." If your two student observers showed high agreement in their ratings when following your instructions as to how to use the rating scale, then it is likely that the second operational definition, if it included your instructions, would also be usable by other researchers. To make a complete operational definition of hyperactivity, it would be necessary to state the rules by which the children were classified or assigned values, how they were observed, and who did the classification.

The *toy-preference* variable seems somewhat easier to operationalize, but there are still some things that the original definition doesn't specify. One researcher might define "toy preference" as which toy the child selected when presented with the entire array and told to choose the one he or she liked best. Another researcher might define it according to the amount of time the child spent playing with each toy when all were continuously available. Notice that these two operational definitions might not yield the same results. For example, a child might choose the pretty doll first, but might subsequently spend a longer time playing with the model farm. In your research, you'll have to use the operational definition that comes closest to what you mean by "toy preference."

RECAPITULATION

for WHAT IS A VARIABLE?

A *variable* is anything that can vary along some dimension. Any variable must have at least two or more different *single values* or *levels*. When you define a variable in a research study, the definition must be so complete that another person would have no problem in repeating your research. Such a complete definition is called an *operational definition*. Any variable can be operationally defined in a number of ways. Supposed differences in the results of different research studies are often simply the result of using different operational definitions.

BEHAVIORAL OBJECTIVES

for WHAT IS A VARIABLE?

1. Describe what is meant by "operationally defining a variable."
2. Describe why it is important to operationally define variables in a research study.
3. Choose a variable yourself and give an operational definition of it.
4. Given a list of variables and of single values of variables, be able to specify which is which (see Application 1, p. 47).
5. Given a set of single values of a variable, devise a name for the variable (see Application 2, p. 47).
6. Given the name of a variable:
   a. operationally define it (see Application 1, p. 48).
   b. give some sample single values for the variable.
7. Given a definition of a variable, point out some ways in which its operational definition is incomplete (see Application 2, p. 49).
8. Given a description of a research study, identify the variables involved and give their operational definitions.

SAMPLE TEST QUESTION

for WHAT IS A VARIABLE?

1. In a study of effects of sex-role stereotyping, a group of 20 boys and 20 girls were tested on what they could remember about a short story they had just read. The experimenter wanted to see whether what the children remembered was influenced by sex-role stereotypes in the story. In the short story were included examples of four different story situations. Two of these were stereotypic: a boy doing things usually associated with boys and a girl doing things usually associated with girls. Two of the story situations were nonstereotypic: a boy doing things usually done by girls and a girl doing things usually done by boys. After reading the short story, the children were given a reading-comprehension test and were scored for their correct answers as to the activities in which the characters in the story had been engaged. The experimenter found that the children correctly recalled the stereotype-appropriate behaviors more often than they recalled stereotype-inappropriate behaviors for a given story character. There was no difference in findings between boys and girls. This study implies that ideas about what is and is not appropriate for a given sex influence memory, even in children.

a.   Identify at least three variables involved in this study.

b.   For each of the three variables, write out the operational definition of the variable as given in the above description of the experiment.

c.   Are there any improvements or clarifications these operational definitions should have? Please specify.

d.   For one of the variables you have identified, give a description of the complete set of single values the variable could have.

SECTION 5: INDEPENDENT AND DEPENDENT VARIABLES

DISTINGUISHING IVs AND DVs

As you worked on the sample test question at the end of the previous section, you may have felt that the different variables you identified functioned in very different ways in the study. The levels or values of some of the variables were specifically created by the experimenter before running the actual experiment. The experimenter decided to make the sex of the children participating in the study a variable by selecting both boys and girls. In addition, the experimenter created the four story situations, determining all the levels of another variable in the experiment. Both of these variables can be seen as *in*put into the experiment. Such variables, whose levels are determined ahead of time by the experimenter, are called **Independent Variables (IVs).**

In contrast, the variable measuring what the children remembered about the story is an *out*put variable for the experiment. While the experimenter determined ahead of time how this variable would be measured, the actual measurements obtained are dependent on the responses of the children and can be known only after running the experiment. What the children remember is, after all, what the experimenter is trying to find out by conducting the research. Such variables representing the output of the experimental process are called **Dependent Variables (DVs).**

Usually it is not too difficult to spot the major IVs and DVs early in the description of a research study, sometimes in the title itself. One general form of descriptive statement that often occurs is: "This experiment was done to establish the effects of *(IV)* on *(DV)*." For example, an experiment might be done to investigate the effects of subject anxiety on learning a list of nonsense syllables. The input to this particular study would be a set number of different levels of subject anxiety as selected or determined by the experimenter. The output would be measurements of each subject's performance on the learning task. The purpose of the experiment would be to establish a cause-effect relationship between the two variables.

The same combination of IV and DV could be given in a different form of statement: "This research study was conducted to see whether *(DV)* was affected by changes in *(IV)*." Specifically, the above experiment might be described as: "This experiment attempted to show whether performance on a learning task was affected

by the level of anxiety of the subjects.'' Even though this statement appears in reverse order, the experimenter still is doing the same thing: manipulating or selecting
subject anxiety level (IV) to determine whether it affects or changes measurements
of the subjects' learning performance (DV).

You have to be careful about picking out IVs and DVs from research descriptions, because a given variable might be an IV in one research study and a DV in
another. For instance, a researcher might be interested in determining whether engaging in a learning task affects a subject's level of anxiety. In this case, the experimenter will determine ahead of time the kinds of learning tasks to which the subjects
will be exposed and will measure as output for the study the level of anxiety produced in the subjects by participating in the learning tasks. Now, the *IV* is the type
of learning task and the *DV* is subject anxiety.

OPERATIONAL DEFINITION OF
AN INDEPENDENT VARIABLE

An IV is operationally defined by specifying the levels (single values) that the experimenter is going to use in the experiment. Since an IV is a *variable,* the operational
definition of an IV must specify at least two levels, although there can be more. In
the sex-stereotyping research study described on page 51, the ''sex-of-subject'' IV
had two levels: boy and girl. The experimenter saw to it that he selected 20 of each of
the two kinds of subject. The second IV, the four levels of story situation, was also
set up ahead of time by the experimenter: he made sure that each of the four sex-
stereotyping situations was represented equally often in the story the children read.

Since most variables can potentially have a large number of levels, you must be
explicit about which levels of the IV you are using when defining a particular IV for
a particular experiment. For example, if we wanted to do a study on the effects of
the consumption of a stimulant (IV) on the speed of working through a set of math
problems (DV), we would specify not only what stimulant we intend to use, but also
all the dosage levels. We might, for example, set up three levels of the IV as follows:
no cups of coffee (no-dose level), one cup of coffee (low-dose level), and four cups
of coffee (high-dose level). Depending on how we designed our experiment, we
might have different subjects for each of the dosage levels or we might study the
same subjects at all three dosage levels. In either case, our DV will be a measurement
of how rapidly each subject works through the set of math problems.

OPERATIONAL DEFINITION OF A DEPENDENT VARIABLE

An operational definition of a DV must include specification of what measures you
are going to take on the subjects, what kind of measurement scale you will be using,
and how you will take the measurement. For example, in the sex-stereotyping study,
the DV was a reading-comprehension score. For a complete operational definition,
the researcher has to describe the test and how it was scored. For example, he might
have used a 40-item test with 10 items relevant to each of the four story situations.
Each child could then score from 1 to 10 for each story situation. This would be an

interval-type measurement of the child's recall. Or he might ask each child to recall an event from the story and then categorize the child according to which of the four story situations he or she chose to recall. This would be a nominal-type measurement of what the child remembered best about the story.

MULTIPLE IVS

Frequently an experiment or research study will use more than one IV or more than one DV. While this increases the complexity of doing the research, it also increases the amount of information that can be gathered from a single study.

Using multiple IVs can quickly make an experiment more complicated to run. Consider the experiment proposed on page 53, designed to determine whether the amount of coffee consumed by a person affects the speed at which a set of math problems can be worked. The major IV, "amount of stimulant consumed," was defined as having three levels. But, as we begin to think about this, we might wonder whether those subjects already used to drinking coffee would react differently to the stimulating effects of a dose of coffee than subjects who did not regularly consume the stuff. So we decide to add a second IV, "customary coffee consumption," and define it as having three levels: rarely or never drinks coffee, moderate consumer (one or two cups a day), and heavy consumer (three or more cups a day). Now we have expanded the experiment to include nine conditions (i.e., rare drinkers who get no coffee, rare drinkers who get one cup, rare drinkers who get four cups, moderate drinkers who get no coffee, moderate drinkers who get one cup, moderate drinkers who get four cups, heavy drinkers who get no coffee, heavy drinkers who get one cup, and heavy drinkers who get four cups).

A friend (?) of ours then suggests that the difficulty of the math problems might also be worth considering. He speculates that a person who had consumed a stimulant might whip through a set of easy problems more quickly, but would be unable to concentrate on hard problems. This tempts us to add a third IV, problem difficulty, which we define as having two levels: an easy set of problems and a hard set of problems. Now there are eighteen ($3 \times 3 \times 2$) conditions in our experiment. An example of one of the conditions would be a moderate coffee drinker (level 2 of IV_2) who is given a heavy dose of coffee (level 3 of IV_1) and is then asked to work an easy set of problems (level 1 of IV_3). Our statistical consultant points out that if we intend to use different subjects for each condition of our experiment, then we'd better find at least 180 subjects, a minimum of ten for each experimental condition. Another so-called friend subsequently muses that the use of stimulants may be helpful to men in solving problems but be harmful to women (whom he feels are sufficiently agitated without any outside help), and accordingly suggests yet a fourth IV for our experiment. When we contemplate having to find ten men *and* ten women for each of 18 experimental conditions, we slug him. Seriously, it is easy to see how careful consideration of a research question could suggest many interesting IVs. Dealing with multiple IVs and deciding how many you can use at the same time is a design issue we will consider in a later chapter.

MULTIPLE DVs

On the other hand, increasing the number of DVs in an experiment usually is less complicated. Each DV we decide to add simply means taking another measure on each subject. When we measure the probem-solving ability of the subjects in the coffee-consumption experiment, we may want to measure not only the speed with which the subjects work through each problem set (DV_1) but also the accuracy (DV_2) of their solutions. Using two measures of problem-solving ability increases the information we can get from the experiment. We might find, for example, that while a stimulant increases the speed of solution of the problems, it decreases the accuracy of the solutions.

RECAPITULATION

for INDEPENDENT AND DEPENDENT VARIABLES

The *Independent Variables* (IVs) in an experiment are those the experimenter manipulates: they represent what the experimenter puts *in*to the experiment. An IV is operationally defined by specifying before the experiment all the levels of the variable that are to be investigated. Often multiple IVs are used, resulting in a multiplicative increase in the total number of experimental conditions created by the experimenter.

The *Dependent Variable* (DV) in a research study is what the experimenter observes and measures about the subjects after they have been affected by the IVs. The DV is some aspect of the subject's behavior that the researcher expects to be altered by the action of one or more of the IVs. The measurement scale to be used and the manner in which the measurements will be taken are defined before the research is begun, but the actual measurements are obtained during the course of the experiment. The DV is the *out*come of the research. Multiple DVs are frequently used, increasing the information obtained from the experiment and permitting investigation of relationships between different DVs.

BEHAVIORAL OBJECTIVES

for INDEPENDENT AND DEPENDENT VARIABLES

1. Describe the concept of an IV.
2. Describe the concept of a DV.
3. Given a series of statements about the general characteristics of varibles, identify which statements refer to IVs, which refer to DVs, which refer to both types of variables, and which refer to neither.
4. Given single sentences summarizing an experiment, identify on the basis of the form of the sentence which part refers to an IV and which refers to a DV.
5. Given a description of an experimental study, identify the IVs and the DVs.

6. Given the name of a variable, make up an experiment in which that variable would be an IV. Give a complete operational definition of your IV.

7. Given the name of a variable, make up an experiment in which that variable would be a DV. Give a complete operational definition of your DV.

SAMPLE TEST QUESTIONS

for INDEPENDENT AND DEPENDENT VARIABLES

1. Describe the concept of an IV. How do you operationally define an IV?

2. Describe the concept of a DV. How does it differ from an IV? What is necessary for the operational definition of a DV?

3. For the following statements, fill in *IV* and *DV* in the appropriate blanks:

   a. This study ascertained the effects of _____ on _____.

   b. This study investigated how _____ was affected by _____.

   c. The current research showed that changes in _____ could be produced by varying _____.

   d. _____ was found in this experiment to be affected by _____.

4. For each of the following variables, make up a statement in which the variable is an IV in an experiment (you'll have to dream up your own DVs for each experiment). For at least one of them go into a complete operational definition of the IV.

   a. hunger

   b. fatigue

   c. activity

5. For each of the following variables, make up a statement in which the variable is a DV in an experiment (you'll have to dream up your own IVs for each experiment). For at least one of them provide a complete operational definition of the DV.

   a. hunger

   b. fatigue

   c. activity

6. Read the following abstract of a published research study from Crawford, Friesen, and Tomlinson-Keasey (1977): Effects of cognitively induced anxiety on hand temperature.

   This study explored the relationship of cognitively induced anxiety and hand-temperature reduction in a nonclinical sample. Forty college students were randomly assigned to either the Anxiety Group or the Pleasant Group. Following a baseline period, individuals in the Anxiety Group discussed with the experimenter topics which were anxiety-producing for them. Individuals in the Pleasant Group discussed topics of a pleasant nature. During those discussions, hand temperatures were recorded from the palmar surface of the third finger on the dominant hand.

ated that hand-temperature decreases were significant only in anxiety-producing topics.*

V and operationally define it.

DV and operationally define it.

elationship found between the IV and the DV.

7. In an experiment on the effects of observing TV violence on subsequent play behavior of children, the researcher decides to compare the effects of two films. One film shows a group of people playing in an active game with several violent incidents occurring between players. The other film shows the same group of people playing the same game but with no violence. The experimenter divides her subjects into three age groups: 3–5 years, 6–8 years, and 9–10 years. She makes sure that there are ten girls and ten boys in each of the age groups. Half of the boys and girls in each age group watch the violent film on TV and half watch the nonviolent film. After observing the film, the children in each age group are asked to play the same game and the number of violent acts displayed by the different children in play is recorded.

   a. Identify the three IVs used in this study. Specify the levels of each IV.

   b. How many experimental conditions will result from using these three IVs? Describe each experimental condition.

   c. What is the DV for this experiment?

SECTION 6: NON-SUBJECT AND SUBJECT IVs

One way you can produce different levels of an IV for your experiment is by direct manipulation of each of your subjects. With this technique, each of your subjects could potentially be assigned to any of the IV levels and you, the experimenter, would decide which level each subject will experience, which fate each one will suffer. In the stimulant experiment described on page 54, the principal IV, "amount of stimulant consumed," is operationally defined by such direct manipulation of the subjects. According to our operational definition of this IV, we are free to assign each subject to whatever level of coffee drinking we desire ("John, you're a no-dose subject; Mary you're a four-cup subject—start drinking"). Such an IV, whose levels are created by direct manipulation of subjects, is called a **Non-Subject Independent Variable.**

Another way of operationally defining an IV allows the experimenter to determine the levels of the IV only by selecting subjects who already possess a stated characteristic and not by direct manipulation of each subject. The second IV in the stimulant experiment, "customary coffee consumption," is of this type. The three levels of this variable were: never or rarely drinks coffee, moderate consumption (averages one to two cups a day), and heavy consumption (averages three or more

*Reprinted by permission of Plenum Publishing Company (copyright © 1977).

cups a day). For this variable we are not free to assign each subject to whatever level we wish; we have to take the subjects as they come with their built-in coffee-drinking habits. It will be necessary to ask each subject (or to find out some other way) what his or her usual coffe consumption is, and we will have to assign each subject to a particular level of the IV according to the answer. This type of IV, in which you are not free to assign subjects to levels but must assign them according to a characteristic they already possess, is called a **Subject Independent Variable.**

Many variables can be operationally defined either way, depending on the wishes of the experimenter. The "amount-of-stimulant-consumed" IV, operationally defined above as a Non-Subject IV, could be redefined as a Subject IV. Instead of forcing our subjects to drink the amount of coffee we specify, we might place the subjects in a room for an hour with coffee freely available. We would then record how much coffee each subject spontaneously drinks in that hour. We might operationally define our "amount-of-stimulant-consumed" IV as having the following levels: none, spontaneously drinks one cup, spontaneously drinks two cups, and spontaneously drinks three or more cups. While we still define the IV levels, we are no longer in control of which subject is placed at which level. If John spontaneously drinks six cups of coffee, we can't arbitrarily assign him to the no-dose level.

CHARACTERISTICS OF NON-SUBJECT IVs

When an IV is operationally defined to be a Non-Subject IV, it is the experimenter who determines what each subject experiences. Potentially the experimenter could assign any subject to any IV level. There is no necessary reason beyond the experimenter's choice why a particular subject experiences a particular IV level. Non-Subject IVs permit an experimenter to assign subjects at **random** (by chance). Or, if the researcher prefers, subjects may be assigned to IV levels on some other basis. The experimenter is in control. In the "effects-of-TV-violence" study described on page 57, the "type-of-film" IV was a Non-Subject IV since the experimenter could determine for each child which film was seen.

CHARACTERISTICS OF SUBJECT IVs

For a Subject IV, the experimenter still defines the levels, but each subject can be placed in only one appropriate level. Random or other arbitrary assignment of subjects to levels is no longer possible. In the same "effects-of-TV-violence" study mentioned above, the "age-of-subject" and "sex-of-subject" IVs are both of this type. It is simply not possible for the experimenter to choose a child arbitrarily and declare that the child will be in the 9–10-year-old group when in fact the child is 7! The "sex-of-subject" IV has the same limitation, since the children must be assigned into its two levels on the basis of their actual sex. The researcher could not assign "John" to the "female" group in the same way she could decide whether or not he is to see the violent film.

Obviously, if we are using a Subject IV, we'll have to take preliminary measures of some sort on the subjects to decide at which level they belong. If "sex of subject" is the IV, we'll have to determine whether each subject is male or female. If "amount of coffee spontaneously consumed" is the IV, we'll have to watch the subjects to see how much they consume in order to assign them correctly.

PROBLEM WITH SUBJECT IVs

Using a Subject IV always carries a built-in limitation which arises from not being able to assign the subjects at random. We cannot be sure that the subjects at the different levels of the IV differ *only* in the way specified by a Subject IV. This situation may give rise to some problems in interpreting the effects of an IV on our DVs. Suppose (and this is just a suppose) that students with higher grade point averages (GPAs) also generally drink more coffee. In selecting subjects for the "amount-of-coffee-spontaneously-consumed" IV, it might happen that our high-dose level (three or more cups spontaneously consumed) also ends up with higher GPA subjects on the average. Now if our DV tells us that the "high-dose" subjects did better on the math problems than the other groups, do we attribute this result to the direct effects of the coffee consumption or to the higher average GPA for that group? We'll discuss some ways to minimize this kind of problem in a later chapter, but it will remain as built-in difficulty of IVs operationally defined as Subject IVs. Unfortunately, some very interesting IVs can only be operationally defined as Subject IVs. Such things as "sex of subject," "IQ," "socioeconomic class," "race," and "ethnic group", are all IVs which we cannot directly manipulate, and the interpretation of their effects will always be limited.

RECAPITULATION

for NON-SUBJECT AND SUBJECT IVs

The levels of an IV to be used in an experiment can be defined by the experimenter in two different ways. If the experimenter is operationally defining the IV in a *Non-Subject* manner, then the experimenter can arbitrarily assign subjects to the IV levels and manipulate the subjects to see that they experience the amount of the IV appropriate to their assigned level. When the IV is operationally defined as a *Subject IV,* the experimenter defines the levels in terms of a characteristic the subjects already possess and then searches for subjects who already have the characteristic required for each level. When using a Subject IV the experimenter must take some initial measure on the subjects to determine at which level of the IV they belong. With a Non-Subject operationaly defined IV, however, the experimenter is free to assign subjects to the different levels of the IV at random or in any other arbitrary way. Many variables can be defined either way, although some—like age, sex, and grade point average—can only be defined as Subject IVs. A Subject IV always is limited in its usefulness by the fact that the subjects at the different IV levels may consistently vary in some other way than that specified by the operational definition of the IV.

BEHAVIORAL OBJECTIVES

for NON-SUBJECT AND SUBJECT IVs

1. Given a list of statements describing Non-Subject and Subject IVs, identify which is which.
2. Describe what is meant by the term "Non-Subject IV." Give an example of a Non-Subject IV and explain how you would divide your subjects among its levels.
3. Describe what is meant by the term "Subject IV." Give an example of a Subject IV and explain how you would divide your subjects among its levels.
4. Given a description of an experiment, identify the IVs as either Subject or Non-Subject IVs.
5. Discuss a limitation on the interpretation of the effects of a Subject IV. How is it possible to avoid this limitation with a Non-Subject IV?
6. Given a list of IVs, operationally define each one as a Subject IV and also as a Non-Subject IV.

SAMPLE TEST QUESTIONS

for NON-SUBJECT AND SUBJECT IVs

1. Identify each of the following statements as characteristic of a Subject IV (SIV) or of a Non-Subject IV (NSIV).
   a. It is possible to assign subjects at random to the different levels of the IV.
   b. The experimenter is able to manipulate the subjects directly into representing different IV levels.
   c. It is necessary to measure something about the subjects to determine which IV level they will represent.
   d. Any subject can potentially be placed at any level of the IV by the experimenter.
   e. It always carries the possibility that the subjects at the different levels of the IV may show consistent differences other than those produced by the IV.
   f. The different levels of the IV are achieved by selecting appropriate subjects.
2. For each of the following research descriptions, identify the IV and state whether it is a Subject or a Non-Subject IV.
   a. The experimenter wants to determine the effect of the subjects' chronological age on the amount of cooperative play in which the subjects engage in a nursery-school setting. The age groups to be studied are: 2 years, 2½

years, 3 years, 3½ years, 4 years, and 4½ years. (By the way, what's the DV here?)

b. The teacher wants to find out whether the effects of a new method of instruction are different for departmental majors as compared to nonmajors. She intends to measure instructional effects by scores on the class final.

c. In a research study on drug effects, each rat will be injected either with a neutral saline solution, a solution containing nicotine, or a solution containing amphetamine. The speed of running a straight alley for food reward will be measured for each rat for three consecutive trials after receiving the injection.

d. In a recent study on the effects of being caught in wrongdoing on subsequent helping behavior, people were observed at a local zoo. Those who were seen to feed bears inappropriate food despite warning signs were identified. Half of these people selected at random were given a mild reprimand ("Please don't feed the animals unauthorized food.") The other half were given a strong, forcefully spoken, reprimand ("Hey, don't feed unauthorized food to those animals. Don't you know it can hurt them?"). As each of the subjects walked away from the bear pits, a lady researcher dropped her purse, spilling its contents. Another researcher observed which subjects stopped to help the lady. It was found that 58 percent of those who had been harshly reprimanded spontaneously stopped, while only 25 percent of those who had been mildly reprimanded stopped. (Based on Katzev *et al.,* 1978).

3. The study described in Question 2d above also had a third "control" group, which consisted of people who had not fed the bears and were not reprimanded. What would have been a more appropriate "control" group to form a third level of the IV as described above? If you compare people who spontaneously feed bears with people who do not, do you have a Subject IV or a Non-Subject IV?

4. For two of the following variables, give both a Subject IV operational definition and a Non-Subject IV operational definition.
   hunger
   fatigue
   activity
   anger

SECTION 7: RELEVANT VARIABLES—CONTROLLED OR CONFOUNDING?

So far everything seems pretty straightforward about doing an experiment. You decide what your IVs and DVs are to be. You operationally define your IV as either a Subject or a Non-Subject IV. You obtain a sufficient number of subjects for each of your IV levels. You see that each subject has the characteristic or is given the experience appropriate to his or her level of the IV. You take DV measures on your subjects. Then you look and see whether your IV has affected your DV. Finally, you interpret your results and draw your conclusions.

But it isn't always that simple. Take, for example, the study described on page 61, which discusses the effects of reprimanding people for wrongdoing on their subsequent helping behavior. If you consider only people who were detected misfeeding the bears and who were then randomly given either a mild reprimand or a harsh one, you clearly have two levels of a Non-Subject IV. A third, obvious level for this IV would be a set of misfeeders who were not reprimanded at all. But the third group actually used in this experiment was formed from people who did not feed the bears to begin with and who therefore received no reprimand. Thus an additional Subject-type variable is introduced into the study, since the experimenter could not assign people to the misfeeding and nonmisfeeding groups at random but had to let them assign themselves. How might this change in the way of operationally defining the IV confuse the interpretation of results? It is possible that bear misfeeders are particularly loving individuals who feel compelled to stretch out a helping hand despite warning signs. Reprimanding them may actually inhibit their natural helpfulness. But without the results for a group of bear *mis*feeders who are *not* reprimanded, we don't know. We just can't assume that people who do not heed warning signs about feeding inappropriate food are automatically the same people who do or that they will respond in the same way to a reprimand.

A group of subjects in an experiment that experiences zero-level of the IV is often called the "control" group. An appropriate **control group** for an experiment should be as much alike as possible to the groups exposed to the other IV levels. The only difference that should exist between groups to be compared is the amount of the IV they experience. In the reprimand study, we could argue that the "no-reprimand" group was not an appropriate control group for the mild- and harsh-reprimand groups, since it differed from those groups not only in whether or not its subjects received a reprimand but also in whether or not the subjects were people who would spontaneously choose to misfeed the bears in the first place.

When you design an experiment, it is necessary to identify possible **Relevant Variables** which may have effects on the DV in addition to the effects produced by your IV. If these Relevant Variables are not accounted for, they may *confuse* your interpretation of the results of the experiment; in other words, the effects of the Relevant Variables may *confound* the effects of your IV. An important part of planning any research is to identify potential Relevant Variables and to control them, eliminating the possibility that their effects will distort the relationship of the IV and DV. If Relevant Variables are left free to vary in the experiment, they are called **Uncontrolled Variables.** When Uncontrolled Variables affect the DV in ways mistakenly attributed to the IV they are called **Confounding Variables.** Either Subject-type or Non-Subject-type Variables are potentially Confounding Variables. We could say for the zoo study that because of the inappropriate "control group," the reprimand IV was confounded by a Subject-type Relevant Variable of willingness to heed signs.

EXAMPLE OF RELEVANT VARIABLES WHICH MAY
AFFECT CONCLUSIONS: THE SPANISH-TEXTBOOK CASE

When the author was an undergraduate in college, members of the modern language department were debating whether it was better to teach second-year grammar out of a text in which explanations were given in English or out of a text in which everything was in the language to be learned. They decided to compare the results of the English-Spanish text they had been using with a new all-Spanish text. Two sections of 15 students each, called the "experimental" sections, were formed from among the best students of the preceding year. These sections were given the new text after an encouraging presentation by the teacher as to how it would be more beneficial although it might be more difficult at first. The "control" sections were two sections of standard size (about 30 students) that were not selected on the basis of previous performance. The students in these sections were given the old text without any special introduction. The same teacher taught all four sections, and all the sections met for the same number of hours per week. When all the sections took the same final, the "experimental" sections were found to have much higher average scores than the "control" sections. The department then adopted the all-Spanish text for future second-year classes. (This really did happen. Does anything about this study and its results bother you?)

ANALYSIS OF THE SPANISH-TEXTBOOK CASE

Obviously, the intended IV for this research study was the type of textbook used by second-year students, and it had two levels: the English-Spanish text previously used and the new all-Spanish text. The DV was the students' scores on the final exam. The researchers found that the students with the all-Spanish text did better on the final. But were they justified on the basis of this study in adopting that text? Was the information underlying their decision worth anything? If you consider the Relevant Variables present in this study, you will find that a number of them were left uncontrolled and very likely confounded the results.

Some of the Relevant Variables were controlled. The same teacher taught all four sections, so the students who used the all-Spanish text did not have the advantage of a better teacher. Also, the classes all met for the same number of hours per week. So far so good, but an important Subject Relevant Variable was not controlled; in fact, it was handled in such a way as to seriously confound the results. The sections that used the all-Spanish text were composed of the best students of the preceding year. It is very likely that these students would have scored higher on the final whichever text they used. Other Relevant Variables that were left uncontrolled that could potentially confound the results were class size, student attitudes as influenced by the introduction, and, possibly, the teacher's enthusiasm for the new text. When a research study is poorly designed and contains a number of Confounding Variables, you might as well not bother to do it. You might just as well base your decisions on your own inclinations. The whole point to doing research is to improve the quality of the information that goes into your decisions, not to produce information to "back up" decisions you have already made secretly.

RECAPITULATION

for RELEVANT VARIABLES—CONTROLLED OR CONFOUNDING?

Any experiment includes variables other than those defined as the IV(s) or DV(s). If these variables are likely to affect the DV they are called *Relevant Variables*. Relevant Variables must be eliminated or *controlled* by the researcher. Uncontrolled Relevant Variables may produce changes in the DV which are mistakenly interpreted as representing effects of the IV. When this happens, the Relevant Variable is called a *Confounding Variable* because its effects confound or are confused with IV effects. The key to designing good research, and to interpreting the research of others, is identification of Relevant Variables and evaluation of whether they have been controlled sufficiently to prevent their effects from confounding those of the IV.

BEHAVIORAL OBJECTIVES

for RELEVANT VARIABLES

1. Describe what is meant by a Relevant Variable. Explain what it means to say you have *controlled* such a variable.

2. Sometimes uncontrolled Relevant Variables can be Confounding Variables. Describe what is meant by a Confounding Variable. Make up an example of a situation where a Confounding Variable could produce changes in a DV which would be mistakenly attributed to an IV.

3. Given a description of a research study, identify Relevant Variables and determine whether or not they are controlled. If they are uncontrolled, speculate as to how they may confound the interpretation of the results of the study.

SAMPLE TEST QUESTION

for RELEVANT VARIABLES

1. A new industrial arts curriculum, which allows increased freedom of choice of projects along with individualized lesson plans, was tried out in a junior high school in Seattle. It was hoped that the new curriculum would not only improve student skills but also would improve the students' view of themselves as active and confident learners. To determine whether this was the case, a researcher compared the 180 students using this curriculum to 340 students from another junior high school in a different area of Seattle which was still using the older industrial arts curriculum. At the end of the school year, all the industrial arts

students in the two schools were asked to fill out a standardized "self-concept" test which could be scored to determine whether each student's self-image was positive or negative. Comparing results from the two schools, the researcher found that the students who had the new industrial arts curriculum on the average viewed themselves as more independent and more creative than did those who had the old curriculum. He concluded that the new curriculum did have positive effects on the way the students viewed themselves, and on that basis recommended it to the school system for incorporation in other schools.

a. What did the researcher intend to be his IV? (If you're not sure, look at his conclusion.) What levels of the IV did he use?

b. What is the DV? How was it operationally defined?

c. What Relevant Variables do you see as possibly uncontrolled in this experiment? (Come up with at least two).

d. For one of the Uncontrolled Variables you identified, describe how its presence might have confounded the results.

e. The researcher potentially has a Non-Subject IV. What problem did he create by assigning subjects to its levels on a nonrandom basis?

SECTION 8: BRIEF REVIEW OF THE LANGUAGE OF SCIENCE

Experiments are designed around variables. A variable is anything that can take two or more different values and, therefore, can be measured. When defining a variable, you must describe the scale on which it is to be measured. This scale is the set of all possible values the variable can have. Measurements can be very crude or very precise depending on what is being measured and on how many measurement categories there are on your scale. *Nominal* measurement scales consist of only two or more unordered categories. For *ordinal* measurement, the possible measurement categories on the scale must fall in some natural order. On *interval* scales, the possible measurement categories are not only ordered, but also possess the property of being equally distant from each other. Nominal and ordinal scales are considered qualitative. Interval scales are quantitative.

When designing an experiment, the experimenter decides which variables, the *IVs,* are to be manipulated in order to determine their effects on other variables, the *DVs.* The IVs are operationally defined by describing the procedure the experimenter goes through to create all the different levels of the IV. IVs can be either *Non-Subject* or *Subject,* depending on whether the experimenter is able to arbitrarily assign subjects to the different IV levels and manipulate their experience, or has to select subjects for the levels because of the amount of the IV they already possess. To increase the information yielded by an experiment, it is possible to use multiple IVs; however, doing this rapidly increases the number of conditions in the experiment and often increases the number of subjects the experimenter needs to find.

DVs are operationally defined by describing how they are to be measured and the scale of measurement that is to be used. The experimenter must take care to ensure that the way the DV is measured is not *reactive,* that the process of measurement does not influence the measures obtained. The type of scale on which the DV is measured will be one of the things determining the way the data from the experiment can be analyzed and the type of conclusions that can be drawn.

The aim of the experimenter is to conclude that changes in the IV produced by the experimenter cause the observed changes in the DV. However, there may be *Relevant Variables* which, if left uncontrolled by the experimenter, can confound the interpretation of the results by making changes in the DV that are not due to the IV. Such variables are called *Confounding Variables.* Experiments based on Subject IVs are often difficult to interpret because of the ever-present possibility of Confounding Variables. Subjects who differ in the way specified by a Subject IV quite possibly differ in some Other Relevant Variable as well.

CAN YOU SPEAK THE LANGUAGE OF SCIENCE?
(3 STUDIES)

If you can meet the behavioral objectives presented for the various sections in this chapter, you should now be able to read research literature and identify IVs, DVs, Relevant Variables, and any Confounding Variables. You should be able to recognize and criticize the operational definitions given for these variables. In addition, you should be able to evaluate the researchers' conclusions in terms of how well they are following the ground rules of scientific method. Try your command of the language of science on some actual research literature.

Study 1 Boren and Foree (1977): Personalized instruction applied to food and nutrition in higher education.

> A personalized competency-based instructional strategy was designed and evaluated as an alternative to the traditional teacher-directed method. Self-paced modules were designed to meet diverse student needs in a university-level food and nutrition lecture-laboratory course. Students were exposed to either a teacher-directed (control, $N = 64$) or experimental self-paced group ($N = 109$). Data from objective pretests and posttests indicated that the control and experimental teaching strategies were similar when cognitive objectives were evaluated. The experimental strategy was superior to the control method in teaching psychomotor competencies. (Abstract at the beginning of the article.)*

You may feel that this abstract contains more than its fair share of jargon. Before asking you questions about it, here's a little translation: "Personalized competency-based instructional strategy" means that the content of the course was broken down into a number of parts. Each part had special written materials and assignments, and the student had to test satisfactorily on one part before going on to the

*Reprinted by permission of the *Journal of Personalized Instruction* (copyright © 1977).

next. "Teacher-directed method" simply means the more usual type of college in-struction with lectures, discussion groups, and standard text materials. "Self-paced modules" are the parts described above which the student could work through at her own rate. "Cognitive objectives" means the usual kind of class tests for verbal knowledge, mostly multiple-choice. "Psychomotor competencies" refers to some skills the students were expected to acquire. In this particular course, students were asked to prepare a meal under set conditions, and they were rated on their perfor-mance by the teacher as the evaluation of their skills. Both the information tests and the rating of meal preparation were done for each student at the beginning (**pretest**) and the end of the course (**posttest**). Now, with this information, reread the abstract and answer the following questions:

1. What was Boren and Foree's IV? How many levels did it have? How were the levels operationally defined? Was it a Subject or a Non-Subject IV?
2. What two DVs did they use? How were they operationally defined? Which DV was probably measured on an interval scale? Which one was measured on an ordinal scale?
3. For which DV did they see an effect of the IV? For which DV did they see no effect?
4. This author can't find, in either the abstract or the article itself, the basis on which students were assigned to the levels of the IV. Does this bother you?
5. From what is given in the article, it seems the teacher knew when she did the ratings which group the student being rated came from. Why should this bother you?
6. Discuss some Relevant Variables that you would have to be sure were controlled before deciding conclusively that this self-paced modular system was indeed better than a lecture-discussion system.

Study 2 Aragona, Cassady, and Drabman (1975): Treating overweight children through parental training and contingency contracting.

Fifteen overweight girls aged 5 to 11 years were randomly assigned to one of three weight-reduction treatments: response-cost plus reinforcement, response-cost only, or a no-treatment control group. In the response-cost plus reinforcement group, parents contracted to facilitate their child's weight loss by carrying out reinforce-ment and stimulus control techniques, completing weekly charts and graphs, and encouraging their child to exercise. The response-cost-only group parents did not contract to reinforce their child's performance. The response-cost program applied to both experimental groups was conducted in weekly meetings in which the parents lost previously deposited sums of money. Twenty-five percent was deducted for missing the weekly meeting, 25 percent for failing to fill out charts and graphs, and 50 percent if their child failed to meet her specified weekly weight-loss goal. At the end of the 12-week treatment period, both experimental groups had lost signifi-cantly more weight than the control group. After an eight-week, no-contact follow-up, some of the lost weight was regained. The response-cost plus reinforcement group was still significantly below the controls. The response-cost-only group was below but just missed significance. A 31-week no-contact follow-up failed to show a treatment effect, but did show a trend toward slower weight gain by the response-cost plus reinforcement group. (Abstract at the beginning of the article.)*

This abstract needs less translating than the previous one. "Reinforcement contracting" means that the parents specifically contracted with their children to give them praise, privileges, and money for carrying out specified exercises and for reducing their caloric intake by specified amounts. This is in contrast to the "response-cost" system which was applied only to the parents. With this information, you should be able to answer the following questions:

1. What was the authors' main IV? How many levels did it have? How were the levels operationally defined? How were people assigned to each of the levels? Was it a Subject or a Non-Subject IV?

2. What was the authors' DV? What measurements were taken? Is this measurement scale nominal, ordinal, or interval?

3. What relation was found between the IV and DV at the end of the program?

4. The authors had a second IV, the time passed since the end of the program. What are the three levels of this IV? What was the effect of this IV on the DV?

5. Can you think of any Relevant Variables that might not have been controlled?

Study 3 Paul (1966): Insight vs. Desensitization in psychotherapy.

In this study Paul was interested in comparing different therapeutic approaches to reducing distress in public-speaking situations. He used a series of personality questionnaires to identify students who were both emotionally reactive under stress and apprehensive about speaking to an audience. He had these students deliver impromptu speeches before an audience which, they were told, would be evaluating them. Before delivering the speech, the students' pulse rate and amount of palm sweating were measured. The students' performances while giving the speech were rated for indications of nervousness and anxiety by observers. The students were also asked for self-ratings about their degree of distress.

The students were randomly assigned to one of four therapy groups as follows:

1. *Insight psychotherapy:* These students had five sessions of therapy with practicing clinicians which focused on gaining insight into each student's speaking problems.

2. *Counter conditioning:* These students had five sessions in which the therapist taught them to relax while thinking about situations connected with public speaking. As therapy progressed they were instructed to shift from thinking about relatively unthreatening situations (like being two weeks away from having to give a talk) to thinking about actual delivery of a talk to a large audience.

3. *Attention-placebo:* These students also had five sessions in which they were given a harmless pill. They were led to believe that the pill would reduce their

---

*Reprinted by permission of the *Journal of Applied Analysis of Behavior* (copyright © 1975) and by Ronald Drabman.

anxiety and then were given a supposedly stressful task to do which was actually a task designed to make them drowsy.

4. *Control:* These students were tested at the same time as the others, but had no therapy sessions.

After the students had their various therapy or control sessions, they were again tested in the same stressful speaking situation as at the beginning of the experiment. The percentage of students in each group that showed reduction in emotional reaction to the second speech is given in Fig. 2.2.

You should be able to answer the following questions about this interesting research study:

1. What was Paul's IV? How many levels did it have and what were they? Is this IV defined on a nominal, an ordinal, or an interval scale? Is the IV a Subject or a Non-Subject IV?

2. Paul used the same five therapists for Groups 1 and 2. He chose them for their ability as good insight therapists. What was he trying to control for by doing this?

FIG. 2.2

Percent of subjects in each of the four groups who showed significant decreases in anxiety as measured by physiological indicators, behavior ratings by observers, and self-reports. (Drawn from data of Paul, 1966, p. 37.)

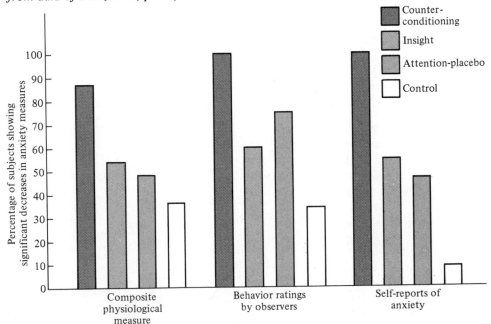

3. One group in the experiment was included to control for subject expectations of success of therapy and also for the subjects' attendance at five treatment sessions. Which group was this?

4. One group controlled for the simple passage of time and for the possibility that repeating the speaking test twice would in and of itself have some effect. Which group was this?

5. What were the three DVs used in the experiment? How was each one operationally defined? Which two are based on ordinal measures? Which one is based on interval measures? Can you see how any of these measures might be reactive?

6. From looking at the three DVs as given in the figure, what would you say about the following?

   a. Does counterconditioning have any other effect than that produced by the subjects' expectations and by paying five visits to a therapist?

   b. Does insight therapy have any other effect than that produced by the subjects' expectations and by paying five visits to a therapist?

   c. Why was it important to include Group 4? Is there any effect of simple repetition of the speaking assignment?

7. Can you suggest any Relevant Variables that Paul may not have controlled?

8. If you are nervous about public speaking, which form of therapy would you seek given the results of this experiment?

(If you can handle these questions, then you are speaking the language of scientific research and are ready to start planning some of your own.)

chapter 3

designing an experiment

Usually research design is covered in statistical textbooks. This mode of presentation leaves students with the unfortunate impression that to understand and utilize experimental design they must first be sophisticated in mathematics and statistics. Actually designing research is mostly common sense after you learn a few basic rules. Research designs can vary from quite simple to very complex. The more complicated they become, the more information they can potentially yield about your research question. However, more complicated designs usually mean more costly research projects. Researchers must balance their resources against the use they hope to make of information yielded by their research and choose a design which best meets their needs. By the end of this chapter and the next one you'll be able to identify designs used by others and also to design some experiments yourself.

SECTION 1: WHAT INFORMATION CAN AN EXPERIMENT YIELD?

EXPERIMENTAL DESIGN

The **design** of a research project is the overall plan for how the research will be performed. When you develop your design you have to specify how many IVs you are going to investigate and how many levels of each IV you intend to use. Your design determines how you will sort your subjects into groups and how many groups you will need. Your design must specify when and how often you will take measures on your DVs. Since the same IVs and DVs can be investigated using many different research designs, you will have to decide which design best suits your needs.

The amount of information you will obtain from your research will be limited by the design you choose. At first glance, you might be tempted to choose a complex design that will yield a maximum amount of information. However, unless you have unlimited resources, you have to weigh the potential information to be gained against the cost of doing your research. More complex designs require more subjects, more experimental conditions, more time to run the experiment, more money to support the research, and more time to analyze the results. If you consider the use you expect to make of the information from your research, you may find that a simpler design is all that is necessary. Whatever design you finally choose, you must keep in mind its limitations on information yield when you interpret your results. Let's take a look at some of the kinds of information that can be yielded from an experimental design.

POSTTREATMENT INFORMATION

The first kind of information we need from any design is information on how the subjects behave just after they have experienced our experimental treatment. But such **posttreatment information** does not by itself provide much evidence about whether or not the subjects' behavior is caused only by our treatment. Without additional information, we have no right to conclude that the subjects are any different after our treatment than they were before it.

PRETREATMENT INFORMATION

One obvious solution to the problem of establishing that the treatment has an effect is to use a design that collects **pretreatment information** from the subjects as well as posttreatment. With this additional information, we can see if there has been a pre-to-post treatment change in the subjects' behavior. If there has been such a change, we can attribute it to our treatment. Or can we, in all cases?

Suppose we were interested in discovering whether giving preschoolers training and practice on a low balance beam improves their motor coordination. We design an experiment in which we pretest a group of children in a day-care center for motor coordination, give them daily practice on the balance beam for a period of two months, and then posttest them. We find that most of the children show improvement in their motor coordination and recommend that the balance-beam activity be included regularly in the day-care program. However, we should be somewhat wary of making this recommendation without stating some reservations. The pre-to-post change might have been caused by our treatment, but it might also have been caused by some other things about which our design provides no information. For one thing, people generally do better the second time they are tested on anything; some of the pre-to-post improvement might simply have resulted from the children having been pretested. Also, these children have been experiencing things other than our treatment. In particular, children of this age group are maturing rapidly. Their improvement in coordination may have occurred simply because they are two months older. If it is important that our recommendation be a good one—for instance, if incorporating the balance-beam practice into the day-care routine is costly or has a high injury potential—we may need a research design that gives us more than just pre- and posttreatment information.

COMPARISON INFORMATION

To get a firmer hold on what may be causing a pre-to-posttreatment change, we will need to add to our design at least one other group to provide **comparison information.** Generally the subjects who receive our treatment are referred to as the **experimental group,** and the subjects who do not receive the treatment are called the control group. By adding this second group, we now have created two levels of a Non-Subject IV with one level assigned a zero value. This control or comparison group has DV observations taken at the same time and under the same conditions as the experimental group. By doing this it is possible to compare posttreatment information between a group that had the treatment and one that did not. For example, if we find that our group of preschoolers who have been practicing on the balance beam has superior motor coordination at the end of two months to a group that has not been practicing, we might feel more secure about saying that the practice made a contribution to their motor coordination.

INFORMATION ABOUT GROUP EQUIVALENCE

How secure should we feel in concluding that the difference between two groups is produced by our treatment of one of them? The degree of faith we can place in our comparison information depends on how much information our design yields on the **equivalence** of the groups used in the experiment. If our experimental and control groups were different to begin with, then the comparison of their posttreatment information might simply reflect built-in group differences rather than the effects of the treatment. For instance, if our experimental (balance-beam practice) children came from the University Day-Care Center and our controls (no balance-beam practice) came from the Downtown Day-Care Center located in a slum area of the city, any posttreatment differences in motor coordination might simply be an indication of overall differences in coordination between children raised under different circumstances. Somehow we need to establish that our two groups of children were equivalent in motor coordination in the first place.

One way of obtaining information about group equivalence is by taking pretreatment observations on the two groups and showing that they were similar in motor coordination at the start of the experiment. However, even if the two groups started out with similar motor abilities, it might happen that the parents of the children in the University Day-Care Center, after hearing of the new gym routine, would work with their children at home to improve their performance. Sometimes groups that are equivalent to begin with lose their equivalence as the experiment proceeds for reasons other than the effects of the treatment.

A different design for this research might establish group equivalence by ensuring that children from both schools were included in the experimental and control groups. This might be done, for example, by assigning children from each school at random (by chance) to the two groups. Doing this would produce experimental and control groups with equivalent mixtures of children from the two schools. Such a procedure would make us feel more secure that posttreatment differences between the experimental and control children were in fact due to the balance-beam program.

INCREASING COMPARISON INFORMATION

We could further increase the information yield from our research by including more than two levels of our IV. This **multi-level comparison information** can be obtained by using different amounts or types of treatment rather than just comparing treatment to no treatment. For our preschoolers we might want to compare daily balance-beam practice with daily calisthenics as well as with a no-practice control. Getting this information would mean a more complicated design, either with three groups of children or with repeated measures on the children as they experience different conditions of the experiment. Whatever the specifics of our design, it would be a more costly experiment. Whether or not we investigate these additional levels of the IV depends on how important that information is to us. If, for example, calisthenics will be cheaper and safer to incorporate into a day-care program, then we might be interested in finding out whether any improvement seen with balance-beam practice was due specifically to the balance beam or just to providing some form of physical activity for the children.

Another way to expand the usefulness of our research is by designing it to yield **follow-up comparison information.** When we want this kind of information, we not only take posttreatment DV observations, we also come back some time after the treatment has ended and again take DV observations on our subjects. Sometimes a treatment has an immediate effect but this effect disappears over time. If it is important to us that our treatments have long-term effects, we will have to provide for follow-up. Follow-up data collection can be difficult and costly; human subjects are free to move about and often are just not there when we want to look at them again. However, for some kinds of research questions, follow-up information is essential.

INTERACTION INFORMATION

Maximum information yield comes from experimental designs that have multiple IVs. When more than one IV is used in the same experiment, we can compare their relative effects. Even more important, we can get information about whether the IVs interact in their effects on the DV. Two IVs are said to interact when the effects of one IV are different for different levels or values of the other IV. If this happens, it is impossible to predict the effects of both IVs together by knowing only their separate effects. Only experimental designs that have two or more IVs can give us such interaction information.

Suppose that for our preschoolers we decided to treat the location of the day-care center as a second IV. Accordingly, we establish two equivalent groups within each center, for a total of four groups in the experiment. One group in each center would have balance-beam practice and the other would not. Now, we can directly compare the motor coordination of children from the two centers to check our suspicion that there may be built-in differences. Of course, we still gain information about the effects of our treatment in this design. In addition, we can find out if there is an interaction between the effects of the Non-Subject treatment variable and the Subject-type location variable. It is possible we'll discover that balance-beam practice results in even greater improvements in motor coordination for the Downtown Day-Care Center children than for the University Day-Care Center group. Without using a design that has both IVs, we would have no way of knowing that our treatment is differentially effective for children from different areas of the city.

RECAPITULATION

for INFORMATION YIELDED BY EXPERIMENTAL DESIGNS

The *design* for an experiment is an overall plan that specifies the number of IVs, the number of levels of each IV, the number of groups, the rules for dividing subjects into groups, and when and how often the DV measures will be taken. The same combination of IVs and DVs can be investigated with different designs. Researchers choose among designs according to what information they need and what resources they have available. All designs yield *posttreatment information* about the behavior of the experimental subjects just after they've experienced the treatment. *Pretreatment information* can be gathered by planning to take initial DV observations on all subjects. *Comparison information* can be obtained by increasing the number of groups in the experiment, using more levels of the IV, using multiple IVs, and taking follow-up observations. Some designs provide *information about the equivalence of groups* to increase the chances that any observed posttreatment differences among groups result only from the treatment. Finally, multiple-IV designs provide *information on interaction effects*. More complex designs yield more information, but are generally more costly to run.

BEHAVIORAL OBJECTIVES

for INFORMATION YIELDED BY EXPERIMENTAL DESIGNS

1. List the different things that must be specified in a research design.
2. List the five general categories of information that might be yielded by a research design.
3. Describe each of the general categories of information that could be yielded by a research design.
4. Describe at least three types of *comparison* information that might be yielded by different research designs.
5. Given the description of a simple research study, list the categories of information its design would yield.
6. Explain what is meant by the words *experimental subject* and *control subject*.

SAMPLE TEST QUESTIONS

for INFORMATION YIELDED BY EXPERIMENTAL DESIGNS

1. The University coach wants to buy Astro-turf, but the deans are giving him trouble about the expense. He decides to do some research to show the superiority of Astro-turf over the regular dirt track. He has all his runners practice on Astro-turf for one week. He then compares their scores for a 100-yard dash on the regular track after the week of practice with their scores on the same track just before the Astro-turf practice. He finds that there has been an improvement in running speed and passes this information on to the deans.

   a. What posttreatment information was obtained?

   b. Was pretreatment information obtained? If so, what?

   c. What comparison information was available from his design, if any? Are there any other kinds of comparisons you think the design should have provided for? Discuss.

   d. Why do you think the deans might refuse him again?

2. On page 66 in Chapter 2 is the abstract of a study comparing the effects of two methods of instruction on learning about food and nutrition in a college home economics course. Reread it and answer the following questions:

   a. What posttreatment information was obtained?

   b. Was pretreatment information obtained? If so, was any pre-to-posttreatment change observed?

   c. What comparison information was available from this design?

   d. Is there any information about group equivalence? If not, how might the absence of this category of information weaken conclusions from the research?

   e. Is there any interaction information? If so, what?

3. In Question 7 on page 57, there is a description of an experiment on the effects of violence in films on children's play activity. Reread this description and answer the same questions as above (2a–2e).

SECTION 2: A SHORTHAND FOR DESIGNING EXPERIMENTS

The wide variety of designs and even wider variety of design names can be overwhelming to a beginning researcher. Often designs that differ only slightly in structure are given very different names. Some writers don't even attempt to name their designs but give confusing verbal descriptions which the reader has to unravel. Using a simple shorthand while learning about designs can make it much easier for you to recognize basic design structure. Actually, designs consist of only a very few elements put together in different patterns. Even when you become knowledgeable about designs, this shorthand can be useful for treading your way through lengthy descriptions of experiments and for planning your own research. The shorthand presented in this book is a modified version of the original one proposed by Campbell and Stanley (1963) and adapted for instruction by Crawford and Kielsmeier (1970).

Another problem for beginning researchers is variation in use of terminology in textbooks and research reports. Each writer seems to have his or her own preferences. In this section we'll introduce you to the most common terms as well as to some frequently used alternatives.

DIVIDING SUBJECTS

A **subject** is a person or an animal that has been recruited in some fashion into your research. When referring to humans, some authors prefer such terms as "research participant," but "subject" is still the more common term. The abbreviation for "subject" is **S**. If you want to specify a particular subject, you can label or **subscript** the S as follows: $S_1, S_2, S_3 \ldots$ or $S_a, S_b, S_c \ldots$. Subjects in an experiment are frequently divided into groups. Formation of a **group** of subjects is represented in our shorthand by a **G**. Again, if you want to refer to a particular group of subjects you can subscript the G: G_e (experimental group) and G_c (control group) or $G_1, G_2, G_3 \ldots$.

The research design specifies how the subjects are divided into groups. In some cases, the experimenter simply takes groups that are already formed. The research discussed on page 66 concerning the effects of type of instruction on learning in a college food and nutrition course is an example of such a design. The researchers simply took students from one year of the course and compared them to students taking the course in a different year. They had no control over which subjects went into which group of the experiment but took the students as they chose to register for the course.

When they can, experimenters prefer to divide subjects into groups on some *random* or unsystematic basis rather than using preformed groups. A random division is one in which each subject has an equal chance of being placed in each group. Random division is a way of increasing the likelihood that the groups are equivalent at the beginning of an experiment. When the design includes formation of the groups by random division of subjects, our shorthand will put an **R** in front of the G. Study 2(d) on page 61, which concerned whether reprimanding people for misdeeds would influence later helping behavior, had a design which randomly divided the misdoers into a mild-reprimand group and a harsh-reprimand group. In our shorthand, we would represent these two groups as follows: RG_m and RG_h.

When a Subject IV is used in an experiment, the subjects must be formed into groups on the basis of some characteristic they already possess. Such a division is called **blocking** the subjects and can be represented by a **B**. On page 74 we planned a multiple-variable study to find out whether a balance-beam practice program (IV_1) could improve the coordination of preschool children and also whether there were any differences in coordination between children from different day-care centers (IV_2). We blocked the children according to the location of their day-care center, and then within each block we randomly formed two groups. Using the shorthand, this could now be represented as follows:

$$
\begin{array}{|c|}
\hline
\begin{array}{cc} & RG_1 \\ B_1 & \\ & RG_2 \end{array} \\
\hline
\begin{array}{cc} & RG_3 \\ B_2 & \\ & RG_4 \end{array} \\
\hline
\end{array}
$$

where B_1 is the University Day-Care Center
and
B_2 is the Downtown Day Care Center.

ADMINISTERING A TREATMENT

A design also specifies when we apply a **treatment** to a group to create a level of a Non-subject IV. In our shorthand, we can represent application of a treatment by a **T.** If we have just a single Non-Subject IV, we can represent its different levels by subscripting the T. For instance, an experiment with just two groups, one receiving a treatment and the other not, could be represented by a T_e for the experimental treatment and a T_c for the control treatment. Using this notation, our multi-variable balance-beam research project could then be abbreviated as:

$$
\begin{array}{|c|}
\hline
\begin{array}{cc} & RG_1 \; T_e \\ B_1 & \\ & RG_2 \; T_c \end{array} \\
\hline
\begin{array}{cc} & RG_3 \; T_e \\ B_2 & \\ & RG_4 \; T_c \end{array} \\
\hline
\end{array}
$$

When one level of the Non-Subject IV consists of not doing anything to the subjects, the shorthand representation can just leave the treatment part of the notation blank. In this case, the above could be simply written as:

$$
\begin{array}{|c|}
\hline
\begin{array}{cc} & RG_1 \; T \\ B_1 & \\ & RG_2 \end{array} \\
\hline
\begin{array}{cc} & RG_3 \; T \\ B_2 & \\ & RG_4 \end{array} \\
\hline
\end{array}
$$

COMBINING TREATMENTS

If multiple Non-Subject IVs are used, then each group will receive some combination of treatments. This can be represented in various ways by subscripting the Ts. For example, if we wanted to broaden the balance-beam research to answer more general questions about the effects of physical activity on the coordination of preschoolers, we might use the two Non-Subject IVs of practice on the balance beam and of doing calisthenics (within one school, please. Let's not complicate things too much.). Then we could design an experiment as follows:

RG_1 T_b T_c where T_b means daily balance-beam practice and T_c
RG_2 T_b means daily calisthenics.
RG_3 T_c
RG_4

Or we might want to use a different form of subscripting which would indicate "no practice" as a form of treatment. If so, we could represent the same design as follows:

RG_1 T_{bc} where b means balance-beam practice,
RG_2 T_{bn} c means calisthenics, and
RG_3 T_{nc} n means no practice on one or the other.
RG_4 T_{nn}

We can say that our two-variable experiment has four **conditions:** T_{bc}, T_{bn}, T_{nc}, T_{nn}.

TAKING DV OBSERVATIONS

The one thing missing at this point from our shorthand is an indication of when the experimenter is planning to make an **observation** of the subjects, or, in other words, when the experimenter intends to take measurements on the various DVs. We'll use an **O** to indicate the *time at which observing is* to be done. In one version of the preschool balance-beam investigation, the DV observations were taken both before and after the treatment. A complete representation of this design for investigating the effects of balance-beam practice on coordination of preschoolers from two different schools would look as follows:

B_1 RG_1 O T O   where B_1 = children selected from the
       RG_2 O   O   University Day-Care Center,
                       B_2 = children selected from the
B_2 RG_3 O T O   Downtown Day-Care Center, and
       RG_4 O   O   T = two months of practice on the balance
                             beam.

RECAPITULATION

for SHORTHAND FOR DESIGNING EXPERIMENTS

The plan of an experiment can be represented by a shorthand which allows us to figure out which design an investigator is using and recognize its limitations. In this shorthand, G represents a group of subjects lumped together on some basis. If the subjects were divided by random processes, then an R will be written in front of the G. If the subjects were divided according to a Subject IV, a process called *blocking,* then a B will be used to indicate each block of subjects. The application of a treatment to a group of subjects will be indicated by a T. Whenever the subjects are observed or measured on the DVs, an O will indicate the time at which the observations occurred. For multi-group, multi-IV, multi-level studies, various combinations of subscripts can be used for G, B, and T.

BEHAVIORAL OBJECTIVES

for SHORTHAND FOR DESIGNING EXPERIMENTS

1. Given one of the shorthand letters (B, G, R, T, and O), explain what it represents.
2. Given a description of a simple experiment, represent its design using the shorthand. If you subscript any letter, make a key explaining your subscripts.
3. Given a shorthand representation of a design, explain the design in words.
4. Distinguish between the terms "subject" and "group."
5. Define the terms "treatment" and "condition."

SAMPLE TEST QUESTIONS

for "SHORTHAND FOR DESIGNING EXPERIMENTS"

1. Describe in words the following design:

$$\boxed{\begin{array}{lcc} RG_1 & T & O \\ RG_2 & & O \end{array}}$$

2. How does the design in Question 1 differ from the following?

$$\boxed{\begin{array}{lcc} G_1 & T & O \\ G_2 & & O \end{array}}$$

3.   If T_A represented eating a meal (and its absence meant not eating) and T_B represented listening to music (while its absence meant not listening), how would you describe the following?

$$
\begin{array}{llll}
RG_1 & T_A & T_B & O \\
RG_2 & T_A &   & O \\
RG_3 &   & T_B & O \\
RG_4 &   &   & O
\end{array}
$$

4.   Reread the Astro-turf study on page 76. Represent the design of this study in shorthand.

5.   Reread the study described on page 68 about the most effective therapy for nervousness while speaking in public. Represent this design in shorthand.

SECTION 3: BETWEEN- AND WITHIN-SUBJECTS DESIGNS FOR IVs

COMPARISON OF BETWEEN- AND WITHIN-SUBJECTS DESIGNS

One important decision you need to make early in planning your research is how you're going to divide up your subjects. So far, most of the designs that we have been discussing have used different subjects for each level of the IV. In this type of design if your IV has, say, three levels, you will need three groups of subjects. This approach is called a **Between-Subjects design** since the comparisons of the effects of different IV levels are made *between* different groups of subjects.

Sometimes you can get more information out of a given number of subjects if you design your experiment so that the comparisons between levels of your IV are made *within* the same subjects. This would mean that the same subjects experience all the levels of the IV and are measured after they have experienced each level. With such a design you need fewer subjects since you are getting your data by taking **repeated measures** on the same subjects. Using the same subjects at each level of an IV is called a **Within-Subjects design.**

On pages 53–54 we designed an experiment to investigate the effects of drinking a stimulant, coffee, on the speed of working through a set of math problems. The principal IV was operationally defined as the amount of coffee we gave the subjects. It had three levels: 0 cups, 1 cup, and 4 cups. Since the experimenter decides how much coffee each subject will drink, it is clearly a Non-Subject IV. If we decide to assign different subjects to each of the levels, it will also be a Between-Subjects design and we will judge the effects of our IV by making DV comparisons between the different groups of subjects. However, we could also use this Non-Subject IV in a Within-Subjects design by having the same group of subjects experience all three levels. If we do this, all our subjects in the experiment will be tested under all three conditions or IV levels. If we want 12 observations at each level of our IV, the Between-Subjects design will require 36 subjects, 12 for each of our three groups. The Within-Subjects design, however, will require only 12 subjects since we observe and measure each subject three times.

ORDER EFFECTS IN WITHIN-SUBJECTS DESIGNS

Obviously, a Within-Subjects design has the advantage of decreasing the number of subjects needed for our research while increasing the amount of information we get from each subject. However, there are some problems you should be aware of when you use such a design. The principal one is the possibility of an **order effect.** If we did the stimulant experiment in a Within-Subjects design it might seem reasonable first to test our subjects (0-cup level), then give them one cup of coffee and test them again (1-cup level), and finally give them three more cups to drink followed by a final test (4-cup level). But suppose we found that their speed of solving math problems improved over the three tests? Isn't it possible that any improvement from test to test resulted simply from taking repeated tests? So we don't know whether the observed change in the DV resulted from the IV or from the uncontrolled variable of repeated tests. One way to correct for this might be to add to the experiment a second control group which would take the tests at the same time but would not be given any coffee. A possible design for this experiment would be:

$$\begin{array}{|llll|} \hline RG_1 & OT_a & OT_b & O \\ RG_2 & O & O & O \\ \hline \end{array}$$
where T_a is 1 cup of coffee and T_b is 3 additional cups.

However, solving the problem this way would mean we'd have to double our number of subjects and lose some of the advantage of a Within-Subjects design.

COUNTERBALANCING FOR ELIMINATION OF ORDER EFFECTS

Another way of compensating for the order effect inherent in Within-Subjects designs is to use a technique called **counterbalancing.** To counterbalance the conditions of a Within-Subjects design you need to figure out all possible orders in which the conditions could be administered. If you have two conditions, this means two possible orders (2 x 1). If you have three conditions, six different orders are possible (3 x 2 x 1). When you expand to four conditions, you'll find that there are 24 possible orders (4 x 3 x 2 x 1)! When counterbalancing conditions, you must make sure that the same number of subjects experience each order of conditions. Then you are no longer favoring one order over another. In the context of the coffee experiment, counterbalancing conditions will probably mean having our subjects come in on three different days to give the effects of the coffee consumed for one condition a chance to wear off. Since we have three levels of our IV, there are six possible orders (0 cup, 1 cup, 4 cups; 0 cup, 4 cups, 1 cup; 1 cup, 0 cup, 4 cups; 1 cup, 4 cups, 0 cup; 4 cups, 0 cup, 1 cup; 4 cups, 1 cup, 0 cup). With 12 subjects we could use each order twice. Now we can say that we have completely counterbalanced the order of conditions and have wiped out any consistent effect on the DV of the order in which the conditions occur. Using counterbalancing you can eliminate confounding order effects without increasing your number of subjects.

SUBJECT IVs ARE USED ONLY IN BETWEEN-SUBJECTS DESIGNS

When your IV is operationally defined as a Subject IV you almost always are forced to use a Between-Subjects design. Since Subject IVs are defined in terms of characteristics already possessed by the subjects, you generally cannot have the same subject appear at more than one level of the IV. If your Subject IV is "sex," for example, you can't (under usual circumstances) test the same subject as both a "male" and a "female." Therefore, an IV operationally defined as a Subject IV can usually be investigated only in a Between-Subjects design.

MULTIPLE-IV EXPERIMENTS

As if things weren't complicated enough, when you have a multiple-IV experiment, you have to decide separately for each IV whether it will be treated as a Within-Subjects or a Between-Subjects variable. The stimulant research we are considering has as its main IV the Non-Subject variable of the amount of coffee the subjects drink during our experiment. In Chapter 2 (page 54) we considered adding a second IV, "customary coffee consumption," to see whether the amount of the stimulant the subject habitually uses interacts with (changes the effects of) the amount we have the subject consume in our laboratory. Since this second IV is defined in terms of habits the subjects bring to the experiment, it is a Subject IV and its different levels must be represented by different groups. Therefore, it can only be treated in a Between-Subjects manner. To create the levels of this IV, the subjects will be blocked according to their habitual coffee usage (rarely or never, 1 to 2 cups per day, 3 or more cups a day).

The Non-Subject IV, the amount of coffee we give the subjects to drink, could, however, be treated either Between-Subjects or Within-Subjects. If we decided to treat it as a Between-Subjects variable, then we could design the experiment shown in Fig. 3.1.

FIG. 3.1

Between-Subjects design for a two-IV experiment.

B_1	RG_1 T_0 O RG_2 T_1 O RG_3 T_4 O
B_2	RG_4 T_0 O RG_5 T_1 O RG_6 T_4 O
B_3	RG_7 T_0 O RG_8 T_1 O RG_9 T_4 O

B_1, B_2 and B_3 are the three levels of the Subject IV_2 and T_0, T_1 and T_4 are the three levels of the Non-Subject IV_1.

This looks like a neat design, but we might wonder where we are going to find enough subjects to fill it. If we wanted 12 subjects per group, we'd have to find 9 x 12, or 108 subjects (and, remember, we have to look for ones with the right coffee-drinking habits!).

Alternatively, we could treat the Non-Subject IV as a Within-Subjects IV. In shorthand, the design for this experiment might be represented as follows:

B_1 T_0 O T_1 O T_4 O B_2 T_0 O T_1 O T_4 O B_3 T_0 O T_1 O T_4 O

where T_0, T_1 and T_4 are three levels of our Non-Subject IV *and are completely counter-balanced across subjects.*

With this design we would need only 3 x 12, or 36 subjects since each subject is to be measured three times. Of course, within each block, we would have to assign two of the subjects to each of the six possible treatment orders to eliminate any order effect. This version of the two-IV design does require counterbalancing, which is a nuisance, but it may be worth it in terms of the reduced number of subjects we have to recruit.

RECAPITULATION

for BETWEEN- AND WITHIN-SUBJECTS DESIGNS

A Non-Subject IV can be treated in either a *Between-Subjects design* or a *Within-Subjects design*. When a Between-Subjects design is used, the comparisons between different levels of the IV are made between different groups of subjects. When a Within-Subjects design is used, the same subjects are repeatedly measured at the different levels of the IV. This permits multi-level comparisons to be made within subjects. A Between-Subjects design will require a larger number of subjects, but a

Within-Subjects design has the problem of *order effects.* Sometimes order effects in a Within-Subjects design can be controlled by *counterbalancing conditions,* a procedure which ensures that an equal number of subjects experiences each possible order of conditions to avoid favoring any one order. A variable operationally defined as a Subject IV can usually be treated only in a Between-Subjects design.

BEHAVIORAL OBJECTIVES

for BETWEEN- AND WITHIN-SUBJECTS DESIGNS

1. Describe in words a Between-Subjects design for an IV with two or more levels.
2. Describe in words a Within-Subjects design for an IV with two or more levels.
3. Explain why a Subject IV is unlikely to be handled with a Within-Subjects design.
4. Given a description of an experiment, identify the IVs, state whether each IV is operationally defined as a Subject or a Non-Subject IV, and then state whether each IV is being used in a Between-Subjects or a Within-Subjects design.
5. Given a description of two IVs as Between-Subjects or Within-Subjects, and given the number of levels of each IV, state the number of conditions (combinations of levels) present in the experiment. Then, upon being told how many observations are required for each condition, decide how many subjects the experimenter will need to find.
6. Given a description of a Within-Subjects IV, specify how it should be counterbalanced.

SAMPLE TEST QUESTIONS

for "BETWEEN- AND WITHIN-SUBJECT DESIGNS"

1. Suppose you had an experiment with two IVs. IV_1 has two levels and IV_2 has four levels.
   a. How many conditions will this experiment have?
   b. Assume that you want observations on 24 subjects for each condition of the experiment.
      1) How many subjects will you need if both IVs are treated Between-Subjects?
      2) How many subjects will you need if IV_1 is Between-Subjects and IV_2 is Within-Subjects?
      3) How many subjects will you need if IV_1 is Within-Subjects and IV_2 is Between-Subjects?
      4) How many subjects will you need if both IV_1 and IV_2 are Within-Subjects (for the moment, you can ignore the necessity of counterbalancing)?
      5) How many subjects will you need if both IV_1 and IV_2 are Subject-type IVs?

2. On page 76 (Question 1) there is a description of an experiment done to demonstrate the usefulness of Astro-turf. Was this designed as a Between-Subjects or a Within-Subjects experiment?

3. On page 57 there is a description of an experiment concerning the effects of violence in TV films on children's play. The experimenter used three IVs as follows: age group (3 levels), sex (2 levels), and type of film seen (2 levels). Reread the description and answer the following:

    a. How many conditions were there in her experiment?

    b. Which of the IVs are Subject IVs?

    c. Which of the IVs are Non-Subject IVs?

    d. For each IV, specify whether it appears in her design as Between-Subjects or Within-Subjects.

    e. If she wanted to have five subjects in each condition of the experiment, what is the total number of subjects she must find?

4. You are interested in determining people's taste preferences among three kinds of soda pop. You decide to compare Pepsi Cola (PC), Coca Cola (CC) and a Diet Cola (DC). Your procedures ask the subjects to sample all three and to choose the one they like best. You're worried that the order in which the colas are sampled might affect the results (your private opinion is that DC will kill the taste for anything else). To control for this you decide to counterbalance the order in which the colas are tasted.

    a. Write down all the possible orders you would use.

    b. If you had 42 subjects, how many would you assign to each order?

5. The following is a description of a study on the effects of removing a gland, the adrenal medulla, on drinking behavior:

    Twenty-four rats were randomly divided into two groups of 12 each. One group had their adrenal glands surgically removed. The other group had "sham operations" which involved similar surgery but without removal of the glands. After recovery from surgery, the amount that each rat would drink in a day was measured for three solutions: plain water, sugar water, and salt water. Each rat was given free access to a different solution on each of three days. Each rat within a surgery group had a different order of solutions.

    a. Describe the design of this research in shorthand.

    b. What are the experimenter's IVs?

    c. Which IVs are Subject IVs and which are Non-Subject?

    d. Which IVs were treated as Between-Subjects and which were treated as Within-Subjects?

    e. If an IV was used Within-Subjects, did the experimenter counterbalance the order of conditions? (If you can't figure out from the description of the experiment, tell the researcher what he should have done.)

SECTION 4: VERY SIMPLE DESIGNS

PILOT STUDIES

The first designs we are going to consider have only a single group of subjects or a single treatment condition. The simplicity of these designs makes them inexpensive to use, but they yield little information. Designs such as these are most likely to be used for what is called a **pilot study,** a small-scale research project that is not expected to yield any final answers. Pilot studies are usually done to check out procedures that are to be incorporated into a more extensive study. The results of a pilot study can considerably improve the planning and increase the chances for success of a subsequent larger-scale experiment. Such pilot work, because of the limited amount of information it yields, is usually not published.

A SAMPLE RESEARCH QUESTION

To emphasize the different kinds of information that can be obtained using different experimental designs, we are going to apply all the designs discussed in this and the next chapter to the same research question. Let's consider the general question: how does consumption of marijuana affect human functioning? This is a question of more than topical interest. Through the ages many different chemical substances have been consumed by human beings in pursuit of analgesia, pleasurable reactions, or religious experience. For as long as people have been ingesting such chemicals, there has been concern with the possible effects of these substances on individual health, physiology, personality, motivation, and performance. Experience with the costly, detrimental personal and societal effects of a socially entrenched substance such as alcohol has increased concern about short- and long-term reactions to any new substance that may become fashionable. In a single research project on the topic, we might look at a practical aspect of the general question, such as whether or not specific warnings should be given to motorists not to drive for a certain number of hours after consumption. Or we might be interested in more basic research questions concerning what types of human behaviors are affected.

IDENTIFYING AND OPERATIONALIZING OUR VARIABLES

In a general sense, we know that marijuana consumption will be our major IV and that some measure of human functioning will be our DV. Before we can consider the design of our research, however, we need to specify these variables in much more detail.

To operationally define our IV, we must decide how the marijuana is to be administered to our subjects. Its consumption in food would probably be easiest to control, but inhalation is the most popular technique at present, and it appears to achieve larger and quicker effects. For these reasons, we decide that the marijuana will be delivered to our subjects by their smoking it in a pipe. Establishing consistent dosages will be a problem as the quality of marijuana available to the average smoker seems to fluctuate. Perhaps we'll decide to use a pure compound of tetra-hydrocannabinol in order to control dosage more exactly. Reading the current literature about marijuana and tetrahydrocannabinol and consulting with chemists may help us make some of these decisions. We are going to have to seek permission to do this research from appropriate authorities since marijuana generally is not legally available. In addition, we are going to have to be very open with our subjects concerning the nature of the research in which they are getting involved. For the moment, let's say that these problems are solved and we decide to administer the substance by inhalation through a pipe using a standardized amount about equivalent to the contents of one marijuana cigarette as smoked by the average user.

We are under an obligation to choose our DVs carefully. This experiment, like many medical experiments, entails some possible risk to the subjects, so it is important to get maximal information from doing it. This is not the type of experiment one would want to repeat too often. We decide, therefore, that we are going to measure a variety of physiological and performance DVs.

Some physiological measures we might take are heart rate and rate of respiration. Some other ones, such as blood pressure, skin temperature, and electrical resistance of the skin, become possible if we have access to the proper equipment. All these physiological variables can be measured on interval scales. To complete their operational definition, we'll need to specify the conditions under which the measures will be taken. This would include such things as specifying that the subjects will be at rest when they are measured and that the measures will be taken in a certain order.

Since there are many kinds of human performance we can measure, and such measurements take time, a good deal of thinking will have to go into our choice of performance DVs. The literature on marijuana effects indicates that a person's judgment of the passage of time may be altered, so we decide to include timing in some of our performance measures. For our performance measure DV_1, we decide to use a **"reaction-time" task** in which we measure how fast a subject can make a simple hand movement in response to a flash of light. For performance measure DV_2, we choose a more complicated task involving response timing and eye-hand coordination. We ask the subject to hold a pointer and to trace with it on a screen a rapidly moving light circling over a complicated path. In this **"pursuit-rotor" task** we can measure for what portion of a minute the subject is able to keep the pointer on the light. For both DV_1 and DV_2 we'll probably need to measure the performances repeatedly and then average the scores. Say that on the reaction-time task we ask the subject to do 50 reactions, and for the pursuit task we measure their "time on target" for five repeated one-minute trials. Since for both DV_1 and DV_2 we are measuring "time," these are also interval measures.

For our third performance DV, we decide to measure a different aspect of human functioning, verbal problem solving. After consulting the literature, we choose an **"anagram" task.** For this task, we give the subjects 20 printed words with the letters mixed up in each word and ask them to unscramble as many words as they can in five minutes. Our measure will be the number of words they can unscramble correctly in the allotted time. This DV_3 is another interval measure.

Finally, the literature suggests that subjects consuming marijuana may be prone to overrate the quality of their performances. Accordingly, when the subjects complete each task, we will ask them to indicate on a seven-point scale how well they feel they did on the task. Since this is a rating measure, this DV_4 will be measured on an ordinal scale.

Having operationally defined four psychological DVs and several physiological ones, we need to specify the order in which they will be measured. We also need to assure ourselves that taking all these measures does not consume an unreasonably long time, fatiguing our subjects and letting the effects of the drug wear off.

Now, with our IV and DVs operationally defined, it is time to plan the design of our research.

DESIGN 1: ONE-SHOT

The **One-Shot design** uses only one group of subjects. These subjects are all given the same treatment, and then they are observed. The shorthand for this design would be:

$$\boxed{G \quad T \quad O}$$

This design can yield information only about the *posttreatment behavior* of our group of subjects. Its simple structure does not give us any comparison information which might indicate whether or not the posttreatment behavior was due to the treatment.

Is this a silly design? The One-Shot design can be seen as analogous to our usual approach to college instruction. We take a group of students who register for a course, treat them to certain educational techniques such as a textbook and lectures, and grade them at the end of the course. The limited information yielded from this design is one of the reasons it is so hard to evaluate the effectiveness of college instruction. This One-Shot design provides little information as to whether or not the instruction had any real effect on the students.

In our marijuana research, it might be a good idea to use this design for a pilot study. We need to check out whether the operational definitions of our DVs are actually feasible. For example, we may have guessed wrong when we constructed our anagram task. If the task is so easy that everyone will solve all the anagrams correctly or so difficult that no one will be able to solve any of them, then we won't get very much useful information from that DV. If our subjects are so stoned by our dosage that they can't stand upright to do the pursuit-rotor task, we may not get very many usable measures on that DV either. A G T O pilot experiment on, say, five subjects might give us the reassuring information that the scores on the anagram task do scatter between 0 and 20 correct and that the subjects can manage to give a recordable pursuit-rotor performance without curling up and going to sleep. Such a pilot study might tell us that in reality it takes a good half-hour to make our observations on all the DVs. If this is too long a time, we may want to eliminate some measures or modify our measurement procedures so that it is more efficient. This simple pilot study might also alert us to the necessity of making the subjects smoke the chemical in a more uniform fashion. We may find that some subjects rapidly consume the marijuana while others drag out the smoking process. If so, we may want to change our instructions to the subjects in our later, more extensive experiment. Such information from pilot work can help us avoid costly mistakes in our larger-scale research project.

DESIGN 2: ONE-GROUP PRE-POST

The **One-Group Pre-Post design** is similar to the One-Shot except that it adds DV observations taken on the group of subjects before the treatment is given. The shorthand for this design would be:

$$\boxed{\text{G O T O}}$$

Adding this initial observation period makes *pretreatment information* available in addition to *posttreatment information*. Now it becomes possible to do *pre-to-post comparisons*.

If we used this design for the marijuana study, we could make Within-Subject comparisons to reveal the effects of the drug treatment. Suppose, for example, that our results showed improvement on the three performance tasks: the subjects reacted faster on the average in the reaction-time task, the subjects were able to track the light for longer periods of time in the pursuit task, and the subjects correctly solved more of the anagrams. We could then conclude that consumption of marijuana improved performance on these tasks. Or could we? If we did so, we'd be stepping beyond the bounds of what this design can tell us because we have no information on the effects of having taken a pretest on posttest scores. It is quite reasonable that people would show faster reactions to the light and better coordination in the pursuit-rotor task simply because they had already practiced these tasks before. For the anagrams test, if we used the same set of anagrams at posttest time, it would be no wonder if subjects did better. Even if we used different items on pre- and post-tests, we might suspect that wrestling once with the problem of unscrambling anagrams might improve anyone's performance of a similar task although the individual items are changed. The   G O T O   design can give us no information about these possibilities.

We might feel a little happier about attributing pre-to-post changes in this experiment to treatment effects if the subjects performed more poorly at posttest time despite the beneficial aspects of practice. In this case, we might claim there were detrimental effects caused by smoking marijuana. Still doubters could argue that the poorer performance the second time around was due to boredom or fatigue. Because of design limitations, our study could not conclusively reject this argument.

DESIGN 3: COMPARING BLOCKS OF SUBJECTS

Pilot studies are often done to see whether some characteristics of the subjects affect DV performance and, therefore, should be eliminated or controlled for in our final experimental design. For example, we might be concerned that the DV performance measures of men and women in the age group we are interested in studying would differ greatly independent of any exposure to marijuana. Accordingly, we might design a pilot study to investigate the single Subject IV, "sex of subject." We would block prospective subjects into groups of "men" and "women" and measure them on our DVs. In this simple design there is no treatment since we do nothing to our subjects other than observe them. A shorthand representation of this design would be:

The information yielded by this design is very limited. We can get only Between-Subjects comparison information for the two groups. The design can tell us whether men and women differ on our DVs, but it tells us nothing about why they differ. There is no information in this design as to whether the two groups of subjects were equivalent on other Relevant Variables when blocked as specified by the operational definition of our Subject IV. The women, for example, might not have taken the tasks as seriously as the men did. Or, perhaps, these tasks are more familiar to men than to women. Or maybe there is some real difference in skill level between the sexes. However, even though this design reveals nothing about why any differences exist, the results of this pilot study could well modify our final research plan. If large differences existed between the men and women tested on these tasks, at the very least we would want to be sure in our final research plan that there were equal numbers of men and women in the experimental (treatment) and control (no-treatment) groups. We might even decide to do a multiple-IV experiment with "sex of subject" as one of our IVs. Or, if our resources were too limited for a multiple-variable experiment, we might decide to limit our final study to males and avoid the issue of male-female differences altogether. On the other hand, if no differences existed in the pilot study between male and female performances on the DV tasks we would be less worried about sex of subject as a possible Relevant Variable in our final research plan.

RECAPITULATION

for "SIMPLE DESIGNS"

Two very simple designs use only a single group of subjects. These are the *One-Shot,* or $\boxed{\text{G T O}}$ *design,* and the *One-Group, Pre-Post,* or $\boxed{\text{G O T O}}$ *design.* The One-Shot yields only posttreatment information. The One-Group, Pre-Post design yields, in addition, pretreatment information and pre-to-post comparison information. Neither design can conclusively establish that the posttreatment observations or the pre-to-posttreatment changes are solely produced by the treatment. In a third simple design, the subjects are blocked into two or more groups according to a Subject IV and then observations are taken on the different groups. This design yields comparison information about existing DV differences between groups. However, without information about group equivalence, such a *blocked design* cannot establish that the Subject IV is the sole variable responsible for observed group differences. Despite their limitations, these designs are very useful for small-scale, inexpensive *pilot studies.* Such pilot research can be used to check out procedures before incorporating them into subsequent larger-scale experiments.

BEHAVIORAL OBJECTIVES

for SIMPLE DESIGNS

1. Give the shorthand representation for:
   a. the One-Shot design.
   b. the One-Group, Pre-Post design.
   c. a Two-Group, Blocked design.
2. List the kinds of information available from an experiment done with:
   a. a One-Shot design.
   b. a One-Group, Pre-Post design.
   c. a Two-Group, Blocked design.
3. Given the shorthand representation for any of these designs, name the design correctly.
4. Given a description of a pilot study:
   a. Write out the shorthand representation of its design.
   b. Name the design.
   c. Describe the information available from such a design.
   d. Evaluate the conclusions of the research in terms of the limitations on information from such a design.
   e. Suggest an improvement in the design.

5. Explain what the term "pilot study" means. Why might one wish to do a pilot study?

6. Explain why the $\boxed{\text{G O T O}}$ design is a Within-Subjects design.

7. Explain why a Two-Group, Blocked design is a Between-Subjects design.

SAMPLE TEST QUESTIONS

for "SIMPLE DESIGNS"

1. Reread the Astro-turf study on page 76.
   a. Represent this design in shorthand.
   b. Give the name of this design.
   c. Describe the information yielded by this design.
   d. Discuss the conclusion that the improvement seen in performance is due to Astro-turf. Why is this conclusion weak?
   e. How might you change this experiment to strengthen conclusions about the effects of practice on Astro-turf?

2. In a pilot experiment on the effects of coffee consumption, you find that all your subjects correctly solve all ten math problems on a test given to them immediately after consuming one cup of coffee.
   a. Give the shorthand representation of this design, specifying what each letter stands for.
   b. Name this design.
   c. What kinds of information can be obtained from this design?
   d. Given the results of this pilot study, what change might you make in the operational definition of the DV to improve the usefulness of results from a subsequent study?

3. (From the *Fables of Aesop* according to Sir Roger L'Estrange, 1967, p. 16.)

   A good woman had a hen that laid her every day an egg. Now she fancy'd to herself, that upon a larger allowance of corn, this hen might be brought in time to lay twice a day. She tried the experiment; but the hen grew fat upon't and gave quite over laying.

   a. What was the design of this experiment? What is the name of this design?
   b. What treatment was applied to the subject?
   c. What was the DV?
   d. What information can be obtained from this design?
   e. What would be your objections if, on the basis of this research, the woman concluded that feeding chickens extra corn did not increase their ability to lay eggs?
   f. Why is this a Within-Subjects design?

SECTION 5: TWO-GROUP DESIGNS FOR NON-SUBJECT IVs

The obvious cure for the limited information about treatment effects available from one-group designs is to add a second group. With this second group in your design you can give a treatment to one group (experimental) and no treatment to the other (control). Or you may want to compare two different treatments, giving the first treatment to one group and the second to the other. In either case, the effect of the treatment can be estimated by comparing the posttreatment behavior of the two groups. In these two-group designs, the Non-Subject (treatment) IV is treated Between-Subjects and has two levels. Most of the designs discussed in this section are called **Independent-Groups designs** since the subjects assigned to one group are different people from those assigned to the other. At the end of this section, we will also consider a special variation of the two-group design in which the subjects in one group are paired or "matched" on some basis with the subjects in the other.

INDEPENDENT-GROUPS DESIGNS

Static-Groups Design

The **Static-Groups design** uses two groups of subjects that have already been divided by some process before the experimenter has access to them. For some reason, the experimenter is not free to assign subjects but simply accepts the pre-existing groups. These groups are not considered to be "blocks" in the design shorthand because they were not intentionally formed to investigate a specific Subject IV. The experimenter gives a treatment to one of the groups and then takes posttreatment observations on both groups. A shorthand representation of such a Static-Groups design might be:

$$
\begin{array}{ccc}
G_e & T & O \\
G_c & & O
\end{array}
$$

This design not only gives *posttreatment information* for the experimental group, as does a One-Shot design, but it also permits us to make *comparisons* between two groups, one of which has been treated differently. The design does not, however, contain any information about group equivalence since the formation of the groups is not under the experimenter's control.

For our marijuana study, we might ask members of a college class to indicate whether or not they regularly use marijuana. Since a relatively small number admit to marijuana smoking, we assign all of the admitted smokers to our experimental group. For a control group, we take student volunteers from the rest of the class.

Our IV, smoking of marijuana, is treated in a two-level, Between-Subjects design, with the experimental group getting one standard dose of marijuana and the control group getting no dose. We test the marijuana smokers on all our DVs just after smoking and compare their results to those of the control group. We find that the experimental subjects do less well than the controls on all three performance tasks. At the same time, the self-ratings of the experimentals indicate that they feel their performances are of higher quality. We conclude that smoking marijuana decreases performance while increasing confidence.

By this point you should be squirming at the thought of the obvious Relevant Subject Variables that have been left uncontrolled in this design. So what if the experimental group did less well than the control group? Smoking a single dosage of marijuana was not necessarily the only difference between these two groups. Possibly, the admitted smokers were different in their performance abilities at the beginning of the experiment, and their poorer performance wasn't due only to the marijuana dose given them as the treatment. This problem reveals a limitation of the Static-Groups design: we have no way of conclusively establishing whether the differences between preformed groups in their DV measures are due to the effect of the treatment or to built-in Subject Variable differences. A Static-Groups design potentially confounds unmeasured Relevant Subject Variables with the Non-Subject (treatment) IV. This design simply does not give satisfactory information about equivalence of groups.

Since this lack of information about group equivalence is such a serious handicap, why use the Static-Groups design at all? In many areas in which you may want to do research, you will not be able to divide the subjects into groups as you wish. In the case of the marijuana study, for example, we may not feel free to assign any marijuana nonsmokers to the experimental group. Similarly, when doing research in educational settings, you may have to use whole classes as the groups in your research and may not be free to divide students on any other basis to suit your research plans. The same is often true of research on clinical populations when the therapy needs of the patients take precedence over any research considerations. Sometimes circumstances force you into using a Static-Groups design. When this is the case, you must be aware of the limitations of this design and include appropriate reservations when stating your conclusions.

Static-Groups, Pre-Post Design

One way to attempt to establish group equivalence when you must use a Static-Groups design is to pretest the subjects in the two groups. The shorthand for this **Static-Groups, Pre-Post design** would then be:

$$\boxed{\begin{array}{llll} G_1 & O & T & O \\ G_2 & O & & O \end{array}}$$

If you pretest both groups on the DV and find that initially they are the same, this would strengthen your argument that a posttest difference between the two groups reveals an effect of your treatment. Including this pretest measurement means that *pretreatment, pre-to-posttreatment change,* and *some group-equivalence information* is available as well as *posttreatment* and *comparison* information.

You may want to measure some things other than the DV when you are attempting to establish that static groups are equivalent. In the case of our two-group marijuana study, we might want to establish that the two groups of subjects (admitted marijuana smokers and nonsmokers) are equivalent on such Subject variables as IQ, sex composition, grade-point average, and age. If our two static groups are equivalent in all these ways, as well as having similar levels of performance on the pretest DV observations, then we would be even more secure in attributing differences at posttest time to the effects of the treatment.

The Static-Groups, Pre-Post design does not give us information about the effects of taking the pretest on posttest performance. Also, it cannot control for any different events that happen to the two groups during the course of the experiment. In the marijuana study, if our design calls for doing the pretest on one day and the treatment and posttest on the next, it is possible that, because of differing life-styles, our subjects may be exposed to different influences during the intervening time. In particular, subjects in the experimental group, composed of admitted smokers, may smoke additional dosages of marijuana on their own. Or it is possible that the experimental-group subjects get less sleep than control-group subjects. If any of these differences occur, then our conclusion that posttreatment observations are due to treatment effects is again weakened. Static groups that appear to be equivalent at pretest time may not remain so.

Randomized-Groups Design

Another way to establish group equivalence is to assign the subjects to the two groups *at random.* This **Randomized-Groups design** greatly reduces the chance that the two groups will differ consistently on some Relevant Subject Variable, since any subject with any particular degree of a given characteristic is equally likely to end up in either group. The shorthand representation for this design would be:

$$\begin{array}{ll} RG_1 & T \;\; O \\ RG_2 & \;\; O \end{array}$$

This design yields *posttreatment information* and two-group *comparison information,* and it also does a better job of establishing *equivalent groups.* Using this design strengthens the conclusion that any difference in posttreatment observations between the two groups is due to the effects of the treatment. It is an Independent-Groups design because different subjects form the two groups. For the same reason, the design is also said to be a Between-Subjects one.

Using this design for our marijuana study, we would probably select all our subjects from students who admitted to the use of marijuana in order to avoid ethical issues about exposing nonusers to the drug. We would then divide these subjects *randomly* into two equal-sized groups. This random division might be accomplished by flipping a coin for each subject, by use of a random-number table, or by some other process which ensures that each subject is assigned to a particular group only by chance.

Random assignment of subjects to groups in an experiment is always good insurance against uncontrolled effects of undetected Subject Relevant Variables such as are likely to occur in a Static-Groups design. As mentioned above, however, practical considerations sometimes prevent random division.

Randomized-Groups, Pre-Post Design

In the **Randomized Groups, Pre-Post design,** group equivalence is established by randomization, but pretests also are taken. The shorthand representation of this design would be:

$$\begin{array}{llll} RG_1 & O & T & O \\ RG_2 & O & & O \end{array}$$

You would use such a design when you were interested not only in posttreatment comparisons but also in comparison of pre-to-post changes. The information yielded by this design would be: *posttreatment information, pretreatment information, comparisons of posttreatment information between groups* (Between-Subjects), *comparison of posttreatment to pretreatment information* (Within-Subjects), *comparison of pre-to-post changes between groups* (Between-Subjects), and *group equivalence.* It differs from the Randomized-Groups design only in the addition of a pretest.

In our marijuana study, the only alteration necessary to change it from a straight Randomized-Groups design to a Randomized-Groups, Pre-Post design would be to give all subjects the pretreatment battery of tests on the DVs. We might try to do this within one session or, since taking the DV measures will take some time (about one-half hour according to our pilot work), we might split the experiment into two sessions, pretesting on one day and having the subjects come back for treatment and posttesting on the second. To be sure that we haven't some Non-Subject uncontrolled Relevant Variables concealed in the woodwork, we had better provide for some neutral activity for our control (no-treatment) subjects that takes the same amount of time as it takes the treatment subjects to smoke their marijuana. We want the two groups of subjects to differ only in whether or not they smoke the drug we give them.

In addition to letting us discuss pre-to-post changes, taking a pretest measurement in a Randomized-Groups design allows us to see whether the randomization process did in fact produce equivalent groups. Sometimes, especially if group size is small, one or two subjects with extreme characteristics will by chance end up in one or the other of the groups. For instance, two subjects in athletic training might have wandered into our marijuana study and by chance been placed in the experimental group. Because of their athletic background, these subjects show extremely good performances on both the reaction-time and pursuit tasks. This would make the experimental group as a whole look better, especially if the experimental group is small in size. Without a pretest, we could not detect that our two groups lack equivalence on this Relevant Variable despite randomization. So, in this sense, the pretest can be seen as an additional check for group equivalence.

While there are advantages to adding a pretest to a Randomized-Groups design, doing so means that the experiment will take longer to run. In addition, the possible effects of pretesting on posttest performance will not be controlled, and we may be adding a confounding variable to our study.

Matched-Groups Design

Sometimes, the nature of the research question is such that it is very important that the two groups be completely equivalent before the experiment, either in terms of a pretest on the DV or in terms of some other Relevant Variable. When this is so, it may be worthwhile to go to the trouble of matching the subjects before assignment to groups. For example, in our marijuana study, if we were worried that individual differences in coordination could obscure the small effects of consumption of marijuana, we might want to use a **Matched-Groups design.**

One way of matching the groups would be to use the pursuit-rotor scores on the pretest as the basis for matching. If we decided to do this, we would give all our prospective subjects this pretest before assignment to groups. We would take the pursuit-rotor scores and use them to rank our subjects from the best to the worst performer. We would then divide these subjects into pairs as follows: the two best, the two next best, . . . the two worst. Within each pair, we would decide at random which member of the pair would go into the experimental group and which one would go into the control. In this **Matched Randomized-Groups design,** assignment to groups is random, but the two groups are no longer independent; each subject in one group has a partner in the other. This approach ensures that the two groups are initially exactly the same on the pursuit-rotor task. It also permits us to use statistical analyses which reduce the effects of individual differences on our comparisons. A shorthand representation of this design would be:

$$\boxed{\begin{array}{l} O \ MRG_1 \ T \ O \\ O \ MRG_2 \quad\ \ O \end{array}}$$

The abbreviation MR can be used to indicate that while assignment to groups is random, the randomization is done within pairs matched (**M**) according to pretest scores.

Subjects can be matched on Subject Relevant Variables rather than on their DV pretest scores. In our marijuana study, for example, we might consider it important that the subjects in the two groups be of equal IQ. In this case, we would obtain IQ scores for our prospective subjects, rank the subjects according to their IQ scores, and then divide them into pairs based on their ranks. Again, within each pair, one subject would be randomly assigned to the experimental group and one to the control. In making a shorthand representation for this design we wouldn't put in an initial O because the basis for matching was not observations on the DV. This type of Material Randomized Groups design could be abbreviated as follows:

$$\left|\begin{array}{l} MRG_1 \ T \ O \\ MRG_2 \quad\ \ O \end{array}\right|$$ where M stands for matching
   pairs according to IQ scores.

Sometimes matching is done because the subjects are genetically related. If (and this isn't too likely) we could find a sufficient number of marijuana-smoking identical twins, we might match our two groups by randomly putting one member of each twin pair in the first group and the other in the second. Then our two groups would be matched for genetic factors. This kind of matching is somewhat more common in animal research, especially that done with animals born in litters. In a matched **littermate** design, for every animal assigned to one group a member of the same litter ("littermate control") is assigned to the other.

Matching may also be done when subsequent random assignment to IV levels is not possible. If you were forced by circumstances to use a Static-Groups design, you might attempt to match on some basis each person in one group to a person in the other. This would increase your chances of having equivalent groups even though you couldn't make subsequent random assignment. Also, when a Subject IV is being used, you might match each person in one block (one level of the Subject IV) on some basis to a person in another block (another level of the Subject IV) to decrease the effect of some Relevant Variable. A **Static-Groups Design with Matching** does not ensure group equivalence, but it does improve the interpretation of results by controlling at least one Relevant Variable.

The information yielded by a Matched Randomized-Groups design is the same as that yielded by the Randomized-Groups design with the added information about group equivalence provided by the matching. When matching is done for a Static-Groups design or between levels of a Subject IV, it decreases the chance of a Confounding Variable affecting the results.

RECAPITULATION

for TWO-GROUP DESIGNS

Adding a second group to an experimental design greatly increases the amount of information available from the design although it also doubles the number of subjects you'll have to find. Two-group designs are mostly *Independent-Groups designs* in which the subjects in one group are different from and independent of the subjects in the other group. These designs are used for investigating Non-Subject IVs with only two levels. Sometimes it is necessary or convenient to use two pre-existing groups that have been formed by some process not under the experimenter's control. Such designs are called *Static-Group designs*. These designs yield posttreatment comparison information between groups but do not establish group equivalence. Adding a pretest to the Static-Groups design makes it possible to check whether or not the groups are at least initially equivalent as far as the DV is concerned, but does not ensure against other Relevant Variables differing between the groups. Group equivalence is usually established in a two-group design by random division of the subjects into groups. A *Randomized-Groups design* greatly decreases the chances that the two groups will differ on any Relevant Variable. If a pretest is included in the design, it would be a *Randomized-Groups, Pre-Post design*. When it is essential that the two groups be exactly the same, they may be matched on some basis. In a *Matched Randomized-Groups design*, the subjects are first divided into matched pairs on the basis of a pretest on one or more of the DVs or on the basis of some Relevant Subject Variable. Within each matched pair, subjects are randomly assigned to the two groups. Using this approach means that the subjects in the two groups are no longer independent of each other and permits comparisons within subject pairs as well as between groups. In summary, the two-group designs discussed in this section can be represented as follows:

Static Groups

G_1	T	O
G_2		O

Static Groups, Pre-Post

G_1	O	T	O
G_2	O		O

Randomized Groups

RG_1	T	O
RG_2		O

Randomized Groups, Pre-Post

RG_1	O	T	O
RG_2	O		O

Matched Randomized Groups		Matched Randomized Groups	
(on basis of DV)		*(on the basis of some Relevant Variable)*	

```
O  MRG₁  T  O
O  MRG₂     O
```

```
MRG₁  T  O
MRG₂     O
```

BEHAVIORAL OBJECTIVES

for TWO-GROUP DESIGNS

1. List the names of all the designs discussed in this section and in Section 4.

2. Given the name of one of these designs, write down the shorthand representation of the design.

3. Given the shorthand for any one of these designs, state its name.

4. Given either the name or the shorthand representation of any one of the designs, describe the information yielded by the design. Mention at least one limitation on information yielded by the design. (To prepare for this objective, you might want to make yourself a chart.)

5. Explain what the new symbol "M" represents. Use a specific example in describing the procedure.

6. Describe a basis on which you may want to match subjects.

7. Explain what it means to say that a design consists of "Independent Groups." List the designs described in this and the preceding section that are Independent-Groups design.

8. Given a description of an experiment:
   a. Identify the IV or treatment variable.
   b. Identify the DVs on which observations are to be taken.
   c. Give the design in shorthand.
   d. Describe the information that can be yielded by the design.
   e. Evaluate the conclusions of the research in terms of the limitations on information of the particular design.
   f. Suggest an improvement in design.

9. Given an experimental question, design a two-group experiment to answer the question.

SAMPLE TEST QUESTIONS

for TWO-GROUP DESIGNS

1. An experimental design is represented as follows:

$$\boxed{\begin{array}{l} MRG_1 \ T \ O \\ MRG_2 \quad\ \ O \end{array}}$$

In this design, T represents a one-hour session on ways to improve testtaking behavior and O represents scores on the final for an Introductory Psychology Class. M was done on the basis of grade point average (GPA).

a. Name this design.

b. In an essay, give a verbal description of this research study, narrating all the steps involved in setting it up.

c. What kinds of information can be yielded by this design?

d. If the subjects were just assigned at random without considering their GPAs, what would be the shorthand representation of the design?

2. Read the following brief design descriptions. State for each design whether it is an *Independent-Groups design* (I), a *Matched-Groups design* (M), or a *One-Group, Pre-Post design* (P-P).

a. The experimenter takes a group of 40 subjects and randomly divides them into two groups of 20. One group drinks unlimited amounts of coffee while solving a long series of problems. The other group has no coffee. Number of correct problem solutions is measured.

b. Each of 40 subjects is tested for problem-solving accuracy and speed before and after drinking three cups of coffee.

c. For a kindergarten class, you find separately for boys and for girls the number who fail to make any solution of a problem, the number who make a time-consuming but obvious solution, and the number who make a difficult but quick solution.

d. A group of ten rats are run in a straight-alley maze and their speed of running is measured. Then all rats are injected with a dose of nicotine. Their running times are again measured.

e. Twenty sets of identical twins are separated at birth with one child randomly assigned to a middle-class home and one to a lower-class home.

f. Two male rats are selected from each of ten litters. Within each pair, one rat is randomly assigned to a group which is given nicotine injections. The other rat from each pair is assigned to a group given injections of saline (a weak salt solution). The running speeds of the two groups of rats are compared.

g. In a study attempting to determine the effects of a period of transcendental meditation on subsequent motor coordination and physiological response to physical stress, the researcher tested practiced meditators and nonmeditator controls both before and after 20 minutes of meditation (for the meditators) and 20 minutes of relaxation (for the nonmeditators). For each of the 20 practiced meditators who volunteered for the study, the researcher found a nonmeditator control subject of the same sex, age, height, weight, and level of customary physical activity.

3. For any of the designs in Question 2 that you identified as "Independent Groups," mark whether they are a Randomized-Groups design (R), a Static-Groups Design (S), or a Blocked-Groups design (B).

4. An experimenter is interested in comparing the effects of instruction in speed-reading techniques with and without the use of an expensive speed-reading training machine. To be certain that his two groups are of equal reading ability to begin with, he measures the reading speed for technical material of all 40 of his subjects. He then establishes 20 pairs of subjects, the members of each pair having approximately the same reading speed. Within each pair he flips a coin to decide which member will be assigned to the "Machine" group and which will be assigned to the "Non-Machine" group. For two weeks, the subjects meet nightly. They all have a half-hour of instruction each night in speed-reading techniques. They have one and one-half hours of practice, the "Machine" group using the machines and "Non-Machine" group using specially designed practice reading materials. At the end of the two weeks, all subjects' reading speeds are again measured for technical materials.

a. Write down the shorthand representation of this design.

b. What is the name of this design?

c. List all the information available from this design. Be specific.

d. What limitation on information does this design have?

e. If the experimenter took the beginning measurements of reading speed, but assigned the subjects randomly without taking into account these measures, what would be the representation of this altered design? What would be the name of this altered design?

5. (From the *New York Times,* reprinted in the Corvallis *Gazette-Times,* June 19, 1978).

Jewish Penicillin "Good for Colds"

Jewish mothers are doing the right thing when they treat their sick with "Jewish penicillin," or chicken soup, according to a study by researchers at Miami's Mount Sinai Hospital. Using 15 subjects and some fairly sophisticated medical testing equipment, Doctors Klumars Sakethop and Marvin A. Sackner have found that the broth is in fact good for colds—or, as they put it, "efficacious for upper respiratory tract infections therapy."

Why is chicken soup so effective? Heat is a therapeutic factor, according to Sackner, but neither he nor his partner could explain why chicken soup was statistically more effective than hot water.

Design a two-group study to test the above question:

a. Write down a shorthand representation of your study, specifying what the letters stand for.

b. What is the name of your design?

c. What kinds of information can be yielded by your design?

d. What, if any, are the limitations on information yielded from your design?

e. Describe your IV.

f. Describe your DV(s).

6. Reread the abstract and description of the Boren and Foree (1977) study given on page 66. With the added information that the two instructional methods were used in different years of the course and that there was no control by the authors over what students registered for what years, do the following:

a. Give the shorthand representation of the design.

b. Name the design.

c. List the kinds of information available from such a design.

d. Describe a limitation on information yielded by such a design.

e. Describe how you would design a better study.

chapter 4

more complex designs

When you start dreaming up ideas for an experiment, you'll often find your curiosity not satisfied with comparing the effects of just two conditions. You may find, for instance, that a more complete operational definition of your IV involves investigating its effects at three or more levels. Accordingly, you might want to design a *single-IV, multiple-level* experiment. Or, since in the real world variables do not usually occur in isolation, you may want to know whether the effect of your IV would be modified by the presence of another IV. Two or more IVs can be investigated at the same time by using a **multivariate or factorial design.** There are other complex designs suited for specific situations. The *Solomon's Four-Group design* allows you to investigate the effects of pretesting while studying the effects of a Non-Subject IV. A *Latin-Square design* can be used when complete counterbalancing is impractical for a multi-level, Within-Subjects experiment. Various *Correlational designs* are available for studies which wish to find out the interrelationships among multiple DV measures. *Single-Subject designs,* which intensively study only a few subjects at a time, may be necessary in clinical studies where a large number of similar subjects are not available. These more complex designs can yield more information but, of course, are more expensive to use than the simpler two-condition designs. Researchers must balance their need for information against available resources when choosing a design for a particular study.

SECTION 1: MULTI-LEVEL DESIGNS

When you operationally define your IV you may find that you wish to investigate its effects at more than two levels. This is simple to do; you just add more conditions to your research design, creating a **multi-level design.** Of course, adding more conditions will increase either the number of subjects you need to find or the number of times you have to observe each subject. Increasing information yield from an experiment always carries a price in terms of the cost of doing the research. So be sure you really want the added information before you start increasing the number of research conditions.

MULTIPLE IV LEVELS IN A BETWEEN-SUBJECTS DESIGN

One way of investigating more levels of your IV is to include more groups in your experiment. Suppose you define your IV as having three levels which you call T_1, T_2, and T_3. If you use three independent groups of subjects you could design the following experiment:

$$
\begin{array}{ll}
RG_1 & T_1 & O \\
RG_2 & T_2 & O \\
RG_3 & T_3 & O
\end{array}
$$

This *Multi-Level, Randomized-Groups* design would yield all the information yielded by the Two-Group, Randomized-Groups design. In addition, it would allow you to make multiple posttreatment comparisons among the different levels of your IV.

For the moment we'll depart from consideration of our own marijuana experiment proposal in Chapter 3 and take a look at some research done by other investigators. The following research compares the effects of marijuana and alcohol on driving a car:

Crancer, Dille, Delay, Wallace, and Haykin (1969): Comparison of effects of marijuana and alcohol on simulated driving performance.

> The effects of marijuana, alcohol, and no treatment on simulated driving performance were determined for experienced marijuana smokers. Subjects experiencing a "social marijuana high" accumulated significantly more speedometer errors than . . . under control conditions, whereas there were no significant differences in accelerator, brake, signal, steering and total errors. . . . subjects intoxicated from alcohol accumulated significantly more accelerator, brake, signal, speedometer, and total errors than under normal conditions, whereas there was no significant difference in steering errors.*

Before we figure out the design of this research, we have to identify the IV and DVs. The IV we could label as "type of drug," defined in this study as having three levels: no drug, alcohol, marijuana. As in our own research project, these authors used several DVs to increase the information they could get from the research. The DVs mentioned in the abstract are: speedometer errors, accelerator errors, brake errors, signal errors, steering errors, and total errors. If we were thinking of replicating this research, we'd have to read more of the article than this abstract to find out the complete operational definitions of the variables. If we did so, we'd find that the alcohol level of the IV was defined as two drinks of 95 percent alcohol in juice with the amount of alcohol adjusted according to the subject's body weight in order to produce a .10 blood alcohol level (legal intoxification) on a Breathalyzer. The

---

*Reprinted by permission of the American Association for the Advancement of Science (copyright © 1969) and Alfred Crancer, Jr.

marijuana level of the IV was defined as two marijuana cigarettes smoked in one-half hour (about 1.5 gm of marijuana of .9% Δ^9-THC). The DV measures were obtained from a driver-trainer simulator using a test film which gives the subjects a "driver's-eye view" of the road while leading them through normal and emergency driving situations.

If independent, preformed groups of subjects were assigned to the different levels of the IV, then the design would be a *Multi-Level, Static-Groups, Between-Subjects design* which could be abbreviated as follows:

$$
\begin{array}{lll}
G_1 & T_m & O \\
G_2 & T_a & O \\
G_3 & & O
\end{array}
$$

If the subject assignment were random, then the design would be a *Multi-Level, Randomized-Groups, Between-Subjects design*. In shorthand, this design would look like:

$$
\begin{array}{lll}
RG_1 & T_m & O \\
RG_2 & T_a & O \\
RG_3 & & O
\end{array}
$$

Finally, if there were some basis on which to match subjects, the authors might want to use a *Multi-Level, Matched-Groups, Between-Subjects design* which would look as follows:

$$
\begin{array}{lll}
MRG_1 & T_m & O \\
MRG_2 & T_a & O \\
MRG_3 & & O
\end{array}
$$

There are many different bases on which you might want to match subjects in an experiment like this. For example, the abstract says that all the subjects were "experienced marijuana smokers." If you thought that their amount of experience might affect the outcome of the experiment, you could obtain from the subjects the information as to how long and how frequently they had been using the drug. Then you could rank them in order according to the amount of their prior usage of marijuana, divide them into triplets with approximately equal experience, and randomly assign one member of each triplet to each of your three groups.

On the other hand, you might want to assure yourself that the groups were really of equal driving ability, and not depend on randomization alone to achieve this. If so, you would pretest subjects on your driving simulator, rank them according to their skill (probably using the DV "total errors"), place them in triplets (the best three, the next best three, . . . , the worst three), and randomly assign members of each triplet to the three groups. This way of handling the matching would not only give you increased information about group equivalence but also would give you pretest information and the basis for pre-to-posttest comparisons within and between groups. The shorthand representation of this kind of *Multi-Level, Matched-Groups, Between-Subjects design* would be:

$$
\begin{array}{lll}
O & MRG_1 & T_m\,O \\
O & MRG_2 & T_a\,O \\
O & MRG_3 & \,O
\end{array}
$$

MULTIPLE IV LEVELS IN A WITHIN-SUBJECTS DESIGN

Actually, Crancer *et al.* (1969) used a design different from any discussed above. They had a lot of restrictions on the type of subject they wanted. They required that their subjects: (1) be experienced marijuana users who had smoked marijuana at least two times a month for the past six months, (2) be licensed drivers, (3) be currently enrolled in school or have a job, (4) be familiar with effects of alcohol, (5) be in good health, (6) not be taking any medication, and (7) not have certain personality problems. With all these restrictions, you can be sure that a large number of subjects would be hard to find! They found 36 subjects (27 males and 9 females) who met their requirements and were willing to participate (for a fee). If the researchers had used a Between-Subjects design, this would have placed only 12 subjects in each of the three groups. They wanted a larger number of observations than this for each condition of their experiment so they choose a different type of design.

Each subject in the Crancer *et al.* study experienced each of the three conditions of the experiment. With this arrangement, comparison of the effects of no drug, alcohol, and marijuana could be made within each subject. This would provide 36 observations for each level of the IV. Obviously, this design had the advantage of maximizing the use of their subjects. It presented some problems, however. One was that repeated testing on the driver simulator might improve performance in and of itself. Another was that the order of experiencing the experimental conditions (alcohol before marijuana as opposed to marijuana before alcohol) might have an effect. The usual way to control for these effects in a Within-Subjects design is to counterbalance the conditions, to have an equal number of subjects experience each possible order of conditions. In a drug experiment, it would also be advisable to let time pass between the different conditions to give the drug a chance to wear off. Crancer *et al.* let two days pass between observations under different conditions. A complete shorthand representation of a *Counterbalanced Multi-Level, Within-Subjects design* for three levels of the IV would be as shown in Fig. 4.1.

FIG. 4.1

Design for a three-level, Within-Subjects experiment.

$$
\begin{array}{l}
RG_1 \ T_o \ O \ T_a \ O \ T_m \ O \\
RG_2 \ T_o \ O \ T_m \ O \ T_a \ O \\
RG_3 \ T_a \ O \ T_o \ O \ T_m \ O \\
RG_4 \ T_a \ O \ T_m \ O \ T_o \ O \\
RG_5 \ T_m \ O \ T_o \ O \ T_a \ O \\
RG_6 \ T_m \ O \ T_a \ O \ T_o \ O
\end{array}
$$

T_o is no drug
T_a is alcohol
T_m is marijuana

This design could be more briefly written as: $\boxed{RG \ T_o \ O \ T_a \ O \ T_m \ O}$ (with T_o, T_a, and T_m counterbalanced across subjects).

This Multi-Level, Within-Subjects design yields the same comparison information for posttreatment effects of multiple IV levels as does the Between-Subjects design. However, the level comparisons are made within the same subjects rather than between different subjects. Since the same subject group is used throughout, there is information on group equivalence, provided that when counterbalancing you assign subjects to the different orders of the conditions at random. If you have enough subjects that several of them (say ten or more) can be assigned to each order of conditions, then you can also make a meaningful between-subjects comparison to see how order of conditions actually affected results. In the Crancer *et al.* study, the six subjects assigned to each order are probably too small a number for meaningful comparisons about order effects. So we should probably just compare the DV measures taken after marijuana and after alcohol with each other and with those taken after no drug. We can be secure when we do this that the counterbalancing means that there will be no consistent order effect confounding conclusions about the Within-Subjects drug effects.

RECAPITULATION

for MULTI-LEVEL DESIGNS

Often we will find ourselves interested in effects of more than two levels of our IV. Accordingly, we can plan an experiment with three or more conditions, each condition representing a level of our single IV. We can define our IV for the experiment as Between-Subjects by using different groups of subjects for each condition. For example, we can add a third group to an Independent-Groups design, such as Static-Groups or Randomized-Groups, or to a Matched-Groups design. The information yielded by these expanded designs is the same as that yielded by the two-group designs, except that we now have multi-level comparison information as well. Multiple levels of an IV can also be investigated with a Within-Subjects design. This design allows us to reuse the same subjects at every level rather than having to divide the subjects into smaller groups. However, in a Within-Subjects design we must allow for the possible effects of repeated observations on the subjects and also for the effects of different orders of conditions. The usual way to control for these problems is to counterbalance the order of conditions across subjects. This means we see that an equal number of subjects, selected at random, experience each possible order of the conditions. A Within-Subjects design allows us to increase the number of observations under each condition without increasing the number of subjects, but it does require that the subjects spend a longer time participating in our experiment.

BEHAVIORAL OBJECTIVES

for MULTI-LEVEL DESIGNS

1. Given the shorthand representation of any of the designs from this section or from Chapter 3:
   a. Describe in words what the design consists of.
   b. Name the design.
   c. List the information yielded by the design.
2. Given the names of designs from this section or from Chapter 3, give the shorthand representation of the design.
3. Given a description of a three-level IV, design an experiment to yield multi-level comparison information:
   a. with the IV defined *Between-Subjects*.
   b. with the IV defined *Within-Subjects*.
4. Describe the process of counterbalancing conditions. Give a specific example. When is this procedure used?
5. Given a particular simple design, describe exactly what would be necessary to add to it to make it into a particular more complicated design.
6. Describe the two problems that must be controlled for when using an IV Within-Subjects.
7. if you are told you have available a specific number of subjects, specify how many will be observed at each level of an IV:
   a. if the IV is defined Between-Subjects.
   b. if the IV is defined Within-Subjects.
8. Given a description of an experiment:
   a. Write down its shorthand representation.
   b. Name the design.
   c. List the information yielded by the design.
   d. Discuss any limitation on information yielded by the design.

SAMPLE TEST QUESTIONS

for MULTI-LEVEL DESIGNS

1. An experiment was done with the following design:

   $$\boxed{\begin{array}{l} RG_1 \; O \; T_1 \; O \\ RG_2 \; O \; T_2 \; O \\ RG_3 \; O \; T_3 \; O \end{array}}$$

   where T_1 was individual tutorial help,
   $\quad\quad T_2$ was group-help sessions,
   $\quad\quad T_3$ was no outside-of-class help,
   and $\quad$ O was the score on a test in an introductory math class

   a. Describe in words what was done in this experiment.

   b. What is the name of this design?

   c. What information would be yielded by this design?

2. The following research was reported in a newspaper, the *Oregon Horse* (June 1978):

   Dr. John Baker at the University of Kentucky did some research on horses chewing wood. He fed three diets: (1) 20 pounds of grass-legume hay; (2) 13 pounds of sweet-feed grain; and (3) 13 pounds of grain followed by cecal infusions* of a chemical 4–6 hours after feeding to lower intestinal acidity. (The horses were) also fed $1'' \times 8'' \times 5'$ white pine boards.

   These were confined, mature horses with developed wood-chewing habits. All the horses chewed wood regardless of the diet. Each horse fed the . . . hay ate 7 pounds of wood in 9 days. The all-grain horses ate 21 pounds, and the all-grain plus infusion ate 19 pounds of wood.
   (*A ''cecal infusion'' is an enema!)

   a. What was Dr. Baker's IV?

   b. What was his DV?

   c. Give the probable design of the experiment in shorthand.

   d. What kind of information was yielded by this experiment (please list).

   e. Was the IV treated Between- or Within-Subjects?

   f. Whatever your answer to (e), redesign the experiment so that the IV is treated in the opposite way and write down your design in shorthand.

3. Reread the study by Aragona *et al.* (1975) described on page 67. This study concerned the best method for helping overweight children to lose weight.

   a. Give the design of this study in shorthand.

   b. What is the name of this design?

   c. What information is yielded by this design?

   d. Was the IV treated Between-Subjects or Within-Subjects?

4. Read the following excerpt from Galanter, Wyatt, Lemberger, Weingartner, Vaughn, and Roth (1972): Effects on humans of Δ^9-Tetrahydrocannabinol administered by smoking.

In the initial part of the experiment, each of the 12 subjects smoked a different one of the following on each of three days: (i) placebo marijuana material alone, (ii) placebo material injected with 10 mg of synthetic Δ^9-THC, or (iii) natural marijuana assayed to contain 10 mg of Δ^9-THC.

a. Write down the probable design in shorthand.

b. What is the name of this design?

c. How many of the 12 subjects will be observed under each condition of the experiment?

d. Write down all the orders of the treatments that should be used. How many subjects would be assigned to each order?

e. If you compare the effects of different levels of the IV, will that be a Within-in-Subjects or a Between-Subjects comparison?

f. If there were sufficient subjects that you could compare the effects of different orders of the levels of the IV, would that be a Between-Subjects or a Within-Subjects comparison?

SECTION 2: MULTIPLE-IV DESIGNS WITH NON-SUBJECT IVs

WHAT CAN YOU LEARN FROM A MULTIVARIATE DESIGN?

Using multiple IVs in a single research study is the same as simultaneously running two or more different single-IV experiments. You can get information about the effect of each IV taken separately. In addition, you can get information about the effects of the IVs when they are used in combination. On page 57 of Chapter 2 (Question 7), there is an example of a three-IV multivariate experiment concerning the effects of watching violence in a film on subsequent play behavior in children. The experimenter used the two Subject IVs of "sex" (2 levels) and "age" (3 levels) and a third Non-Subject IV of "type of film viewed" (2 levels). Combining these three IVs in one experiment produced 12 experimental conditions. The two Subject IVs, of course, had to be treated Between-Subjects and the researcher also chose to treat her Non-Subject IV in a Between-Subjects manner. As a consequence, the 12 conditions of her experiment had to be represented by 12 independent groups of subjects, each consisting of five children.

There were three **overall effect** or "main-effect" comparisons of DV measures that she could make in this experiment, one comparison for each IV. She could compare the 30 boys in the study to the 30 girls to find out if overall (ignoring the other two IVs) boys show more violence in play than girls. She could compare the 20 children of 3–5 years of age with the 20 children of 6–8 years of age and each of these age groups in turn with the 20 children of 9–10 years of age to see whether there was an overall effect of age on violent play. Finally, if she combined children of both sexes and all ages, she could compare the 30 children who saw the violent film to the 30 who saw the nonviolent one to see whether there was a main effect of the type of film viewed on play behavior. Thus her single multivariate experiment could yield comparison information the same as if she had done three separate studies investigating "age," "sex," and "type of film seen" as possible factors affecting children's play behavior.

In addition to the main-effect comparisons available for each of the separate IVs in a multivariate experiment, a new kind of information emerges as a result of investigating IVs simultaneously. This information is called **interaction** information. Several specific kinds of interaction information are available from the film-violence study. For instance, the violent film might have the overall or main effect of increasing violent acts of play. In addition, it might be observed that boys (whether they've seen the film or not) generally play more violently than girls. The new information available from looking at both of these variables in combination is that the film might be more effective in stimulating violence in boys than in girls. If so, there is an interaction in the effects of these two variables. Specifically, it might be that the violent film increases violent play in girls by 20 percent but among boys by 100 percent. This differential effect of the film on the two sexes could only be discovered in an experiment simultaneously investigating both IVs. Similar interactions could be looked for between the effects of age and seeing the film (possibly older children are more affected by seeing violence than younger children are) or between the effects of age and sex (the difference in amount of violence between the sexes might increase with age).

When you use a multiple-IV design you have comparison information about the main (overall) effect of each IV separately. In addition, you have two-way interaction information for each pair of IVs. If you use more than two IVs simultaneously you also have information about higher-order interactions (three-way, four-way) but interpretation of these is more difficult and best left for advanced statistics courses.

DEVELOPMENT OF A MULTIVARIATE OR "FACTORIAL" DESIGN

Devising IVs for an experiment is like eating peanuts: once you've operationally defined one IV, it's hard to keep from adding another. In Chapter 3 we planned a simple, two-condition experiment investigating the effects of a single "social" dosage of marijuana on physiological measures and both motor and verbal performance. More than likely, there are other variables we would like to investigate. We can think of several Non-Subject Variables that might alter the effectiveness of smoking the drug. For instance, we might be curious as to how long the effects lasted and want to test our subjects at various lengths of time after smoking. Or we might wonder whether the surroundings in which the drug is smoked have any influence on its effect, especially since it has been speculated that some of the drug's effects are due to suggestion. Since in the real world people often mix the substances they self-prescribe, we might want to know whether or not other substances that may be consumed at the same time can alter the drug's effect. There are also several Subject Variables that might interest us: experienced marijuana smokers may react differently to the drug than nonexperienced ones. The sex or age of the smoker may be a factor in the drug's effect. The attitude of the person consuming the drug may change its effectiveness.

Coming across the Crancer *et al.* (1969) study on driving performance (described on page 106) might suggest to us that in our own research we investigate both marijuana and alcohol at the same time. Crancer *et al.* did their study with a single IV (type of drug) investigated at three levels. We decide to go one step further and develop a two-IV or two-factor design which will let us see the effects of these drugs in combination as well as separately. We've already defined our first IV, marijuana consumption, as having two levels: no dose and a "standard cigarette" dose. We decide to define the second IV, alcohol consumption, also to have two levels: no dose and a dose half of what Crancer *et al.* used (since our marijuana dose is about half theirs).

Conditions of a Multivariate Design

A convenient way of figuring out the conditions for a multivariate experiment is to draw up something called a **factorial table.** In such a table the levels of one IV, or **factor,** are listed across the top of the table while the levels of the other factor are listed down the side. Each cell or square in the body of the table then represents one of the experimental conditions. In Fig. 4.2, a 2×2 factorial table is used to find out the conditions or treatments that would arise from combining our two drug variables. From this factorial table you can see that we would have to create four conditions or treatments for our experiment: no alcohol and no marijuana, marijuana alone, alcohol alone, and marijuana and alcohol together.

FIG. 4.2

A 2×2 factorial table

		IV$_2$: Alcohol	
		No dose	One dose
IV$_1$: Marijuana	No dose	T$_1$	T$_2$
	One dose	T$_3$	T$_4$

Assigning Subjects so that All IVs Are Between-Subjects (Completely Randomized Design)

Now that we know from the factorial table what treatments or conditions we have to create, we need to decide how we are going to divide up the subjects. One approach would be to treat both of the IVs in a Between-Subjects manner. In such a design, we would need four groups of subjects, one for each condition. If we had a total of 40 subjects to divide up, this would mean that we would assign 10 at random to each condition. A multivariate or **factorial design** in which a different group of subjects is assigned at random to each condition of the experiment is called a **Completely Randomized design.** This design in shorthand would look as follows:

$$
\begin{array}{llll}
RG_1 & T_1 & O \\
RG_2 & T_2 & O \\
RG_3 & T_3 & O \\
RG_4 & T_4 & O \\
\end{array}
\qquad \text{or} \qquad
\begin{array}{llll}
RG_1 & & O \\
RG_2 & T_a & O \\
RG_3 & T_m & O \\
RG_4 & T_{am} & O \\
\end{array}
$$

Assigning Subjects so that One of the IVs Is Within-Subjects (Mixed Design)

Maybe we don't feel that 10 observations per condition will be sufficient. We've tried, but we can't round up any more subjects willing to participate. So we decide that we must treat at least one of the IVs, or factors, Within-Subjects. If we decide to treat the alcohol IV Within-Subjects and keep the marijuana IV Between-Subjects, then we could have 20 observations per condition. The same 20 subjects would experience both the no-dose and one-dose alcohol levels. This division of subjects is indicated in the factorial table in Fig. 4.3

If we do the experiment this way, we have to be sure that half of the subjects in each marijuana-level group have the no-alcohol-dose condition first while the other

FIG. 4.3

A 2 × 2 factorial table, showing subject assignment for a mixed design.

		IV$_2$: Alcohol (Within-Subjects)		
		No dose		One dose
IV$_1$: Marijuana	No dose	20 Subjects (T$_1$)	(Same) ⟶	20 Subjects (T$_2$)
(Between-Subjects)	One dose	20 Subjects (T$_3$)	(Same) ⟶	20 Subjects (T$_4$)

half have the one-dose alcohol condition first. In other words, we must see that the alcohol conditions are counterbalanced for each marijuana group. We might represent this design in shorthand as follows:

RG_1 T_1 O T_2 O (with T_1 and T_2 counterbalanced across subjects)
RG_2 T_3 O T_4 O (with T_3 and T_4 counterbalanced across subjects)

Such a design involves taking repeated measures on the same subjects for the IV defined Within-Subjects while using randomized groups for the levels of the IV defined Between-Subjects. It is, therefore, called a **mixed design** because it is *partially a randomized design* and *partially a repeated measures design*.

Of course, we could do the experiment the other way, defining the marijuana IV Within-Subjects and the alcohol IV Between-Subjects. Again we would randomly divide our subjects into two groups of 20. This time there would be a different group of subjects for each level of the alcohol variable. Each of these groups would be exposed to both the no-dose and one-dose levels of marijuana. A factorial table for this design is given in Fig. 4.4.

FIG. 4.4

A 2 × 2 factorial table, showing subject assignment for a mixed design.

IV$_2$: Alcohol (Between-Subjects)

		No dose	One dose
IV$_1$: Marijuana	No dose	20 Subjects (T_1)	20 Subjects (T_2)
(Within-Subjects)	One dose	(Same)↓ 20 Subjects (T_3)	(Same)↓ 20 Subjects (T_4)

With the subject assignment diagrammed in Fig. 4.4, we would have to counterbalance the order of the marijuana conditions within each alcohol group. As many subjects, selected at random, would have to be tested with marijuana first and no-marijuana second as would need to be tested in reverse order. The shorthand for this design would be:

RG_1 T_1 O T_3 O (with T_1 and T_3 counterbalanced)
RG_2 T_2 O T_4 O (with T_2 and T_4 counterbalanced)

It is important to keep track of which of your IVs in a mixed design are Between-Subjects and which are Within-Subjects for two reasons. One is that you may need to counterbalance the order of conditions for the IV defined Within-Subjects. The other is that the statistical analysis you eventually do on your data will be somewhat different for mixed designs depending on which IV is handled Between-Subjects and which Within-Subjects.

A Completely Repeated-Measures Design With Both IVs Within-Subjects

Finally, if our subjects were very patient, or were well paid, or like the free booze and smokes, we could create a factorial design which would use all subjects in all conditions. Each of our 40 subjects would be tested under each of the four conditions. This is called a **repeated-measures design.** A simple shorthand representation of this design might be:

$$RG \; T_1 \; O \; T_2 \; O \; T_3 \; O \; T_4 \; O \; \text{(with treatments counterbalanced)}$$

To completely counterbalance the treatments in this repeated-measures design we would need to have 24 different treatment orders equally represented! (Or as close to equal as we can get with 40 subjects. Maybe we should find eight more if we want to use this design.) To remind ourselves of this we can look at a more detailed representation of the design which indicates the counterbalancing (see Fig. 4.5).

FIG. 4.5

Shorthand representation of a 2 × 2 factorial done completely Within-Subjects.

$$
\begin{array}{l}
RG_1 \; T_1 \; O \; T_2 \; O \; T_3 \; O \; T_4 \; O \\
RG_2 \; T_1 \; O \; T_2 \; O \; T_4 \; O \; T_3 \; O \\
RG_3 \; T_1 \; O \; T_3 \; O \; T_2 \; O \; T_4 \; O \\
RG_4 \; T_1 \; O \; T_3 \; O \; T_4 \; O \; T_2 \; O \\
. \; \text{(You should be able} \\
. \; \text{to fill in the intervening} \\
\;\;\; \text{orders)} \\
. \\
. \\
RG_{24} \; T_4 \; O \; T_3 \; O \; T_2 \; O \; T_1 \; O
\end{array}
$$

INTERACTION INFORMATION

Whichever of the three versions of our factorial (multivariate) design we decide to use, we will gain information about the main effect of alcohol, the main effect of marijuana, and, in addition, will be able to see if the two substances interact in their effects. Does the presence of alcohol change the amount of effect caused by marijuana? Does the presence of marijuana change the amount of effect caused by alcohol?

Two IVs Which Both Have an Effect and Interact as Well

The DV we are measuring as an indication of verbal performance is the number of correct solutions of 20 anagrams (mixed-up words). A possible set of results for the anagrams measure in our alcohol-marijuana experiment is given in Table 4.1. Looking at this table we can see that overall there is a main effect of smoking marijuana. The two conditions without marijuana averaged 16 anagrams correct while the two with marijuana averaged only 9. Similarly, alcohol shows a main effect. The two conditions without alcohol averaged 17 correct and this decreased to 8 correct with one dose of alcohol.

Table 4.1   Average Number of Anagrams Solved for a List of 20

| | | IV$_2$: Alcohol consumption | | |
		No dose	One dose	(Overall)
IV$_1$: Marijuana consumption	No dose	18	14	(16)
	One dose	16	2	(9)
	(Overall)	(17)	(8)	

Looking at the separate conditions rather than the overall effects, let us see if there has been any interaction between the drugs. When no alcohol is present, one dose of marijuana reduces the number of anagrams solved by only two points (18 to 16). However, when alcohol is present, the effect of going from no dose to one dose of marijuana is a loss of 12 points. It certainly looks like the effects of marijuana are altered by the presence of alcohol. A similar inspection of Table 4.1 for the effects of alcohol in the absence and presence of marijuana will show that marijuana also changes the effects of alcohol. Clearly these two substances interact in their effects on anagram solution.

It is often easier to see whether or not the effects of two IVs interact from looking at a graph of the results. Figure 4.6 gives two alternative ways that the results in Table 4.1 could be graphed to reveal interaction information. The DV measures in such a graph are always given on the y-axis. The levels of one of the IVs are marked off on the x-axis. The levels of the other IV are represented by separate lines on the graph. Either IV can go on the x-axis, so there are two ways you can graph the results of any two-factor experiment.

In either version of the graphs in Fig. 4.6, you can see that the two lines are not parallel (do not maintain an equal distance between them). The lines would cross each other if they were extended. This is a visual indication that the effects of the two IVs interact.

FIG. 4.6

Average number correct on anagrams task graphed as a function of marijuana (IV$_1$) and alcohol (IV$_2$) dosage.

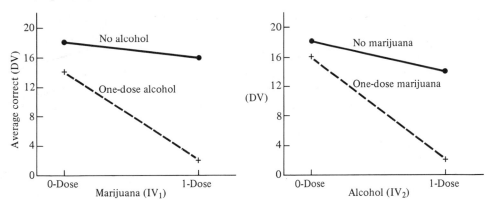

Two IVs Which Both Have an Effect but Don't Interact

One possible outcome of a two-factor experiment is that both factors affect the DV, but the effects of one IV are the same at all levels of the other IV. In this case we would say that the two IVs were operating independently in affecting the DV and did not interact. Table 4.2 contains the results of an experiment in which both marijuana and alcohol have effects, but the two substances do not interact.

Examining Table 4.2 reveals that one dose of marijuana decreases verbal performance by four points whether alcohol is present or absent. Similarly, the amount of decrease in performance (five points) produced by alcohol is the same for both marijuana dosages. Neither IV changes the effect of the other.

The results from Table 4.2 are graphed in two different ways in Fig. 4.7. From either of these graphs, we can see that the lines lie parallel to one another. This is a visual indication that the effects of the two IVs do not interact.

Table 4.2   Average Number of Anagrams Solved for a List of 20

		IV$_2$: Alcohol consumption		
		No dose	One dose	(Overall)
IV$_1$: Marijuana consumption	No dose	18	13	(15.5)
	One dose	14	9	(11.5)
	(Overall)	(16)	(11)	

FIG. 4.7

Average number correct on anagrams task graphed as a function of marijuana (IV₁) and alcohol (IV₂) dosage.

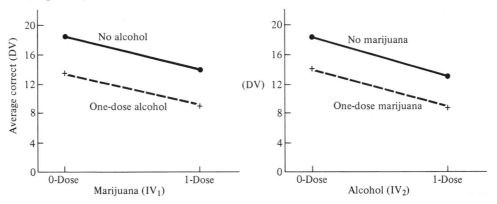

EXPANDING FACTORIAL DESIGNS

Of course, if you are ambitious, you can use more than two levels for either of your IVs in a factorial experiment. The total number of experimental conditions will still be the product of the number of levels of each of your factors. A design, for example, with three levels of one factor (IV₁) and four levels of another (IV₂) would have a total of 12 experimental conditions (3 × 4).

A factorial design can also have more than two factors. Again the number of conditions in the experiment will be the product of the number of levels of each of the factors. The smallest three-factor design you can have would, for instance, have eight conditions (2 × 2 × 2). As well as yielding main-effect comparison information for each of the factors in the design, multifactor designs give you a considerable amount of information about the interactions between the effects of every possible pair of variables.

RECAPITULATION

for MULTIPLE-IV DESIGNS WITH NON-SUBJECT IVs

Two or more Non-Subject (experimenter-manipulated) IVs can be combined in the same experiment. Such a multivariate design is also called a *factorial design*. When multiple IVs are used, the total number of conditions possible in the experiment is the product of the number of levels of each IV. The conditions resulting from the combination of two IVs can be represented in a two-way *factorial table* with the levels of one IV (or factor) forming the rows and the levels of the other IV forming the columns. If both of the IVs in a two-factor design are treated Between-Subjects, then a separate group of subjects must be randomly assigned to each condition and the design is said to be *completely randomized*. If one of the IVs is defined Within-

Subjects, then a single group of subjects is repeatedly measured under every level of that variable. In this case, only as many different groups of subjects are necessary as there are levels of the other, Between-Subjects, IV. Such a *mixed design* could be said to be *partially randomized and partially repeated measures.* If both IVs in a two-factor experiment are treated Within-Subjects, then one group of subjects will be repeatedly measured under all experimental conditions. This design would be a *completely repeated measures design.* A factorial experiment yields information about the *interaction* of effects of different IVs as well as main-effect comparison information for each IV separately. If an interaction exists, the effects of one IV will be different when measured at different levels of the other IV. A graph of results from a two-factor experiment will show nonparallel lines if such an interaction is present.

BEHAVIORAL OBJECTIVES

for MULTIPLE-IV DESIGNS WITH NON-SUBJECT IVs

1. Given a shorthand representation of any of the designs from this section, or from Section 1:
   a. Describe in words what the design consists of.
   b. Name the design.
   c. List the information yielded by the design.

2. Make a factorial table for a two-factor experiment, specifying all the conditions produced by the combination of the factors. You can pick the factors and specify how many levels each one has.

3. For a specific two-factor experiment, explain how you would divide up the subjects if:
   a. both IVs were Between-Subjects.
   b. IV_1 was Between-Subjects and IV_2 was Within-Subjects.
   c. IV_1 was Within-Subjects and IV_2 was Between-Subjects.
   d. both IVs were Within-Subjects.

4. Given a specific description of a two-factor experiment, explain how you would counterbalance conditions if
   a. IV_1 was Within-Subjects and IV_2 was Between-Subjects.
   b. IV_1 was Between-Subjects and IV_2 was Within-Subjects.
   c. both IVs were Within-Subjects.

5. Explain the difference between a *completely randomized design,* a *completely repeated-measures design,* and a *mixed design.*

6. Given graphs of results from two-factor experiments, say whether:
   a. IV_1 is having any effect.
   b. IV_2 is having any effect.
   c. the effects of IV_1 and IV_2 are interacting.

7. Given the description of an actual experiment:

   a. Write down its design in shorthand.

   b. Name the design.

   c. List the information yielded by the design.

   d. Describe any limitations there may be on information from the design.

8. For a given multiple-IV experiment describe each kind of overall or "main-effect" information that would be available and then describe the specific kinds of interaction information that could be obtained.

9. Given an operational definition of one or more IVs, design an experiment to investigate the effects of the IV(s), specifying which IVs you are treating as Between-Subjects and which as Within-Subjects.

SAMPLE TEST QUESTIONS

for MULTIPLE-IV DESIGNS WITH NON-SUBJECT IVs
---

1. A six-week weight-control study involving 60 overweight volunteers was set up as follows:

   IV_1 (use of an "appetite-inhibiting" drug)
         Level 1—placebo (fake pill the subject thinks is real)
         Level 2—commercial appetite-control drug

   IV_2 (type of program)
         Level 1—nothing
         Level 2—weekly weigh-ins, inspirational talks, and recommended-diet sheets
         Level 3—same as Level 2, but subjects lose part of an initial money deposit each week they do not lose at least two pounds.

   O—weight in pounds

   The design for this study is given in Fig. 4.8.

   a. If both IVs are defined Between-Subjects, describe this research in words. Specify all conditions, tell how many subjects were assigned to each condition, and identify the DV and its scale of measurement.

   b. What would be a name for this design?

   c. What kinds of information would be yielded by this design? Be specific as to main effects and interactions.

2. Suppose the results of the weight-reduction study described in Question 1 were as given in Fig. 4.9.

   a. What was the effect of IV_1?

   b. What was the effect of IV_2?

   c. Was there any interaction of the two IVs?

   d. Would you take this drug if you wanted to lose weight?

   e. What method seems to be the most effective in helping subjects to lose weight?

FIG. 4.8

Designs for a 2×3 multivariate experiment

Factorial table

IV₁ (Drug)

		1	2
		1	2
	1	T₁	T₂
IV₂ (program)	2	T₃	T₄
	3	T₅	T₆

Shorthand design

RG₁ O T₁ O
RG₂ O T₂ O
RG₃ O T₃ O
RG₄ O T₄ O
RG₅ O T₅ O
RG₆ O T₆ O

FIG. 4.9

Weight loss in pounds graphed as a function of drug administration (IV₁) and type of program (IV₂).

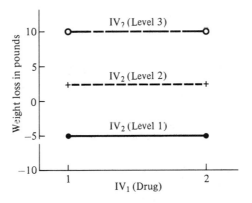

3. You suspect that some of the disruptive effect of consumption of alcohol on performance has something to do with the subject's expectations. You decide to use the pursuit-rotor task, an eye-hand coordination task in which the subject has to follow a rapidly moving light with a pointer, as your performance measure. You operationally define your alcohol IV as having three levels: none, the equivalent of one shot of whiskey, and the equivalent of two shots of whiskey. Whatever the level of alcohol, it is presented to the subject in a strongly flavored drink which prevents the subject from tasting whether or not any alcohol is present. Your second IV has two levels: you either tell the subjects that the drink contains very little alcohol and will not affect them very much or you tell them that the drink is really very strong and they can expect it to have a large effect. You have 30 volunteers for this study.

   a. Make up a factorial table representing all the conditions of this experiment.
   b. Suppose you treat both IVs Between-Subjects:
      1) How many groups of subjects will you have in the experiment?
      2) How many subjects can you assign to each group?
      3) Give your design in shorthand.
      4) What kind of multivariate design is this?
   c. Suppose you treat the alcohol IV Within-Subjects and leave the expectation IV Between-Subjects.
      1) How many groups of subjects will you have in your experiment?
      2) How many subjects will there be in each group?
      3) Describe how you will counterbalance conditions.
      4) What kind of multivariate design is this?
   d. Suppose you treat the alcohol IV as Between-Subjects and the expectation IV as Within-Subjects.
      1) How many groups of subjects will you have in your experiment?
      2) How many subjects will there be in each group?
      3) What kind of multivariate design is this?

FIG. 4.10

Time on target graphed as a function of alcohol dosage (IV₁) and expectation (IV₂).

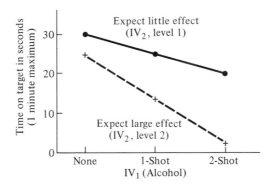

4. Suppose that for the experiment described in Question 3 you got the results seen in Fig. 4.10.
   a. Describe the overall effect of alcohol (ignoring expectations).
   b. Describe the overall effect of expectations (ignoring alcohol dosage).
   c. Do alcohol consumption and expectations interact? If so, how?
   d. Which condition has the most destructive effect on performance?

    e. What is the DV? What is its scale of measurement?

    f. Redraw the graph in Fig. 4.10 with the expectation IV (IV$_2$) represented in the x-axis and the levels of the alcohol IV (IV$_1$) represented as three separate lines.

SECTION 3: MULTIPLE-IV DESIGNS WITH A SUBJECT IV

Often when you want to add an IV to your experiment it is because you suspect that some characteristic of your subjects may interact with the effect of your main Non-Subject IV(s). For example, one criticism that has been made of the Crancer *et al.* (1969) marijuana vs. alcohol study is that all the subjects in the experiment were faithful marijuana users. Kalant (1969) suggests that such subjects might have a vested interest in not letting marijuana have too much effect on their driving performance and in exaggerating the effects of alcohol. In other words, Kalant is saying that the prejudice of the subjects was an uncontrolled Relevant Variable in the Crancer *et al.* study which may have confounded interpretation of the results. Kalant suggests:

> . . . it would have been desirable to include a second group of subjects who were experienced drinkers and probably biased in favor of alcohol. (p. 640)

FACTORIAL EXPERIMENTS WITH A SUBJECT IV

We could follow up Kalant's suggestions by adding a Subject IV to our marijuana experiment. Let's define this IV as having two levels: regular marijuana smokers and regular alcohol drinkers. This is clearly a Subject IV since the subjects assign themselves to its levels by habits they already possess. The experimenter is not free to assign subjects at random to levels of this variable. When we select our subjects to represent the levels of this IV, we probably should avoid those people who regularly use both substances since we won't be sure where to assign them.

    If an IV is operationally defined as a Subject IV, then it must appear in our design Between-Subjects. As we've discussed earlier, it is usually not possible to take repeated measures on the same subjects at different levels of a Subject IV. It is very unlikely that we could quickly change a confirmed marijuana smoker into a confirmed alcohol drinker so that we could measure the same person at both levels. Therefore Subject IVs will not appear in a multivariate design Within-Subjects.

    For a two-factor experiment, let's combine our Subject "type-of-user" IV with a Non-Subject "drug" IV. The "type-of-drug" IV we define for this experiment as having three levels: no drug, alcohol, and marijuana. Combining these two variables would give us a 2×3 factorial design with six conditions. We can represent these conditions by the factorial table given in Fig. 4.11.

FIG. 4.11

Factorial table for a 2×3 design.

IV$_2$: Type of drug

		None	Alcohol	Marijuana
IV$_1$: Type of user	Marijuana smoker			
	Alcohol drinker			

Randomized Blocks

Our Subject-type IV must be Between-Subjects. Our Non-Subjects IV (IV$_2$) can be treated as either Between- or Within-Subjects. If we define IV$_2$ as Between-Subjects we could design our multivariate experiment as shown in Fig. 4.12.

FIG. 4.12

Design for a 2×3 Randomized Blocks experiment.

B$_a$	RG$_1$ T$_a$ O RG$_2$ T$_m$ O RG$_3$ T$_o$ O
B$_m$	RG$_4$ T$_a$ O RG$_5$ T$_m$ O RG$_6$ T$_o$ O

where T$_a$ is one dose of alcohol,
T$_m$ is one dose of marijuana, and
T$_o$ is one dose of nothing.

This type of multivariate design is called a **Randomized-Blocks design.** The subjects are first blocked according to a subject characteristic (Subject IV) and then within each block they are randomly assigned to treatments (Non-Subject IV). A Randomized-Blocks design yields all the usual information (posttreatment, multi-group and multi-level comparison, and group equivalence) plus information about the interaction of a treatment effect with a subject characteristic.

Repeated-Measures within Blocks

Alternatively, we could define our Non-Subject IV Within-Subjects. We might want to do this if we find that it is difficult to round up enough marijuana smokers and alcohol drinkers who are willing to participate in our study. If we define IV$_2$ as a Within-Subjects IV, all the subjects in each block would experience all the drug conditions, in counterbalanced order. A complete representation of this design would be as shown in Fig. 4.13.

FIG. 4.13

Design for a 2×3 repeated measures experiment.

B_a	RG_1 T_o O T_a O T_m O
	RG_2 T_o O T_m O T_a O
	RG_3 T_a O T_o O T_m O
	RG_4 T_a O T_m O T_o O
	RG_5 T_m O T_o O T_a O
	RG_6 T_m O T_a O T_o O
B_m	RG_7 T_o O T_a O T_m O
	RG_8 T_o O T_m O T_a O
	RG_9 T_a O T_o O T_m O
	RG_{10} T_a O T_m O T_o O
	RG_{11} T_m O T_o O T_a O
	RG_{12} T_m O T_a O T_o O

Or, if you really know what "counterbalanced" means, you could represent this design more briefly as:

B_a T_o O T_a O T_m O
B_m T_o O T_a O T_m O

with T_o, T_a, T_m completely counterbalanced within each block

INTERPRETATION OF INTERACTION BETWEEN SUBJECT AND NON-SUBJECT VARIABLES

If Kalant's (1969) suspicions were correct, we'd expect to find an interaction between our Subject IV (type of user) and our Non-Subject IV (drug) in their effects on subject performance as measured by one or more of our DVs. We might find, for the pursuit-rotor task, for example, results such as are given in Fig. 4.14. Clearly, the two lines in Fig. 4.14 aren't anywhere near parallel. Kalant's guess about the importance of the subjects' biases might be correct if we got results like these. The subjects show their worst performance for the drug they do not normally use. Also, it looks like overall the alcohol users perform worse than the habitual marijuana smokers.

If we got the results graphed in Fig. 4.14, we would say that the subject characteristic did make a difference and did interact with the drug variable. However, as with any Subject IV, we're limited in how far we can go with our interpretation. It might be the case that the group of habitual alcohol users is older than the group of marijuana users. If this were true, then the overall poorer performance of the alcohol users could be partly a result of age. Or it might be the case that subjects are less affected by a substance their bodies are used to than by an unfamiliar substance. It

FIG. 4.14

Time on target in a pursuit-rotor task as a function of type of user (IV₁) and type of drug consumed (IV₂).

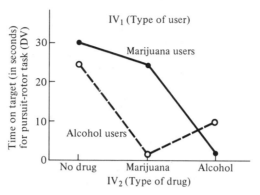

may be, as Kalant suggested, that the subjects are biased against the substance they don't normally use and strive to show their worst performance when given that drug. A limitation of using a Subject IV is that there is always the possibility that a related factor is actually causing the observed effects on the DV. Matching could reduce the effects of some of these factors, like that of age, but we would still be uncertain whether we have matched the groups on all the relevant factors. What we have is the bare fact that the habitual alcohol and the habitual marijuana users respond differently to our Non-Subject drug IV; and we don't really know why.

EXPANDED RANDOMIZED-BLOCKS DESIGN: A CASE STUDY

Of course, a person can go hog-wild on this multivariate designs. Consider, for instance the design given in shorthand in Fig. 4.15.

The design shown in Fig. 4.15 looks horrendous. Closer examination reveals that it is nothing but a four-factor experiment. Two of the factors are Subject IVs. One, with three levels, is a variable having to do with the subject's habitual usage of substances. Subjects are blocked into these three levels, and since there must be different subjects at each level, this part of the design is Between-Subjects. The second Subject IV is age, again defined in three levels. Since a subject can't be two ages at the same time, there must be different subjects at each level and this also is Between-Subjects. A third IV, alcohol administration, is a Non-Subject variable since the experimenter determines who gets alcohol and who doesn't. It is apparently being treated Between-Subjects since different subjects are randomly assigned to its two different levels. The fourth IV, marijuana administration, is again a Non-Subject variable since the experimenter controls who smokes marijuana in the experiment

FIG. 4.15

Shorthand summary of a $3 \times 3 \times 2 \times 2$ Randomized-Blocks design.

B_A	B_1	RG_1 T_a O RG_2 T_m O RG_3 $T_a T_m$ O RG_4 O			
	B_2	RG_5 T_a O RG_6 T_m O RG_7 $T_a T_m$ O RG_8 O			
	B_3	RG_9 T_a O RG_{10} T_m O RG_{11} $T_a T_m$ O RG_{12} O			
B_M	B_4	RG_{13} T_a O RG_{14} T_m O RG_{15} $T_a T_m$ O RG_{16} O			
	B_5	RG_{17} T_a O RG_{18} T_m O RG_{19} $T_a T_m$ O RG_{20} O			
	B_6	RG_{21} T_a O RG_{22} T_m O RG_{23} $T_a T_m$ O RG_{24} O			
B_O	B_7	RG_{25} T_a O RG_{26} T_m O RG_{27} $T_a T_m$ O RG_{28} O			
	B_8	RG_{29} T_a O RG_{30} T_m O RG_{31} $T_a T_m$ O RG_{32} O			
	B_9	RG_{33} T_a O RG_{34} T_m O RG_{35} $T_a T_m$ O RG_{36} O			

where:
T_a is one dose of alcohol,
T_m is one dose of marijuana,

B_A are habitual alcohol drinkers,
B_M are habitual marijuana smokers,
B_O use neither,

B_1, B_4, and B_7 are under 20 years old,
B_2, B_5, and B_8 are between 20 and 35 years old, and
B_3, B_6, and B_9 are all over 35 years old.

and who does not. It, too, is being treated Between-Subjects and different subjects are assigned to the groups experiencing its two levels.

How many conditions does this monstrosity have? Just take the product of the number of levels of each of its four factors. For this experiment that would be $3 \times 3 \times 2 \times 2$, or 36 conditions. If 10 observations were wanted for each condition, that would mean finding 360 subjects. And, don't forget, they've got to be subjects of the right age and with the right drug-consumption habits. Just any subject kidnapped off the streets won't do since they have to meet the requirements of the two Subject IVs.

Why might someone want to get involved in something this complicated? Look at the information this experiment could yield if it were carried out according to plan. There would be group equivalence information for all Non-Subject defined IVs since subjects were randomly assigned to the different levels of these factors. There would be posttreatment information on 36 different groups. There would be main-effect comparison information for four different IVs. There would be two-way interaction information between all possible pairs of variables. It would be possible to find out for each of these factors whether its effect on the DV was modified by any of the other factors.

Since the blocking factors, the two Subject IVs, put such restrictions on who could be used for a subject, it might be necessary to change this design and treat one or both of the Non-Subject IVs as Within-Subjects. If either the alcohol or marijuana IVs were treated Within-Subjects the number of subjects needed would be decreased by half. If both Non-Subject IVs were Within-Subjects then only 90 subjects would be needed. There would still be ten observations per condition, since each subject would be used four times. Of course, if either or both of these factors were Within-Subjects, it would be necessary to counterbalance the order of the repeated measures across subjects to avoid uncontrolled order effects and uncontrolled effects of repeated testing.

RECAPITULATION

for MULTIPLE-IV DESIGNS WITH A SUBJECT IV

A Randomized-Blocks design is a factorial in which one or more factors are operationally defined as Subject IVs. Since different subjects must be selected for the different levels of a Subject IV, then these variables can be treated in the design only Between-Subjects. When you use a Randomized-Blocks design, the subjects are first blocked according to the Subject IV(s) and then within each block they are randomly assigned to the levels of the Non-Subject IV(s). The Non-Subject IVs can be defined either Between-Subjects or Within-Subjects, provided that the designer uses counterbalancing with any Within-Subjects designs. Randomized-Blocks designs yield posttreatment information for all groups, multi-level comparison information for each of the IVs, group equivalence information for the Non-Subject IVs, information about the overall effects of both Subject and Non-Subject IVs, and interaction information indicating whether the action of any one IV is modified by any of the others. Interpretation of the effects of Subject IVs must always carry the reservation that the groups representing different levels of a Subject IV may lack equivalence on other variables than the Subject IV used to block them.

BEHAVIORAL OBJECTIVES

for MULTIPLE-IV DESIGNS WITH A SUBJECT IV

1. Describe how a Randomized-Blocks design is a special type of factorial design.
2. Given a shorthand representation of any of the designs discussed up to this point:
   a. Explain in words what the shorthand means.
   b. Name the design.
   c. List the information yielded by the design.
   d. Identify the IVs involved in the design and state whether they are
      1) Subject- or Non-Subject.
      2) Between-Subjects or Within-Subjects.
3. Given operational definitions of two or more factors (IVs) that could be combined in a multivariate experiment:
   a. Make up a factorial table representing the conditions of the experiment.
   b. State the number of conditions in the experiment.
   c. Identify which IVs are Subject and which are Non-Subject.
   d. Decide how many total subjects you'd need to provide a stated number of observations per condition:
      1) if all variables were defined Between-Subjects.
      2) if one or more specified Non-Subject IVs were defined as Within-Subjects.
   e. When IVs are defined Within-Subjects, describe how counterbalancing should be done.
4. Given a description of a research study:
   a. Identify the DVs and state what kinds of scales they are being measured on.
   b. Identify the IVs, and:
      1) state which IVs are Subject and which are Non-Subject.
      2) state which IVs are being treated Within-Subjects and which are being treated as Between-Subjects.
   c. If it is a multivariate design, represent the conditions of the experiment in a factorial table.
   d. Represent the design in shorthand.

e. Name the design.

f. List and describe the information available from this type of design.

SAMPLE TEST QUESTIONS

for MULTIPLE-IV DESIGNS WITH A SUBJECT IV

1. On page 51 there is a description of a proposed study concerning the effects of sex-role stereotyping on reading comprehension of boys and girls. Reread this study and answer the following:

    a. Write out a factorial table showing how the four story situations were created.

    b. Identify the three IVs used in the experiment.

    c. For each IV, state whether it is a Subject or a Non-Subject IV.

    d. Which IV(s) was treated Between-Subjects?

    e. Which IV(s) was treated Within-Subjects?

    f. What is the DV in this experiment? On what kind of scale is it being measured?

    g. If 40 children took part in this study, and each one was scored for his or her recall of each of the four story situations, how many scores (observations) would result from the study?

2. Suppose you were interested in whether the sex and perceived occupation of speakers influenced the way people reacted to what they had to say. You compose a script describing the social, economic, and technical reasons why nuclear power plants should be built. You make separate recordings of a man reading the script and of a woman reading the script. You then make two tapes for each reader, one introducing the speaker as a "self-employed, free-lance writer" and the other as a "renowned physicist and engineer." You have a standardized attitude questionnaire on feelings about nuclear power that you intend to give your subjects immediately after they listen to one of the tapes. In addition to finding out whether the different tapes have any effect on attitudes, you are also curious as to whether sex of the listener makes any difference.

    a. Identify the three IVs in this research.

    b. Specify which IVs are Subject and which are Non-Subject.

    c. Design an experiment incorporating these IVs, and write down the design in shorthand.

    d. Which IVs did you treat as Between-Subjects? Which as Within-Subjects?

    e. How many conditions are there in your experiment?

    f. How many subjects will you need in your experiment if you decide you want 12 observations per condition?

    g. Describe the information you expect to be yielded from this experiment.

SECTION 4: SOME OTHER INTERESTING RESEARCH DESIGNS

While we've covered a fair number of designs, there are many more available. Some designs were created to solve particular research problems or to yield a special kind of information. In this section, we'll consider four types of research designs that are useful for special situations: Solomon's Four-Group, Latin Square, Correlational, and Single-Subject designs.

SOLOMON'S FOUR-GROUP DESIGN

The **Solomon's Four-Group design** is useful when you want pretest information but are very concerned about the possible effects of pretesting on your subjects. You decide that having or not having a pretest should in itself be another IV in your research. You might feel this way if your DV measure consists of some sort of test of performance or an attitude survey. In both cases, answers the second time around often change just from the subjects having taken the test before. Solomon's Four-Group design controls for this pretesting effect by having half the subjects receive a pretest and half not receive it. To set up Solomon's Four-Group design, you first randomly divide the subjects into four groups, two of which receive the pretest and two of which do not. Then you give the experimental treatment to one of the groups that was pretested and to one of those that was not. A shorthand representation of this design would be:

$$
\begin{array}{llll}
R\ G_1 & O & T & O \\
R\ G_2 & O & & O \\
R\ G_3 & & T & O \\
R\ G_4 & & & O
\end{array}
$$

This design yields posttreatment information for four groups, pretreatment and pre-to-postcomparison information for two groups, comparison information about the effects of pretesting, comparison information about the effects of the treatment, and interaction information as to whether treatment effects are influenced by pretesting.

LATIN-SQUARE DESIGNS

A **Latin-Square design** is an incomplete factorial design, a multivariate design that does not have all the orders of conditions that would result from complete counterbalancing of IVs treated Within-Subjects. Sometimes, you may have too few subjects to carry out a completely counterbalanced design. Remember that as few as four conditions can be ordered in 24 different ways. Sometimes, too, you may want to investigate order effects as an IV in your research in addition to just controlling for them as a nuisance Relevant Variable. However, you may not have enough sub-jects to assign to all the different orders so that you can make meaningful compari-sons between them. A Latin-Square design specifies which ones of the possible orders you should use if you can't use all of them.

Setting up a Latin-Square design is best explained by an example. Suppose you have three different conditions (A, B, and C) that you need to counterbalance for an IV handled Within-Subjects. For these three conditions, there would be six possible orders. You can represent this completely counterbalanced design by a table with three columns representing the conditions and six rows representing the possible orders as follows:

A B C   (order 1)
A C B   (order 2)
B A C   (order 3)
B C A   (order 4)
C A B   (order 5)
C B A   (order 6)

For a Latin Square incomplete factorial of three conditions, you would select three of these orders such that each condition occurred once in each row and once in each column. Either of the following sets of orders would be a Latin Square of these three conditions:

A B C   (order 1)   A C B   (order 1)
B C A   (order 2)   or   C B A   (order 2)
C A B   (order 3)   B A C   (order 3)

If you decided to use a Latin-Square design instead of a completely counter-balanced design for a three-condition experiment, you would need to divide your subjects at random among only three rather than six orders. If, for example, you could only round up 30 subjects for your research and you wanted to compare dif-ferent orders for order effects, you might feel a lot happier making these compari-sons among three groups containing ten subjects each than among six groups each with only five subjects.

The advantages of a Latin-Square arrangement increase as the number of con-ditions in the experiment increases. For a four-condition Within-Subjects experi-ment, a Latin-Square design would require four orders of conditions rather than the 24 of the complete factorial. If the experiment had five conditions, a Latin Square would use only 5 rather than 120 orders. Let's consider our marijuana-alcohol re-search project. We had operationally defined three performance measures, an atti-tude measure, and some physiological measures as our DVs. There is some possi-bility that the order of taking these measures might affect results since doing them takes time and the drug effects may wear off. To completely counterbalance for order of taking these measures, we would have to use 120 different test orders and would need to split the subjects in each experimental group randomly among these different test orders. Suppose we had only 25 subjects in each experimental group.

In this case, it would be better to use a Latin-Square arrangement in which we had five subjects each experience one of five different orders of testing on the DVs such as is given in Table 4.3.

If you use such an incomplete factorial as the Latin-Square design, you do lose some information about order effects since you do not use every possible order. However, if you have too few subjects to represent all the possible orders equally with a reasonable group size, you've already lost this information anyway.

Table 4.3   A Latin-Square for Order of Measuring Five DVs

Order 1:	Physiol.	Pursuit task	Anagrams	Reaction time	Attitude
Order 2:	Pursuit task	Anagrams	Reaction time	Attitude	Physiol.
Order 3:	Anagrams	Reaction time	Attitude	Physiol.	Pursuit task
Order 4:	Reaction time	Attitude	Physiol.	Pursuit task	Anagrams
Order 5:	Attitude	Physiol.	Pursuit task	Anagrams	Reaction time

CORRELATIONAL RESEARCH

Often when you measure multiple DVs, you may find that some of them seem to vary in the same way. In our marijuana-alcohol study, for instance, we may discover that the subject who does well at the pursuit-rotor task also has a fast response on the reaction-time task. Looking over the scores of our subjects on these two DVs we might find that they are so strongly related, or "correlated," that knowledge of a subject's score on one DV permits us to predict with a high degree of accuracy what his or her score will be on the other DV. If this is the case, we may want to eliminate one DV measure altogether, thereby decreasing the overall amount of time we have to spend in taking measurements.

How you go about correlating the measures on two DVs will be described in the next chapter. Whenever you have multiple DV measures in an experiment, you have the possibility of getting correlational information about the DVs as well as the other information about IV-DV relationships yielded by the particular experimental design.

In some types of research, there are no IVs. The experimenter is unable to manipulate any variable either directly or by selection. In this situation, the researcher simply takes a number of DV measures and sees which correlate with which. Such an approach is often used in personality research and in attitude studies. In our own marijuana research project we might, for example, have investigated the question of the relation between marijuana consumption and performance by asking our subjects to estimate their usual marijuana consumption (DV_1), by determining grade point average (GPA) in school (DV_2), by checking on their driving records (DV_3), and by determining their degree of participation in sports (DV_4). We could then correlate these four measures and find out if any of them vary together.

Correlation information always carries a limitation on its interpretation that, unfortunately, some researchers neglect. Just because two variables vary together or correlate does not mean that the variations in one variable cause the variations in the other. Establishing a correlation between two DVs is not the same as establishing a cause-effect relationship between an IV and a DV. If we found that there was a correlation between marijuana consumption and poor driving records, would we be justified in saying that consumption of marijuana causes deterioration of driving skills? Since all we have is a correlation between two DVs, we'd be just as justified in saying that being upset over poor driving performance increases marijuana consumption.

While correlation information is not conclusive, it is often suggestive. The existence of a strong correlation between two DVs may suggest a fruitful area for an investigator to do further research and establish an IV-DV relationship. Correlation between substance abuse and poor driving records was the starting point for Crancer *et al.* to design their experimental study in which they directly manipulated consumption of drug substances (IV) and observed driving performance (DV). Their failure to find that marijuana consumption in their experiment had much effect on driving suggests that a marijuana-driving performance correlation may be due to some other common causative factor (like age of subjects or general life-style).

This limitation on the interpretation of correlative information is similar to the limitation we discussed earlier on interpreting the effects of Subject IVs. When you operationally define a variable as a Subject IV you are imposing more control on the variable than when you just measure it as a DV in a correlational study. By doing so you are improving the chances that the variable you specify is the one causing changes in the DVs. But, as we discussed before, there is always the possibility with any Subject IV that some other uncontrolled Relevant Subject characteristic is also present, confounding your interpretation of a relationship between the Subject IV and the DV. For instance, in our marijuana-alcohol study, when we select our groups of habitual marijuana and habitual alcohol users we might find out that we have also sorted people by age, the alcohol users tending to be older persons. If we then find out that the alcohol users are poorer performers on a driving task we might attribute to substance abuse an effect that more properly should be attributed to age!

SINGLE-SUBJECT DESIGNS

Up to now all the research we've described has involved comparisons among groups of subjects. Even when we've made Within-Subjects comparisons, we have made them for several subjects. This approach is usually necessary because we want to be sure that a treatment that works for one subject also works for others before we start making any sweeping statements about IV-DV relationships. Also, when the treatment effect we are looking for is rather small, we don't want it obscured by unrelated individual differences in our subjects. Increasing the number of subjects we measure decreases the effect of such unsystematic individual variations and makes it easier to see a treatment effect.

There are some research questions, however, that are capable of investigation through taking a large number of measures on a few subjects rather than relatively few measures on a large number of subjects. Some characteristics of human behavior show relatively few individual differences among normal individuals. For example, most aspects of hearing and vision are highly similar among undamaged humans. Usually studies in these areas use only a few subjects and take many careful measures on each of them. The measures taken on one subject are expected to virtually duplicate the measures taken on another.

Another situation in which a study may use a **single-subject design,** or at least a very few subjects, is when the process under investigation is reversible. In a field of learning called operant conditioning, for example, studies of the effects of the consequences of a response on the rate of repetition of that response are often done on only a few subjects studied over a long period of time. This is because the response rate can be repeatedly increased and decreased by the experimenters' manipulations, demonstrating over and over again in the same subject the role of different kinds of positive and negative consequences. Similarly, studies of drugs that have consistent effects across individuals often use a few subjects and repeatedly return the subject to **baseline** (pretest) behavior between administration of different drug dosages. This procedure is called a **reversal design.**

Doing research in a clinical setting often means that you are limited to a very few subjects, especially if the condition you are studying is uncommon. Clinical researchers must accept the idea that therapy for the patient is the major issue. This consideration may eliminate the possibility of no-treatment controls, or controls being given a treatment to make them worse. One approach would be to alternate periods of therapeutic intervention with periods of nonintervention and then see for each patient whether the repeated intervention periods result in more change than the nonintervention ones. Another technique is the use of the **multiple-baseline** approach. In this single-subject procedure, several different behaviors the therapist wants to change are identified and observed. The therapist tries to modify only one of these while continuing to observe the subject's other behaviors. After a period of time, the therapist extends the intervention to another behavior while still continuing to observe all the behaviors. And so on. If for the different baselines it is found that each behavior started to change at the time the therapist specifically began working on it, then this is a strong indication that the therapist's actions are indeed responsible for the modification of the patient's behaviors.

This is only a brief introduction to doing research with a very few or with single subjects. Success with this approach depends on adequately controlling experimental conditions so that there are few individual differences among the subjects. When interpreting the results of such studies it is necessary to ask yourself whether the single subject is indeed a good representative of people in general.

RECAPITULATION

for OTHER INTERESTING DESIGNS

Some designs give you special information or are applicable to specific situations. *Solomon's Four-Group design* treats the having or not having of a pretest as another IV and thereby provides information about the effects of pretesting on the subjects and about the interaction of pretesting with the effect of the treatment. The shorthand for Solomon's Four-Group design is:

$$
\begin{array}{llll}
R & G_1 & O\ T\ O \\
R & G_2 & O\quad\ \ O \\
R & G_3 & \quad\ T\ O \\
R & G_4 & \quad\quad\ O
\end{array}
$$

The *Latin-Square design* is an incomplete factorial which is used to obtain information about the effects of the order of repeated exposures of subjects to different conditions. It is used in place of a completely counterbalanced design. To set up a Latin Square, use only those orders of conditions that result in a given condition occurring once in each row and once in each column in a list of all the orders. The number of orders necessary for a Latin Square will be the same as the number of conditions that are to be ordered. The shorthand for a three-condition Latin-Square design might be:

$$
\begin{array}{l}
RG_1\ T_1\ O\ T_2\ O\ T_3\ O \\
RG_2\ T_2\ O\ T_3\ O\ T_1\ O \\
RG_3\ T_3\ O\ T_1\ O\ T_2\ O
\end{array}
$$

In such a design the effects of the different treatments are determined from Within-Subjects comparisons while the effects of the different ordering of treatments are determined from Between-Subjects comparisons.

Correlational research is possible when the experimenter can obtain a number of DV measures on the same subject and wishes to see if the measures vary together. In many correlational studies there are only DVs; the experimenter cannot directly manipulate any variable as an IV. The interpretation of results from correlational research must be limited by the fact that correlational relationships are not necessarily causal relationships. Although researchers sometimes fall into the trap of inferring IV-DV causation from a DV-DV correlation, there are too many relevant Subject Variables over which the experimenter has no control for this to be a safe conclusion.

Although treatment effects are usually estimated by comparing groups of subjects, some research questions lend themselves to intensive investigation in *single subjects*. If there is little individual difference between subjects in regard to what is being studied, a single representative subject may give results generalizable to a larger group. If the IV-DV relationship being studied is a reversible one, the same treatment can be repeatedly applied to the same subject and the subject used as its own control (*reversal design*). In other situations, it is possible to monitor several DVs and change them one at a time to repeatedly demonstrate the effectiveness of a treatment within a single subject (*multiple-baseline design*). Single-Subject designs are of special interest to researchers working in clinical settings who may not be able to gather large groups of subjects or to assign subjects to nontreatment conditions.

BEHAVIORAL OBJECTIVES

for OTHER INTERESTING DESIGNS

1. For each of the four research procedures discussed in this section (Solomon's Four-Group, Latin Square, correlational approach, Single-Subject studies), describe the special situation for which you might want to use the design.
2. For a Solomon's Four-Group design:
   a. Identify it from description of an experiment.
   b. Give the design in shorthand.
   c. Describe the information yielded by the design.
   d. Indicate the special kind of information yielded by the design.
3. For a Latin-Square design:
   a. Identify it from a description of an experiment.
   b. Give the design in shorthand.
   c. Specify the information yielded by this design.
   d. Lay out the Latin-Square.
   e. State whether treatment comparisons are being made Within- or Between-Subjects.
   f. State whether the effects of different orders are being determined by Within- or Between-Subjects comparisons.
4. For a correlational research study:
   a. Identify the type of study from a description.
   b. Describe what it means to say that two DVs are "correlated."
   c. Explain why saying that two variables are correlated is not the same as saying that one variable is causing the other.
5. For Single-Subject research studies:
   a. Recognize the description of one.
   b. Describe the circumstances under which a Single-Subject study might be desirable.
   c. Explain what is meant by a:
      1) reversal design.
      2) multiple-baseline design.

SOME SAMPLE TEST QUESTIONS

for OTHER INTERESTING DESIGNS

1. As part of a conference on the role of museums in education, techniques were discussed on the ways to improve the amount of information a viewer could get from looking at a museum display. Personnel from one museum devised a "personal guide" system which consisted of a cassette tape recorder hooked to a "punch board." Questions were posted as part of the exhibit to which the viewers could respond by inserting a metal stylus into the appropriate hole on their boards. When the answer to a question was incorrect, the tape started and the viewer was given the correct answer with explanatory information. It was felt that this system would have some of the advantages of each viewer having a personal guide. Museum visitors were enthusiastic about these "guide machines."

Since the guide machines were expensive, it was decided to see if they were really effective. In an initial study, viewers of a special exhibit were pretested before visiting the exhibit by a "testing machine" which gave them 20 multiple-choice questions one by one and told them their final number correct. The people then viewed the exhibit with a guide machine. At the end of the exhibit, they were again tested by the testing machine with 20 new questions selected at random. Visitors to this exhibit showed large pre-to-post gains in number of correct answers.

Before recommending widescale purchase of the guide machines, researchers at another museum decided to do a more extensive study. In this second study, it was decided at random for each visitor to a special exhibit whether or not to pretest. Guide machines were then distributed at random to half of the people who had been pretested and to half who had not. Viewers were all posttested as they left the exhibit. The results of this second experiment are given in Table 4.4.

After seeing the results of this second experiment the researchers recommended to their museum that a single "testing machine" be placed at each exhibit. Visitors were encouraged to "see what they knew" about the subject of an exhibit before visiting it.

a. For the first study:

1) represent the design in shorthand.
2) name the design.
3) specify the kinds of information available from the design.
4) why might you still be reluctant to invest in the guide machines?

Table 4.4 Average Number Correct Answers on the Posttest

	No pretest	Pretested
No guide	10	17
Guide	17	18

   b. For the second study:
     1) represent the design in shorthand.
     2) name the design.
     3) what kind of special information is yielded by this design that was not yielded by the first study?
   c. Why did the researchers decide not to invest in the individual guide machines although the results of the second study did indicate they were effective?

2. The adrenal gland has to do with regulation of salt elimination from the body. Removing it eventually increases the body's need for salt. Much research has been directed at whether or not an animal can regulate the intake of salt to compensate for the loss of function of this gland. In one study 40 rats had their adrenals removed. The 30 survivors of the operation were then assigned at random to test groups of 10 each. Each rat was tested on three successive days by being given unlimited access to either plain water, a sugar solution, or a salt solution. Each day the amount the rat drank was recorded. The order of giving the solutions was shown in Table 4.5.

   a. Represent the design of this experiment in shorthand.
   b. Name this design.
   c. List all the information provided by this design.
   d. Were all possible orders of the solutions used? If not, what are the missing orders?
   e. Is the comparison of the amount of each solution drunk a Within- or Between-Subjects comparison?
   f. Is the comparison of the effects of different orders a Within- or a Between-Subjects comparison?
   g. Why didn't the experimenter give all rats the same order of solutions? Explain.

Table 4.5 Order of Testing

		Days	
Test group	1	2	3
1	Water	Salt	Sugar
2	Salt	Sugar	Water
3	Sugar	Water	Salt

3. Excerpt from Manheimer, Mellinger, and Balter (1969): Marijuana use among urban adults.

   . . . . The study was conducted among adults in San Francisco during 1967–1968. Personal interviews were held with 1104 men and women, all 18 years of age or older. In order to obtain a representative cross-section of San Francisco's population, strict probability sampling was employed. The personal interview lasted an average of 1.4 hours. The interviewer began by asking some general questions about physical and mental health and about ways in which respondents had handled various problems. The interview then proceeded gradually to the more sensitive questions about the use of psychotherapeutic drugs. At the end of the interview, respondents were asked if they had ever tried any other mood-changing drugs, including marijuana and LSD. . . . Young men or women are much more likely to have used these drugs than older men or women . . . . White women under 35 are twice as likely as Negro women of the age group to have tried marijuana . . . . Marijuana users among student populations have often claimed that smoking marijuana is an alternative to drinking. The present study shows that use of marijuana and alcohol tends to be positively (related) in the general population . . . . *

a. What kind of study is this?

b. Identify the IV(s) in this study, if there were any.

c. Identify at least four DVs in this study.

d. Given the results of this study:

   1) Would you say that being young causes people to use marijuana? Explain.

   2) Would you say that drinking alcohol increases marijuana usage? Explain.

   3) Would you say that being "white" causes a person to use marijuana? Explain.

SECTION 5: BRIEF REVIEW
OF EXPERIMENTAL DESIGNS

Once you have proposed your research question and have operationally defined your IVs and DVs, you are ready to design your research. A research design includes specification of how your subjects are to be divided into groups, when and what treatments will be administered to the groups, and when you will take your DV measurements. Designs can vary from very simple ones, costing relatively little to carry out in terms of the experimenters' time and resources, to very complex designs that require abundant resources and a large number of subjects. The experimenters must decide beforehand exactly what information they need and choose the least complicated design that will yield that information.

   Some of the kinds of information that are available from different designs are: *posttreatment information* about how subjects behave just after treatment, *pretreatment information* about how subjects behave at the start of the experiment, many kinds of *comparison information* revealing the effects of the treatment, and *information about group equivalence* necessary to establish that posttreatment differences between groups are indeed due only to treatment effects. Special designs can yield information about such things as *interaction effects* among multiple IVs,

---

*Reprinted by permission of the American Association for the Advancement of Science (copyright © 1969).

effects of taking pretreatment measures on subsequent measures, *effects of the order* of multiple treatments, and *correlations* among multiple DV measures.

When designing a research study, one important decision is whether to treat Non-Subject IVs Between-Subjects or Within-Subjects. If an IV is treated Between-Subjects, then different groups of subjects are necessary for the different levels of the IV and multi-level comparisons are made between groups. If the IV is treated Within-Subjects, then all subjects are tested at all levels, increasing the amount of information obtained from any one subject. Multi-level comparisons are then made within each of the subjects, each subject serving as its own control. When IVs are treated Within-Subjects, it is necessary to be concerned with the possibility of effects of the order in which each subject experiences the multiple conditions. The usual way to control for such order effects is to counterbalance the conditions across subjects, eliminating any systematic effects of order.

The simplest designs have only one group of subjects. The *One-Shot design* simply observes subjects after they have experienced the experimental treatment. The *One-Group, Pre-Post design* observes the subjects both before and after a treatment. Another simple design just observes two groups of subjects blocked according to a Subject IV without applying any treatment to see whether the *blocked groups* differ on some DV. Such simple designs are useful for pilot studies but severe limitations on the information they can yield about treatment effects mean that the results of such studies are usually not published.

Addition of a second group to a design makes possible comparison of posttreatment effect for the experimental group with that of another group who had no treatment or a different treatment. Subjects can be assigned to two independent groups at random (*Randomized-Groups design*) or they may be already formed into two independent groups by processes not under the experimenters' control (*Static-Groups design*). In some versions of these *Independent-Groups designs*, pretests are administered as well as posttests. In a special case of two-group designs, the groups are not independent but are matched on some basis, either according to a pretest or on the basis of some other Subject characteristic. In such a *Matched-Groups design,* each subject in one group has a matched partner in the other group and the groups are no longer independent.

To be secure in attributing posttreatment comparison differences between groups to the effects of the treatment, the design must yield information about the equivalence of the groups. Random assignment of subjects to groups is a common way of achieving equivalence. Pretesting on the DV and demonstrating that two groups are initially the same is another way. Sometimes the two approaches are combined. To ensure equivalence on an important Relevant Subject Variable, the groups can be specifically matched for that variable. Static-Groups designs, although sometimes forced on the researcher by circumstances, always weaken interpretation of treatment effects because of the possibility of the existence of some confounding Relevant Subject Variable which creates either initial differences between the groups or causes the groups to lose equivalence during the course of the experiment.

Multi-level comparison information can be obtained by investigating the IV at more than two levels. These levels can be represented by different groups of subjects in a Between-Subjects design; or they can be represented by repeated measures of the same subjects in a Within-Subjects design. Counterbalancing is necessary for any IV that is handled Within-Subjects.

Designs can also be made more complex by simultaneous investigation of two or more IVs. In such *multivariate or factorial designs,* the total number of experimental conditions is the product of the number of levels of each IV (factor) and rapidly increases as more IVs are added. The IVs can be operationally defined as either Subject or Non-Subject in type. If they are Non-Subject, the experimenter must decide whether to treat them in the design as Within-Subjects or Between-Subjects. If they are Subject IVs, they can be treated only Between-Subjects with subjects blocked into different groups according to the operational definition of the IV. Such multivariate designs yield information about the interaction effect of two IVs as well as comparison information about the effects of each IV separately. Interaction information tells us whether the action of one IV on the DV(s) is modified by the simultaneous action of other IVs.

There are special designs which are useful when particular kinds of information are needed. *Solomon's Four-Group design* treats the giving of a pretest as a second IV and allows us to see whether the operation of pretesting is having any effect in and of itself or is possibly interacting with treatment effects. The *Latin-Square design* is an incomplete factorial yielding information about the effects of different orders of conditions without complete counterbalancing. *Single-Subject* designs, using techniques such as repeated reversals of treatment effects and multiple-baselines, allow intensive investigation of a few subjects and are useful in clinical settings. *Correlational* studies are often done when the experimenter cannot directly manipulate any IVs. They involve the measurement of multiple DVs to see whether any of them tend to vary together. Correlational designs do not yield direct information about treatment effects, but they are often a rich source of ideas for future experiments.

SECTION 6: ARE YOU FAMILIAR WITH EXPERIMENTAL DESIGNS?

If you can meet the behavioral objectives at the ends of the sections in Chapters 3 and 4, you should be able to identify and critically evaluate designs used in actual research studies. Moreover, given a potential research question you should be able to design some research of your own with full knowledge of the information you can expect your study to yield. Try your skills on the following studies.

Study 1: News report from the AP wire (reprinted in Corvallis *Gazette-Times,* July 24, 1978).

The moderate amounts of artificial sweeteners used by human beings do not cause cancer, a major study in Baltimore has concluded.

The Baltimore study involved 519 patients with bladder cancer at 19 Baltimore-area hospitals between 1972 and 1975. It also involved 519 other people, called controls, who were matched for age, sex, and other factors but did not have bladder cancer. . . .

In their study, Kessler and Clark questioned cancer patients and the matched controls about their consumption of artificial sweeteners in carbonated and non-carbonated soft drinks, iced tea, and other liquids, and in salad dressings, candy, ice cream, pastry, gelatin, chewing gum, and other foods.

Both patients and controls were questioned also about their smoking habits, occupational history, diabetes, and other factors that might have been involved.

Those who conducted the interviews did not know which subjects were cancer patients and which were not. They found no significant differences in the amounts of food or beverages containing cyclamate or saccharin consumed by the patients or controls.

This study is a good example of the level of scientific sophistication our daily newspapers now expect from their readers. With your research background you should be able to answer the following questions.

a. What is defined as the IV in this study?

b. Is it a Subject- or a Non-Subject IV?

c. Is it treated Within- or Between-Subjects?

d. What is the major DV of the study?

e. Can you represent this design in shorthand? What name would you give this design?

f. What kinds of information can be yielded by this design?

g. Why did they match the two groups on so many factors?

h. Why did they make sure that the interviewers did not know which subjects were cancer patients and which were not?

i. Do you have any reservations about their conclusions?

Study 2: Description of study by Bandura (1965): Influence of model's reinforcement contingencies on the acquisition of imitative responses.

Children were randomly assigned to one of three groups in such a way that each group contained equal numbers of boys and girls. The children observed a filmed model who exhibited a sequence of unusual physical and verbal aggressive responses. In one treatment condition, the model was severely punished following the aggressive behavior; in the second, the model was generously rewarded with treats and praise; and in the third there were no consequences to the model for the aggressive behavior. After seeing one of the movies, the children were placed in a situation where they could imitate similar aggressive acts. The degree to which they imitated was measured. The children in the model-punished group showed much lower rates of imitation than did children in the model-rewarded or no-consequencces groups. Girls showed consistently less imitation of the aggressive behaviors than boys. The suppressing effect of the model-punished condition was much greater for the girls than for the boys.

a. What are the IVs in this study? Operationally define each of them and state the number of levels of each.

b. What are the total number of conditions in this experiment?

c. Identify the IVs as Subject or as Non-Subjects.

d. For each IV, was it treated Between-Subjects or Within-Subjects?

e. What was the DV? Give its operational definition.

f. Give the design of this study in shorthand.

g. What is the name of this design?

h. List all information that can be yielded by this design.

i. Was there any evidence reported of an interaction effect? Explain.

j. If a TV show portrays violent behavior, what does this study suggest should be included in the plot to minimize imitation of violence by child viewers?

Study 3: Description of Werner, Minkin, Minkin, Fixsen, Phillips, and Wolf (1975); Intervention package: An analysis to prepare juvenile delinquents for encounters with police officers.

> These researchers felt that whether or not a young boy is defined as a "delinquent" during an interaction with a policeman depends on the boy showing some rather specific behaviors. The four behaviors they identified as especially important in making a good impression were: facial orientation (looking at the policeman), politeness in short answers, expressions of reform, and expressions of understanding and cooperation. Over 18 sessions with each of three boys, the researchers used an instruction-demonstration-practice-feedback training procedure directed at changing these specific behaviors. During these sessions they monitored the occurrence of all four behaviors. In session 5 they started to train for facial orientation; in session 7, they began training for polite answers; in session 11, reform expressions; and in session 14, cooperation expressions. All three subjects were pre- and posttested by a videotaped interaction with a "policeman."

a. What kind of study is this? What is the specific name of the design used?

b. If the training procedure is effective in modifying specific behaviors:

    1) in what session would you expect to see an increase in the proportion of times a boy maintains appropriate facial orientation?

    2) in which session would you see an increase in the rate of giving polite responses to questions?

    3) in which session should you see an increase in the rate of making expressions of reform?

    4) in which session would you see increased expressions of understanding and cooperativeness?

c. Given the research design used, what would you require in terms of agreement among the results of the three subjects in the study?

describing what you've found

This chapter and the next should not be regarded as replacements for a course in statistics or a good statistical reference book. Instead, you'll learn what the statistics mean, how to interpret them, and how to choose them. This kind of knowledge often seems to slip by students taking a statistics course, perhaps because they're too busy wrestling with numbers and formulae to sit back and ask themselves what it means. Doing statistics on the results of research is worthwhile only insofar as we can interpret these statistics, translate them into words, and can arrive at logical conclusions about what the research proves and does not prove.

As an accompaniment to Chapters 5 and 6, you should acquire a beginning statistics text. Look for one that explains how to calculate such statistics as means, standard deviations, percentiles, z-scores, t-tests, chi-square tests, and correlations, and is written in terms you can understand. A good statistics book will have several useful statistical tables in the back. A few such books are mentioned at the end of Chapter 6, but almost any statistics book that you can understand will do. The major problem with many of the available statistics books is that they short change variables that are not measured on interval scales. So you may have to find a second book which covers "nonparametric" statistics appropriate for nominal and ordinal scales. Have a statistics book or two around, but don't get hung up on calculating statistics. If you know what you want in the way of statistics, you can always hire a statistician or use a computer program to do the actual figuring!

SECTION 1: A CONSUMER'S GUIDE TO STATISTICS

The word "statistics" has an ominous sound to many people. They don't understand statistics, can't calculate them, and feel badgered when confronted by them. Yet statistics are hard to avoid. Even if you seldom read research journals, statistics will be constantly shoved at you in the popular press and on TV. Again and again in your daily personal, political, and occupational roles you'll be called upon to make decisions involving statistical information. Unless you can defend yourself by knowing how to interpret statistics and how to tell when they're being misused, you'll be taken advantage of; you'll be making decisions based on information that is not necessarily very good.

Why are statistics necessary at all? Why can't we just look at a situation and see the facts for ourselves? One of the most fascinating things about human beings is their biases; their built-in ways of misinterpreting the world. In many ways humans do not so much "believe what they see" as "see what they believe." Even training as a scientist will not inoculate you against certain kinds of errors in interpreting evidence. Tervsky and Kahneman (1974) report that, in situations involving uncertainty, trained scientists make much the same types of errors as nonscientists in interpreting facts when they rely on their intuitive judgment instead of applying statistics. Both scientists and nonscientists allow themselves to base their decisions on irrelevant, worthless information. All of us tend to jump to conclusions from too little data; do not really understand what is implied by the word "chance"; and put as much faith in our predictions of future events as our evaluations of past ones. We also like to invent cause-and-effect explanations for coincidences; let personal contact with single instances outweigh evidence obtained from a wider number of observations; and exclude information that is inconsistent with preconceived ideas. In short, all of us need to make intelligent use of statistics to help compensate for our set ways of thinking and limited perception.

In gathering information we must always be on guard against ourselves, particularly against the ease with which we can fool ourselves. We could extract from the history of human knowledge example after example where investigators ignored statistical considerations and fooled themselves (and a lot of other people!) into accepting false information. One story will suffice (Gould, 1978a). In the first half of the last century a Philadelphia physician, Samuel George Morton, amassed the largest pre-Darwinian collection of human skulls representing all racial groups. He wanted to replace speculation about racial differences in intelligence with good hard fact. He assumed that cranial capacity (the space in the skull) was a rough index of general intelligence; an assumption we'd quarrel with nowadays, but one considered reasonable at the time. He laboriously measured the cranial capacity of over 600 skulls. The results supported his view of racial differences in intelligence and of separate creation of the races of man as different species. He was highly respected in his day. At his death in 1851 the *New York Tribune* reported that "probably no scientific man in America enjoyed a higher reputation among scholars throughout the world than Dr. Morton" (Stanton, 1960). His theory of the separate creation of races was used as a scientific argument for the continuation of slavery. It has been periodically revived by other theorists about race.

Morton's skull collection has long since been dispersed, but he did publish all his original measurements along with information about how he made them. Over a century later, Gould (1978a) reanalyzed Morton's own data and found that Morton was guilty of numerous errors, errors that always went in the direction of supporting his preconceived theories about racial differences. To be blunt about it, Morton had distorted his data from beginning to end. He selected data that fit his theories and threw out data that did not. All his mathematical and measurement errors were in the direction of favoring his theories. Reanalysis of Morton's data with appropriate statistical procedures produced no consistent differences in cranial capacity between racial groups. Any differences between subgroups within a general racial grouping were adequately explained by differences in overall body size. Was Morton a charlatan who deliberately manipulated his data? Gould (1978a) thinks not:

> Yet, through all this juggling, I find no indication of fraud or conscious manipulation. Morton made no attempt to cover his tracks, and I must assume that he remained unaware of their existence. He explained everything he did, and published all his raw data. All I discern is an a priori conviction of racial ranking so powerful that it directed his tabulations along preestablished lines. Yet Morton was widely hailed as the objectivist of his age, the man who would rescue American science from the mire of unsupported speculation.* (p. 509)

Consumers of science beware! Honest intentions and scientific credentials are not automatic safeguards against misinterpretation of what we observe. Use of appropriate statistical procedures can go a long way toward helping us overcome our initial biases.

DESCRIBING WITH STATISTICS

Our first task in analyzing data from our research is to describe it, to summarize it. We must find a way to summarize that accurately conveys to others the exact nature of all our results. At the same time, we must keep our description brief enough so that it is possible for our audience to come to some other interpretation than, "My, isn't this a lot of numbers." We have to reduce our often-voluminous data to a comprehensible amount of information. We must treat our data in such a way as to both inform the reader what we found out and make clear how we got from our raw data to our interpretation of results.

It might seem that the best way to be honest and accurate about our results is to report them fully, to give all our raw data. If you ever read one of the massive reports that issue from government agencies, you'll soon drop this idea. Your audience simply doesn't have the time (or the interest) to wade through page after page of numbers. In fact, one way you can lie with statistics is to flood your report with undigested and unsummarized data. You can then make wild interpretations which will go unchallenged because you give *too* much information for your audience to check your logic. After all, it took over 125 years for someone to challenge Morton's interpretation of his results, and then it took a good deal of time to go back through Morton's raw data and produce unbiased and accurate summaries.

The first step in summarizing the results of any research is to identify the DV and to figure out its scale of measurement. The type of scale is the principal determinant of what summary statistics we may use. The next step is to obtain a frequen-

---

*Reprinted by permission of the American Association for the Advancement of Science (copyright © 1978) and Stephen Gould.

cy distribution for the DV measures. This is a simple matter of tabulating for all the possible DV measurement categories how many times each measure actually occurred in the results of the research. Such a frequency distribution can be presented either in a table or a graph.

We then need some single value to represent our "average," or most typical, DV measure. In statistics, such a measure is referred to as a **measure of central tendency** and is a convenient way of representing an entire frequency distribution. The way we find this measure of central tendency will depend on the scale of measurement used for our DV. It also, in some cases, will depend on characteristics of the frequency distribution of our results.

We'll need something other than a single typical measure to convey accurately to our audience the nature of our frequency distribution. When we report just an "average" for our data, our audience will have no way of knowing whether the individual observations were all close to this average or whether the DV values were actually widely scattered. So, in addition to a measure of central tendency, we need a measure of how much the results varied; that is, a measure of the variability of the frequency distribution. The **measure of variability** that will be appropriate will again depend on the scale of measurement used for our DV and on characteristics of our frequency distribution. If we choose our measure of central tendency and our measure of variability correctly, it should be possible for our audience to approximately visualize the entire frequency distribution from just these two **descriptive statistics**.

Another useful type of summary statistic is one that indicates the degree of association or **correlation** between two DVs. This summary statistic indicates how closely the results on one DV can predict the results that will be obtained for another DV used to measure the same subjects. The particular type of correlation used will depend on the scales of measurement of both of the DVs and also on the frequency distribution of measures for each DV.

MAKING INFERENCES WITH STATISTICS

The second function of statistics is to allow us to arrive at conclusions from our data and to indicate how reliable these conclusions are. For example, in deciding whether or not a difference we have found between the average results of a treatment group and those of a nontreatment group is real and would occur again, we have to allow for the possibility of the difference having occurred by chance. In deciding whether or not to make something of a correlation between two DVs, we have to decide whether there really is an association or whether we may be observing a coincidence not likely to happen again. We not only need to describe our results, we also want to have an idea of how likely it is that the same results would be gotten again if the experiment were repeated. Results that are one way one time and another way the next are not of much use. We want trustworthy information on which we can base decisions for the future.

Inferential statistics are always designed around the pessimistic idea (hypothesis or assumption) that our results are due only to chance. When we want to reject this idea and conclude that our results are real and repeatable, an inferential statistical test will tell us what the probability is that we are wrong in saying that our results aren't just due to chance.

Inferential statistical tests come in an almost bewildering variety, and calculations involved sometimes seem very messy. However, the general procedure for doing an inferential statistical test is much the same for all tests. You begin by assuming that your results are due only to chance; you do (or hire someone else to do) the calculations for the appropriate test; you obtain a "test statistic" from your calculations; you look this statistic up in a table; and you find the probability that you'll be wrong if you reject the idea of chance. To be confident about your results, you want the probability that you are wrong to be very small. Selection of the appropriate test in each situation requires knowledge of the design of the experiment, the scale of measurement of the DVs, and the frequency distribution found for each DV. Actual calculation of the inferential statistical test can be done by someone else or by a computer just so long as you know what test you need.

RECAPITULATION

for A CONSUMER'S GUIDE TO STATISTICS

There are certain logical errors that are very common for humans to make when arriving at a conclusion from the results of their observations. Most of these errors can be avoided if appropriate use is made of descriptive and inferential statistics. *Descriptive statistics* are necessary for summarizing results and quickly conveying our research findings to others. *Frequency distributions, measures of central tendency, measures of variability,* and *correlations* of multiple DVs are all useful for describing data. *Inferential statistics* tell us the degree of certainty with which we can predict getting the same results in future experiments. Inferential statistical tests are constructed around the *hypothesis* that our results occurred only by chance and are not likely to be repeated. When we reject this idea, an inferential test will tell us the probability that we are wrong in doing so. The appropriate inferential test must be selected according to our research design, our scale of measurement of the DV(s), and characteristics of the frequency distribution of DV measures.

BEHAVIORAL OBJECTIVES

for A GUIDE TO STATISTICS

1. Describe at least two kinds of descriptive summary statistics.
2. List the factors that must be considered when choosing an appropriate descriptive summary statistic.
3. Distinguish between descriptive and inferential statistics.
4. Describe the hypothesis (assumption) around which an inferential statistical test is constructed.

5. List the factors that must be considered when choosing an appropriate inferential statistical test.

6. Describe the purpose of doing descriptive statistics on your data.

7. Describe the purpose of doing inferential statistics on your data.

8. Given a list of characteristics of either descriptive or inferential statistics, identify which is which.

SAMPLE TEST QUESTIONS

for A GUIDE TO STATISTICS

1. For the following statements, write *D* after those that are relevant to descriptive statistics, *I* after those that are relevant to inferential statistics, and both letters after those that are relevant to both kinds of statistics:

   a. measures of central tendency

   b. measures of variability

   c. hypothesis (assumption) of chance

   d. summarizes already obtained research results

   e. correlation

   f. predicts direction of future results

   g. must know the research design to select

   h. must know the scale of measurement of the DV to select

   i. may need to know characteristics of the frequency distribution to select

   j. probability statements can be connected to the statistic

2. Review questions on Morton's research:

   a. What was the DV in Morton's research?

   b. What type of scale would this DV be measured on?

   c. What was the IV in Morton's research?

   d. Was his IV a Subject or a Non-Subject IV?

SECTION 2: FREQUENCY DISTRIBUTIONS

The initial step in describing data is to make up a *frequency distribution* of the number of times each DV measure occurs. This is a simple procedure. First we list all the possible measurement categories defined for the DV and then we check off a category each time it occurs in our observations. When we are through we will have a tabulation of how the observations on our subjects are distributed among the possible measurement categories.

FREQUENCY DISTRIBUTIONS FOR INTERVAL SCALES OF MEASUREMENT

The number of possible measures is usually very large for interval scales of measurement. Potentially, many interval scales run from zero to infinity. In the study of preschooler activity levels discussed in Chapter 2 (page 31), the DV measure of the number of switches a child makes among a set of toys was an interval measure. A tabulation of the frequency of occurrence of the different values of this measure was started in Table 2.4 (page 33), but we soon decided that there were too many DV categories to continue tabulating each category separately. We then combined adjacent measurement categories into measurement classes. We can do this and still have an interval scale of measurement as long as the classes are of equal size and remain, therefore, equidistant on our scale.

How Many Classes Do You Want?

Deciding how many classes you should have and how to define the class limits is something of an art for which there are no really hard-and-fast rules. If you use too large a **class size**, one which lumps too many measurement categories together, you'll get a frequency distribution that shows little about the data. In Table 5.1, the preschooler data from Table 2.4 is tabulated with a class size of 30 switches.

Table 5.1   Number of Switches between Toys Recorded for 24 Preschoolers

Number of Switches	Frequency
0–29	23
30–59	1
60–89	0
Total	24

Not much information can be obtained from looking at this frequency distribution. All we can see is that one child made more than 30 switches and the rest made fewer. Too large a class size means too few classes to give any detail about the distribution of results.

Too small a class size, such that only one or two observations fall in each class, also makes it hard to get any usable information about the characteristics of a frequency distribution. From the information given in Table 2.4 we'd have a hard time figuring out any overall distribution characteristics. For instance, it's not obvious which part of the DV scale has the most observations.

The number of classes you need depends to some extent on how much detail you want to preserve. As a rule of thumb, plan to have at least ten classes. To decide on a class size, find the difference between your largest DV measure (42 switches for your preschool study) and your smallest (3 switches) and divide by ten. This would suggest a class size of 3.9 for the toy-switch data. However, for the convenience of your audience, you should make your class size a whole number. It would get a little confusing if your classes ran: 0–3.8, 3.9–7.7, 7.8–11.6, 11.7–15.5, etc. A class size of four would be better. If they'll provide sufficient detail, class sizes of five or ten or multiples thereof produce frequency distributions that are easier for people used to the decimal system to read. If we used a class size of five on the toy-switch data, then its frequency distribution would look as in Table 5.2.

Table 5.2   Number of Switches between Toys Recorded for 24 Preschoolers

Number of Switches	Frequency
0– 4	2
5– 9	6
10–14	7
15–19	2
20–24	4
25–29	2
30–34	0
35–39	0
40–44	1
45–49	0
Total	24

From this distribution we can see that most of the children fall in either the 5–9 or the 10–14 category, with a few children making more switches. We can also see that there was one child who made a really extreme number of switches when compared to the rest of the group. With a class size of five, this distribution both gives us enough detail and allows us to see some overall characteristics of the distribution.

Setting Your Class Limits

Class limits must be set in such a way as to leave no uncertainty about which measure goes in which class. If we had defined our classes for Table 5.2 as 0–5, 5–10, 10–15, 15–20, etc., there would be seven observations that we wouldn't know what to do with. Does Martin's score of 15 switches belong in the 10–15 or the 15–20 class? To avoid this ambiguity, you always carry out your *real class limits* to one more decimal place than your observations will actually have. Thus the real class limits for Table 5.2 might be: −.5 to 4.5, 4.5 to 9.5, 9.5 to 14.5, etc. You might just as justifiably set them at: +.5 to 5.5, 5.5 to 10.5, 10.5 to 15.5, etc., although if you did so, you'd better hope that no child makes zero switches! You must adopt some such rule for your real class limits and use it consistently, not only in your initial tabulation, but also in any calculations you later make based on the frequency distribution.

Frequency Histograms

Often a pictorial version of a frequency distribution will communicate results more immediately to an audience than a tabular one. A **frequency histogram** can be drawn from a tabulated frequency distribution. Such a histogram plots the frequency of occurrence of each DV measure versus the DV measurement-scale categories or classes. A frequency histogram for the distribution given in Table 5.2 would look as in Fig. 5.1. We can quickly see from Fig. 5.1 the same kinds of information we could get from taking the time to examine Table 5.2. Most of the children made between 5 and 15 toy switches while one child showed an extremely large number, more than one per minute.

FIG. 5.1

Frequency histogram of number of switches between toys in a half-hour period made by 24 preschoolers.

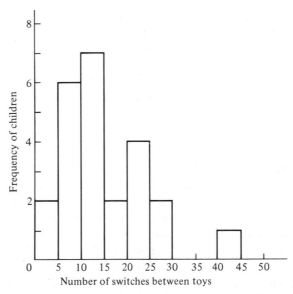

Figure 5.2 shows a frequency histogram based on Table 5.1, the one for which we used a horrendously large class size. Notice how much less information about the distribution is conveyed by this second histogram.

FIG. 5.2

Frequency histogram of number of switches between toys in a half-hour period made by 24 preschoolers.

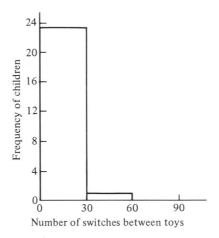

Drawing Attractive Frequency Histograms

When drawing a frequency histogram (or any other graph, for that matter), both axes should be fully labeled. The *x*-axis must clearly specify both the DV and its units of measurement. For readability, the axes shouldn't be cluttered with too many numbers. A general rule of thumb is to space numbers along the two axes so that the body of the graph comes out approximately square. By this rule, neither of the two histograms in Fig. 5.3 is artistically very pleasing or makes very good use of the available space.

Comparing Frequency Distributions

Often we'll want to compare frequency distributions for different groups or conditions. This cannot be done directly unless the total frequencies or sample sizes are the same for both distributions. When they are not equal, it is better to report the proportion or percent of the total frequency that falls in each class rather than the actual frequency of observations. Suppose, for example, that in a study of another preschool class, we found that eight children fell in the 25–29 switches category, whereas in the original study only two fell into this category. Before we jump to the conclusion that there are a lot more high-activity children in the second preschool group, we'd better ask ourselves how many total children were observed in the second study. If our answer is "102 children," then the eight children falling in the 25–29 switches class represent only 7.8 percent (8/102) of the total. Since the two children who were in this class in your original study represented 8.3 percent (2/24) of the total number observed, then there really isn't very much difference between

FIG. 5.3

Frequency histogram of number of switches between toys in a half-hour period made by 24 preschoolers.

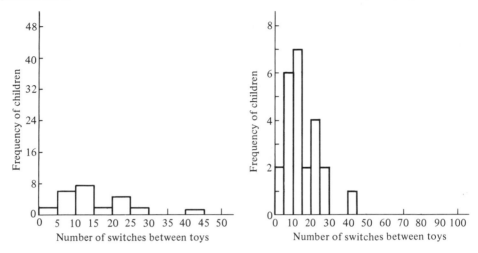

the two preschools in terms of how many children make between 25 and 29 switches when faced with the toy collection. Since in the second study we looked at about four times as many children as in the first, we would expect to have about four times as many children fall into each of the classes of the DV if the two preschools have similar children. Whenever you compare frequency distributions, you must be sure the total frequencies or sample sizes are the same, or else you must convert your class frequencies for each distribution to **proportion** or percents of the total frequency.

Frequency Polygons

Another graphic way to represent frequency distributions for intervally scaled DVs is by means of a **frequency polygon.** For this type of graph, the frequency of observations in each class is represented by a point placed over the midpoint of that class and lines are drawn connecting the points. The **midpoint** for each class is found by adding together the upper and lower real class limits and dividing by two. When graphing such a polygon, you must remember to return your lines to zero frequency at the ends and not leave the polygon floating in space above the *x*-axis. The frequency histogram given in Fig. 5.1 is redrawn as a frequency polygon in Fig. 5.4.

Just as for frequency histograms, whenever you are likely to be comparing two frequency polygons, be sure that the total frequencies, or sample sizes, for the two polygons are the same. Or, better yet, get in the habit of converting your raw frequencies to percents or proportions of the total frequency so you can stop worrying about equal sample sizes when you want to make comparisons.

FIG. 5.4

Frequency polygon of number of switches between toys in a half-hour period made by 24 preschoolers.

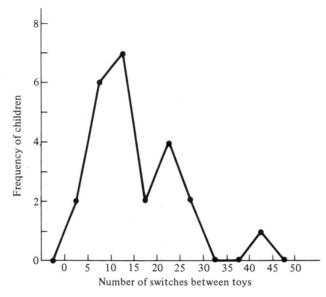

FREQUENCY DISTRIBUTIONS FOR ORDINAL SCALES OF MEASUREMENT

You construct a frequency distribution for an ordinal scale of measurement in the same way as for an interval scale, except that usually you won't be combining measurement categories into bigger classes. Since the measurement categories of an ordinal scale are not equidistant, there is no rationale for adding them together. The activity ratings you asked your student colleagues to make for the children in the preschool study discussed in Chapter 2 are ordinal measures. A frequency distribu-

Table 5.3 Ratings of Activity Levels for 24 Preschoolers (1 is inactive and 5 is extremely active)

Rating-Scale Values	Frequency of Children	Proportions	Percents
1	0	.00	0
2	9	.38	38
3	7	.29	29
4	6	.25	25
5	2	.08	8
Total	24	1.00	100

tion of the raw activity ratings from Table 2.1 is given in Table 5.3. For ease of comparing this distribution with observations from other studies, the proportions and percents of total frequency are given in the table along with raw frequencies.

Bar Charts for Ordinally Scaled Measures

A **bar chart** can be made for an ordinal-scale frequency distribution which is similar to the frequency histogram used for interval data. The values defined for the measurement scale are placed in order along the x-axis the same as for an interval scale, but the spacing is arbitrary. Usually we space the categories at equal distances, but this is only a convention since for an ordinal scale we do not know whether the measurement categories are in fact equidistant. We could just as reasonably space the categories at random distances as long as we kept them in correct order. The bars in the graph are not placed next to each other as in the frequency histogram because, again, we cannot assume that there is an underlying continuum of equally spaced measures. A bar chart based on the data in Table 5.3 is given in Fig. 5.5.

FIG. 5.5

Proportions of 24 preschoolers assigned different activity ratings.

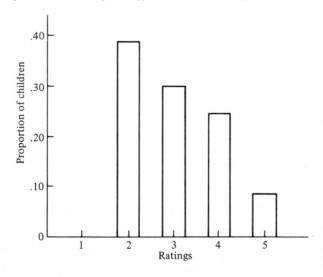

With bar charts we can visually compare two frequency distributions by plotting bars from a second group next to the bars representing our original group. Suppose we have available data from 65 preschoolers in a special program for neurologically impaired children and we wish to compare these data with those from the 24 "normal" preschoolers. Since the total frequencies of the two samples are unequal, we will have to compare proportions or percents. From Fig. 5.6 we can see that the second group of preschoolers (the neurologically impaired group) seems to have a

FIG. 5.6

Proportions of 24 normal preschoolers (white bars) and 66 neurologically impaired pre-schoolers (shaded bars) assigned different activity ratings (1 is inactive and 5 is extremely active).

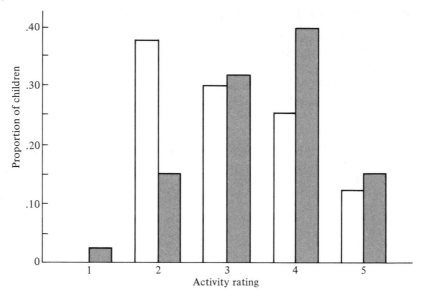

much greater proportion of children with high activity ratings than did the first group of normal children.

You cannot convert the bar chart for ordinally scaled data into a polygon as you can a histogram for interval data. Doing so would imply an underlying continuum of equidistant categories which ordinal scales do not possess.

FREQUENCY DISTRIBUTIONS FOR NOMINAL DATA

When your DV is defined by a nominal scale of measurement, you can tabulate the number of subjects assigned to each measurement category just as for ordinal and interval data. You can also calculate the proportion of the total sample assigned to each category if you intend to make comparisons with other frequency distributions. The only difference in the way you handle nominally scaled measures is that you can place the measurement-scale values in any order since nominal scales have no inherent order. In Table 2.6 (p. 40) results are given for measurement of which toy your preschoolers selected when they were given their choice among five toys. These data are given again in Table 5.4 along with proportions and percents. Notice that a different ordering of toys is used this time. Any order would be just as acceptable.

Table 5.4   Toy Selections by 24 Preschoolers

Toy Selected	Frequency	Proportion	Percent
Book	2	.083	8.3
Hammer	3	.125	12.5
Truck	3	.125	12.5
Gun	8	.333	33.3
Doll	8	.333	33.3
Total	24	1.00	100.0

Bar Charts for Nominally Scaled Measures

The data in Table 5.4 could be presented graphically as a bar chart similar to the one we did for the ordinal rating data. However, the ordering of the measurement categories along the *x*-axis would now be at the whim of the artist. Let's draw a bar chart for these results that permits a direct comparison with a second set of results. Suppose we repeat the toy-selection measure on the 66 neurologically impaired preschoolers. For each of the two groups, we find the percent of children in the group choosing each toy. The comparison of the two sets of measures is given in Fig. 5.7.

FIG. 5.7

Percent of children selecting a given toy for 24 normal preschoolers (white bars) and 66 neurologically impaired preschoolers (shaded bars).

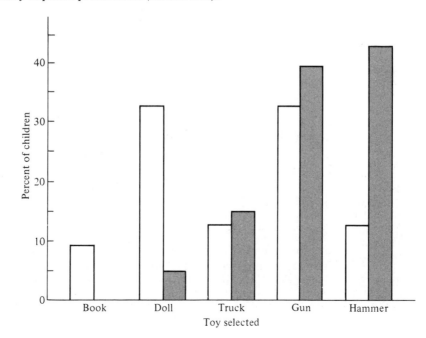

Looking at Fig. 5.7, a bar chart of nominal measurements of two groups of pre-schoolers, we would say that there appears to be some difference in the toys selected by these children. In particular, the neurologically impaired children were far more likely to choose a hammer (42.4 percent) than were the normal preschoolers (12.5 percent). At the same time, the neurologically impaired children were far less likely to select a doll (4.5 percent) than were the normal children (33.3 percent).

Two-Way Classifications

Often, when categorizing subjects according to a nominally scaled DV, we also measure them with a second nominal variable to see if the two variables are related. For instance, we may suspect that sex of child is related to toy preference. So for each of the children we record the sex as well as the toy selected. Some possible results of such a **two-way classification** are given in Table 5.5. This table indicates that the pattern of toy selection is very different for boys and girls.

Table 5.5   Two-Way Classification of 24 Preschoolers by Sex and by Toy Selected

TOY	SEX		Total
	Male	Female	
Book	0	2	2
Hammer	3	0	3
Truck	2	1	3
Gun	6	2	8
Doll	1	7	8
Total	12	12	24

After looking at Table 5.5 we might realize that it would be a good idea to pay attention to sex of child in our neurologically impaired sample. Since the normal boys seem to prefer the gun and hammer and reject the doll, if there were an excess of boys in the neurologically handicapped group, this alone might be a partial explanation of the seeming high preference for gun and hammer of the impaired children. When we look at the sex ratio of our neurologically impaired group, we find it composed of 46 boys and 20 girls. A two-way classification of this group by sex and by toy selected is given in Table 5.6

If we want to compare Tables 5.5 and 5.6 directly, we must convert our frequencies to proportions or percents since our sample sizes are unequal. Not only are the total preschool samples of unequal size, but also the male/female ratios are different for the two samples. Therefore, we need to convert our frequencies to per-

Table 5.6 Two-Way Classification of Neurologically Impaired Preschoolers by Sex and by Toy Selected ($N = 66$)

TOY	SEX Male	SEX Female	Total
Book	0	0	0
Hammer	18	10	28
Truck	8	2	10
Gun	20	5	25
Doll	0	3	3
Total	46	20	66

cents of males and percents of females within each group if we are going to keep the data from the sexes separate. Table 5.7 gives these percents.

Looking at Table 5.7, it's a good thing we did compare the proportions calculated separately for each sex. When sex is taken into account, the two groups of children do not look as different as they did before. The high concentration of boys in the neurologically impaired group weighted the choice of toys toward the gun and hammer. In fact, the only striking differences that we now see are the greatly increased preference of the neurologically impaired girls for a hammer and the compensating decreased preference for a doll. The neurologically impaired boys look much the same in their toy preferences as the normal boys. Comparing proportions is necessary whenever you have unequal sample sizes.

Table 5.7 Percents of Males and of Females Who Select a Given Toy for Both Normal ($N = 24$) and Neurologically Impaired ($N = 66$) Preschool Samples

TOY	University Day-Care Center SEX Male	Female	Combined	TOY	Neurologically Impaired Children SEX Male	Female	Combined
	($N = 12$)	($N = 12$)	($N = 24$)		($N = 46$)	($N = 20$)	($N = 66$)
Book	0.0	16.6	8.3	Book	0.0	0.0	0.0
Hammer	25.0	0.0	12.5	Hammer	39.1	50.0	42.4
Truck	16.6	8.3	12.5	Truck	17.4	10.0	15.2
Gun	50.0	16.6	33.3	Gun	43.5	25.0	37.9
Doll	8.3	58.3	33.3	Doll	0.0	15.0	4.5
Total	100.0	100.0	100.0	Total	100.0	100.0	100.0

RECAPITULATION

for FREQUENCY DISTRIBUTIONS

When analyzing data, the first step is to obtain a *frequency distribution* of the occurrence of each DV measure separately for each condition of the experiment. When we do this for interval data, we will often find it convenient to combine adjacent measurement categories into larger, equal-sized *classes*. We try to select a class size such that there are at least ten classes that will fall within the range of our DV measures in order to have sufficient detail in our frequency distribution. We also try to adjust class size so that the *class limits* are multiples of whole numbers, making it easier for our audience to read our frequency distributions and graphs. The frequency distribution for an interval measure can be graphed as a *frequency histogram,* with class limits equally spaced on the *x*-axis and class frequencies on the *y*-axis. It can also be graphed as a *frequency polygon* with points representing the class frequencies centered over the *midpoints* of the classes equally spaced along the *x*-axis. These points are then connected by straight lines. Frequencies for each class may be converted to *proportions or percents of the total frequency* before graphing a histogram or polygon. This facilitates comparison with other frequency disrtibutions that may not have the same total sample size. Frequency distributions for ordinal data are graphed as *bar charts*. The order of the measurement categories on the *x*-axis of a bar chart is determined by the ordinal scale. Bar-chart measurement categories are equally spaced along the *x*-axis because of custom, not because they represent equidistant categories. Frequency distributions for nominally scaled DVs can also be represented as bar charts, but the order in which the measurement categories are placed on the *x*-axis, as well as their spacing, is up to the artist. For purposes of comparing between distributions, the raw frequencies of either ordinal or nominal bar charts can be replaced by proportions or percents of the total frequency, the same as for intervally scaled data. Often nominal or ordinal frequency distributions are made simultaneously for two DVs in a *two-way classification table.*

BEHAVIORAL OBJECTIVES

for FREQUENCY DISTRIBUTIONS

1. Given either ordinal or nominal data, make up a completely labeled frequency distribution.
2. Given interval data, decide on a class size and select real class limits. Then make up a completely labeled frequency distribution of the data.
3. Describe the considerations that go into selecting a class size and real class limits for an intervally scaled DV.
4. Explain when it is desirable to report proportions or percents of the total frequency for each measurement class rather than raw frequencies.
5. Given a frequency distribution, draw an appropriate, completely labeled, artistically satisfying graph representing the frequency distribution. Provide it with

an informative caption. Show it to a friend and ask him or her to tell you what it means.

6. Given a table or a graph summarizing a frequency distribution, identify the scale of measurement, identify the type of graph, and describe in words what the table or graph communicates about the results.

7. Describe what is meant by a two-way classification frequency distribution for nominal or ordinal data. Make up an example, complete with numbers.

8. Given a list of characteristics or terms, identify them as being true of one or more of the following: frequency histograms, frequency polygons, bar charts for ordinal data; bar charts for nominal data; two-way classifications.

SAMPLE TEST QUESTIONS

for FREQUENCY DISTRIBUTIONS

1. Make up the appropriate graph to represent the data in Table 2.2 (page 33). Be sure your graph is completely labeled, has an informative caption, and is artistically pleasing.

2. Go back to the original preschool activity data in Table 2.1 (page 31). Make a two-way classification frequency distribution for the DVs of teacher's rating and student observers' ratings. Write down some intelligent comments about what this two-way classification tells you about agreement between the teacher and the student observers in characterizing the children's activity.

3. The following is taken from McKay, Sinisterra, McKay, Gomex, and Lloreda (1978): Improving cognitive ability in chronically deprived children.

This study selected a group of three-year-old children in Colombia who were from impoverished families and whose low body weight and stature indicated a history of nutritional deficiency. All the children used in this study were declared neurologically normal by medical examinations. The children were divided into four groups by a random process. T_4 children had four successive years of an intensive preschool program which included nutrition and hygiene as well as educational activities. T_3 children had only the last three years of this program, being delayed in entering it for one year. T_2 children had only the last two years of the program, and T_1 children participated only for the last year before they entered the regular school program.

All these children were tested at eight years of age for IQ using the Stanford-Binet test. This was at the end of their first year in the regular school program and one year after the termination of the special preschool program. Two reference groups, not in the experiment proper, were also tested with the Stanford-Binet at the same time. The T_0 reference group consisted of children from impoverished homes that had not had body weight or height evidence of malnutrition at the original screening and were therefore not included in the preschool program. The HS reference group was composed of children also of average weight and height from middle-class homes. The results of these IQ measurements are given in the frequency-distribution graphs shown in Fig. 5.8.

FIG. 5.8

Mean scores on the Stanford-Binet Intelligence Test at 8 years of age. (McKay et al., 1978)

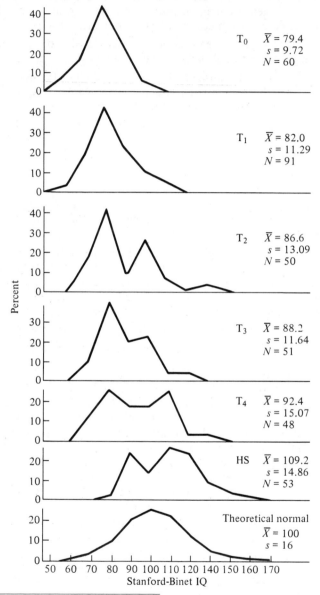

Reprinted by permission of the American Association for the Advancement of Science (copyright © 1978).

a. What is the DV in this study?

b. What kind of scale is this DV being measured on?

c. What is the design (write it down in shorthand) of the four-group experiment that was the core of this research?

d. Are the comparisons being made in this study Between- or Within-Subjects?

e. What specific type of graph is being used here?

f. What did they put on the y-axis of these graphs? Why was this done?

g. Looking at T_1 to T_4:

   1) What would you say about the effects of participation of children from impoverished homes in this preschool program?

   2) Is this a Subject-type or a Non-Subject-type comparison?

h. Compare T_4 with T_0.

   1) What would you say about the effects of participation of children from impoverished homes in this preschool program?

   2) Is this a Subject-type or a Non-Subject-type comparison?

i. Compare HS with T_0.

   1) What might you say about the effects on IQ of the social class into which one is born in Colombia?

   2) Is this a Subject-type or a Non-Subject-type comparison?

4. For the following list of characteristics, identify each as being true of one or more of the following: frequency histograms (FH), frequency polygons (FP), bar charts for ordinal (BC-O) or nominal (BC-N) data, two-way classifications (2-W).

a. x-axis scale is marked off for adjacent, equidistant classes.

b. Graph representing the frequency distribution for interval data.

c. Graph representing a frequency distribution for nominal data.

d. Order of categories on the x-axis is arbitrary (at the whim of the artist).

e. Can replace the frequency for each class with the proportion of the total frequency falling in that class.

f. x-axis categories are in a necessary order, but the distance between them could be varied.

g. Graphical representation of an ordinal frequency distribution.

h. May need to decide on class size and class limits.

i. Alternative graph to a frequency histogram.

j. Frequencies are indicated over the midpoint of each class.

k. Simultaneous classifications on two DVs.

SECTION 3: MEASURES OF CENTRAL TENDENCY

WHAT IS A MEASURE OF CENTRAL TENDENCY?

Comparing whole frequency distributions is somewhat awkward, especially when we have several groups or conditions to consider. What we need is some statistic that can represent or summarize a whole distribution in a single number. This statistic should tell us the most typical value of the DV shown by our group of subjects. In terms of a frequency distribution, we need to know on which value of the DV the distribution tends to center. There are several descriptive statistics that can indicate the "central tendency" of a distribution. To decide which of them is appropriate for a particular case, we need to know the scale on which the DV was measured and the shape of the frequency distribution resulting from our measurement process. Sometimes, the purpose for which we want to report the measure of central tendency will also be a consideration in its selection.

MEASURES OF CENTRAL TENDENCY FOR INTERVAL SCALES: MEAN, MEDIAN, AND MODE

Mean

The **mean** of a set of DV measures is simply the sum of the subjects' DV values divided by the total number of subjects. Since calculating the mean involves the addition of different DV values or categories, the mean can only be properly calculated for intervally scaled data. The mathematical operations involved in calculating the mean assume the measurement categories to be equidistant, an assumption that is not true for ordinal or nominal scales.

The mean is a measure of central tendency that uses all the data; all the DV values are involved in its calculation. The mean has the special property of being the "mathematical center" of the distribution. You can take each of your DV scores and convert it into a "deviation score" by subtracting the mean from it. This **deviation score** tells you by how much a particular DV score differs from the mean of all the DV scores. If you then add up all your deviation scores, keeping track of whether they are positive or negative, you'll find they sum to zero. The mean for the distribution is the only number that has this property. Subtract any other constant number from your DV measures and the resulting difference scores will not sum to zero. (If you prefer to check things out for yourself, try the following: The mean for the six numbers 3, 4, 5, 6, 7, and 8 is 5.5. Subtract 5.5 from each of these six numbers and add the resulting deviations. They should sum to zero; and if they don't, you'd better check your math. Now, try subtracting another number, say 4 or 7, from each of the six scores and add up these resulting difference scores. You'll find they won't sum to zero. How many different numbers you try depends on how stubborn you are, but you'll find that only the mean score will produce deviation scores that sum to zero.)

Whether or not the mean is the best statistic to describe intervally scaled DV measures depends on the shape of the frequency distribution. If the distribution is symmetrical (the two halves are the same shape) and humped in the middle, then the mean is a good representative value. However, not all frequency distributions are symmetrical or have a single hump in the middle. Take another look at the IQ distributions plotted in Fig. 5.8 for the disadvantaged children in the Colombian preschool research program. There are some good reasons why the authors didn't simply report the means of their intervally scaled DV (IQ score) and instead gave their audience a chance to look at the actual distributions. Only the theoretical IQ distribution is symmetrical. The distributions for actual data collected in the research program are decidedly asymmetrical (*not* symmetrical) in some possibly interesting ways. For example, the untreated children (T_0) not only have a lower mean IQ, they also have a higher concentration in the lower end or lower **tail of the distribution.** Actually there is no shift from T_0 to T_1 (children who had one year of the preschool program) in the location of the major peak of the IQ distribution, but there is a shift of children into the upper end (upper tail) of the distribution which increases the mean value slightly. Even more interesting is the comparison of the distributions for the T_2 to T_4 groups. The location of the major **peak** does not change, but a second peak of higher IQs steadily emerges. It looks like the preschool treatment may be affecting some of the children and not others. The distribution for the HS group, composed of middle-class children, also shows two peaks, again as if it contained basically two groups of children. If the authors had just reported the means of these groups we'd have no way of knowing that these individual distributions had this two-peak property and would have assumed they were all shaped like the theoretical curve.

When the frequency distribution is asymmetrical or has multiple humps, the mean may not be the most representative statistic. Using it may give a false impression of the most typical DV value. If the distribution is asymmetrical, it is said to be skewed. A **skewed distribution** with a few extreme values added to the upper tail will have a mean which will lie above the distribution's peak. A skewed distribution with a few extreme values added to the lower tail will have a mean which lies below the distribution's peak. If the frequency distribution is based on a fairly small set of observations, then only one or two **extreme values** may pull the mean far away from the most typical scores. In this case, the mean will no longer be a good single representative value for the distribution. A distribution with two humps rather than one is called a **bimodal distribution.** The mean for such a distribution, if it is a score falling between the two humps, may not represent very many of the actual DV values. The mean works best as a measure of central tendency for interval data whose frequency distribution is close to symmetrical and is **unimodal.**

Figure 5.9 contains sketches of several possible frequency distributions for intervally scaled data. Look these over and ask yourself the following questions: Which ones are symmetrical and can best be represented by the mean score? Which ones are skewed? Which ones are bimodal? Which ones are both bimodal and skewed?

FIG. 5.9

Sample frequency distributions for internally scaled measurements.

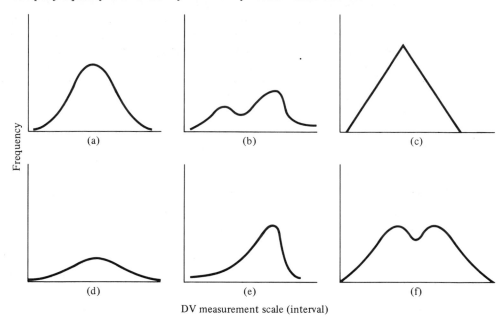

DV measurement scale (interval)

MEDIAN OR 50th PERCENTILE

So, what do you do if the frequency distribution for your intervally scaled measure is badly skewed? There is a measure of central tendency that you can use which is "distribution-free" a measure which can still be interpreted the same way no matter what the shape of the distribution. This measure is called the **median** or *50th percentile.*

The median score for any distribution is that DV value that is larger than half of the DV values in the distribution and less than those DV values forming the other half of the distribution. The median cuts off the upper 50 percent of the observations from the lower 50 percent. Thus if it is said for a group of people that the median age is "13" you know that 50 percent of the people in this group are 13 years or less in age and 50 percent are 13 years or more in age, no matter what the actual shape of the frequency distribution. The median score is that DV value that cuts the area of a frequency histogram or polygon into two equal portions.

Obviously, if the frequency distribution is symmetrical, the median and the mean will be the same value and the mean will also cut the area under the distribution into halves. If the distribution becomes skewed by having extreme values in the upper tail, the mean will be increased more than the median, and the mean will no longer cut the distribution into an upper and lower 50 percent. If the distribution is skewed by having a few extremely low values, this will pull the mean down further than the median. The mean is more influenced by a few extreme values in a distribution than is the median.

There are more sophisticated measures of skewness, but a good practice when reporting statistics for interval data is to report both the mean and the median. Then your audience can see for themselves which of your distributions are symmetrical (same mean and median) and which are skewed one way or the other.

Mode

There is a third measure of central tendency that can lay claim to being a "typical value" for a distribution. This is the measurement category or class that has the highest frequency; the DV value that was obtained for the greatest number of subjects. This measure is called the **mode** or "modal class." In the case of a symmetrical distribution with a single hump, the mode will be the same value as the median or the mean. If there are a few extreme DV values increasing the height of one or the other tails of the distribution, the mode, like the median, will remain relatively unchanged while the mean will be pulled toward the extreme values.

The mode comes into its own as a measure of central tendency for interval data when a distribution has multiple humps. In the Colombian preschool study discussed earlier (page 165, Sample Test Question 3), the most accurate description of the distributions would be to say that they were bimodal. With increased length of experience in the preschool program the lower mode remains at an IQ score of 80, similar to the average IQ score of untreated children, but a second mode increasingly appears at higher IQ scores. Often such bimodal distributions imply that there are at least two frequency distributions being added together, which would lead the researchers to do further studies isolating the multiple factors involved. When frequency distributions in your research consistently show more than one mode, it is only fair to communicate this to your audience.

MEASURES OF CENTRAL TENDENCY FOR ORDINAL SCALES: MEDIAN, MODE

Median

When your DV is measured on an ordinal scale, the appropriate measure of central tendency is obtained by *ranking* the DV measures or placing them in order from lowest to highest. The DV measure that corresponds to the middle rank is then the median, since half of the DV scores are equal to or greater than it and half are equal or less. When you have an even number of DV measures, the convention is to take the DVs with the two middle ranks, add them together, and divide by two to obtain the median. If we returned to the preschool activity study of Chapter 2 (page 30), we could find the median activity rating the student raters assigned to the children by ranking the 24 children from highest rating to lowest. We would find (try it for yourself) that the 12th-ranking child and the 13th-ranking child were both assigned the DV category value of "3." Thus we could say that the median rating given these children by our student raters was "3," or "moderately active."

The mean would not be an appropriate summary statistic for ordinal data since calculation of it assumes that the DV measurement categories are equidistant and can be added together or subtracted from one another. Calculation of a mean score for ordinal data is probably one of the most common mathematical violations in research reports, so watch out for it!

Mode

Since the mode is simply that DV measurement category that has the highest frequency, it, too, can be calculated for ordinal data. The median is generally preferable to the mode as a summary statistic because the mode ignores the fact that the DV measures are ordered. However, in cases of weak-ordinal scales with a very small number of categories (say, five or fewer), the mode is often the statistic reported since it is likely to be the same as the median. The teacher's ratings of the children in our preschool study form an ordinal scale since the three categories (withdrawn, normal, hyperactive) do represent a natural order when applied to activity levels. However, since only three categories were used, determining the modal category ("normal," with 15 of the 24 children) will give you the same result as ranking all 24 measures and finding out that the 12th- and 13th-ranking children would both fall in the "normal" category. Even when there are a sufficient number of categories on an ordinal scale to make calculation of the median meaningful, it's a good idea to report modes in addition if the frequency distribution is bimodal or if the mode is a very different score from the median.

MEASURES OF CENTRAL TENDENCY FOR NOMINAL SCALES: MODE

For a frequency distribution of nominally scaled data, the mode is the only possible measure of central tendency. Calculation of a mean requires equidistant categories, and calculation of a median requires ordered categories, neither of which is possessed by a nominal scale. For a nominally scaled DV, the "typical" value is the one that occurred most frequently.

To illustrate how modes are used in summarizing nominal data, let's return to the information on toy selection by preschoolers. The frequency distributions of toy selections are given in Table 5.7 (page 163) for both normal preschoolers and for the neurologically impaired sample. A bar chart visually presenting these distributions is given in Fig. 5.7 (page 161). For the normal kids there are two modal toys: a gun and a doll. For the neurologically impaired children the modal toy was a hammer, with a gun a close second. If we consider the toy choices separately for the two sexes, the modal choice for normal boys was a gun and for normal girls, a doll. For the neurologically impaired children, the modal toy selected by boys was also a gun, but the modal choice for the girls was a hammer rather than a doll.

RECAPITUATION

for MEASURES OF CENTRAL TENDENCY

Measures of central tendency are used when we want to compare distributions on the basis of their single most typical or most representative value. Three measures of central tendency are the *mean, median,* and *mode.* The mean is the arithmetic average of a set of numbers and can be calculated only for intervally scaled data. The median, or *50th percentile,* is that DV value that is larger than half of the observed DV values and less than the other half. The median can be determined for either interval or ordinal DV scales. The mode is the DV measurement class or category that occurs most frequently and can be obtained from frequency distributions done for either interval, ordinal, or nominal scales. Choice of the appropriate measure of central tendency depends on knowledge of the scale of the measurement of the DV being summarized and also of characteristics of the frequency distribution. For intervally scaled data, a distribution that is badly *skewed* or has a few very *extreme values* will be better represented by the median than the mean. Extreme values pull the mean away from the peak of the distribution where most of the observations are clustering. When an interval or ordinal distribution has multiple *peaks,* it is valuable to report the modes of the distribution as well as its mean or median. For intervally scaled data that has a symmetrical frequency distribution, the mean, median, and mode will all be the same value.

BEHAVIORAL OBJECTIVES

for MEASURES OF CENTRAL TENDENCY

1. Define the descriptive statistics: mean, median, and mode. Explain how each one is calculated.
2. Describe the circumstances under which:
   a. the mean would be the appropriate measure of central tendency.
   b. the median would be the appropriate measure of central tendency.
   c. the mode would be the appropriate measure of central tendency.
3. Given sketches of frequency distributions, describe them in terms of their symmetry, skewness, and bimodality.
4. Explain, with examples, the concepts of "skewness," "asymmetry," and "bimodality" of frequency distributions.
5. Given the operational definition of a DV and a description of the frequency distribution resulting from measurements of this DV, choose the most appropriate measure of central tendency and defend your choice.
6. Given the summary of the results of a research study, identify the measure of central tendency used and discuss why it was (or was not) the most appropriate one for the researcher to report.
7. Given a list of terms or characteristics, identify whether they are true for the mean, the median, or the mode.

SAMPLE TEST QUESTIONS

for MEASURES OF CENTRAL TENDENCY

1. Look at Table 2.1 (page 31) which gives the raw data for the preschooler activity study. If you rank the 24 toy-switches scores from highest (42) to lowest (3) you will find that the 13th-ranking score is 12 toy switches and the 12th-ranking score is 11 toy switches. If you add the 24 actual scores up and divide by the total number of children, the resulting answer you will get is 14.1. If you look for the scores that occurred most frequently, you'll find that 11 switches and 20 switches each occurred three times. If you refer to Table 5.2 (page 154), you will find that when these data are grouped, the modal class is one of 10–14 toy switches.

    a. What is the mean number of toy switches made by these children?

    b. What is the median of these data?

    c. Describe the relationship between the mean and the median for these data.

    d. What would your answer to (c) lead you to say about the shape of this distribution and the possibility of the existence of extreme values? (Look at Fig. 5.1, page 155, to see if you're correct.)

    e. What is the mode of these data? (Watch out! There are two possible answers depending on whether you use the raw data from Table 2.1 or the frequency distribution given in Table 5.2.)

    f. What would you choose as the best measure of central tendency for this distribution? Explain your choice.

2. Refer to the McKay *et al.* (1978) study summarized for Sample Test Question 3 on page 166.

    a. Make up a neat, titled, clearly labeled table that would permit us to compare the average results of the different groups in their experiment.

    b. Explain why you think McKay *et al.* were not content with presenting just a summary table of their average results but chose to draw the actual frequency distributions as well.

3. The following information is from Pronko and Bowles (1949): Identification of cola beverages. III. A final study.

    In this study on the identification of different cola beverages, each one of 96 subjects was presented in counterbalanced order with 1 oz. each of Hyde Park, Kruger, and Spur Colas, three relatively unadvertised cola drinks available in their community. They were told to identify each one of these cola drinks as best they could. They rinsed their mouths out with water between each sample. The results are given in Table 5.8.

    a. Give the design of this study in shorthand.

    b. Is it a Within-Subjects or Between-Subjects comparison when you compare the identification of the three different colas?

    c. Why did they counterbalance order of presentation of the colas?

    d. What was their IV? How many levels did it have?

Table 5.8 Showing the Distribution of 288 Identification Responses When Each of the 96 Subjects Was Presented in Turn, but in Counter-Balanced Order, with One 1-oz. Sample Each of Hyde Park, Kruger, and Spur Cola (Pronko and Bowles, 1949, p. 606)

Brand of Beverage Given Subject	*Frequency of Subjects' Identification Responses*										
	H.P.	*K.*	*S.*	*C.C.*	*Pep.*	*R.C.*	*7-Up*	*Dr. Pep.*	*Cleo.*	*Other*	*Total*
Hyde Park	0	0	0	39	27	24	1	1	0	4	96
Kruger	0	0	0	30	39	22	1	0	1	3	96
Spur	0	0	0	34	33	22	2	1	1	3	96
Total	0	0	0	103	99	68	4	2	2	10	188

e. What was their DV? What kind of scale was it measured on?

f. What kind of frequency-distribution table is this?

g. What is the most typical DV value for overall identification of colas?

h. If you look separately at the identifications done for Hyde Park, Kruger, and Spur Colas, do they all have the same modal values? If not, what are the modes for each of these distributions taken separately?

i. What would these results lead you to say about the ability of these subjects to identify colas correctly by taste?

4. The State Board of Higher Education is considering the possibility of book-purchase grants to students. They estimate that $100 is needed per quarter to cover book costs. The administration of your college says that on the average students can come up with $80 without borrowing and recommend that $20 per student be budgeted for book grants. The student government estimates, however, that the typical student can come up with only $60 without borrowing and estimates that the grant program should be budgeted at $40 per head. The administration and student government estimates of the amount the typical student has readily available to spend on books are made from the same frequency distribution and neither group made any math errors. What's going on here?

a. Which estimate of the student money available for books is most likely a *mean* estimate?

b. Which estimate of the money a student has available for books is most likely a *median* estimate?

c. How can these two measures of central tendency for the same distribution be different? Explain.

d. Which measure of central tendency do you feel would be the most justifiable "average" to use in this case? Back up your choice (Are you a student or an administrator?).

5. The following statements are true for one or more of the following: Mean ($\bar{X}$), Median (X_{50}), or Mode (M). Indicate by each statement which one or ones of the central tendency measures it is true for.

a. The sum of all the differences between it and the scores on which it is based will be zero.

b. It will be the same as the mean for a symmetrical frequency distribution.

c. Possible to calculate for interval data.

d. Most appropriate for interval data that is badly skewed.

e. Not particularly influenced by a few extreme values.

f. Can have more than one value for the same frequency distribution.

g. Possible to calculate for ordinal data.

h. Appropriate for nominal data.

i. Is the measure of the most typical score for a set of DV measures.

j. All of the DV measures are directly involved in its calculation.

k. Splits the area of a frequency polygon or histogram into two equal halves.

l. Mathematical center of a set of intervally scaled DV measures.

m. Will be increased faster than the other measures if a few DV values are added to the upper tail of your distribution.

n. Should be reported for bimodal data.

o. May be used as the appropriate summary statistic for ordinal DVs with three or fewer categories.

p. Will be the same as the mean for a symmetrical bimodal frequency distribution.

q. Can report it along with the mean to give some idea of a distribution's skewness.

r. Can be found by ranking DV measures and giving it the value of the DV measure in middle rank.

s. Ignores any order in DV measurement categories.

SECTION 4: MEASURES OF VARIABILITY

If we are trying to summarize a frequency distribution completely, we need not only a statistic to tell our audience where on the DV scale the observed scores tend to center, but also a second statistic to indicate how closely the scores cluster. Some frequency histograms have very high skinny peaks with most of the scores closely grouped around the average score. Others are much more spread out, much flatter. Figure 5.10 shows four frequency distributions with the same mean but, nonetheless, very different shapes. To describe these distributions fully, we need a statistic which will increase as the data gets more variable and the frequency distribution flattens and spreads out along our DV scale.

FIG. 5.10

Four frequency distributions with the same mean and the same total sample size but different variabilities.

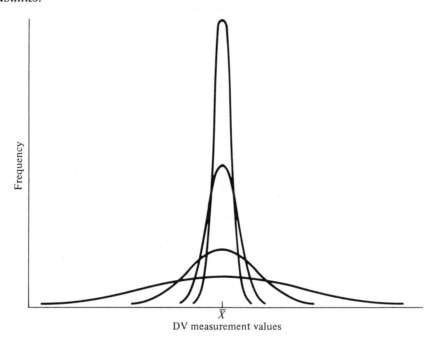

DV measurement values

MEASUREMENT OF VARIABILITY FOR "NORMALLY DISTRIBUTED" INTERVAL DATA

The "Normal" Distribution

A **"normal" distribution** is one whose shape can be specified by one particular mathematical equation. It is bell-shaped and unimodal with the greatest frequency in the center. Its two sides are symmetrical around the middle. As you go away from its center, the frequencies become smaller and smaller, the curve approaching closer and closer to the x-axis, but, theoretically, never touching it. Any particular normal curve can be completely drawn from knowledge of only two statistics: the mean of the distribution and a number called the **standard deviation.** The four distributions graphed in Fig. 5.10 are all "normal" distributions with the same mean but with different standard deviations. It is unfortunate that the name "normal" got stuck to this particular shape of distribution. In the early work on frequency distributions, the DVs used by investigators just happened to produce distributions of this shape. There are lots of other distribution shapes which occur naturally so don't get the idea that observations on all interval DVs must be distributed this way or else be "abnormal." Another name for the normal distribution is "Gaussian," but that name never became popular.

When observations on intervally scaled DVs are normally distributed, a whole host of useful statistical procedures developed for normal distributions becomes available. If the frequency distribution of your intervally scaled DV is decidedly non-normal, however, you should not use these statistics.

Difference or Deviation Scores

The problem of obtaining a measure of variability of interval data was approached by statisticians in several different ways. One possible way to get a measure of variability for a distribution would be to determine the size of the differences of each score from the mean and to average these differences. A distribution of low variability would have small differences and one with high variability would have large differences. The difficulty with this approach is that the sum of all the differences from the mean of any distribution will always be zero! To get around this difficulty, it was proposed to forget about the signs when averaging, a procedure called taking the **absolute value** of each of the difference scores. This procedure yields a number, called the "average deviation," which increases in size as the variability of a distribution increases. If you read older articles in the research literature, you may find "average deviations" reported as the sole measure of variability.

The Variance and the Standard Deviation

Definition of a "Variance":   Nowadays, the **variance** has replaced the "average deviation" as a way of reporting variability of a normal distribution. To obtain this measure, instead of averaging the absolute-difference scores, you average the squares of the difference scores. The resulting number grows rapidly with increasing variability. Squaring the deviation scores eliminates their signs just as did the older procedure of taking absolute values. The official definition of the descriptive variance is "the average of the squared deviations of each score in a distribution from the distribution's mean."

Definition of a "Standard Deviation":   Usually, instead of reporting the variance, researchers report the "standard deviation," which is just the positive square root of the variance. This number is now considered the most appropriate measure of variability for a normally distributed, intervally scaled DV.

Calculation of the Variance and the Standard Deviation: Statistics books abound showing a variety of complicated "calculational formulas" for the variance and standard deviation. These formulae successfully disguise the underlying simplicity of their definitions from most students. They are derived for use with mechanical calculators, which are rapidly becoming museum pieces. If you have only a few DV values to summarize, you can easily calculate their variance by directly following the above verbal definition. First you find the difference of each score from the mean of all the scores. Then you square each of these differences. Next, you add up the squares. Finally, you take the average of the squares by dividing this sum by the total number of scores (sample size or "N"). If you have more than a few numbers, however, this process becomes tedious. In that case, you may need to use a pocket electronic calculator or a computer program.

The Descriptive Variance and Standard Deviation: If all you wish to do is to describe the data you have gathered and have no secret ambitions of ever regarding your observations as representative of some larger set of possible measures, then it's O.K. to divide by the sample size (N) when calculating the variance. This is called the **descriptive variance** or, sometimes, the **biased variance.** The standard deviation calculated from this would be called the "descriptive standard deviation."

The Inferential Variance and Standard Deviation: The truth is that most researchers have some pretensions to glory and wish to regard their results as an indication of what would be found if the research were repeated. In this case, a modification of the variance is reported, known as the **inferential variance.** This number is slightly larger than the descriptive variance since in calculating it you divide by one less than the sample size (N-1) rather than by the sample size (N) itself. This version of the variance is also called the **unbiased variance.**

The distinction between the descriptive and inferential variances is only important when the sample sizes are small. If N is a large number, there is little mathematical difference between the values of the two types of variance and even less between the two types of standard deviation. Division by 100, for example, produces an answer only slightly larger than division by 99. If you subsequently take square roots, this difference further diminishes.

Which Variance (or Standard Deviation) Does Your Calculator Give?   Often the instructions that come with a pocket calculator or computer program are reticent about which type of variance is being calculated! Some of them divide by N in the final step of the calculation and some divide by N-1. When you have small samples of data, you need to know which kind you are getting. It is incorrect to report the descriptive variance if you are going to be drawing implications for the future from your results and need the inferential. You can run a test case to see which variance (or standard deviation) is being calculated. Try your electronic calculator or computer program on the example in Fig. 5.11.

Relationship of the Standard Deviation to Percentiles

If your frequency distribution is "normal" in its shape, then the standard deviation can yield a great deal of information. In particular, you can use the mean and standard deviation of a normally distributed, intervally scaled DV to estimate the **percentiles** of the distribution.

One percentile that you already know about is the 50th, or median. If a distribution is symmetrical, the mean lies at the 50th percentile and, of course, a normal

FIG. 5.11

Example of calculating the descriptive and inferential variances.

> Sample scores: 1, 2, 3, 4, 5
> Sample size (N): 5
> Sample mean: 3
> Deviations from the mean: $-2, -1, 0, +1, +2$
> Squared deviations from the mean: 4, 1, 0, 1, 4
> Sum of squared deviations from the mean: 10
> Variance (descriptive or "biased"): $10/5 = 2$
> Variance (inferential or "unbiased"): $10/4 = 2.5$
> Standard deviation (descriptive): $\sqrt{2} = 1.41$
> Standard deviation (inferential): $\sqrt{2.5} = 1.58$

distribution is symmetrical. Other percentiles are also useful. You might want to know for any given DV value what percent of the measurements obtained were greater than that value and what percent were less. A score of "40" on a math test for Susie becomes a lot more meaningful if you are also given the information that 40 is the 75th percentile of the distribution of all the math test scores. Then you know that Susie scored better than 75 percent of the other children taking the same test (and worse than 25 percent). Percentiles of a distribution correspond to areas under parts of a frequency histogram or polygon. If you drew a vertical line at the DV score corresponding to the 75th percentile, you would divide the frequency polygon (or histogram) into two parts; a lower one containing .75 of the total area under the curve and an upper one containing .25. Knowing what areas of the distribution lie below or above a particular value of an intervally scaled DV will be very important in doing statistical tests of inference, as you'll discover in the next chapter.

For any "normal" frequency distribution, a DV value that lies one standard deviation above the mean automatically lies at the 84th percentile. The DV value equal to the mean less one standard deviation is the value for the distribution's 16th percentile. Therefore, for any normal distribution we can say that 68 percent (84 percent – 16 percent) of the observations, or about 2/3 of them, will fall between the mean minus one standard deviation and the mean plus one standard deviation.

If you go two standard deviations above the mean along your DV scale, then your corresponding DV value will lie at the 98th percentile, providing your observations follow a normal distribution. The DV value corresponding to two standard deviations below the mean will be at the 2nd percentile. Therefore, 96 percent of any normal distribution will be between the DV measures corresponding to two standard deviations below the mean and two standard deviations above the mean.

You can see from the preceding discussion how useful the standard deviation can be as a descriptive statistic for normal distributions. Not only is it a measure of variability, it also allows us to estimate easily any percentile we may need for a particular observation without having to return to raw scores. However, keep in mind that this relationship between the standard deviation and the percentile is true if, and only if, the frequency distribution for which we calculate the standard deviation is in fact a normal distribution.

INTERVAL DATA, NONNORMAL DISTRIBUTIONS

Can We Use the Standard Deviation for Nonnormal Distributions?

The more skewed (asymmetrical) our frequency distribution is, the less its standard deviation can tell us. For one thing, the relationship between standard deviations and percentiles is disrupted, and we can no longer accurately estimate percentile values by knowing the mean and standard deviation. No longer do 68 percent of the scores necessarily fall between the mean plus and minus one standard deviation or 96 percent between the mean plus and minus two standard deviations. Still, if the frequency distribution, although not normal, is smooth and unimodal with a mode falling within one standard deviation from the mean, the mean plus and minus one standard deviation will include at least 55 percent of the cases, and the mean plus and minus two standard deviations will include at least 89 percent (Freeman, 1965, p. 62). Thus, the standard deviation may still be a useful measure of variability for unimodal distributions that are only slightly skewed.

Percentile-Based Measures of Variability

If the frequency distribution is badly skewed or bimodal, we may want a measure of variability that makes no assumption about the normality of the data, a measure that is "distribution-free." In this case, we must calculate the percentile values directly from the raw data, just as we directly calculate the median (50th percentile) for an asymmetrical distribution rather than assuming it equal to the mean. The procedure for calculating percentiles directly from frequency distributions of raw data can be found in almost any beginning statistics book. When you calculate any particular percentile, you are looking for that DV value below which a certain percent of your observations fall.

The **decile range** is one distribution-free measure of variability. It is found by taking the difference between the DV measure corresponding to the 90th percentile and that corresponding to the 10th. The middle 80 percent of the distribution will be located within the decile range.

The **interquartile range** is the difference between the DV value that corresponds to the 75th percentile and the DV value that corresponds to the 25th percentile. The interquartile range encloses the middle half of the observations.

The **semi-interquartile range** is simply the interquartile range divided by two. The median plus and minus the semi-interquartile range encloses the middle half (approximately) of the distribution.

All these percentile-based measures of variability remain true in terms of the proportion of the distribution they enclose, no matter what the shape of the frequency distribution. That is why they are called "distribution-free" measures of variability.

MEASUREMENT OF VARIABILITY FOR ORDINAL SCALES

Percentiles can be obtained for ordinally scaled DVs just as for intervally scaled ones. To determine the 90th percentile, for example, we would rank our ordinal observations from highest to lowest and determine that ordinal DV value below which 90 percent of our observations fell. If there were 50 total observations, then whatever DV value was 5th in rank would be our 90th-percentile value. Exact procedures for doing this are described in statistics books such as Freeman's *Elementary Applied Statistics* (1965).

The variability measure used for ordinally scaled DVs can be either the *decile range,* which encloses the middle 80 percent of the observations; the *interquartile range,* which encloses the middle 50 percent; or the *semi-interquartile range,* which equals half the interquartile range. All of these range measures of variability will increase as the ordinal DV measures become more variable and the frequency distribution broadens.

MEASUREMENT OF VARIABILITY FOR NOMINAL SCALES

The **variation ratio** is a statistic useful for summarizing the variability of DVs measured on nominal scales. It is simply the proportion of the total frequency that falls outside the modal class. It tells us how good the mode is as a typical value for the distribution. When the variation ratio is small, we know that most of the observations fell in the modal class. When it is large, we know that while one class did have a greater frequency than the others, still many of the observations were not in that class.

If we return to our toy-selection data for the preschoolers that was summarized in Table 5.7 (page 163), we can determine the variation ratios as well as the modes for our different groups. These statistics are given in Table 5.9. From these descrip-

Table 5.9 Summary Statistics for Toy Selection of Two Groups of Preschoolers

Group	Sample Size	Modal Toy Selected	Variation Ratio
Normal boys	12	Gun	.50
Normal girls	12	Doll	.42
Impaired boys	46	Gun	.56
Impaired girls	20	Hammer	.58

tive statistics, we can see that while there was a typical toy selected by each category of preschooler, a substantial number of children, in most cases the majority, chose a different toy. This weakens our statement of how typical the modal choices are for these groups.

The descriptive statistics appropriate for nominal scales are often used for weak-ordinal scales when the total frequency of cases is small or the number of DV categories is few. For instance, it is rather difficult to calculate percentiles for only ten cases distributed on a three-category scale. In this situation, we might provide more information by reporting the mode and variation ratio rather than the median and decile range.

RECAPITULATION

for MEASURES OF VARIABILITY

Frequency distributions differ in their variability; that is, in how closely their scores tend to cluster around a central value or spread out along a DV scale. A *measure of variability* is one that will increase in size as the distribution becomes more spread out. The *variance* and its positive square root, the *standard deviation,* are appropriate measures of variability for normally distributed, intervally scaled DV measures. A *"normal" frequency distribution* is one that follows a symmetrical, unimodal, bell-shaped curve that can be fit by a special equation. The *descriptive variance* of a set of intervally scaled data is the average of the sum of the squared deviations of each observation from the mean. The *inferential variance,* a number slightly larger than the descriptive variance, is reported when the researchers intend to use their results to predict future results. If a distribution is normal, 68 percent of it will lie between one standard deviation below and one standard deviation above the mean, and 96 percent of the distribution will lie between two standard deviations below and two standard deviations above the mean.

If the frequency distribution for an intervally scaled DV is strikingly nonnormal in its characteristics, then one of the *percentile-based measures* of variability should be used. The *decile range,* the 90th minus the 10th percentile, encloses the middle 80 percent of the distribution. The *interquartile range,* the 75th minus the 25th percentile, encloses the middle 50 percent of the distribution. The *semi-interquartile range* is half of the interquartile range.

Ordinally scaled DVs must be summarized by statistics based on percentile values obtained directly from the *ranking* of the raw data. The median (50th percentile), which corresponds to the ordinal DV measure with the middle rank, is used as the measure of central tendency. Any one of the percentile-based variability measures suggested above for nonnormal, interval data can be used as the appropriate measure of variability for ordinal scales.

The measure of variability for nominally scaled DVs is the *variation ratio,* the proportion of cases falling outside the modal class. The variation ratio is also a useful measure of variability for weak-ordinal scales with few categories and/or a small total number of observations.

BEHAVIORAL OBJECTIVES

for MEASURES OF VARIABILITY

1. Explain each of the following and give a general description of how it is calculated: descriptive variance, inferential variance, standard deviation, interquartile range, semi-interquartile range, decile range, variation ratio.

2. Describe the measure of variability and the measure of central tendency best suited to each of the following situations:
   a. interval data, normal or close-to-normal distribution.
   b. interval data, badly skewed distribution.
   c. ordinal data.
   d. ordinal data, few categories (weak-ordinal).
   e. nominal data.

3. Describe the characteristics of normally distributed data. Sketch a "normal curve."

4. Tell what proportion of a distribution (assume it's a normal distribution):
   a. lies between plus and minus one standard deviation of the mean.
   b. lies between plus and minus two standard deviations of the mean.
   c. lies within an interquartile range.
   d. lies within a decile range.

5. Given a list of statements, identify for which one(s) of the following the statements are true: variance, standard deviation, semi-interquartile range, decile range, interquartile range, variation ratio.

6. Given the description of the results of an experiment, choose an appropriate measure of variability and defend your choice.

7. Given the description of an actual experiment, identify the measure of variability used, and say why it was or was not appropriate.

SAMPLE TEST QUESTIONS

for MEASURES OF VARIABILITY

1. Refer to the results of the McKay *et al.* (1978) study reported on page 166.
   a. What measure of variability was reported here?
   b. Discuss the reasons this type of measure of variability would be appropriate to these data.
   c. Discuss the reason(s) this measure of variability might not be appropriate to these data.
   d. How does the variability of the untreated (T_0) group and the group that had one year of treatment (T_1) compare with that of the:

    1) theoretical normal distribution for all children.

    2) HS group.

    3) T_4 group (children with four years of treatment).

2. Refer back to the Pronko and Bowles (1949) study on taste identification of cola beverages (page 174, Sample Test Question 3).

    a. Make a table that shows separately for each of the three brands sampled (Hyde Park, Kruger, and Spur) the typical identification of each and the variability of identification.

    b. Looking at your summary descriptive statistical table, do you think there is good evidence that the three local colas are differently identified?

    c. Justify your selection of a particular type of measure of central tendency and a particular type of measure of variability for these data.

3. If you have a pocket calculator, does it give a descriptive or an inferential variance?

4. For the following statements, identify which one(s) of the following terms they characterize: mean ($\bar{X}$), median (X_{50}), mode (M), variance (V), standard deviation (SD), interquartile range (IQR), semi-interquartile range (SIQR), decile range (DR), variation ratio (VR).

    a. Equals the 50th percentile.

    b. Proportion of observations falling in all other categories than the one with the highest frequency.

    c. Appropriate measure of variability for intervally scaled data that are approximately normally distributed.

    d. The mean plus and minus it encloses 68 percent of the distribution for normally distributed, interval data.

    e. Average of squared deviations from the mean.

    f. Must consider when calculating them whether you are using them to describe a sample or to make inferences from a sample to a wider group.

    g. Equal to one another for any symmetrical distribution.

    h. Most appropriate measure of central tendency for a skewed distribution of intervally scaled data.

    i. Appropriate measure of central tendency for ordinally scaled data.

    j. Class (or mid-point of the class) with the highest frequency of observations.

    k. Appropriate measure of central tendency for nominally scaled data.

    l. Measure of variability based on percentiles.

    m. 50th percentile no matter what the distribution shape.

    n. Distribution-free statistics.

    o. Appropriate measure of variability for ordinal distributions.

    p. 90th percentile minus the 10th.

    q. Normal distribution descriptive statistics.

r. Appropriate measure of variability for badly skewed distributions of intervally scaled measures.

s. Square root of the average of squared deviations from the mean.

t. One-half of the difference between the 75th percentile and the 25th.

u. Measures which increase in size as the variability of a distribution increases.

v. Cuts the area of any distribution in half.

SECTION 5: *z*-SCORES AND STANDARD SCORES

When our DV is an interval one, and the frequency distribution is normal or reasonably close to normal, we can use the mean and standard deviation to figure directly the percentile value of any individual score without having to go to the trouble of ranking all the scores. All we need to do this is a table that is printed at the back of most statistics books. This table will be called something like: "Areas under the Normal Curve," "Normal Curve Table," or "*z*-Score Table." These tables may vary somewhat in form, but they all give the same information; they all can tell us what proportion of the area under a normal curve will be cut off by different DV values.

Giving the percentile value of a DV score is a much more meaningful way of describing a person's performance than giving the **raw score.** As we discussed in Section 4, saying that Susie has a score of "40" on a math test doesn't communicate very much. However, saying that her math score was at the 75th percentile for her third-grade class conveys much more about her math performance. In order to change Susie's raw score to a percentile you have to be able to figure out something called a "*z*-score."

GOING FROM RAW DATA TO A "*z*-SCORE"

The "*z*-score" for any particular DV value is simply a number telling us how many standard deviations a raw DV score is above or below the mean of the entire distribution. Suppose on her class's spelling test Susie had a score of 30. The mean score on this spelling test for the whole class was 40, and the standard deviation was 5. We could characterize Susie's score by saying that it was two standard deviations below the mean and assign her a *z*-score of -2. Another child, Mary, with a score of 43 on the same test would be 3/5ths of a standard deviation above the mean and, accordingly, would have a *z*-score of $+.6$. The relationship between the interval scale of this raw DV measure and the *z*-scale could be diagrammed as in Fig. 5.12.

If you know how to read a *z*-table, you can find out that Susie's *z*-score of -2 cuts off only the lower .0128 (1.3 percent) of a normal distribution while Mary's *z*-score of $+.6$ cuts off .7257 (73 percent). It looks like Susie is pretty near the bottom of her group as a speller while Mary is doing better than nearly three-quarters of the other children. Our description of Susie's and Mary's spelling performances is greatly improved by reporting *z*-scores or percentiles rather than giving the raw test scores.

FIG. 5.12

Correspondence between scores on a spelling test and z-scores if the test mean is 40 and the test standard deviation is 5.

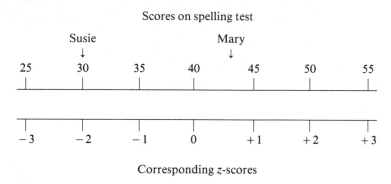

Life would be a lot simpler if all z-tables were in the same form. Unfortunately, they are not, and consumers of statistics must be alert to this. For some devilish reason, most z-tables report the area that lies between the mean and a particular z-score. Table 5.10 is an abbreviated example of this kind of z-table. This way of showing things has the annoying consequence of forcing us to do some calculations, if we want to use the z-table to figure percentiles. The percentile, remember, corresponds to *all* of the distribution which lies *below* a particular z-score. Since we know that the mean cuts a normal distribution in half, the area lying below the mean must be .5 (50 percent). You can use this fact to figure your percentiles based on the partial areas given in the z-table. If the z-score is greater than zero (positive), all you

Table 5.10 Abbreviated Normal Curve Table (Areas given are between the mean and the indicated z-score.)

z-Score	Area between Mean and z-Score
0.00	.0000
(0.43)	(.1667)
0.50	.1915
(0.60)	(.2257)
1.00	.3413
1.50	.4332
2.00	.4772
2.50	.4938
3.00	.4987

need to do is to add .5 to the area given in the table. If the *z*-score is less than zero (negative), you will need to subtract the area given in the table from .5 to find the area left in the lower tail. Rather than trying to remember when to add or subtract, it is better to draw a little sketch of the normal distribution, such as is done in Fig. 5.13. You can then locate your *z*-score approximately on this distribution. According to the description at the beginning of the table as to what area of the normal curve is being reported, you can shade in that area on the sketch. Then you can easily see for your *z*-score whether you need to add to or subtract from .5 to get the percentile.

FIG. 5.13

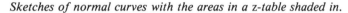

Sketches of normal curves with the areas in a z-table shaded in.

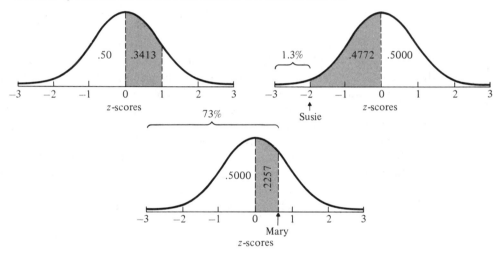

GOING FROM A PERCENTILE TO A RAW SCORE

Sometimes you need to work in the opposite direction. You may want to determine what the corresponding raw DV value would be for a certain percentile. In this case, you can enter the normal distribution table with your area and find the corresponding *z*-score. Then, remembering that what a *z*-score tells us is how many standard deviations we are from the mean, you can use this *z*-score to calculate the desired raw score. Suppose for the spelling test we wanted to know what test score corresponded to the bottom third of the class, having decided beforehand that the worst third of our students would be given special tutoring. This would be the 33rd percentile, corresponding to an area of .3333 in the lower tail of our distribution of spelling scores. The only *z*-table we can lay our hands on is one like Table 5.10 which gives just the area between the mean and a particular *z*-score. Since we want a different area, that of the lower tail, we subtract .3333 from .5000 (if you don't follow this, make a sketch) to find the area that will be listed in the table. This leaves us with an area of .1667 between our z-score and the distribution mean. We look up this area and find that it corresponds to a z-score of .43. It would be a −.43, of course, since it is for the lower half of the distribution. So the raw score corresponding to the 33rd percentile would lie .43 standard deviations below the mean. The spelling test, remember, had a mean of 40 and a standard deviation of 5. The DV value we want must be less than 40 (the mean) and greater than 34 (one standard deviation below the mean). It actually is *37.85* (40 − (.43)(5)). We would decide that any child with a score of less than 38 would be earmarked for further spelling instruction. It certainly looks like our Susie gets some tutoring.

STANDARD SCORES

The z-score is obviously a very useful descriptive statistic, but the fact that it involves decimals and negative numbers makes some people nervous. One trick is to convert the z-score to yet another number, called a **standard score.** Most commonly, the mean of a set of standard scores is arbitrarily made to be 100 and the standard deviation something like 10. Raw scores are converted to z-scores using the mean and standard deviation of the distribution of raw scores. These z-scores are multiplied by 10 (the new standard deviation) and then have 100 (the new mean) added to them. In Fig. 5.14 we apply this process to the spelling test.

FIG. 5.14

Correspondence between scores on a spelling test, z-scores, and standard scores.

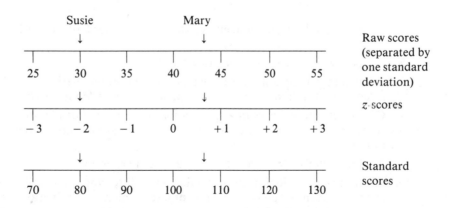

IQ scores are standardized scores. The actual test scores are converted via z-scores to standard scores with a mean of 100 and a standard deviation of between 10 and 20 depending on which IQ test you are talking about. If an IQ test uses a standard deviation of 10, then you can immediately figure out that someone with an

IQ of 130 on this test is three standard deviations above the mean of the population on which the IQ test was standardized. Consulting a z-table would tell you that this corresponded to a percentile value of 99.87 percent, meaning that only .13 percent of the population of people would score higher.

RECAPITULATION

for z-SCORES AND STANDARD SCORES

Interval data that is normally distributed can be converted to *z-scores* by subtracting the mean from each score and then dividing this difference by the standard deviation for the sample. A z-score tells you how many standard deviations a particular score is from the mean. These z-scores can be looked up in a table to find how much of the distribution would lie below and above the corresponding raw score. Thus the z-score can be used to determine the *percentile* of the *raw score* (the percent of observations with values equal to or less than that score). The z-scores may also be converted to *"standard scores"* which have an arbitrary mean and standard deviation. This is done by multiplying each z-score by the new standard deviation and then adding the new mean to it. When reporting an individual's score on a test, it is much more meaningful to give a z-score, a standard score, or a percentile than to give the raw score. Such derived scores express the person's performance relative to that of the whole group.

BEHAVIORAL OBJECTIVES

for z-SCORES AND STANDARD SCORES

1. Given a sketch of a normal curve, identify its: lower half, upper half, lower tail, upper tail, mean, middle portion.

2. Explain what is meant by a "raw" score.

3. Given a mean and a standard deviation for a normal distribution, figure out the z-score or standard score for any single raw score from the distribution.

4. Given a mean and a standard deviation for a normal distribution, convert a z-score or a standard score into the corresponding raw score from that distribution.

5. Explain what a "z-score" is. Give a specific example.

6. Given a z-score, look it up in a table and tell to what percentile value it corresponds. Given the percentile value of a score along with the raw-score-distribution mean and standard deviation, use a z-table to convert the percentile to a raw score.

7. Given a verbal description of someone's test performance expressed as a z-score or a standard score, explain what it means.

SAMPLE TEST QUESTIONS

for z-SCORES AND STANDARD SCORES

1. In going over the file of a boy named Bob, newly admitted to your Summer Remedial Education Program, you find that on the end-of-the year, gradewide tests given in his school he scored 27 in math, 42 in reading comprehension, and 31 in drawing skills. You call his school and obtain the following information:

Test Subject	Mean Score for all Third-Graders	Standard Deviation for all Third-Graders
Math	27	2
Reading	50	4
Drawing	25	3

   a. Calculate Bob's z-score for each of the tests.

   b. Find a z-table somewhere and figure out the corresponding percentiles.

   c. What assumption did you make when you carried out step (b)?

   d. Discuss Bob's abilities in the different subject areas on which he was tested.

   e. How would you plan Bob's summer curriculum in the remedial program?

2. Refer to the McKay *et al.* (1978) study reported on page 166.

   a. Consider a child from the T_1 distribution with an IQ score equal to its mean (82).

      1) What would be the z-score for this child if he were a member of the theoretical IQ distribution (mean of 100, standard deviation of 16)?

      2) What percentile would this child's score correspond to in terms of the theoretical distribution of IQ? (You'll need a z-table. Before you start fooling with it, ask yourself whether your resulting percentile should be more or less than 50 percent.)

   b. Consider a child from the HS distribution with a score lying at its mean (109.2). Where would this "average child" from the HS sample fall on the distribution obtained for the T_0 children (mean of 79.4, standard deviation of 9.7)? What percent of the T_0 children does the average HS child exceed in IQ?

3. If you were told that a person had a "standard score" on a test of 169:

   a. What would you need to know to convert this standard score to a z-score?

   b. What would you then do to convert the z-score to a percentile?

   c. What further information would you need to convert the z-score to the raw score on the original test?

SECTION 6: MEASURES OF CORRELATION

Whenever we measure subjects with two or more DV scales, we may want to know whether the measures on the different scales are associated with one another. It may be that knowledge of a subject's measurement on one DV scale will allow us to predict what measure we'll get for the subject on a second DV scale. Does the type of job a person holds, whether blue-collar or white-collar, allow us to predict whether or not that person will have a heart attack? Many studies have reported an association between a person's job category and occurrence of cardiovascular problems. Does knowledge of a person's drug-using habits enable us to make a better-than-chance guess about his or her ethnic identity? The San Francisco survey we discussed on page 141 found that for young adult women, whites were more likely to have used marijuana than blacks.

Much of our daily lives is controlled by predictions that people have made about us based on such associations or "correlations." If, for example, you are a young, urban-dwelling, unmarried, cigarette-smoking male, you will pay more for your car insurance, no matter what your personal driving skill may be. This is because insurance rates are based on correlations, and strong correlations have been found between accident rates and the variables of age, place of residence, sex, marital status, and cigarette smoking. Your chance of employment may be modified by your score on personality tests, the results of which have been found to correlate with success in particular jobs. When you go to the vocational counselor at your community college you may be given, among other things, a "vocational-interest" test in which you are asked a lot of questions about what you like to do that seem to have no direct relation to any possible work future. You may think your counselor spaced out altogether when he suggests you consider medicine because you like golf! But, these interest tests were devised by observing correlations between success in certain occupations and the pattern of outside interests.

CHARACTERISTICS OF A STATISTIC OF CORRELATION

A statistic that expresses the degree of correlation between two variables should be one that grows larger when measures on two variables are highly associated and smaller when there is no association. In addition, a statistic of correlation should have a direction, for two ordered variables can be associated either in a positive or a negative manner. If, for example, we held body weight constant, there would be a high predictive association across individuals between height and waist measurements. However, this association would be negative: the taller a person of a given weight is, the skinnier we can predict he or she will be. We can say there is a high correlation since from knowing height we can make a very good guess as to waist measurement. We call the correlation negative since the more the people have of one DV the less we can predict they'll have of the other.

Statistics of correlation vary between 0, indicating no correlation, and 1, indicating perfect correlation. For ordered variables (ordinal or interval), the correlation statistic needs a sign, − or + , indicating whether the correlation is negative or positive. Many (but not all) correlation statistics are given the abbreviation *r*. If two variables are "perfectly correlated" then a correlation statistic calculated for them will be near −1 or +1. Few DVs show perfect correlation unless they are just two different measures of the same thing. For example, measurement of a person's height in inches and in cm should have a perfect **positive correlation** of +1 unless we are unusually sloppy in how we do our measurements. The correlation between outdoor air temperature and the size of our heating bill over a year should show a near-perfect **negative correlation.** A near-zero correlation is likely to be found between our height and the size of our heating bill.

CHOICE OF A STATISTIC OF CORRELATION

In choosing the appropriate statistic of correlation for two DVs, we need first to know *what types of scales the DVs are measured on.* Are we correlating two intervally scaled variables? Are we correlating an intervally scaled variable with an ordinally scaled one? Since there are three scales possible for our DVs, there are six possible combinations of them (interval-interval, ordinal-ordinal, nominal-nominal, interval-ordinal, interval-nominal, ordinal-nominal). If you can identify the scale of each of the two DVs you want to correlate, you can make use of a book like Freeman's *Elementary Applied Statistics* (1965) which devotes a chapter to each of the possible combinations of scales and shows you how to correlate them.

When dealing with interval scales, we must also ask ourselves whether or not the data are normally distributed. The most popular statistic of correlation for interval scales assumes both of the DVs being correlated have normal frequency distributions and may be a misleading number if this assumption is not true for one or both variables. *Therefore, in doing interval-interval correlations we must check the shapes of our frequency distributions before choosing a statistic of correlation.*

If we are dealing with ordinal scales, we need to assess whether or not we can rank the individuals on each DV according to their scale values without a great number of "tied ranks" (two or more persons with the same DV value). If one of the ordinal scales has only a few categories to assign to the subjects, we will find that when we attempt to rank or order subjects we'll have a large number of subjects assigned the same scale value to whom we must give the same ranking. This is referred to as a "tie in rank." Some of the statistics of correlation devised for ordinal scales can't handle tied ranks very easily. *So, if one of the variables you are correlating is ordinal, you must ask yourself whether you can rank subjects on it without a large number of ties in rank.*

Sometimes, we will want to correlate two DVs measured on different scales. One way of doing this is to reduce the scale of the more complicated one to the level of the less complicated one. If we have an interval DV and an ordinal DV, we can change the interval one to ordinal by ranking and then use an ordinal-ordinal statistic of correlation. If we have a weak-ordinal scale with only a few categories which we want to correlate with a nominal scale, we can treat the ordinal-scale values as if they were only nominal and do a nominal-nominal type correlation. However, whenever we simplify a scale in this way we are losing some of the information in our data and are making a less sensitive measure of the degree of association between our two variables. If we have such a combination of scales, we must ask ourselves whether we can afford to simplify one of the scales or whether we'd better find a correlation statistic appropriate to the mixture of scales.

SCATTERPLOTS

If the two DVs that we want to associate are measured on ordered (ordinal or interval) scales, we can draw a graph called a **scatterplot** to get a visual impression of their degree of association. In Fig. 5.15 are examples of scatterplots for several different degrees of correlation.

FIG. 5.15

Sample scatterplots for different degrees of correlation between two DVs.

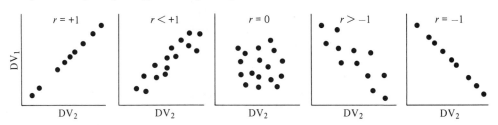

The guidelines for drawing scatterplots are simple. It doesn't matter which variable we put on which axis since both variables are DVs. Just as in drawing frequency histograms (or any other graph), we should make sure that the body of our finished graph is roughly square in shape to give a true visual impression of the degree of association. This means spacing the categories for each variable so that the entire range of observations takes about the same distance along its axis. Let's do some scatterplots for the multiple DV measures reported in Table 2.1 (page 31) taken on the activity of preschool children. Since your purpose in that study was to develop different ways of measuring the children's activity level, you'd hope that the different DV measures would correlate fairly well.

First, let's look at the association between the teacher's categorization of children on a three-point scale and the ratings assigned the children by your student observers. Since both of these DVs were ordinal, the equal spacing between the categories in the graph is for convenience. Since both measures are DVs, we can assign either one to the x-axis and the other to the y-axis as we wish.

From the scatterplot of these data in Fig. 5.16, we can see that there is a positive correlation between the teacher's assessment of the children's activity category and the ratings given by the student observers, but this correlation is by no means perfect. Note that of the nine children given a 2 by the student observers (slightly active), over half were described by the teacher as normal rather than withdrawn. Of the five children given a 4 by the student observers, two were called hyperactive by the teacher and the rest normal. Knowing the student-observer ratings does not allow us to guess with complete accuracy what the teacher's assessment will be, but our guesses would certainly be better than chance. To find out the exact amount of correlation, we need to do an ordinal-ordinal correlation, and it must be one that is not bothered by tied ranks since our two ordinal scales have relatively few categories, and several children fall into the same category.

FIG. 5.16

Scatterplot showing the degree of association between teacher's categorization and student-observer ratings of the activity of 24 preschoolers.

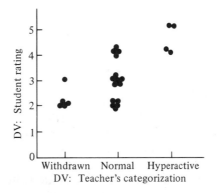

We could also look at the degree of association between the number of toy switches the children made, your third DV, and the ratings assigned by the student observers. In this case, we'd be associating an interval with an ordinal scale. Again, it doesn't matter on which axis we plot which variable, and the equal spacing of our ordinal categories will be arbitrary. Looking at these data plotted in Fig. 5.17, it again appears that there is a positive correlation between these two measures of the children's activity levels. In order to find the exact degree of correlation, we would have to calculate the appropariate correlation statistic for an interval-ordinal association.

FIG. 5.17

Scatterplot showing the degree of association between the student-observers' ratings of activity and the number of toy switches observed for 24 preschoolers.

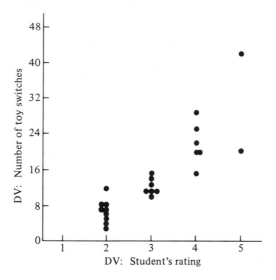

PEARSON'S PRODUCT-MOMENT COEFFICIENT OF CORRELATION FOR INTERVAL-INTERVAL ASSOCIATIONS

Pearson's product-moment correlation is probably the most commonly used (and misused) descriptive statistic of correlation in the research literature. It is based on calculation of the variances for each DV separately as well as their "covariance," or tendency to vary together. Obviously, then, it should only be used for DV measures for which calculation of the variance is appropriate, that is, intervally scaled DVs with approximately normal frequency distributions. Unfortunately, for many researchers, this seems to be the only type of correlation statistic they know, and you will see it mistakenly used for either nonintervally scaled measures, or for interval measures that are either not normally distributed or for which there are too few measures to make any reasonable guess about how they are distributed.

Any statistics book will tell you how to calculate Pearson's correlation coefficient. Doing so is little more complicated than calculating the variance for each DV separately. Figure 5.18 shows two scatterplots of association between intervally scaled variables with their accompanying correlation coefficients. The first example investigates the degree of association between students' cumulative GPA (grade point average) in college and their self-report of the number of hours they spend outside class each week studying. The second association examined for the same students is between their self-report of how many hours per week they spend in social activities and the number of hours they spend studying. The actual scores for these three DVs are given in Table 5.11.

FIG. 5.18

Scatterplots of estimated hours spent studying versus GPA and versus estimated hours spent in social activities.

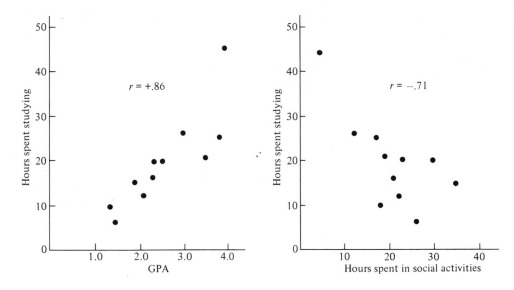

Table 5.11   Student GPAs and Self-Reports of Hours per Week Spent in Studying and Social Activities

Student	GPA	Hours Studying		Hours in Social Activities	
		Number	Rank	Number	Rank
A	2.35	20	5.5th	23	4th
B	2.10	12	9th	22	5th
C	3.80	25	3rd	17	9th
D	3.95	45	1st	4	11th
E	1.38	10	10th	18	8th
F	2.50	20	5.5th	30	2nd
G	3.50	21	4th	19	7th
H	1.90	15	8th	35	1st
I	3.00	26	2nd	12	10th
J	2.25	16	7th	21	6th
K	1.42	6	11th	26	3rd

From looking at the scatterplots in Fig. 5.18, we can see that for these students the estimated number of hours of study is positively correlated with GPA. There also appears to be a negative correlation, perhaps not as strong, between the estimated number of hours spent studying and the estimated number of hours of social activity. The correlation coefficients, +.86 and −.71, support our visual impressions of the degree of association.

"SPEARMAN'S RHO" FOR ORDINAL-ORDINAL CORRELATIONS BETWEEN RANKED DATA

Another correlation coefficient you will frequently see is **Spearman's rho,** also known as the "rank-order" correlation coefficient. This is an ordinal-ordinal correlation, but it is often used to correlate intervally scaled DVs the distributions of which are possibly not normal. Sometimes with intervally scaled data, Pearson's r can give you a mistaken impression of the degree of association between two DVs if there are a few extreme values on one or both of them. Consider the correlation between estimated number of hours spent studying and number of hours of social activity graphed in Fig. 5.18. If you removed subject D (he said he studied 45 hours a week and partied only 4 hours) from the scatterplot, the remaining points would still show a negative association, but one that looks much less strong. Subject D seems to be having a very large influence on the Pearson's correlation. You might want a correlation coefficient more representative of the rest of the group and not so heavily influenced by a single saintly subject.

A solution to this problem of skewed distributions for interval data is to rank the subjects on each DV from highest to lowest and correlate their ranks, according to Spearman's formula. The rankings for the students' estimates of their hours spent studying and their hours spent in social activities are also given in Table 5.11. In the case of "tied ranks," of individuals all sharing the same rank, each subject is given the rank that is the average of the tied ranks. Thus if subjects X, Y, and Z were all tied for ranks 8, 9, and 10, then each one of them would be assigned rank "9" and the next subject in order would be given rank 11. Notice that for number of hours spent studying there is such a tie between subjects A and F for ranks 5 and 6. They are both assigned rank 5.5 and the next subject (J) is given rank 7.

The Pearson's r calculated for the association between the actual number of hours spent studying and the actual number of hours spent in social activities was −.71 (Fig. 5.18). If, instead, the ranks of these two DVs are correlated with Spearman's formula, the correlation coefficient drops to −.62. This discrepancy between the two correlation coefficients indicates that, as we suspected, the one extreme case of subject D inflated the value of Pearson's r.

When you have relatively few observations on your intervally scaled DVs and are concerned that extreme values might produce misleading correlations, it is often useful to calculate and to report both Pearson's correlation coefficient for the raw data and Spearman's correlation coefficient for the ranks. When the two are fairly close in value you can feel reasonably sure that you do not have a spurious correlation produced by a few deviant values.

Spearman's rho is useful as well for correlating DV measures that consist of nothing more than having your scoring system rank the subjects on a variable from most to least without ever assigning interval measures at all. However, if your DV measure is an ordinal scale with many fewer categories (measures) than the total number of subjects, there will be too many "tied ranks" for calculation of Spearman's rho and you'll have to seek a correlation such as **Goodman and Kruskal's coefficient of association** that can handle tied ranks.

NOMINAL-NOMINAL AND OTHER
TYPES OF CORRELATION

There is not much sense in going through the multitude of correlation coefficients statisticians have devised for every possible combination of scales and every possible special situation. It is sufficient for us to know that there are a variety and that we must use the one appropriate for our mixture of scales. Table 5.12 gives at least one suggestion for each of the possible combinations of scales. Once you've identified what you need for your research, find a statistics book that describes how to do the correlation and see whether your data meet the restrictions of the particular correlation model.

Table 5.12   Correlation Coefficients for Different Combinations of DV Scales

	Nominal	*Ordinal*	*Interval*
Nominal	Guttman's coefficient of predictability	Wilcoxon's model for nominal-ordinal association	Correlation ratio
Ordinal	----------------------------	Goodman and Kruskal's coefficient of ordinal association Kendall's tau } not good for Spearman's rho } tied ranks	Jaspen's coefficient of multiserial correlation
Interval	----------------------------	--	Pearson's *r* (Spearman's rho if data are badly skewed)

USING THE CORRELATION COEFFICIENT
TO MEASURE RELIABILITY OF A DV SCALE

Correlation coefficients can be used to establish the **reliability** or consistency of a DV scale. If we've done nothing to change our subjects, we'd like to know that repeatedly using our DV scale would result in each subject scoring the same in relation to the rest of the group. For a given experiment, we may need to measure subjects repeatedly with the same test or we may want to develop two different but equivalent forms of a test. Before we can use the scores from these tests to establish anything else of interest, we have to demonstrate that the test-retest correlations are high and that our DV scale continues to measure the same thing about our subjects. Much care is taken to establish that tests are reliable when developing intelligence tests, attitude surveys, and tests of academic performance.

The question of reliability of our measurement process also arises when we use more than one observer. We don't want our DV measure to change just because a different person is doing the observing. We can establish "inter-observer reliability" by having our observers score some of the subjects simultaneously but independently. If there is a high correlation between their observations, we can feel much more secure that our different observers are actually observing the same things about the subjects.

USING THE CORRELATION COEFFICIENT
TO MEASURE VALIDITY OF DV SCALES

The **validity** of a DV scale is more difficult to determine than its reliability. Validity estimates how well a DV is measuring what it claims to measure. One way of establishing validity is to measure the "same" thing a number of different ways. For example, in the preschool study discussed in Chapter 2 (page 30) you used three different ways of measuring activity levels of the children. We can use correlation coefficients to "validate" these three scales against one another. First, we can see how well the teacher's verbal categorization of the children agreed with the student-observer ratings. The scatterplot for the association of these two DV scales is given in Fig. 5.16. Since both of the scales are ordinal ones with relatively few categories, Table 5.12 suggests we use Goodman and Kruskal's coefficient of ordinal association. Doing the appropriate calculations (Freeman, 1965, p. 85) results in a correlation coefficient of +.92. Next we can see whether our third way of measuring activity—the number of toy switches made by a child in one-half hour—also correlates with the teacher categorizations and with the student ratings. Reference to Table 5.12 suggests that this interval measure can best be correlated with an ordinal measure by using Jaspen's coefficient of multiserial correlation. Doing so (Freeman, 1965, pp. 131–139), we find that the number of toy switches correlates +.94 with the student ratings and +.93 with the teacher categorizations. The high agreement among these three different scales is a good indication that all our DVs are measuring the same aspect of the children.

There is not much point in attempting to validate DV measures that are not in and of themselves reliable. When developing any technique for measuring behavior, the first step is to establish the reliability of the technique. The next step is to validate the measurement process against other DVs thought to be measuring the same thing.

INTERPRETING CORRELATIONS

Correlation coefficients may be the most misinterpreted and overinterpreted descriptive statistics reported in research literature. Taken at face value, all a correlation coefficient does is describe the degree of association found between two DVs in a particular research setting for a given set of subjects. When trying to decide what conclusion you should come to about your own or someone else's results from looking at correlation coefficients, the first step is to see whether the appropriate type of correlation coefficient was calculated for the DV scales. Pearson's r statistic in particular is often used inappropriately to correlate either ordinal or badly skewed interval data.

Researchers often slip too easily from reporting a descriptive correlation coefficient to interpreting it as a prediction of future association between two DVs. This interpretation cannot in fact be made without doing a further inferential statistical test of the correlation, to be discussed in the next chapter. Descriptive correlation coefficients, especially if calculated for a relatively small number of subjects, can easily change their value when the same DVs are measured on a different set of subjects or even when measured again on the same set of subjects.

Another factor to consider is the actual size of the correlation. A correlation coefficient that may have been shown by an inferential test to be repeatable may still be too small in size to have any usefulness in prediction. If you have two DVs that correlate with a correlation coefficient of "r" then only "r^2" of the variations of one of them can be explained by the pattern of variations in the other and $(1 - r^2)$ of the variation is left unexplained. This means that a correlation of, say, .5 between two DVs actually means that knowing the variations in one of the DVs will explain only 25 percent (.25) of the variations in the other, leaving 75 percent of the variation unexplained. This is why persons developing reliable tests require correlations of at least .85 or more between two forms of the same test before they declare them to be reasonably equivalent. You may run across studies that make a big deal of correlations of .2 or .3 because inferential statistical tests have shown them to be real and repeatable. Nonetheless, such small correlations have relatively little predictive value. For a correlation coefficient to have practical meaning, it should be of fairly large size.

Even if a correlation is real and reasonably large, we should never make the mistake of acting as if finding a correlation between two DVs was the same as establishing a causal relationship between an IV and a DV. In the example discussed on page 196, where we looked at the association between grade point average (GPA) and reported number of hours of studying, it would be all too easy to talk about higher GPAs as a necessary result of increased time spent studying. Since all we have is a correlation, it would be just as logical to say that getting good grades encourages students to study more (or at least *say* they study more) while getting poor grades discourages them. A correlation coefficient merely describes the association of two DVs, it says nothing about the causal direction of the relationship nor does it reveal whether or not some third, unmeasured variable is causing the changes in both of the measured variables. If you want to see whether a two-way association between two DVs can be interpreted as a one-way causal relationship between an IV and a DV, you'll have to design and carry out the appropriate experiment.

RECAPITULATION

for MEASURES OF CORRELATION

Whenever we measure more than one DV for a group of subjects, we can find out whether the subjects' measurements on the different DVs are associated, that is, whether they tend to vary together. A *scatterplot,* which represents the values of one DV on one axis and the second DV on the other, can be graphed to give a visual picture of the degree of association between two DVs. The descriptive statistic expressing the degree of association between two DVs is the *correlation coefficient.* If increasing measures on one DV predict increasing measures on the second, then the correlation coefficient will be close to $+1$. If a reverse relationship exists, that is, if an increased measure on one DV is associated with a decreased measure on the second DV, then the correlation will be negative and will approach -1. If no association exists, if knowledge of a subject's measure on one DV gives you no clue as to what his or her measure will be on the second DV, then the correlation will be 0.

There are many different kinds of correlation coefficients. Choice of the appropriate one will be determined primarily by the scale of measurement of each of the DVs being correlated. In choosing a correlation coefficient, it may also be necessary to consider the frequency distribution of observations on each of the DVs and/or the number of values (categories) possible for each DV. Two commonly used correlation statistics are *Pearson's r,* used for correlating two normally distributed intervally-scaled variables, and *Spearman's rho,* which is an ordinal-ordinal correlation coefficient between ranked observations. Spearman's rho is sometimes used for intervally scaled data that is not normally distributed, reducing the influence of extreme values by changing them to ranks. Table 5.12 lists some other kinds of correlation coefficients appropriate for different combinations of DV scales.

Correlation coefficients can be used to calculate the *reliability* of a single DV measurement scale by indicating whether repeated DV measures on the same set of subjects give the same results. They can also be used to determine the *validity* of two different DV measures that claim to be measuring the same aspect of the subjects. Care should be taken not to overinterpret correlations. If they are to be used as the basis for predicting future associations between two variables, inferential statistical tests must be done to confirm that the correlations are repeatable. Since the predictive value of a correlation (r) varies as its square (r^2), small correlations, even if statistically repeatable, may not in fact have much predictive power. Finally, existence of a correlation between two DVs should not be misinterpreted as a causal relationship. Something other than either variable may be simultaneously "causing" the variations in both of the measured DVs.

BEHAVIORAL OBJECTIVES

for CORRELATIONS

1. Given two ordered DV measures for each member of a set of subjects, draw a completely labeled, appropriately scaled, informatively captioned scatterplot for the data.

2. Given a scatterplot of the association of two DVs, describe the correlation between them as zero, negative, or positive; and estimate the size of the correlation as none, little, moderate, high, or perfect.

3. Describe the range of values possible for a correlation coefficient.

4. Describe the factors that determine choice of the appropriate correlation coefficient to describe the association of two DVs.

5. List the circumstances under which the Pearson's product-moment correlation coefficient (r) would be appropriate.

6. Given a set of intervally scaled measures, rank them from highest to lowest. Be sure you can handle tied ranks.

7. Describe Spearman's rho. Describe the circumstances under which you might decide to use it to correlate two intervally scaled DVs.

8. Given a description of two DVs, recognize their scales and use Table 5.12 to choose an appropriate correlation coefficient.

9. Given a particular value of a correlation coefficient for two DVs, write out your interpretation of the degree of association between the two variables.

10. Given someone else's selection and interpretation of a correlation coefficient for a specific situation, point out any weaknesses in reasoning.

SAMPLE TEST QUESTIONS

for CORRELATIONS

1. For the preschool study described on page 30 and in Table 2.1:
   a. Draw a scatterplot of the association between the teacher's categorization of the children's activity levels and the number of toy switches shown by each child.
   b. What type of correlation coefficient would you need to summarize this association?
   c. From looking at the scatterplot, what would you say about the degree and direction of association of the two DVs?

2. Rank the GPAs in Table 5.11 from highest to lowest. If you correlated these ranks with the ranks of either of the other two DVs from Table 5.11, what kind of correlation would you use?
   a. What size and direction of correlation would you predict there would be between GPA rank and the ranks of the number of hours spent studying.

b. What size and direction of correlation would you predict there would be between the ranks of the GPAs and the ranks of the number of hours spent in social activities?

3. Professor Pigge feels that education hurts a woman's eventual functioning as a mother. He administers his "Maternal Interest Inventory" (MII) to high school, college undergraduate, and college graduate women. The data from his pilot study are given below.

Subject:	A	B	C	D	E	F	G	H	I	J	K	L	M	N	O	P
Years of Education:	9	20	10	10	15	11	19	20	14	12	13	16	18	11	15	17
Score on the MII:	100	50	90	95	70	95	50	55	85	85	80	75	55	85	65	60

a. What kind of scale did he use to measure each of his DVs?

b. What type of correlation coefficient would you feel appropriate for these data? Discuss your choice.

c. Draw a scatterplot for these data.

d. From looking at your scatterplot, which of the following would you say would be a likely value for the correlation coefficient?
   −1.0   −0.9   −0.1   0.0   +0.1   +9.0   +1.0

e. If you decided to do a rank-order correlation on these data, you'd have to rank the subjects from 1 to 16 on each of the DVs. Proceed.

f. What is the name of the correlation coefficient you'd use to correlate these ranks?

g. Professor Pigge concludes from his pilot study that increasing years of education destroys a woman's interest in being a mother. He suggests that for the good of the family, women be educated only to elementary school levels. As further support for his conclusions, he points to the increasing divorce rates that have kept pace with the educational gains of women. Other than the problem of a small sample size, what weaknesses are there in his conclusion?

chapter 6

analyzing research results

Descriptive statistics are necessary to tell us what we've found. However, we usually want to go beyond description and use our results as a basis for speculation and prediction. We may want to regard our limited group of subjects as representative of people in general. We may want to predict that what we found in our particular study will be found again. The most exciting part of doing research is finding out things that will hold true beyond the narrow limits of what we can practically look at in any one study. Inferential statistics is a set of procedures that allows us to decide whether our results are real and repeatable or due only to chance and not likely to happen again.

SECTION 1: THE GENERAL PROCEDURE FOR ANY INFERENTIAL STATISTICAL TEST

THE NEED FOR INFERENTIAL STATISTICAL TESTS

There is one factor that must always be considered to influence the set of DV measures we obtain in any one research project. It is variously labeled "chance," "unsystematic variation," "sampling error," or "random error." Chance enters into our observations in several ways. Subjects are of course influenced by many fluctuating factors over which we have no control. This means that any set of people we choose to study will have individual differences. There are also chance factors introduced by the environment and by the way we take our observations. In practice, we will never be able to measure all the people whose behavior we want to speculate about. Also, we will not be able to measure any one person again and again forever under all possible circumstances. Thus the set of DV measures we actually get will have in them some unsystematic or chance variation that we can't get rid of. This creates a serious problem, for when we compare two sets of DV measures, how can we be certain that differences between them are real and repeatable rather than simply reflecting chance variations? Inferential statistics allow us to estimate the probability that the differences we observe are real and not simply due to chance.

SAMPLES AND POPULATIONS

When we regard a particular set of DV measures as representative of a larger possible set, we call the measures we have actually taken a **sample** and the larger set of possible measures a **population**. For example, we might want to do an experiment on 20 of our fellow college students selected at random and regard them as a sample of the larger population of all college students at our school. Since members of a population vary among themselves, a second random sample from the same population would show some differences from the first, simply because it consists of different individuals. The chance variation between random samples from the same population is called **sampling error**. The existence of sampling error will cause us problems when we want to interpret the meaning of differences between samples in our research. If an experimental and a control group differ on DV measures, are these differences real? It may be that the experimental and control measures are just two samples of the same population, and the differences between them are due only to sampling error. We need inferential statistics to help us answer this question.

EXAMPLES OF THE INSIDIOUS WORKINGS OF CHANCE

Watch Out Who You Play Dice With

Suppose you've been gambling with your brother and strongly suspect him of using loaded dice. After all, he's cleaned you out of all your pocket money for three weeks running. Deciding to put your education to some good use, you "borrow" his pair of dice and proceed to run some experiments with them. You start by taking one die, rolling it 24 times, and recording which side comes up each time. You get the following results:

Side	1	2	3	4	5	6
Number	||	||||	⊬|	|||	⊬	||||

Is this die suspect? If the die were not loaded and all six sides were equally likely, you would expect each side to come up about one-sixth of the time, or four times each in 24 rolls. Here, side 1 comes up only twice and side 3 comes up six times. Maybe you'd better try again. Another 24 rolls get you the following.

Side	1	2	3	4	5	6
Number	|||	||	⊬	|||	||||	⊬||

This really looks suspicious. Side 6 came up almost twice as often as it should, and you distinctly remember your brother getting more double sixes than you thought fair. However, looking back at your previous sample of 24 rolls makes you suspect that these fluctuations might be the result of sampling error. If you could measure all of the rolls in the die's lifespan—the entire population of its rolls—perhaps they'd average out with each side coming up one-sixth of the time. Since samples will vary at random, how can we ever tell if a die is loaded? Even having one side come up every time is a possible chance result of rolling the die for a limited sample of 24 rolls.

When Do We Go Out on a Limb with Research Results?

In the dice example above, we worried about sampling error as a possible explanation of the differences between two frequency distributions obtained for a nominal variable consisting of the six faces of a die. The same sampling-error issues can arise for samples of ordinal or interval measures. In Chapter 4, we discussed several studies designed to test the effects of consumption of social levels of alcohol and marijuana on different kinds of human performance. Suppose that using a Randomized-Groups design we found that a "marijuana" group of subject did a little better on a DV measure of verbal ability than a no-drug control group. Ten marijuana subjects averaged 16 (out of 20) correct on an anagram (word unscrambling) task, and ten no-drug controls averaged only 13 correct. When we designed the experiment, we randomly divided our subjects into these two conditions. Therefore, we assume that the two groups were the "same" before the experiment began. However, before we announce that marijuana has facilitating effects on performance of a verbal task, we'd better make sure that the difference between the two samples in mean number of anagrams solved is not just a sampling error resulting from taking two random samples from the same population.

Chance

In both of the examples above we need some way of excluding chance effects due to sampling error before we proclaim our results. Before you accuse your brother of cheating, you need to be very sure that the dice actually are loaded (especially if he's bigger than you are). Before we claim beneficial effects for marijuana, we need to be very, very sure that the difference found between our two groups wasn't due only to random variations expected for repeated samples taken from the same population. We need something more than statistics that just summarize and describe. Humans, remember, are strongly biased in favor of believing that chance events are real. We must have a "human-proof" way of establishing that what looks real isn't just chance.

THE GENERAL FORM OF ALL STATISTICAL TESTS

An inferential statistical test is built around the assumption that the only thing operating to produce variations in data is chance. The initial assumption of any statistical test is that any apparent effects of the IV on the DV result only from sampling error. This may seem a pessimistic assumption, but it's necessary to oppose our natural tendency to ignore the operation of chance in human affairs.

A particular inferential statistical test is constructed for a specific experimental design, and it is appropriate to a specific scale of DV measurement. Many tests also assume a specific type of frequency distribution of the DV measures. Considering all these factors, the statistician builds a mathematical model which predicts all possible results that could be produced in a specific situation by the operation of chance alone.

Given the basic model, an inferential test statistic can be calculated for any particular experiment. This test statistic is usually a ratio. Its numerator (top) is some measure of the difference between what would be expected by chance and what actually happened in the samples. The denominator (bottom) is some measure of the overall variability of the DV measures. Thus we can increase the size of a test statistic in two ways. One is to have a very large difference or discrepancy between what we actually get and what we could get by chance—a good indication that chance isn't the only explanation. Another way to increase this calculated test statistic is to *de*crease the overall variability of our DV measures, something most effectively done by increasing the size of our samples and by not being sloppy when we take our measures.

Using the mathematical model, the statistician can calculate for us the probability that the test statistic will take a certain value if only chance is operating. Most tests are designed in such a way that the larger the test statistic, the lower the probability that it could be produced only by sampling error. For example, if we found that a test statistic calculated for our research results would be produced solely by chance only 1 in 10,000 (.0001) times, we might feel that it would be unreasonable to maintain the initial assumption of chance.

So that statistical consumers don't have to keep recalculating the chance probabilities of different test statistics, these values are recorded in convenient tables, and we rarely have to return to the original mathematical models. Usually these tables don't report all possible values of the test statistic, but just those corresponding to particular probabilities, such as 1 in 10 (.10), 1 in 20 (.05), 1 in 100 (.01), and 1 in 1000 (.001). Since for most inferential statistical models sample size is a factor in the size of the calculated test statistic, tables give different values of test statistics appropriate to different sample sizes.

An inferential statistical test lets us reject the idea that chance or sampling error was the sole explanation of our results whenever our calculated test statistic is larger than the statistic given in the table. When we make such a rejection, the probabilities given in the table let us indicate how sure we are of our decision to reject the idea of chance. When you accost your gambling brother over the issue of the loaded dice, you can tell him, "Sir, I have only a 1-in-20 ($p < .05$) chance of being wrong when I call you a louse!" Similarly, we can hedge our bets when proclaiming the beneficial effects of marijuana by noting that there still is a 1-in-100 ($p < .01$) chance that the difference between the two groups is due only to sampling error.

STEPS IN DOING AN INFERENTIAL STATISTICAL TEST

Choosing the Test

Usually, we'll choose our inferential statistical test when we plan the research. Two major considerations in choosing statistical tests are the *design* of the experiment and the *scale of measurement* of the DV(s). Both of these, of course, are decided before the research is ever carried out. Another factor that sometimes has to be taken into consideration is the shape of the frequency distributions resulting for the DV measures, something we can't know until we complete the research. This factor sometimes alters our initial choice of a statistical test. In the last section of this chapter there is a *decision tree* (Fig. 6.3) that will help you choose a test if you can answer questions about the experimental design, the scale of measurement of the DV(s), and the frequency distribution of DV measures.

Setting Up Our "Null" or "Chance" Hypothesis

Having chosen our test, we next develop a **null hypothesis**. This is a statement that explains our results as being due only to chance factors or sampling error. The exact wording of this hypothesis will vary somewhat for experiments of different designs, but its meaning will be the same: nothing happened in our experiment beyond what can be explained by chance fluctuations in the data.

Let's consider the question of whether Brother's dice were loaded or biased. If the dice were not biased, your expectation would be that on the average the six faces on a die should come up an equal number of times when the die was repeatedly rolled. Your null hypothesis would be that any difference between this expectation and the number of times each face actually came up would be due to chance or sampling error. Since you had decided to do only 24 rolls, your specific null hypothesis would be that on the average each of the six faces would turn up four times, and any deviation from this in your results would be due only to your limited sample size.

For the study on the effects of marijuana, which involved an intervally scaled DV, we would word our null hypothesis differently. Our null expectation would be that the average scores for the marijuana group and for the no-drug control group reprsented nothing more than two samples randomly picked from the same population. Under this null hypothesis, any difference found between the means for the two groups would be due to sampling error and not to the action of our IV, marijuana administration.

Setting Our Level of Significance

In most cases, our hope is that we will reject the null hypothesis and establish that our IV did have some effect on the results beyond what could reasonably be called sampling error. When we reject our null hypothesis, we need to know the probability that we are making a mistake in doing so. It is customary not to report exact error probabilities for rejecting the null hypothesis, but to use one of a standard set of probabilities, or **levels of significance**. For most scientific journals, $p < .05$ (less than 1 chance in 20 of being wrong) is the maximum risk anyone is willing to accept for rejecting a null hypothesis. Sometimes $p < .10$ (less than 1 in 10 chances of being wrong) is acceptable, especially if the results are presented as only pilot work. Of course, $p < .01$ (less than 1 in 100) or $p < .001$ (less than 1 in 1,000), represent even less chance of being in error when rejecting the null hypothesis. The "significance" of our results is said to be greater, the lower the probability that we are mistaken in rejecting the null hypothesis.

Calculating Our Test Statistic

Having selected the appropriate test, we can proceed to calculate (or have someone else calculate) the **test statistic** for our data. The calculation should not be done blindly. From looking at our descriptive statistics we should already have some idea of whether our results are very different from the null expectation. We are then in a better position to catch errors in calculation (such as misplacing a decimal point). We don't want to be caught in the embarrassing position, for example, of having two mean scores that are practically the same, each accompanied by relatively large variabilities, which we illogically declare to be "significantly different" at the .001 level! If our inferential statistics do not bear out our expectations from the descriptive statistics, we'd better check our calculations.

Determining the Level of Significance of Our Test Statistics

For most statistical tests we'll need two pieces of information before looking up the significance of our calculated test statistic. One is the test statistic itself, and the other is a value called the **degrees of freedom** of the test statistic. Any description of procedures for calculating the test statistic will also tell us how to determine this second number or, in more complicated tests, pair of numbers. The degrees-of-freedom value in simpler tests will usually be one less than the sample size ($N - 1$). With this information we can seek out the table appropriate to our test, which may be a "z-table," a "t-table," an "F-table," a "U-table," a "χ^2-table," or what have you. Starting with the lowest level of significance acceptable to us, say .05, we can find from the table the **critical value** of the test statistic for our particular degrees of freedom. The critical value is that value of the test statistic that would be expected to happen with a probability of .05 if the null hypothesis were true. If our calculated test statistic is equal to or larger than this, then the probability of such a statistic occurring only by chance would be $p < .05$, a probability sufficiently small that it might lead us to reject the null hypothesis. Having achieved significance at this level, we check our test statistic successively against the larger critical values given for .01 and .001. When we report a test statistic as being "significant at the .05 level ($p < .05$)," our audience will *automatically* assume that it was not significant at the more stringent .01 level ($p < .01$), but that it fell somewhere in between ($.05 > p > .01$). We must report the best level of significance exceeded by our calculated test statistic.

Coming to a Conclusion

Our conclusion will be either that we accept our null hypothesis, and attribute any fluctuations in our results to chance, or that we reject it. If we reject the null hypothesis, we must state the level of significance, because that tells our audience our risk in making the rejecton. In a research report we state our conclusion in terms of what we investigated. Instead of merely saying, "The null hypothesis was (or was not) rejected at $p < .05$," we make a statement that reminds our audience of the ideas we were testing. In the case of the gambling brother, you might say, "There is no evidence at the $p = .05$ level of significance that the die was loaded. I'm sorry I called Brother a louse." For the marijuana study, we might report, "The marijuana group solved significantly ($p < .05$) more anagrams than did the control group, which had not received any drug."

Statistical tests help us come to a conclusion, but they do not make decisions for us. Even if Brother's dice are fair, maybe you should stop playing with him. Even if the marijuana smokers did significantly better than the controls on the anagrams task, we may not feel that a gain of three anagram solutions out of 20 represents a goal for which we'd push marijuana. **Statistical significance** is a *minimum* requirement; it is necessary to have it before talking about your results as being due to something other than chance. However, the social or biological "significance" of your findings depends on other considerations, once you have established statistical significance.

RECAPITULATION

for INFERENTIAL TEST PROCEDURES

The observations we make in any one experiment are only a *sample* of a much wider set (*population*) of observations that could be made. If we wish to use our results for prediction or speculation, we must first exclude the possibility that differences in the results are due to unrepeatable chance factors, such as *sampling error*. We can do this by using the appropriate inferential statistical test constructed on the assumption (*null hypothesis*) that our results are due solely to chance or sampling error. If the *test statistic* calculated for our data has a very small probability of occurrence, given the "chance-only" assumption, then we can reject the null hypothesis with a specific probability of being incorrect in doing so. Although there are a wide variety of statistical tests available, the steps in doing any statistical test are the same. First, we choose a test appropriate for the scale of measurement of our DV(s), for the design of our experiment, and for the characteristics of the frequency distributions we found for our DV(s). Next, we construct a null hypothesis tailored to our particular experiment. Then we decide what *level(s) of significance* we will require to reject the null hypothesis. The usual levels of significance are $p < .05$ (one chance in 20 of being wrong), $p < .01$ (1 in 100), $p < .001$ (1 in 1000), and, sometimes, $p < .10$ (1 in 10). Next we calculate our test statistic and determine its *degrees of freedom* according to the instructions given for the test. Finally, we compare our calculated test statistic with the critical values we find in tables for the different levels of significance and degrees of freedom. If our calculated test statistic exceeds the *critical value* for a particular level of significance, then we can reject the null hypothesis with a probability of being wrong that is less than that level of significance.

BEHAVIORAL OBJECTIVES

for INFERENTIAL TEST PROCEDURES

1. List the steps involved in doing any inferential statistical test.
2. List the three things that need to be considered in choosing an appropriate statistical test.
3. Given a test statistic and its accompanying degrees of freedom and given an appropriate statistical table:
   a. Look up the test statistic and see at what level(s) it is significant.
   b. Explain how you would interpret the significance of the statistic.
4. Explain what a null hypothesis consists of.
5. Given a description of a simple experimental situation, work out a verbal null hypothesis for it.
6. Explain what is meant by the term "level of significance." List the usual levels of significance reported in the research literature.

SAMPLE TEST QUESTIONS

for INFERENTIAL TEST PROCEDURES

1. A researcher wants to test whether a certain drug will affect learning. The experimental condition required that the subjects consume a pill containing the drug, wait 15 minutes for the drug to take effect, and then learn a list of ten nonsense syllable pairs. The researcher recorded for each subject how many errors were made until the subject finally had one run in which all ten nonsense syllable pairs were correct. The control condition was exactly the same as the experimental condition, except that the pill contained only sugar and not the drug. Ten subjects were randomly assigned to each condition.
   The researcher obtained the following results:

Group	N	$\overline{X}_{errors}$	S.D.
Drug	10	18	5.1
No drug	10	23	4.6

   The test statistic calculated for these data (let's call it "M") was found to be 2.30, and the accompanying degrees of freedom were figured as $(N_1 - 1) + (N_2 - 1)$, or 18.
   a. What is the design of this study? Write it down in shorthand. Is the comparison for the IV going to be a Between-Subjects or a Within-Subjects comparison?
   b. What DV measure was taken on each subject? What scale of measurement was this?
   c. Write out the null hypothesis for this experiment.

    d. Below is a portion of the appropriate table for the test statistic "M". What are the appropriate critical values to compare the test statistic against? Is the calculated test statistic significant? If so, at what levels(s)? What does it mean to say that the test statistic is significant at this level?

    e. State the conclusions that could be drawn about this research.

Excerpt from the Table for Statistic "M"

Degrees of Freedom	Significance Levels			
	.10	.05	.01	.001
16	1.746	2.120	2.921	4.015
17	1.740	2.110	2.898	3.965
18	1.734	2.101	2.878	3.922
19	1.729	2.093	2.861	3.883
20	1.725	2.086	2.845	3.850

2. An experiment was done on the recognition of cola beverages by taste alone. Each subject was given three colas to taste and was asked to label each one as Pepsi Cola, Coca Cola, or Royal Crown Cola. Each subject was categorized as having either 0 correct, 1 correct, or 3 correct. (Do you know why no one was labeled as having 2 correct?)

Chance probabilities for this kind of task would be: 1/3 should get 0 correct by guessing; 1/2 should get 1 correct by guessing; and 1/6 should get all 3 correct by guessing.

The data for a sample size of 72 came out as follows:

	0 Correct	1 Correct	3 Correct
Expected by Chance	24	36	12
Observed Frequencies	22	35	15

The test statistic (let's call it "S") was calculated to be 0.94 with 2 degrees of freedom.

    a. What is the design of this experiment? Write it down in shorthand.

    b. Is the comparison of colas being made Between- or Within-Subjects?

   c. What might you want to counterbalance and why?

   d. What is the DV and what are its possible levels?

   e. Write down your null hypothesis. Just looking at the descriptive table above, do you expect to reject the null hypothesis?

   f. Below is a portion of the appropriate table for the "S" statistic. What are the appropriate critical values to compare your calculated test statistic against? Is the calculated test statistic significant? If so, at what values?

   g. State your conclusions about this research.

Excerpt from the Table for Statistic "S"

Degrees of Freedom	Significance Levels			
	.10	.05	.01	.005
1	2.71	3.84	6.64	7.88
2	4.61	5.99	9.21	10.60
3	6.25	7.82	11.34	12.84
4	7.78	9.49	13.28	14.86
5	9.24	11.07	15.09	16.75

SECTION 2: INFERENTIAL TESTS FOR INTERVAL MEASURES (TWO-CONDITION DESIGNS)

Several simple experimental designs consist of only two conditions, for instance, an experimental condition and a control. If the DV in the experiment is interval and its frequency distribution is reasonably normal, we will describe the results by giving two means with their accompanying standard deviations. Then the question arises as to whether the two means are different only because of chance or whether they indicate a real difference in the effects of the two conditions. We need inferential statistics to answer this question.

SELECTING THE APPROPRIATE TEST, THE "t-TEST"

When our design has two conditions and our scale of DV measurement is interval, we can consider using the *t*-test as our inferential statistical test. Unless our frequency distributions are badly skewed or otherwise decidedly not normal, the *t*-test is a good choice. However, next we need to decide which of two types of *t*-test our design requires us to do.

t-Test for Independent Samples

If our design is a Between-Subjects one, with a different group of subjects representing each condition, we can use a *t*-test **for independent samples** to analyze the data. Such a test is appropriate for any Independent-Groups design, whether a Static-Groups, Blocked-Groups, or Randomized-Groups design.

The *t*-test for independent samples compares the difference between the means of the two conditions to the overall variability of the data. If the difference between the means is large and the variability of the data relatively small, then the calculated *t*-value will be large.

t-Test for Paired Samples

In either a Within-Subjects design or a Matched-Groups design, a score in one condition can be *paired* with a score in the other. In a Within-Subjects, pre-post design, for example, there is both a pre- and a postscore for each subject. Treatment effect can then be estimated for each subject by obtaining the difference between pre- and postscores. In a Matched-Groups design, where each experimental subject has a matched control subject, the effect of treatment can be estimated for each pair by finding the difference between the experimental and control subject scores. A *t*-**test for paired samples**, also known as the *t*-**test for correlated samples**, compares the average of such difference scores to their variability. Again, if the average difference between paired scores is large and the variability of these differences small, the resulting calculated *t*-value will be large.

SETTING UP OUR HYPOTHESES

For any inferential test we need to set up a null hypothesis about what could be expected by chance alone. We accompany this with an alternative or "research" hypothesis that states the idea we will accept if forced to reject our original null hypothesis.

Hypotheses for the t-Test for Independent Samples

The general idea of our null hypothesis is that any difference found between the means of our two conditions is due only to chance or sampling error. For a design with an experimental (E) and a control (C) group, this null hypothesis (abbreviated H_0) can be briefly expressed by saying "$Mean_E = Mean_C$" or else "$Mean_E - Mean_C = 0$." If our calculated *t*-value is too large, we will reject this null hypothesis. Since it's only fair that when we reject something we accept some other idea in its place, we will also need to state an **alternative** or **research hypothesis**. The appropriate alternative hypothesis (abbreviated H_A) for a two-group comparison is that the two means are not equal ($Mean_E \neq Mean_C$) or, stated another way, that their difference is non-zero ($Mean_E - Mean_C \neq 0$).

Hypotheses for the t-Test for Paired Samples

For a Within-Subjects or Matched-Groups design we do the *t*-test on the difference scores. Our null hypothesis is that the real mean of the difference scores is zero, and any departure from this in the data is just sampling error. Although individual pairs of scores may show random differences, over the long run our null hypothesis predicts that these differences will average out to zero (H_0: $Mean_{dif} = 0$). The alternative hypothesis, of course, is that the differences are real and will not average out to zero if the experiment is repeated again and again (H_A: $Mean_{dif} \neq 0$).

DETERMINING ACCEPTABLE LEVELS OF SIGNIFICANCE AND CRITICAL t-VALUES

The statistical model for the two-condition *t*-test produces a theoretical distribution of *t*-values that would be expected if the null hypothesis of chance were in fact true. Such a distribution is given in Fig. 6.1, which shows that although near-zero positive and negative *t*-values are very likely under the null hypothesis, values larger than about +2 and smaller than −2 are rather unlikely.

The exact *t*-values expected by chance change with the degrees of freedom, a number that is dependent on sample size. The particular distribution graphed in Fig. 6.1 is for a situation in which there are 15 degrees of freedom (a total sample size of 16). Suppose for this particular situation that you wanted to find out the size of *t*-values that would be expected less than 5 percent ($p < .05$) of the time if the null hypothesis were true. Since the distribution is symmetrical, you would have to chop off 2.5 percent in each of its tails to exclude a total of 5 percent of the distribution. A *t*-value of +2.131 would cut off the upper 2.5 percent of the distribution, and a *t*-value of −2.131 would cut off the lower 2.5 percent. Therefore you could say that, for this situation, a *t*-value larger than +2.131 or less than −2.131 would be expected less than 5 percent ($p > .05$) of the time *if* all that was operating in the experiment

FIG. 6.1

Distribution of critical t-*values with 5 percent of the area cut off in the upper and lower tails by* t-*values of +2.131 and −2.131 (degrees of freedom = 15).*

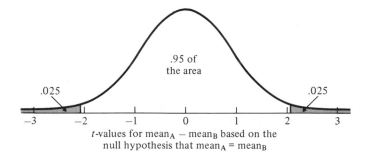

was chance. An absolute (unsigned) t-value of 2.131 would be called the critical t-value for a significance level of .05.

If you were willing to take a greater risk of being wrong in rejecting your null hypothesis, you could use a smaller critical t-value. Suppose you were willing to run a 10-percent risk of being wrong in rejecting the idea of chance. Then you could use critical t-values of $+1.753$ and -1.743 to cut off 5 percent in each tail (a total of 10 percent). However, if you felt more conservative and wanted to run only a 1-percent ($p < .01$) risk of being wrong, you would have to use a larger critical value and reduce the areas cut from the chance t-value distribution to only 0.5 percent in each tail. For Fig. 6.1, this means you would have to use a critical value of 2.947 (both positive and negative) to cut off only 0.5 percent of the distribution in each tail.

CALCULATING THE t-VALUE FOR OUR EXPERIMENT

Before we actually do the calculations, we must be sure we're using the correct t-formula. An independent-groups t is calculated for a Between-Subjects design, and a paired t (correlated t) is calculated for the difference scores produced by a Within-Subjects or Matched design. The t-value we calculate using the appropriate formula will have either a positive or a negative sign.

The book that gives us the formula for calculating t-values will also remind us how to find the accompanying value for degrees of freedom. For an Independent-Groups situation, the total degrees of freedom value is the sum of the degrees of freedom for each sample: $(N_E - 1) + (N_C - 1)$. For a paired t, the value of the degrees of freedom is one less than the number of difference scores (one less than the total number of pairs).

DETERMINING THE LEVEL OF SIGNIFICANCE OF OUR
CALCULATED t-VALUE

Once we have our calculated t-value and our degrees of freedom, we can use a t-table to find the risk we will be taking if we reject our null hypothesis. First, we look up the critical t-value listed for $p = .05$. If our calculated t-value is smaller, we decide that the results are "nonsignificant," and we accept our null hypothesis. However, if our calculated t-value is larger (more positive or more negative) than that listed for .05, we next find the critical t-value given for the next better level of significance, $p = .01$. If our calculated t-value is also larger than this critical t-value, we can find the critical value listed for $p = .001$. Then, if our calculated t-value fails to exceed the critical value for this .001 level, we can report our results as "significant at the .01 level." In other words, we are running a less than 1/100 risk of being wrong if we say that the difference between our means was not due to chance. More extensive t-tables would allow us to report the exact probability of any t-value's occurring by chance. However, this amount of detail is usually not required, and the significance of results is generally reported in relation to the .05, .01, and .001 levels.

Knowing our degrees of freedom is crucial to proper use of a *t*-table. As the number of degrees of freedom decreases, the size of the critical *t* necessary for any particular level of significance increases. If we use small samples in our research, it will take a larger calculated *t*-value to obtain statistical significance.

COMING TO A CONCLUSION

If our calculated test statistic does not exceed the critical *t*-value for our lowest acceptable level of significance (usually $p = .05$), we declare our results to be "nonsignificant" and accept the null hypothesis. Accepting the null hypothesis means we stop talking about the difference in the means of our two conditions as representing any real difference.

If our calculated test statistic does exceed the critical value for $p = .05$ or for an even better level of significance ($p = .01$, $p = .001$, etc.), we can reject our null hypothesis. Now we can talk about the difference in the DV means as representing a real and repeatable effect of our IV. Whenever we discuss this difference, we attach to it an indication of the minimum probability at which the results were significant ($p < .05$, $p < .01$, $p < .001$, etc.). This tells our audience how much faith they can place in our decision to reject the null hypothesis.

Although $p = .05$ is the usual cutoff for "significance," some situations may call for using either smaller probabilities of risk (higher levels of significance) or larger probabilities (lower levels of significance). For example, the medical community, when considering adoption of a new drug, may not be satisfied unless the risk of being wrong is less than 1 in a 1000 ($p < .001$). On the other hand, in circumstances where a "wrong" decision would not cause serious problems, our audience might even be interested in a result that was "significant" at only $p < .10$.

"Statistical significance," though gratifying to the researcher, is only a minimal requirement for deciding what to do with the results. An IV effect can be real and repeatable without being large enough to be of much importance. For instance, a new type of reading instruction might produce a significant ($p < .05$) increase in children's reading comprehension scores. However, if the actual average size of the gain in terms of means was only 3 percent and the new approach required much more of the teacher's time, we might not feel the new method was worth using, despite its statistically significant effect. It's necessary to consider both descriptive and inferential statistics when coming to a conclusion.

AMPUTATING A TAIL FROM THE t-TEST

"Two-Tailed" t-Tests

Whenever there are only two conditions in a design, we have an option for wording the test hypotheses. The most common way is to state the alternative or research hypothesis "nondirectionally" by making no prediction about the direction of the effect we expect from our IV. Our null hypothesis is simply that the means of our two conditions do not differ except by chance, and our alternative hypothesis is that they do differ. This way of stating the hypotheses means that we will reject the null hypothesis for either a large positive t-value *or* a large negative t-value. Since the sign of our calculated t-value is determined by the direction of the difference in the means, we reject the null hypothesis either if the mean of our experimental condition is greater than that of our control condition ($\text{Mean}_E - \text{Mean}_C > 0$) or if it is less ($\text{Mean}_E - \text{Mean}_C < 0$). When we want to reject the null hypothesis for any difference in means, regardless of its direction, we have to divide our significance level between the two tails of the t-distribution, as in Fig. 6.1. Thus a t-test done with nondirectional hypotheses is called a **two-tailed test**.

"One-Tailed" t-Tests

There may be situations, however, in which we want to make a directional prediction in our alternative or research hypothesis. For example, we may have reason to predict that our experimental DV measures will exceed those of our control condition. Perhaps the experiment has been done before. Perhaps we don't care about the possibility that the effect will come out the opposite way. For a Between-Subjects, two-condition t-test, we might state in our alternative hypothesis that Mean_E will be greater than Mean_C ($H_0: \text{Mean}_E > \text{Mean}_C$). For a Within-Subjects or Matched-Groups design we might state in our alternative hypothesis that the average of the difference scores for each experimental value minus its paired control value would be greater than zero ($H_A: \text{Mean}_{E-C} > 0$). Alternative hypotheses like these raise the problem of what to do with the other direction of outcome possible for the experiment. Our null and alternative hypotheses for any test have to cover *all* possible outcomes, even those we don't expect. The undesired direction of outcome is simply dumped into the null hypothesis. Thus for an Independent-Groups t-test, the one-tailed null hypothesis might be that the mean of the experimental group will be equal to *or less than* that of the control group ($H_0: \text{Mean}_E \leq \text{Mean}_C$). For the paired t-test, our null hypothesis might be that the average of the difference scores (experimental minus controls) would be equal to *or less than* zero ($H_0: \text{Mean}_{dif} \leq 0$).

Predicting a direction in the alternative hypothesis allows us to use a critical t-value taken from only one tail of the t-distribution. Fig. 6.2 shows a situation in which a directional prediction has been made. In this case the prediction is that the calculated t-value will be larger than a positive critical value. All the probability for rejecting the null hypothesis is put into just the upper tail. If a .05 level of significance (which would cut off 5 percent of the distribution) were used, the critical t-value for the situation (15 degrees of freedom) graphed in Fig. 6.2 would be $+1.753$. Any calculated t-value less than this, even a very large negative number, would mean acceptance of the null hypothesis.

Using a directional alternative hypothesis doesn't change anything about how you calculate your t-value. All it changes is what t-value is considered critical for any given level of significance. Comparing Figs. 6.1 and 6.2, we can see that for a significance level of .05, the absolute size of the critical t is less for a **one-tailed test** than for a two-tailed test. If you want to use one-tailed hypotheses for your research,

FIG. 6.2

Distribution of critical t-*values with 5 percent of the area cut off in the upper tail by a* t *of* +*1.753 (degrees of freedom = 15).*

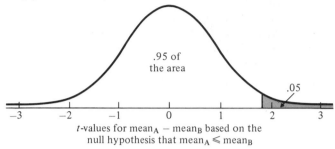

.95 of
the area

.05

t-values for mean$_A$ − mean$_B$ based on the
null hypothesis that mean$_A$ ≤ mean$_B$

you'll need to find a one-tailed *t*-table. (When such a table is unavailable, you can use the more common two-tailed *t*-tables, but you have to divide the stated probability levels in half. For example, the critical value given for $p = .10$ in a two-tailed table is the same as would be listed for $p = .05$ in a one-tailed table.)

Advantages and Disadvantages of a One-Tailed t-Test

The major advantage of one-tailed hypotheses for a *t*-test is that a smaller size of difference between means will be declared statistically significant. It is easier to get significance with a one-tailed test, provided things come out in the predicted direction.

However, one-tailed hypotheses can put us at a disadvantage. Suppose the results come out the exact opposite of what we predicted. We said the experimental DV values would be larger than the controls, but they all come out much smaller! Nevertheless, we are stuck with our null hypothesis. The only way we can establish that there is a large negative effect of our IV is to repeat the experiment (this time with appropriate hypotheses). We can't change our hypotheses after the fact to cover this unexpected outcome. Models for inferential statistical tests require that we state our hypotheses *before* we collect the data.

Therefore one-tailed, directional hypotheses should be used only when we have good reason, such as the results of earlier research, to predict a certain outcome or when we decide beforehand that we don't care about an effect that goes in the opposite direction. For example, in testing the effects of a new instructional method in the classroom, we might not care if the method is harmful rather than merely ineffective. If the method does not improve instruction, we will not recommend its use. In this situation one-tailed hypotheses would be adequate for our purpose.

Unless researchers say otherwise, it is usually safe to assume they have used the more common two-tailed *t*-test. When you do a one-tailed test on your own data, it's necessary to inform your audience specifically and to give them the reasons why you chose to do so.

VARIANTS OF THE t-TEST

Testing for an Expected Mean Value

In some situations we may have collected information on a single group and want to compare it with some theoretical or "normative" value. For example, we might give a third grade class a nationally standardized test of reading comprehension and obtain a mean score of 106. Since we know the test was designed to have a theoretical mean of 100, we wonder whether the class is doing significantly better than the average student on whom the test was standardized. It is possible to do a variant of the *t*-test which allows us to test the idea that our single group mean is or is not the same as some particular value. As for the two-condition *t*-tests, we can of course make up either one-tailed or two-tailed hypotheses for such a **t-test for an expected mean value**.

Testing a Correlation to See If It Is Significant

Another variant of the *t*-test tells us whether or not a correlation coefficient (r) calculated between two intervally scaled DVs is real and likely to happen again. After all, two variables may be correlated in a particular experiment just by chance. A two-tailed null hypothesis would be that the correlation is really zero and that any difference from zero is just sampling error (H_0: $r = 0$). The alternative hypothesis would be that the correlation is different from zero (H_A: $r \neq 0$). In most basic statistics books, there are formulas to convert the Pearson's product-moment correlation to a *t*-value, which then can be looked up in a regular *t*-table. For convenience, there are also tables (Freeman, 1965) that allow us, provided we know our degrees of freedom, to look up correlations directly and see whether they are significant. As for other kinds of *t*-tests, we can choose to set up directional hypotheses for the **t-test for a correlation** and do a one-tailed test. For instance, we might predict that a positive correlation exists between reading speed and reading comprehension for children (H_A: $r > 0$). Then our one-tailed null hypothesis would have to be that the correlation would be zero or negative (H_0: $r \leq 0$).

RECAPITULATION

for DOING t-TESTS

A *t-test* can be used to analyze the results of any two-condition design, provided that the DV measurements are interval and the frequency distribution is approximately normal. An *independent-groups t-test* is appropriate for a two-condition, Between-Subjects design, such as Static-Groups, Blocked-Groups or Randomized-Groups. For a Within-Subjects or Matched-Groups design, a *paired t-test (correlated t-test)* is done. The hypotheses for any *t*-test must be specified before it is done. *Two-tailed hypotheses* predict no special direction of outcome for the research. The two-tailed

null hypothesis is simply that the difference between the means of the two conditions is due only to chance (H_0: $Mean_E = Mean_C$). The two-tailed alternative
hypothesis is that the means of the two conditions are really different (H_A:
$Mean_E \neq Mean_C$). If the researchers have reason to predict the direction of the
effect ahead of time, they may instead use a pair of *one-tailed hypotheses*. In this
case the alternative hypothesis states a direction (H_A: $Mean_E > Mean_C$), and the
null hypothesis includes all other possible outcomes (H_0: $Mean_E \leq Mean_C$).
Once the appropriate type of *t*-test is selected and the hypotheses are written out,
a *calculated t-value* is obtained by use of the appropriate formula, and the accompanying value for degrees of freedom is figured out. A *t*-table lists the *critical
t-values* for rejection of the null hypothesis at any given level of significance (p
$= .10$, $p = .05$, $p = .01$, etc.). If the calculated *t*-value is larger than the critical value, then the results are declared significant at that level, and the null hypothesis is rejected. The level of significance tells us the probability that we are
wrong in rejecting the null hypothesis and accepting the alternative. A variant of
the *t*-test allows us to test the idea that the mean of a single sample of DV measures is or is not a particular value. The *t*-test can also be used to determine
whether a correlation coefficient calculated for two DV measurement scales is
statistically significant and likely to be obtained again.

BEHAVIORAL OBJECTIVES

for DOING t-TESTS

1. Describe the circumstances that would lead you to select a *t*-test to analyze your data.
2. Distinguish between a *t*-test for independent samples and a *t*-test for paired (correlated) samples.
3. Distinguish between a calculated *t*-statistic and a critical *t*-statistic.
4. Describe the difference between a one-tailed and a two-tailed *t*-test. Explain the circumstances under which you would want one or the other.
5. Describe how each of the following would affect a calculated *t*-statistic.
   a. The difference between the means of two samples was increased.
   b. The variability of the data within the samples was increased.
6. Describe how each of the following would affect the value of the critical *t* neces-sary for statistical significance.
   a. The degrees of freedom for the test are increased.
   b. The probability for declaring the *t* statistically significant is decreased from .05 to .01.
   c. The level of significance is increased.
   d. For a significance level of .05, the test is changed from one-tailed to two-tailed.

7. Given the description of a two-condition experiment:
   a. Identify whether or not a *t*-test is appropriate.
   b. Decide whether the hypotheses should be one- or two-tailed, given the researcher's stated expectations.
   c. Decide whether the *t*-test should be the one for independent or for paired samples.
   d. Write out the appropriate null and alternative hypotheses.
8. List the designs for which a *t*-test would be appropriate.
9. List the things you need to know when you set out to check a calculated *t*-statistic against a table of critical values of *t*.
10. Given a calculated *t*-value along with its degrees of freedom in the context of a description of an experiment:
    a. Look up the *t*-value in a table and decide whether or not it is significant.
    b. State your conclusions in terms of the appropriate null and alternative hypotheses for the experiment, indicating whether you used a one- or two-tailed set of hypotheses and stating the probability that your conclusions are wrong.
11. Given a correlation with its degrees of freedom resulting from a particular experiment:
    a. State your null and alternative hypotheses according to whether you should do a one- or two-tailed test.
    b. Decide from a table of critical correlations the significance level of your correlation.
    c. State your conclusions fully.
12. Given a series of statements, identify them as referring to one or more of the following: *t*-test of independent samples, *t*-test of paired samples, *t*-test for correlations, one-tailed test, and two-tailed test.

SAMPLE TEST QUESTIONS

for DOING t-TESTS

1. In a study on the Mueller-Lyer Illusion (a visual illusion in which putting "fins" at the end of a straight line changes its apparent length), the researchers wanted to find out whether results found in a previous study about the effects of orientation of the visual stimulus on the size of the illusion could be replicated using a different experimental design. The shortening version of the illusion, in which placing ingoing fins on the ends of a line make it look shorter (↔), was used.

   The earlier study had each of 30 subjects estimate line length for the illuson in both horizontal and vertical orientations. These results are given in Table 6.1. In their replication of this study, the researchers randomly divided 100 college subjects into two groups of 50 each. One group estimated line length for the illusion positioned horizontally, and the other group estimated it for the vertical position of the illusion. The results of this second study are given in Table 6.2.

Table 6.1 Shortening Effect in Inches on a 24″ Line with Ingoing Fins at its Ends
(Study 1)

	Horizontal	Vertical	
N	30	30	
$\overline{X}$	2.03	1.72	degrees of freedom = 29
S.D.	.90	.75	t statistic = 3.82

Table 6.2 Shortening Effect in Inches on a 24″ Line with Ingoing Fins at its Ends
(Study 2)

	Horizontal	Vertical	
N	50	50	
$\overline{X}$	2.11	1.79	degrees of freedom = 98
S.D.	.60	.49	t statistic = 2.92

Answer the following questions.

  a. What is the DV in each of these experiments?
  b. For each experiment, identify the type of design used.
  c. Discuss why the t-test might be appropriate for the data from these experiments.
  d. For each design, specify which version of the t-test should be used.
  e. One of these studies should use a two-tailed hypothesis, and the other could use a one-tailed. Decide which is which and explain your decision.
  f. Considering your answer to (e), set up the null and alternative hypotheses appropriate to each study.
  g. Given in Table 6.3 are portions of t-tables. Check the statistical significance of the calculated t-statistics for each study, keeping in mind your answer to (e).
  h. State the conclusions for each study fully.

2. Identify each of the following statements as characteristic of one or more of the following: one-tailed hypotheses (1); two-tailed hypotheses (2); t-test for independent samples (t-ind); t-test for paired samples (t-pair); and/or t-test for a correlation ($t - r$).

  a. The null hypothesis is that the means of the two groups will be the same.
  b. H_0: $\text{Mean}_{\text{dif}} = 0$.
  c. The null hypothesis is that the average of the difference scores will be equal to or less than zero.

Table 6.3 Portions of Tables for the *t*-Distribution

Degrees of Freedom	Significance Levels					
	One-Tailed			Two-Tailed		
	.05	.01	.005	.05	.01	.001
26	1.706	2.479	2.779	2.056	2.779	3.707
27	1.703	2.473	2.771	2.052	2.771	3.690
28	1.701	2.467	2.763	2.048	2.763	3.674
29	1.699	2.462	2.756	2.045	2.756	3.659
30	1.697	2.457	2.750	2.042	2.750	3.646
40	1.684	2.423	2.704	2.021	2.704	3.551
60	1.671	2.390	2.660	2.000	2.660	3.460
120	1.658	2.358	2.617	1.980	2.617	3.373

    d. The alternative (research) hypothesis is that the correlation is greater than zero.

    e. We are doing this research to establish whether or not training in voluntary relaxation decreases test anxiety.

    f. Of interest in this project is whether or not training in speed reading techniques affects comprehension of written material.

    g. The null hypothesis is that any difference between the correlation of these two DVs and zero correlation is due to sampling error.

    h. The alternative (research) hypothesis is that $\bar{X}_A$ is greater than $\bar{X}_B$.

    i. The statistical test will be done on the difference scores of matched pairs of subjects.

3. Refer to the study described in Question 3 on p. 165 concerning the effects of a preschool program on the IQs of children in Colombia. Reread the description of this study. Suppose you wanted to test the significance of the difference between the IQs of the T_1 (one year of the program) and the T_4 (four years of the program) children.

    a. What kind of *t*-test would be needed? (To answer this you must know what type of design you are dealing with.)

    b. Decide whether you would use a one-tailed or a two-tailed hypothesis.

       1) Defend your decision.

       2) Write out the appropriate null and alternative hypotheses.

    c. The calculated *t* for this comparison is 4.54 with 137 degrees of freedom. Given your answer to (b), look up this *t* statistic in Table 6.3, and decide on its significance.

    d. Fully state your conclusions in terms of the type of test you selected and your null and alternative hypotheses.

    e. Are there any reasons you might be uncomfortable with a *t*-test for these data? Explain.

SECTION 3: INFERENTIAL TESTS FOR INTERVAL MEASURES (DESIGNS WITH MORE THAN TWO CONDITIONS)

When we want to increase the information we'll get from an experiment, one approach is to use more than two conditions in the design. We may want to investigate a single IV at more than two levels, or we may decide to use more than one IV. When our DV measures are intervally scaled and the frequency distributions are reasonably normal, we'll choose to describe the effects of the different research conditions by means and standard deviations. If we want to interpret the differences among our means as representing effects of our IV(s), we'll have to face the problem of sampling error or chance variation. After all, taking repeated random samples from one and the same population will result in differences in sample (condition) means that do not represent real and repeatable effects produced by our different conditions. We need an inferential statistical test that allows us to decide whether the differences among our condition means represent something more than just chance.

SELECTING THE APPROPRIATE TEST, THE "ANALYSIS OF VARIANCE"

The existence of more than two conditions in our design and the fact that the scale of DV measurement is interval would lead us to consider doing an **Analysis of Variance** on our results. Such an analysis involves calculation of one or more **F-ratios,** which can then be checked against table *F*-values for their statistical significance. Determining an *F*-ratio involves calculating variances; therefore an Analysis of Variance can be done only when we are willing to assume that the DV measures approximate a normal distribution.

    There are many different types of Analysis of Variance. In Chapter 4 we discussed several designs that contained more than two conditions or two groups. There are single-IV designs, which can be either Within-Subjects or Between-Subjects. There are designs with more than one IV, in which interaction effects between IVs can be obtained in addition to finding out the effect of each IV separately. These multiple-IV designs can be further complicated by defining some of the IVs as Non-Subject and some as Subject (or Blocked). The Non-Subject IVs can be treated either Between- or Within-Subjects. The exact way *F*-ratios are calculated depends on such design details. Learning about all the different specific kinds of Analysis of Variance requires one or more advanced statistics courses. However, a statistician will be able to find the appropriate analysis for you if you can clearly communicate the characteristics of your design. In fact, it's best to consult a statistician before actually collecting data to be sure that there is an available analysis that is appropriate for your particular complex design.

In the rest of this chapter, we will consider only two broad categories of Analysis of Variance. One is the analysis for a single-IV design, which will give us only one *F*-ratio to interpret but may require that we do an additional **multiple-comparisons test.** The other involves analyzing multivariable designs, which will yield us several different *F*-ratios from a single analysis. In this case we will have to interpret *F*-ratios for interaction effects as well as those for the separate IVs. Analysis of Variance is a more complicated statistical technique, but you'll find that many of the underlying issues are similar to those discussed for the simpler *t*-test.

STATISTICAL MODEL FOR THE F-RATIO

When we have samples of DV measures from more than two conditions, we need an inferential test statistic based on descriptive statistics from all our samples. This test statistic must simultaneously take into consideration all our sample means and all our sample variances. If the means for the different conditions in our experiment represent only random samples taken from a single underlying population, we would expect the sample means to cluster pretty closely around a single population mean. In this case the variation of these sample means would be relatively small. On the other hand, if the conditions of the experiment do have differential effects on the DV, we would expect the means for the different conditions not to cluster around a single value and to show instead a great deal of variation. What we need is some way of determining whether the variation of the sample means is too large to be explained by repeated random sampling from one population.

Estimating chance variation is a little complicated since the expected variation of means for random samples from the same population is influenced both by sample size and by the variability of the underlying population. The smaller the size of samples and the larger the population variability, the more chance variation we can expect among sample means. Sample size is known for any particular experiment, so taking it into account is no problem. The variability of a theoretical population of measures, however, is something we don't know and can't directly determine. The best we can do is try to estimate this variance by combining the variances calculated for our individual samples.

The test statistic used in an Analysis of Variance compares the variance of the sample means to an estimate of the variance of the population. The population variance is estimated by combining the variances of the individual samples. If the variance of the means is close in value to the estimated population variance, then the assumption that all the means come from samples from the same population is a good one. If the variance of the means is much larger than the estimated population variance, it is likely that at least some of the means come from samples from different populations. This would indicate that the IV is having a real effect on the DV. The test statistic calculated in an Analysis of Variance, designated F, is simply a *ratio* of the "between-samples" variance of the means to the combined "within-samples" variance. When these two variances are equal, the F-ratio will be equal to 1, and the assumption that all the samples come from one and the same population will be supported. When the F-ratio is much larger than 1 we will doubt that the samples all come from the same population.

SETTING UP HYPOTHESES
FOR AN ANALYSIS OF VARIANCE

Single-IV Designs

Just as for a t-test, the Analysis of Variance is constructed on the assumption that the null hypothesis is true. It is assumed that any variation among the means for the different conditions is no more than would be expected from sampling error. In terms of the F-ratio, the null prediction is that F will be close to 1. The alternative hypothesis is that the variation among the means is greater than could be expected by chance, and the differences among the means are real and repeatable. If the F-ratio calculated for a particular set of means is sufficiently greater than 1, we may want to reject the null hypothesis.

Multiple-IV Designs

A multivariate design permits us to run several inferential statistical tests in one analysis. This means that we have several sets of null and alternative hypotheses. First, we consider each IV separately as if it were the only one in the experiment. This is called finding the **main effect** of each IV. Suppose we were doing a study on the effects of three levels of distraction (IV_1) on test performance (DV), and that we were also interested in the effects of sex of subject (IV_2). First we would compare the mean performances for the three levels of distraction (both sexes combined). Our null hypothesis would be that these three means were essentially the same, and our alternative hypothesis would be that the difference in performance at the three distraction levels was real. Next we could take a look at the overall effect of the Subject IV of sex. We could calculate an overall mean for males (combining all levels of distraction) and compare it with an overall mean for females. Our second set of test hypotheses would then consist of a null hypothesis stating that the performance of the two sexes differed only by chance, and our alternative hypothesis would be that the two means really differed. We have as many "main-effect" sets of test hypotheses as we have IVs in our research design.

In addition, multivariate designs give us interaction information. For each possible kind of interaction, our null hypothesis will be that the effects of an IV on the DV are *not* changed by the presence of the other IV. Our alternative hypothesis is that one IV changes the effects of the other. For the example described above, our null hypothesis about the interaction would be that the effects of distraction on performance were the same for both sexes. Our alternative hypothesis would be that distraction affected male test performance differently than female.

Thus a simple two-IV (two-way) Analysis of Variance allows us to investigate three sets of null and alternative hypotheses. The main effect of each IV taken separately can be studied, as well as the possibility that they interact. A three-IV Analysis of Variance (A × B × C) would give us three main-effect sets of test hypotheses, one for each IV, plus three more sets of hypotheses for the two-way interactions (A × B; A × C; B × C), and an additional set for a three-way interaction! In other words, a three-way Analysis of Variance can allow us to do seven statistical tests all at once. Multivariate studies result in multiple test hypotheses and allow us to reach conclusions about several issues at the same time.

CALCULATING F-RATIOS

It is more difficult to calculate F-ratios than to calculate t-values, especially for complicated multivariate designs. Computers are therefore very useful for doing Analyses of Variance. A stage in the process of calculating an F-ratio is to obtain something called a **Mean Square** (which is *not* an "angry conservative" but a variance estimate). The ratio of two Mean Squares gives a single F-ratio. Each F-ratio must have *two* accompanying values for degrees of freedom. One degree-of-freedom value belongs to the numerator Mean Square. The numerator Mean Square is calculated from the means that are being compared, and its degrees-of-freedom value equals one less than the number of means. Therefore the value for degrees of freedom associated with the numerator is usually a small number. The denominator Mean Square (also known as the **error term** in some circles) has an accompanying degrees-of-freedom value that is larger and somewhat more difficult to calculate. It is the sum of the degrees of freedom of those sample variances that are combined in estimating the population variance. Whether or not we can figure out these degrees-of-freedom values on our own, we must be sure that we have both of them when we check the significance of a calculated F-ratio against critical values listed in an F-table.

DETERMINING THE SIGNIFICANCE
OF A CALCULATED F-RATIO

An F-Table lists the critical F-values necessary for significance at some single probability level (such as $p = .05$). The critical value for a particular F-ratio is found by locating both the numerator degrees of freedom (usually given in columns across the top of the table) and the denominator degrees of freedom (generally running down the side of the page). If our calculated F-ratio exceeds the critical value listed for the appropriate pair of degrees-of-freedom values, then we can reject the null hypothesis at that level of significance. If we want to check our F-ratio against a higher level of significance (such as $p = .01$ or $p = .001$), we will have to find another F-table. (Some F-tables give critical values for two levels of significance in the same table by listing the ones for a higher level in a different-sized type.) Each F-ratio calculated in a multivariate analysis has its own appropriate pair of degrees-of-freedom values. The null hypothesis for that particular F-ratio is accepted or rejected, depending on whether the calculated value is smaller or larger than the critical F value. In a multivariate analysis, some of the F-ratios may be nonsignificant, some may be significant at $p < .05$, and some may be significant at even higher levels. We have to check each F-ratio separately to find out.

Since in Analysis of Variance our alternative hypotheses do not state a direction of difference among the means, we do not have to worry about the issue of making one- or two-tailed comparisons, as we did for the t-test. If we reject a null hypothesis in an Analysis of Variance, our alternative is simply to conclude that the means being compared come from different populations.

COMING TO A CONCLUSION FROM THE ANALYSIS OF VARIANCE

To come to an intelligible conclusion from an Analysis of Variance, we have to look at both the descriptive and the inferential statistics. First we examine the main effect found for each IV separately. If an IV's F-ratio is significant, we reject the null hypothesis associated with that IV and conclude that the overall DV means representing the levels of that IV are really different. We have to look at the overall means themselves to determine the direction of the effect. If another IV's F-ratio is not significant, we accept its null hypothesis and conclude that this IV does not affect the DV. If an interaction effect is significant, we have to look at the means of the different conditions to discover the nature of the interaction. For example, the study of the effects of distraction and sex of subject on performance might show that both main effects were significant, and that there was a significant interaction as well. Looking at the three overall means for the levels of distraction might tell us that the effect of increasing distraction was to decrease performance significantly. The two overall means for the two sexes might reveal that the females performed significantly better on the task than the males. To determine the meaning of the significant interaction, we would have to look at the six means for each of the experimental conditions. Examination of these means might show that distraction had a much larger effect on women than it did on men. For example, females might perform a great deal better than males under conditions of low distraction, but only slightly better under conditions of high distraction. The results of an Analysis of Variance are only understandable if we examine the actual means being compared.

EXAMPLES OF ONE-WAY ANALYSES OF VARIANCE

Interval data from a Single-IV, Multi-Level design can be analyzed by a one-way Analysis of Variance. The one-way analysis is the same whether the IV is defined as Between- or Within-Subjects. In Chapter 4 we discussed the Crancer *et al.* (1969) study in which three levels of a single drug administration variable were investigated in a Within-Subjects design. Using counterbalanced orders, Crancer *et al.* measured all their 36 subjects after no-drug (control), alcohol, and marijuana consumption. They recorded a number of DV measures of performance on a simulated driving task. For such a design, you would perform a separate Analysis of Variance for each DV measure.

Crancer *et al.* reported no significant differences in steering errors among the means for their three groups. A hypothetical Analysis of Variance for such data might look as in Table 6.4. Let's see what information is available from such a table.

Table 6.4   Analysis of Variance of Steering Errors

Source of Variation	Mean Square	Degrees of Freedom	F
Drug IV (between means)	248.3	2	1.16 (2, 105)
Error (within samples)	214.0	105	
Total		107	

We know from the design of the research that estimating the drug (IV) effect will involve comparing three means. Table 6.4 shows the degrees of freedom for this comparison as $3 - 1 = 2$. Each of these means is based on 36 observations. The *Mean Square Error,* a term often used for the denominator of the *F*-ratio, is a combination of the variances of each of the three samples, and its degrees-of-freedom value is the sum of the separate degrees of freedom for each sample, or $(36 - 1) + (36 - 1) + (36 - 1) = 105$. The *F*-ratio for the drug IV doesn't look too promising; it's so close to 1 that we will probably accept the null hypothesis and conclude that the drug IV doesn't affect steering errors. To be on the safe side, we'd better look it up in a table anyway. The *F*-table we find doesn't have any entries for 2 and 105 degrees of freedom, but it does for 2 and 100 and for 2 and 125, so we can make do. For 2 and 100 the critical *F* for $p = .05$ is 3.09, and for 2 and 125 it's 3.07. Our hunch is correct; the drug IV *F*-ratio of 1.16 is nowhere near significant. We have to conclude that for steering errors there are no differences among the samples other than sampling error.

For another DV, speedometer errors, Crancer *et al.* reported significant effects. A hypothetical Analysis of Variance for this outcome of the experiment is given in Table 6.5. The *F*-ratio in this table certainly looks more promising. It exceeds the critical *F* of about 3.09 that we found listed for the .05 level. Further checking reveals that it does not exceed the critical *F* of 4.82 listed for 2 and 100 degrees of freedom at the .01 level. We conclude that we can reject our null hypothesis with a $p < .05$ of being wrong. It looks like the drug IV, which did not affect steering errors, did significantly affect errors in speed. We would have to look at the means themselves to say what the effect was.

Table 6.5 Analysis of Variance for Speedometer Errors

Source of Variation	Mean Square	Degrees of Freedom	F
Drug IV (between means)	612.6	2	3.64 (2, 105)
Error (within samples)	168.3	105	
Total		107	

Multiple Comparisons after a One-Way Analysis of Variance

At this point you may feel a little dissatisfied. We established in Table 6.5 that the drug IV had a significant effect on speedometer errors, but you may want to know whether alcohol and marijuana produced equal effects. There are a number of multiple-comparison tests we can use *after* doing the appropriate Analysis of Variance. Some of these involve making all possible comparisons; others involve making only specific comparisons, such as comparing several experimental groups against a single control group. Lee (1975, pp. 300–304) presents a good discussion of the alternative tests that are available. For example, we could use the *Newman-Keuls test* (Lee, 1975, p. 302) to check the significance of all the differences possible among the three means. We might find from this test that both the alcohol and the marijuana groups made significantly more errors than the control group, but that there was no significant difference between the alcohol and marijuana groups in speedometer errors.

TWO-WAY ANALYSES OF VARIANCE

When we use a design with multiple variables, not only can we estimate the main effect of each IV, but we can also get a measure of the interaction of the IVs. In Chapter 4 we designed a four-group experiment to test the effects of both alcohol and marijuana on a number of DVs. In Table 4.1 and Fig. 4.6 we looked at a possible outcome of this experiment for the DV of number of correct solutions for a 20-item anagram test. This four-group study had ten subjects randomly assigned to each group. The conditions the four groups were subjected to resulted from combining a two-level alcohol variable with a two-level marijuana variable. An Analysis of Variance that might result for these data is given in Table 6.6.

Each of the three F-ratios in Table 6.6 has the same pair of degrees of freedom, so we need find only one set of critical values from our F-tables. For the combination of 1 and 36 degrees of freedom, the .05 level has a critical F of 4.11, and the .01 level has a critical F of 7.39. Comparing the calculated F values from Table 6.6 with these critical values, we can reject the null hypothesis that marijuana has no effect at the .05 level and the null hypothesis that alcohol has no effect at the .01 level. In addition to having both main effects significant, we find that the interaction is significant at the .01 level. The interaction we saw between the effects of these two IVs

Table 6.6   Analysis of Variance for Correct Anagrams Solutions

Source of Variation	Mean Square	Degrees of Freedom	F
Main effect 1: alcohol	405.00	1	7.64 (1, 36)
Main effect 2: marijuana	245.00	1	4.62 (1, 36)
Interaction	517.00	1	9.74 (1, 36)
Error (within samples)	53.03	36	
Total		39	

in Fig. 4.6 is therefore statistically significant and likely to be found again. Mixing alcohol and marijuana is much more detrimental to the anagram task than could be predicted by adding their separate effects. This is something we can find out only by doing a multivariate study.

ANALYSES OF VARIANCE WITH MORE THAN TWO FACTORS

As we discussed in Chapter 4, multivariate designs can get very complex, especially if we treat some of the IVs as Within-Subjects and some as Between Subjects, or combine Subject and Non-Subject IVs. When a design is partially randomized and partially repeated measures, we can have multiple "error" terms, and the appropriate denominator for the F-ratio will depend on which main effect or interaction we are considering. However, the interpretation of the F-ratios, once calculated, is the same. If they are significant for a main effect, it means that the IV affected the DV. If they are significant for an interaction, it means that the IVs in the interaction alter each other's effects.

WHY NOT USE MULTIPLE t-TESTS?

Occasionally we'll find in the literature a study in which the significance of differences among means in a multigroup experiment is estimated by **multiple t-tests.** This must have sneaked by the editors. For example, a six-condition experiment reports 15 t-statistics calculated for each of the possible pairwise combination of six sample means. The authors then go on to tell us which of the comparisons were "significant" and to draw numerous conclusions. However, some of their "significant differences" are most likely spurious (not true), for the researchers are not sticking to the probability model underlying the t-test (for more explanation, see Cochran and Cox, 1957, p. 75).

Suppose that in a study with six groups you had assigned ten subjects to each group and measured each subject once on your DV. The total number of observations you would have from your experiment is 60, and the total number of degrees of freedom is one less than that, or 59. When you perform inferential statistical tests on your data, you cannot use up more than the total number of degrees of freedom you have. However, if you do multiple pairwise comparisons of the six sample means using the formulas for the *t*-test of independent groups, you will use 18 (10 − 1 + 10 − 1) degrees of freedom for each pairwise comparison. This means that if you do all possible 15 tests on your six means, you will have used a total of 270 (18 × 15) degrees of freedom! By doing so you are pretending you have 271 pieces of data instead of the 60 you actually collected. Such multiple comparisons of means must be done using tests designed for the purpose after completion of an Analysis of Variance.

RECAPITULATION

for MULTICONDITION ANALYSES OF VARIANCE

The *Analysis of Variance,* based on the *F-ratio,* is used for normally distributed, interval data collected from experiments whose designs have more than two conditions to be compared. The *F*-statistic is the ratio of a variance calculated between sample means to a variance estimated from the within-sample variances. These variances are often called *Mean Squares.* Each part of the *F*-ratio has its own associated value for degrees of freedom, and checking the significance of a calculated *F*-statistic involves finding the critical value of *F* specified by a pair of degrees of freedom. When the variance of the sample means exceeds the population variance estimated from sample variances, the resulting *F*-ratio may be sufficiently large that the null hypothesis that all the samples come from the same population will have to be rejected. The *one-way Analysis of Variance* is used for multicondition designs with only one IV. This analysis of variance produces only a "between-conditions" variance estimate and a "within-conditions" variance estimate (also known as an *error term*), the ratio of which gives a single *F*-statistic. If it is desirable to further determine statistical significance of pairwise comparisons of multiple sample means, there are several *multiple-comparison tests* available for use after doing the Analysis of Variance. Multiple *t*-tests should not be used on data collected from multicondition designs. Analyses of variance on multiple-IV designs produce several *F*-ratios. There will be an *F*-statistic for the *main effect* of each IV taken separately. There will also be an *F*-statistic for each interaction between IVs. Depending on the exact construction of the design, especially if Between-Subjects (randomized) and Within-Subjects (repeated measures) IVs are combined, there may be more than one error term for the design. However, the interpretation of the *F*-ratios in rejecting specific null hypotheses remains the same. For each main effect you either accept or reject the null hypothesis that the overall means representing each level of that IV come from the same population. For each interaction term you either accept or reject the null hypothesis that the effect of one IV on the DV is not changed by the actions of another IV.

BEHAVIORAL OBJECTIVES

for MULTICONDITION ANALYSES OF VARIANCE

1. Demonstrate, for three or more sample means, how doing multiple between-samples t-tests (for which the degrees of freedom equal $N_1 - 1 + N_2 - 1$) overestimates the total degrees of freedom in the data ($N_{tot} - 1$).

2. List the requirements for doing an Analysis of Variance.

3. Describe the numerator and denominator of an F-ratio.

4. Describe the two variance (or Mean Square) estimates you calculate in a one-way Analysis of Variance.

5. Describe the different kinds of variance estimates (Mean Square estimates) you get from a multiple-IV Analysis of Variance.

6. Given an F-statistic with its two accompanying degrees of freedom, look it up in an F-table and evaluate its significance.

7. Given Analysis of Variance results from an experiment, interpret the F-ratios in the table and write down the conclusions that can be made about the data.

8. Write out the null hypothesis for a one-way Analysis of Variance.

9. Write out the null hypothesis for a multivariate Analysis of Variance:
   a. For a main effect.
   b. For an interaction.

SAMPLE TEST QUESTIONS

for MULTICONDITION ANALYSES OF VARIANCE

1. Consider a design with three randomized groups of 20 subjects each. Suppose all possible pairwise comparisons were done between the means of these groups, using the t-test for independent samples (degrees of freedom $= N_1 - 1 + N_2 - 1$).
   a. How many pieces of data have the researchers actually collected?
   b. How many total degrees of freedom have they used in making all their pairwise comparisons?
   c. What is a problem with doing this type of analysis, given your answers to (a) and (b)?

2. From Milton (1959): Sex differences in problem solving as a function of role appropriateness of the problem content.

   In this study 24 undergraduate men and 24 undergraduate women were each given a set of 20 problems to solve. Half of the problems had content appropriate to the masculine role and half had problem content appropriate to the feminine role. The mean number of problems solved out of 10 are given separately for the four experimental conditions in Table 6.7. The results of an Analysis of Variance on these data are given in Table 6.8.

Table 6.7   Mean Number of Problems Solved

| Problem Content | Sex of Subjects | | Overall |
	Men	Women	
Masculine	5.71	3.29	4.50
Feminine	4.99	3.83	4.41
Combined	5.35	3.56	

Source: Reprinted with permission of the publisher from G. S. Milton, "Sex differences in problem solving as a function of role appropriateness of the problem content."

Table 6.8   Analysis of Variance of Number of Problems Solved

Source of Variation	Degrees of Freedom	Mean Square	F-Ratios
Sex	1	77.04	14.36 (1, 46)
Error I	46	5.37	
Problem content	1	.18	.08 (1, 46)
Problem X Sex	1	9.37	4.42 (1, 46)
Error II	46	2.12	
Total	95		

a. What is the DV in this study?

b. What were the IVs? For each IV you identify, specify:

  1) Whether it is a Subject or a Non-Subject IV.

  2) Whether it is treated as Between-Subjects or Within-Subjects.

  3) Whether it represents randomized groups, repeated measures, or blocked groups.

c. Give the design of this study in shorthand. What is its name?

d. Looking at the means in Table 6.7:

  1) Would you predict an effect of sex?

  2) Would you predict an effect of problem content?

  3) Would you predict a significant interaction between sex and problem content?

e. From Table 6.8, which sources of variation represent main effects, and which source of variation represents an interaction?

f. The critical F-value for the .05 level at 1 and 46 degrees of freedom is 4.05; and for the .01 level, 7.21.

  1) At what level is the IV of sex significant? What conclusions would this lead you to? (Be specific.)

2) At what level is the IV of problem content significant? What conclusion would this lead you to? (Be specific.)

3) At what level is the combination of the two IVs significant? What conclusion would this lead you to? (Be specific.)

g. The original research hypothesis of Milton was: "When the characteristics of problems are altered to make them less appropriate to the masculine sex role, the sex difference in problem solving skill will be reduced." Explain how his results did or did not support this idea.

3. Consider the study reported on wood chewing in horses as described on p. 111 (Test Question 2).

a. What type of analysis might be appropriate for these data and why?

b. State the null and alternative hypotheses for an inferential statistical test of these data.

d. Why might you want to do an additional multiple-comparison test of these data? What do you expect to be the results of applying the appropriate tests to these data?

SECTION 4: INFERENTIAL TESTS FOR ORDINAL MEASURES

NONPARAMETRIC STATISTICS

Inferential tests designed for samples of ordinal measures are said to be **distribution-free** because they do not require that any assumptions be made about the distribution of the population from which the samples were taken. Inferential statistics based on the normal distribution, such as the t-test and F-test, are called **parametric statistics.** Such tests assume that the underlying population consists of normally distributed interval measures that can be summarized by certain **parameters of the distribution,** namely, the mean and standard deviation. When an inferential test does not require that the population of measures conform to certain distribution parameters, then it is said to be a **nonparametric test,** another way of saying that the test is distribution-free. Whenever your DV measures are ordinal or are interval measures that are not normally distributed, the appropriate statistical test would be one of the nonparametric, distribution-free tests.

THE VARIETY OF ORDINAL INFERENTIAL STATISTICS

Those who are familiar with the t-test and the F-test for normally distributed interval data may be bewildered by the variety of tests available for use with ordinal data. Ordinal measurement scales come in many forms. They may consist of only a few categories and be barely distinguishable from a nominal scale. On the other hand, an ordinal scale can consist of the rankings of a sample of interval data and can have as many ordinal rank categories as there are different values of the interval measure.

Different statistical tests have been devised for the few-category and many-category situations, as well as for different research designs. We'll cover only a few of the more common tests here. For analysis of research involving nominal, ordinal, or nonnormally distributed interval DV scales, you'll need to have a good nonparametric statistics book handy for reference. The classic in the field is Siegel (1956), *Nonparametric statistics for the behavioral sciences.* Some other possibilities are listed in the final section of this chapter. Nonparametric statistics are generally not well covered in most basic statistics books.

One difficulty in using nonparametric statistics is that they are not well developed for complex designs. We'll discuss a couple of nonparametric "analyses of variance" that can handle Multi-Level, Single-IV designs. However, you must curb your enthusiasm for adding IV after IV to your research if your DV measurement scale is to be ordinal rather than interval. Otherwise you may have a hard time finding a test to analyze your data! Even if your measurement scale is interval, it is better to stay away from multivariate designs unless you can find a sufficient number of subjects to gather at least 10 observations in each condition of the experiment. Very small samples of interval data are often better analyzed by nonparametric statistics, and there just aren't any nonparametric tests that can easily handle complex multivariate designs.

THE POWER OF A TEST

When a parametric (normal distribution) inferential test *is* appropriate for our data, a nonparametric test will be less sensitive in detecting the effects of an IV on a DV. In other words, a nonparametric test may fail to reject our null hypothesis when the appropriate parametric test would reject it. This is the meaning of the statement that nonparametric tests have less **power** than parametric tests, provided that the assumptions of the appropriate parametric test are met. For small samples, the power of parametric and nonparametric tests is about the same, but as sample size increases, the nonparametric test becomes progressively less powerful than the appropriate parametric test. For this reason it is very important that you know the type of measurement scale you are using and the characteristics of the distribution of measures you obtain. Using parametric statistics when they don't apply can lead to mistaken conclusions, but using nonparametric statistics when parametric statistics are appropriate can mean that you perform a less powerful test and underestimate the significance of your data.

PECULIARITIES OF NONPARAMETRIC TESTS

Ranking

Most of the tests for ordinal measures require that all the DV measures be ranked, or put in order from most to least. Then a test statistic is computed from these ranks. Ranking of data can get messy for a large sample of DV observations measured on a scale with only a few categories. For example, if 100 subjects are measured on an ordinal scale consisting of only five categories, obviously a lot of people will have the same measurement. It will be impossible to put them neatly in order and assign them all different ranks from 1 to 100. The solution is to say that people who are assigned the same DV measures are all **tied** for the same rank. Table 6.9 gives an example of how to assign an **average rank** to subjects tied for the same measure.

The 35 people in Table 6.9 who were all assigned the DV ordinal value of 1 occupy ranks 1 to 35. Each is given the rank of 17.5, which is the average of their beginning and end ranks. The next 15 people, all of whom were given the DV scale value of 2, occupy the next 15 ranks, ranks 36 to 50, and they are all considered tied for rank 43, the average of 36 and 50. And so on. Many ordinal tests require that we first carry out such a ranking of our subjects according to the DV measures assigned to them. Some tests may also require a **correction for ties** or may even warn us that they are not useful tests if there are a large number of such ties.

Table 6.9   Rankings of 100 Subjects Measured on a Five-Category Ordinal Scale

Ordinal Measure	Frequency of Subjects	Beginning Rank	Ending Rank	Average Rank	Number Tied
1	35	1	35	17.5	35
2	15	36	50	43	15
3	25	51	75	63	25
4	15	76	90	83	15
5	10	91	100	95.5	10
	100				

Small Samples Versus Large Samples

Some of the tests for ordinal data have a version for small samples (usually those less than 20) that is different from the version for large samples. In some cases the test may not be appropriate at all if samples are smaller than some stated size. When using nonparametric statistics, it's necessary to read the descriptive information at the beginning of the test instructions to be sure which version of the test you want—or whether you want it at all!

Special Tables

Ordinal inferential tests result in calculated test statistics, just as do the *t*-test and the *F*-test, and you'll need the appropriate table to check their significance levels. A book that describes how to do a particular test will usually have the necessary table. The exact form of these tables will vary, so you must figure out what the author means by the various letters used in the table headings. In general the tables will report the critical test statistics for the common levels of significance (.05, .01) and will tell you whether they are for one-tailed or two-tailed tests. In looking up the critical test statistic for ordinal tests, you will have to take into account either sample size or degrees of freedom, as specified by the test instructions. (Some of the ordinal test-statistic tables are "backwards." They are set up so that you reject the null hypothesis when the critical test statistic is *less than,* rather than *greater than,* the value in the table. Even statisticians like to introduce some variety into life.)

Sometimes, especially for large samples, the test instructions will tell you to convert your calculated test statistic to a z-score. After doing this, you can look up the calculated z-score in any z-table (table of the normal distribution) to see whether it falls in the region of rejection for the null hypothesis, as specified by your level of significance and whether your hypotheses are one- or two-tailed. For example, suppose we were doing a one-tailed, nonparametric test and the calculated test statistic converted, according to formulas given with the nonparametric test, to a z of 1.65. A check of a table of z-scores would tell us that this z had only a .0495 probability of occurring by chance. We could then reject our null hypothesis at $p < .05$ for a one-tailed test. (Could we reject this null hypothesis at the .05 level if the test hypotheses were two-tailed?)

TWO-CONDITION, INDEPENDENT-GROUP DESIGNS

If our data are ordinal and our design involves two independent groups, such as occurs in Static-Groups or Randomized-Groups designs, then we need an ordinal inferential statistical test analogous to the t-test for independent groups. Our null and alternative hypotheses will be similar to those for the corresponding t-test, except that our hypotheses will now be stated in terms of comparison of medians rather than of means. Since there are two medians to be compared in a two-group design, our hypotheses can be either directional (one-tailed) or nondirectional (two-tailed), just as for the t-test.

Median Test

The **Median test** (Siegel, 1956, pp. 111–116) will indicate whether it is likely that two independent samples, not necessarily of the same size, have been drawn from the same population or from populations with the same median. It is a fairly simple test to do. It requires that you combine both samples and find the overall median for all your data. Then, for each sample separately, you count up how many scores are above the overall median and how many are below. Obviously, if one sample has most of its scores above the overall median and the other sample has most of its scores below, this test should reject the null hypothesis that both samples come from populations with the same median. The particular inferential test statistic you calculate depends on the sizes of your two samples. This test has relatively low power for large samples.

Mann-Whitney U-Test

The most powerful of the nonparametric tests is the **Mann-Whitney U-Test** (Siegel, 1956, pp. 116–127). Similar to the *t*-test for independent groups, it tests whether or not two samples are drawn from the same population. However, it does not require that the population measures be intervally scaled or that the population be assumed to be normally distributed. The null and alternative hypotheses, as for the *t*-test, can be either one- or two-tailed. A two-tailed null hypothesis for this test would be that the two samples came from the same population (H_0: Median$_E$ = Median$_C$). The two-tailed alternative hypothesis would say that they came from different populations with different medians (H_A: Median$_E \neq$ Median$_C$).

The test statistic calculated in the Mann-Whitney is called the **U**-statistic. It can be calculated only if there are relatively few ties in rank and the samples are small (less than 25). Critical values of U are listed in "*U*-tables." It's necessary to read test instructions carefully when interpreting U. Most U tables are set up so that the null hypothesis is rejected when the calculated U is *less* than the critical value of U listed for a given significance level! Also, before checking your calculated U you have to be certain whether you have a one-tailed or a two-tailed *U*-table, since both kinds are available.

When sample sizes are large (greater than 20) and/or there are many ties in rank, you must convert your *U*-statistic to a *z*-score. Along with the formulas for this conversion will be included a "correction for ties," which will take care of the problem of tied ranks. Once you have your *z*-score, you can look it up in a *z*-table to see whether it is large enough to reject your null hypothesis. If your hypotheses were one-tailed, for example, you would need a *z*-score of $+1.64$ or more to reject the null hypothesis at the .05 level, whereas if your hypotheses were two-tailed, the *z* would have to be ± 1.96 for rejection with $p < .05$.

TWO-CONDITION PAIRED-SAMPLES DESIGNS

If our data are ordinal measures or nonnormal interval measures and they were gathered from a two-condition design involving either repeated measures within the same subjects or matched measures for pairs of subjects, then we need an ordinal inferential statistical test analogous to the *t*-test for paired (correlated) samples. Just as for this type of *t*-test, ordinal inferential statistics for repeated measures or matched pairs involve determining the direction of difference within each pair of scores. As for the *t*-test for paired samples, the null and alternative hypotheses are set up concerning the differences within each pair, and they can be worded to be either one-tailed, predicting a certain direction of difference, or two-tailed.

Sign Test

This **Sign test** (Siegel, 1956, pp. 68–75) has relatively low power but has the compensating virtue of being easy to do. If this test comes out significant, we can be sure that a more powerful test appropriate to the data will also come out significant.

For a Sign test, all you do is compare each observation in sample A with its paired observation in sample B. Each time the sample A observation in a pair is bigger than the sample B observation, you give the comparison a *plus*. Each time the sample A value is less than its paired sample B observation, you give the comparison a *minus*. Pairs that have the same value in both samples are thrown out of the analysis. For a two-tailed Sign test, your specific null hypothesis is that the number of pairs with pluses is equal to the number of pairs with minuses. Your alternative two-tailed hypothesis is that they are not equal (either more or less pluses than minuses). Of course, you can also set up the Sign test hypotheses as one-tailed if you want to predict before the experiment that one sample will yield consistently larger DV measures than the other. As with the *t*-test, whether your hypotheses are one- or two-tailed makes a difference only at the end of the test when you determine the critical value for your test statistic.

The table available for interpreting the results of a Sign test tells you for any given total number of pluses and minuses what the probability is for obtaining a particular number of one type of sign. The probabilities are usually listed for the less frequent sign, the sign that occurs less often for your pairs. When your total number of pluses and minuses exceeds 25, you can calculate a *z*-score from knowing only the number of the less frequent sign and the total number of pluses and minuses (Siegel, 1956, p. 72). You then use a *z*-table to determine the probability, keeping in mind whether your test hypotheses were one- or two-tailed.

Wilcoxon's Matched-Pairs, Signed-Ranks Test

A test that is applicable to the same design situations as the Sign test and the *t*-test for paired samples is **Wilcoxon's Matched-Pairs, Signed-Ranks Test** (Siegel, 1956, pp. 75–83). Since it takes into account the relative size of the differences between paired sample-A and sample-B scores in addition to their signs, it uses more of the information in ordinal and nonnormal interval data than does the Sign test. It involves not only finding the signs of differences within pairs of scores but also ranking the differences according to their relative sizes. Just as for the *t*-tests, the *U*-test, and the Sign test, Wilcoxon's test can be done with either one- or two-tailed hypotheses. A two-tailed null hypothesis would be that the median difference score would be zero (H_0: Median$_{E-C}$ = 0). A one-tailed null hypothesis might be that the median difference score was equal to or less than zero (H_0: Median$_{E-C} \leq 0$) if the alternative hypothesis was that it was greater than zero (H_A: Median$_{E-C} > 0$).

Just as for the Sign test, pairs of scores with no difference between them are discarded from the Wilcoxon analysis. The remaining difference scores are then ranked according to absolute size without regard to sign. Difference scores with tied ranks are each given the average rank, as demonstrated in Table 6.9. After the scores are ranked, the ranks of all the positive differences are summed and compared with the sum of the ranks of all negative differences. These two sums will be about the same if the median difference score is zero. If one sum exceeds the other, it indicates that difference scores of one sign are larger than the other. Generally the symbol **T** is used to indicate the "smaller sum of like-signed ranks," and tables of T are available to check its significance. (Like U in the Mann-Whitney U-test, T is significant at a given level only if it is equal to or smaller than the critical T listed for the total number of signed difference scores you are testing.) If your total number of signed difference scores is more than 25, you'd have to convert your calculated T-statistic to a z-score (Siegel, 1956, p. 79) and use a z-table to determine the probability that would let you reject or accept your null hypothesis.

Wilcoxon's T-test is a much more powerful test than the Sign test, and for small samples it is close in power to the t-test, even when the conditions of the t-test are met. It is a good all-purpose test whenever you have a Within-Subjects, Repeated-Measures or a Matched-Groups design in which the DV is measured on an ordered scale.

MULTICONDITION DESIGNS WITH ORDINAL MEASURES

As mentioned in the introduction to this section, ordinal inferential statistical tests are not well developed for complex multivariate designs. Let's look at two analyses that are available for Single-IV, Multi-Level designs.

The **Kruskal-Wallis One-Way Analysis of Variance by Ranks** (Siegel, 1956, pp. 184–193) tests the null hypothesis that three or more independent samples come from the same or identical populations. It can be used for a Single-IV, Between-Subjects design after the DV measures have been ranked.

For a Single-IV, Within-Subjects or Matched-Subjects design, a different analysis is necessary. The **Friedman Two-Way Analysis of Variance by Ranks** (Siegal, 1956, pp. 166–173) is used for such Repeated-Measures or Matched-Measures designs.

Each type of Analysis of Variance by Ranks has its appropriate test statistic and test-statistic table. Interpretation of a significant test statistic is the same as interpretation of a significant F in the parametric Analyses of Variance.

HINTS FOR DOING NONPARAMETRIC STATISTICAL TESTS

If you are unfamiliar with a particular test, first read carefully the introductory material to see whether the test is really applicable to your own situation. If you decide it is the test you want, then work through at least one example that appears to be close to your situation. Explanations of test procedures and formulas are sometimes confusing, but if you can follow the author's example and come up with the same numbers, you'll be more likely to analyze your own data correctly. Be sure you understand the instructions for using the particular table given for the test. There are many different formats for statistical tables, even ones for the same test! Remember that selecting the correct statistical test for your data is more important than being able to do the calculations; for that you can get help from someone else.

RECAPITULATION

for INFERENTIAL TESTS FOR ORDINAL MEASURES

Nonparametric or *distribution-free* inferential statistical tests are necessary for ordinally scaled measures or for interval measures that are not normally distributed. There are a variety of nonparametric tests appropriate to different designs and different measurement situations. Common to most of these tests is the necessity of ranking the DV measures and solving the problem of *tied ranks* when a number of subjects are given the same DV value. Many nonparametric tests have different versions for small and large samples, and they require either special tables or formulas for converting the test statistic to a *z*-score. Nonparametric tests vary in *power,* or the ability to reject the null hypothesis at a given significance level. Two-condition, nonparametric tests can be either one- or two-tailed, depending on the null and alternative hypotheses. For a two-condition, Independent-Groups design, such as the Static-Groups or Randomized-Groups designs, it is possible to do either the *Median test* or the more powerful *Mann-Whitney U-Test.* For a two-condition design involving either repeated Within-Subjects measures on a single group of subjects or matched groups of subjects, either the *Sign test* or the *Wilcoxon T-test* is appropriate. Both of these tests are based only on those pairs of scores for which the value in one condition is more or less than its paired value in the other condition. The Wilcoxon test takes into account the magnitude of each difference as well as its direction and is a more powerful test. Nonparametric inferential statistics are not well developed for multicondition designs. The *Kruskal-Wallis One-Way Analysis of Variance by Ranks* can be used for a Single-IV, Between-Groups design. The *Friedman Two-Way Analysis of Variance by Ranks* can be used for a Single-IV, Within-Subjects or Matched-Subjects design.

BEHAVIORAL OBJECTIVES

for INFERENTIAL TESTS FOR ORDINAL MEASURES

1. Distinguish between parametric and nonparametric tests.
2. List the six ordinal tests presented in this section.
3. Given a list of characteristics of the different ordinal tests, identify which tests they apply to.
4. Given either interval or ordinal data, rank the data, dealing with the problem of tied ranks.
5. Given a description of a measurement situation, identify which analysis would be appropriate for the data, and set up the null and alternative hypotheses.
6. Explain what is meant by the "power" of an inferential statistical test.
7. Given the name of any of the six tests discussed in this section, describe the situation for which it would be appropriate.
8. Given the results of an ordinal statistical test with its level of significance, state the conclusions the test would allow you to make.

SAMPLE TEST QUESTIONS

for INFERENTIAL TESTS FOR ORDINAL MEASURES

1. For each of the following statements, identify the test or tests to which the statement refers as: Median test (med), Mann-Whitney (U), Sign test (sign), Wilcoxon (T), Kruskal-Wallis (K-W), Friedman (Fr).

   a. Data must be ranked first, and the analysis done on the ranks.

   b. Appropriate for a two-group, Matched-Subjects design.

   c. Has relatively low power.

   d. Involves both ranking of sizes of differences and determination of their signs.

   e. For large samples, the calculated test statistic is converted to a z-score.

   f. Appropriate for a three-group, Within-Subjects (repeated-measured) design.

   g. Use when you have more than two conditions in the experiment.

   h. Can be either one-tailed or two-tailed.

   i. Used for the same design situation as the t-test for independent groups.

2. After your subjects have completed relaxation training either with or without feedback from a muscle-tension biofeedback device, you ask them to rate their agreement or disagreement with the statement: "I felt successful at relaxing during the training sessions." The subjects can use ratings from 1 (strong disagreement) to 5 (strong agreement). You have 10 subjects in the no-feedback group and 10 subjects in the feedback group.

   a. What test would you use for the rating data if the subjects had been randomly assigned to the two groups? What would your hypotheses for this test be?

   b. What test would you use for the rating data if the subjects in the two groups had been matched on some basis? What would your hypotheses for this test be?

3. Suppose the overall results for the 20 subjects responding to the rating question described in Question 2 were as follows:

Rating	Frequency
1	0
2	1
3	1
4	12
5	6
	20

   What rank would you assign to subjects who rated this question with a 4? (In answering this, complete the table above in the same form as Table 6.9.)

4. In a study on the effects of different speech therapies on increasing spontaneous talking in speech-delayed preschoolers, the investigator recorded the amount of time the child spontaneously talked to his or her mother in a final one-hour ob-

servation period. Three different therapies were being compared, with different children assigned to each group. The original intention had been to analyze the "time speaking" data by an Analysis of Variance (*F*-test). However, the researcher was informed that duration or time data usually are not normally distributed. Furthermore, she had only six children in each of her groups. What test would you recommend that she use and why?

SECTION 5: INFERENTIAL TESTS FOR NOMINAL MEASURES

When our DV measures are nominal, we can summarize the measures by finding for each measurement category on our scale the number of subjects who were given that measure. To write a null hypothesis for an inferential statistical test, we need to determine what the **expected frequency** in each category on our DV scale would be if only chance processes were operating. Our alternative hypothesis would be that our **observed frequency** distribution is different from what would be expected under the null hypothesis. In most tests of nominal data the hypotheses are stated in this either-or fashion, so we don't have to choose between one- and two-tailed hypotheses. Either our observed frequencies are the same as our expected frequencies, or they are not. As for other inferential statistical tests, we need a test statistic that will allow us to reject the null hypothesis when more than chance is affecting the frequency distribution of our DV measures.

CHI-SQUARE

The most common test statistic for doing an inferential test on nominal data is called **chi-square** and is symbolized χ^2. It is a statistic that is calculated from the differences between observed frequencies and the frequencies expected under the null hypothesis. When the discrepancy is large between what happens in our research and what is expected by chance, this chi-square statistic will also be large. To see whether we can reject our null hypothesis, we will look up our calculated test statistic in a chi-square table, taking into account its degrees of freedom. As for the *t*-value, *F*-ratio, and *z*-score, when our calculated chi-square is larger than a critical value in the table, we will reject our null hypothesis and accept the alternative hypothesis.

The chi-square test is relatively easy to do, with only a few things to watch out for. You must be careful about setting up the appropriate null hypothesis so that you know what you are rejecting. When the degrees of freedom are small, you have to remember to use a *correction factor*. In fact, if your sample size is too small, you may not be able to do the test at all. The Chi-Square test assumes that observations are taken independently, and when you take repeated observations on the same subjects for the same DV, you will have to find the appropriate variant of chi-square to analyze your data.

THE ONE-WAY CHI-SQUARE, OR TEST OF "GOODNESS OF FIT"

Sometimes we will have the observed frequency distribution for only one sample of nominal data. We want to see how well the distribution of observations in our single sample "fits" what we expect from a particular null hypothesis. Often, our null hypothesis will be simply that the nominal categories on our DV scale should occur equally often. At other times our null hypothesis will be appropriate to some other set of probabilities resulting from chance. For such situations we can use a one-way Chi-Square test (Siegel, 1956, p. 42).

Example 1: Testing Honesty of a Single Die

Remember your sneaky brother and his (possibly) crooked dice discussed in Section 1 of this chapter? If we considered the null expectation for an unloaded die, we would expect the six faces of the die to come up equally often; we would expect each one to come up one-sixth of the time on the average. If our sample consisted of 30 rolls of the die, we would expect the faces of the die to come up five times each under the null hypothesis. To do a one-way Chi-Square test of these data, we could set up a table as follows:

Die Faces

	1	2	3	4	5	6
Expected frequency under the null hypothesis	5	5	5	5	5	5
Observed frequency						

We would then roll the die 30 times and record how many times each face came up. Calculating chi-square involves finding the amount of difference between each observed and each expected frequency. The chi-square statistic will be a small number if the observed and expected frequencies are nearly the same, a large number if they are very different. To determine degrees of freedom, we subtract 1 from the number of DV categories (K) used in the calculation of chi-square. This is usually symbolized as $K - 1$, and for this example it would be $(6 - 1)$, or 5. A chi-square table tells us that the critical chi-square at the .05 level of significance for 5 degrees of freedom is 11.071. If our calculated chi-square is larger than this, Brother is in trouble.

The Minimum Expected Frequency Must Be 5

You may have noticed that between Section 1, when we first discussed this "experiment," and the present section, we increased the number of rolls in our sample. We did so because the Chi-Square test must have an expected frequency of at least 5 in each DV category. If we had stuck to a sample of only 24 rolls, we would not have had a large enough expected frequency in each category to carry out this statistical analysis.

Example 2: Testing Joint Honesty of a Pair of Dice

The null hypothesis for the one-way Chi-Square test is not always that all categories will occur equally often. Sometimes a different probability model is needed. For instance, if we wanted to check the honesty of both of Brother's dice simultaneously by rolling them both together, we would use a different null or chance hypothesis. The possible sums of the numbers on two dice are not equally likely. For example, the sum 2 can occur in only one way: a 1 has to come up simultaneously on both dice. The sum of 3, however, can occur in two ways: either a 2 can appear on die A with a 1 on die B, or the other way around. The expected chance probabilities for the *sum* of the faces on two dice are given below.

Sum of Two Dice Faces

	2	3	4	5	6	7	8	9	10	11	12
Expected probability	1/36	2/36	3/36	4/36	5/36	6/36	5/36	4/36	3/36	2/36	1/36

The expected frequency for each nominal category under the null hypothesis would be its chance probability times the total number of rolls in the sample. If we're going to respect the requirements of the Chi-Square test, we'll need a pretty large sample. Since categories 2 and 12 have only a 1/36 chance of occurring, we'll need to roll the pair of dice 180 times to have the necessary expected frequency of 5 under the null hypothesis for these two categories! If we persist, we can set up our one-way table for the Chi-Square test as below, roll the dice 180 times to get our observed frequencies, and check Brother's honesty.

DV Categories: Sum of Values on Two Dice

	2	3	4	5	6	7	8	9	10	11	12
Expected frequencies under the null hypothesis for 180 rolls	5	10	15	20	25	30	25	20	15	10	5
Observed frequencies											

Testing Brother's dice this way increases the number of categories on the nominal scale to 11; thus we have $(11 - 1)$ or 10 degrees of freedom. The chi-square table tells us that a critical chi-square of 18.307 is needed for significance at the .05 level for 10 degrees of freedom. If our calculated chi-square is larger, we can reject our null hypothesis and accept the alternative idea that "pure chance" isn't the only thing governing Brother's dice.

Chi-Square Correction Necessary with Only One Degree of Freedom

The one-way Chi-Square test on a single sample is an easy test to do. The tricky part is getting the correct null hypothesis and figuring out the expected frequencies. Then we need to be sure that our sample size will be large enough so that the smallest of the expected frequencies will be 5 or more. Almost any basic statistical text gives the formula for the one-way Chi-Square test. The only thing we will need to watch for are situations in which the degrees of freedom will be only 1 (situations in which we have only two categories on the nominal DV scale). In this case we need a version of the chi-square formula containing a correction, usually called a "correction for continuity" or **Yates's correction**. (This correction involves subtracting 1/2 from each difference score before squaring.)

TWO-WAY CHI-SQUARE TEST FOR TWO INDEPENDENT SAMPLES

Often in a measurement situation using nominal variables, we want to see whether the measures on one nominal variable are independent of the measures taken on another. For instance, in Section 2 of Chapter 5, we reported measures of toy preference for samples of both normal and neurologically impaired preschoolers. We examined the resulting frequency distributions in various ways and decided, from the descriptive statistics, that boys in the two groups seemed to show about the same distribution of preferences, but girls did not. We can set up two-way frequency classifications separately for boys and for girls to check what we see in the descriptive statistics. For each of the two-way classifications given in Tables 6.10 and 6.11, our null hypothesis would be that the neurologically impaired and normal children showed the same relative distribution of toy preference.

Almost any basic statistics text gives the formula for calculating a two-way chi-square. For a two-way Chi-Square test of either Table 6.10 or Table 6.11, the null hypothesis would be that both the neurologically impaired and the normal children showed the same relative distribution of preferences. For example, if 21/58, or 36 percent, of all the boys preferred the hammer, then about 36 percent of the boys in each group taken separately should prefer the hammer. This would mean that the expected frequency for the neurologically impaired groups would be 16.6 (36 percent of 46 neurologically impaired boys), and the expected frequency for the normal boys would be 4.3 (36 percent of the 12 normal boys). Using the two-way chi-square

Table 6.10 Two-Way Classification of Toy Preferences for 58 Boys

| | Toys | | | | | |
Group	Book	Hammer	Truck	Gun	Doll	Total
Neurologically impaired	0	18	8	20	0	46
Normal	0	3	2	6	1	12
Total	0	21	10	26	1	58

Table 6.11 Two-Way Classification of Toy Preferences for 32 Girls

| | Toys | | | | | |
Group	Book	Hammer	Truck	Gun	Doll	Total
Neurologically impaired	0	10	2	5	3	20
Normal	2	0	1	2	7	12
Total	2	10	3	7	10	32

formula, we would find that the calculated chi-square is 4.33 for the boys and 14.08 for the girls. The degrees of freedom for a two-way chi-square would be the product of the degrees of freedom for each variable taken separately. Another way of expressing this is that for a two-way classification the degrees of freedom will be the number of columns in the table minus 1 times the number of rows minus 1. For either the sample of boys or that of girls the degrees of freedom will be $(5 - 1) \times (2 - 1)$, or 4. From a chi-square table, we find that at the .05 level the *critical value of chi-square* for four degrees of freedom is 9.488. It looks as though our suspicions from the descriptive statistics are correct: we can accept the null hypothesis for the boys, but for the girls we reject it and accept the alternative idea that the normal and neurologically impaired girls have different patterns of toy preference.

Watch for Expected Frequencies of Less Than 5

But just a moment. Remember the requirement that the expected frequencies should be at least 5 in each category for the Chi-Square test. Certainly this is not true for the "book" category; this category did not occur at all for either sample of boys. A category that is not used at all is eliminated from the Chi-Square test. Doing so would reduce our degrees of freedom to three but would not change the calculated chi-square value. If we looked up the critical chi-square for 3 degrees of freedom at the .05 level, we would still find that the table value, 7.815, was larger than our calculated value for the boys, and we would still accept the null hypothesis.

Even for the girls, who did select toys from every category, our expected frequencies will be less than 5 in some categories, mostly because of our very small sample of normal girls. Before we publish these data, we'd better take larger samples so that all the conditions of the Chi-Square test are met. One very common statistical violation found in the published literature is Chi-Square tests done on samples that are too small, producing many categories that have expected frequencies lower than 5.

Correction for Having Only One Degree of Freedom

The calculation of a two-way chi-square is little different from the calculation of a one-way chi-square, once we have figured out our expected frequencies under the null hypothesis. The degrees of freedom for a two-way chi-square will be the product of the degrees of freedom for each of the variables. When each of the variables in the two-way Chi-Square test has only two categories, the resulting degrees of freedom will be 1 and it will be necessary to use a correction, as for the one-way Chi-Square test.

USING CHI-SQUARE FOR REPEATED SAMPLES FOR THE SAME VARIABLE

Sometimes our research design will call for taking repeated measures of a single group of subjects before and after we have exposed them to a treatment. What interests us in this case is whether or not our treatment changes their distribution on a nominally scaled DV. For instance, we could observe the frequencies of a group of people planning to vote "yes" or "no" on an issue both before and after they had heard a speech on the topic. We would want to see whether the speech had any effect on the distribution of their votes. The results of such a study might be as shown in Table 6.12.

Table 6.12 Influence of a Speech on Votes of 58 People

	Vote "Yes"	Vote "No"	Total
Before speech	13	45	58
After speech	29	29	58

The Before- and the After-Speech values are not independent, because they represent repeated measures of the same subjects on the same DV. With such a repeated-measures, Within-Subjects design we would need a special variant of the Chi-Square test devised by McNemar (Siegel, 1956, p. 63), one especially designed for two repeated measures on a single group of subjects.

If we did repeated measures on a single group of subjects more than twice, we would need a test that is an extension of McNemar's test, called the Cochran Q-test (Siegal, 1956, p. 161). Remembering all these specific test names is not important. However, it is important to recognize that when we repeatedly measure a single group of subjects on the same nominal DV, we will need to find a special variation of the Chi-Square test designed specifically for repeated measures.

RECAPITULATION

for INFERENTIAL TESTS FOR NOMINAL MEASURES

Chi-square is the inferential test statistic calculated for most cases involving nomianlly scaled DVs. A *one-way Chi-Square test* allows us to test whether or not an *observed frequency distribution* for a single nominal DV matches an *expected frequency distribution* based on our null hypothesis. The null hypothesis is constructed on the assumption that the DV frequencies will be determined only by chance probabilities. The degrees of freedom for a one-way chi-square are the number of DV categories minus 1. Our calculated chi-square is significant when it exceeds the critical value in the table for the appropriate degrees of freedom and level of significance. A *two-way Chi-Square test* can be used to determine whether the frequency distributions of two variables are independent of each other. The null hypothesis is that they are—in other words, that the expected relative frequency distribution for one variable is the same for every level of the other variable. The degrees-of-freedom value for a two-way chi-square is the product of the degrees of freedom for each of the variables involved in the two-way classification. If the calculated chi-square is larger than the appropriate table value, then the null hypothesis is rejected, and the distributions of the two variables are said to be dependent on each other. When there is only one degree of freedom for chi-square, a *correction factor* must be added to the chi-square formula. Also, the Chi-Square test requires that there be a *minimum expected frequency of five* in any category, a requirement that is especially important if the test is done on only a few categories. Meeting this requirement may involve combining categories or measuring larger samples. The Chi-Square test is designed for independent samples. For repeated measures of the same subjects on the same DV, a special variant of the Chi-Square test will be needed.

BEHAVIORAL OBJECTIVES

for INFERENTIAL TESTS FOR NOMINAL MEASURES

1. Given the description of an experiment along with its results, identify whether it should be analyzed by:

    a. A one-way Chi-Square test.

    b. A two-way Chi-Square test.

    c. A variant of the Chi-Square test suitable for repeated measures of the same subjects on the same DV.

2.   Give the null and alternative hypotheses for a one-way Chi-Square test (either in general or for a specific situation).

3.   Give the null and alternative hypothesis for a two-way Chi-Square test (either in general or for a specific situation).

4.   Given a calculated chi-square and its degrees of freedom, look it up in a chi-square table and determine its significance.

5.   Given the frequency distribution for one or two variables, set up the appropriate one-way or two-way classification necessary for doing a Chi-Square test on them.

6   List those chi-square situations in which a "correction" will be needed and should be included in the chi-square formula.

7.   Discuss the minimum expected frequency requirement for a Chi-Square test, and suggest what can be done when this requirement is not met by the data.

8.   Given the description of an experiment and the results of a Chi-Square test, interpret the meaning of a significant chi-square.

SAMPLE TEST QUESTIONS

for INFERENTIAL TESTS FOR NOMINAL MEASURES

1.   For the 66 neurologically impaired preschoolers described in Table 5.6 (p. 163):

    a. Set up a two-way classification of sex and toy preference.

    b. State your null and alternative hypotheses for a statistical test of these data.

    c. What should you do with the "book" category? Do you think the "doll" category will have expected frequencies large enough to analyze?

    d. From looking at the data, do you think that a Chi-Square test would show that sex of subject has a significant relationship to toy preference for these children?

2.   If you toss a coin three times in a row, the chance probability that you will get three heads is 1/8, the probability that you will get two heads is 3/8, the probability that you will get only one head is 3/8, and the probability that you will get no heads at all is 1/8. Suppose you watch someone do a series of three tosses 40 times in a row and want to check whether the number of heads produced in each three-toss series is what you would expect from chance.

    a. What kind of Chi-Square test would you use?

    b. What would your null hypothesis be?

    c. What would your expected frequencies be under the null hypothesis?

      d. What degrees-of-freedom value would you use to check chi-square?

      e. Would you need a correction term in your formula for chi-square?

      f. Have you met the requirements of minimum sample size for chi-square?

      g. What would you conclude if the chi-square calculated for your data was greater than the critical value for the .01 level at the appropriate degrees of freedom?

3. Table 5.8 (p. 175) gives the frequency of subjects' identification of three relatively unknown colas as one of the major brands. Consider only the 270 subjects who identified the colas as Pepsi, Coca Cola, or Royal Crown. To begin with, you are interested only in whether or not these three major brand names were used equally often by these subjects.

      a. What kind of Chi-Square test would you use?

      b. What would your null hypothesis be?

      c. What would be your expected frequency of the identifications Pepsi, Coke, and Royal Crown?

      d. What would your degrees of freedom be for this test?

      e. Do you need a correction factor?

      f. Are the minimum requirements of sample size met?

      g. The calculated chi-square for these data is 8.16. The critical chi-square at the appropriate degrees of freedom for the .05 level is 5.99. What do you conclude?

4. Use the data in Table 5.8 to see whether the three different colas sampled by the 270 subjects produced different patterns of identification of them as the three major brands. (Note that you are leaving out of the analysis the 18 subjects who identified these colas as something else.)

      a. Set up the appropriate classification table.

      b. What kind of Chi-Square test do you need?

      c. What would your degrees of freedom be for this test?

      d. Are the requirements of minimum sample size met?

      e. Would you need a correction factor in your formula for chi-square?

      f. The calculated chi-square for these data is 3.43. The critical chi-square for the appropriate degrees of freedom at the .05 level is 9.488. What do you conclude?

SECTION 6: HINTS ON CHOOSING THE RIGHT INFERENTIAL TEST

CHOOSING YOUR STATISTICS

Choosing the right descriptive and inferential statistics to use on your data actually involves knowing the answers to only a small set of questions. First and foremost, you must correctly identify the scale on which your DV was measured. Next, you need to know how your measures distributed themselves along your scale. Finally, you need to know the details of your design. Answering a series of simple questions about your DV and your design will usually single out which statistical test will be appropriate. The questions, as well as the implications of their possible answers, are given in Fig. 6.3 in a *decision tree*. Following the path dictated by your answers to such simple questions as "Is your IV Between- or Within-Subjects?" will quickly lead you to a suggested test that meets the requirements of your data and your design.

CALCULATING INFERENTIAL STATISTICS

Calculating the test statistic required for the particular test you choose will require finding the formulas and procedures for the test in a statistics reference book or else consulting a statistician. To calculate your own statistics, you'll need access to at least two books. One should be a good basic statistics book, such as is used in an introductory statistics course. If you can locate one slanted toward your own field of interest, you will find it easier to read, and its examples will be more relevant. There are available a large number of introductory statistics books, all covering approximately the same material, and your choice of one should be based on whether or not you can follow its explanation of test-statistic calculations. At the end of this section we list a few basic statistics books that are reasonably readable.

Unfortunately, you'll also need a second book covering nonparametric statistics. Introductory statistics books simply do not include enough nonparametric tests and tables. There are only a few nonparametric books to choose from. Siegel's 1956 book is still the most comprehensive, but his explanations may be a little too advanced. The other books in the list were written with the student in mind.

If you want to do Analyses of Variance, you'll need to obtain (and be able to understand) one of the more advanced statistical books. Frankly, those of us doing research rarely calculate our own Analyses of Variance. We use a computer or consult a statistician to do the lengthy calculations correctly. However, we still need to be able to explain the details of our multivariate designs to ensure that the right Analysis of Variance is used. It's also nice to be able to interpret intelligently the results of the analyses in our research reports. The list at the end of this section includes a few advanced statistics books that cover the whole range of possible Analyses of Variance and are good reference books (though not exactly bedtime reading).

It can be very frustrating when you can't find exactly the statistical table you need. The different statistics books give different collections of the authors' favorite tables. Having a good statistics handbook containing a large number of tables can be a great help. One of the most useful of these is given in the list.

Remember that before you calculate any inferential test statistic, you should have a good idea from looking at the descriptive statistics on the data how your analysis is going to come out. If the descriptive statistics suggest that there is little or no difference between two samples, then you should be suspicious of an inferential test that says the difference is significant at the .01 level! It is very easy to misunderstand a formula or to misplace a decimal, even when you think you have double-checked

FIG. 6.3

Decision tree for choosing a statistical test.

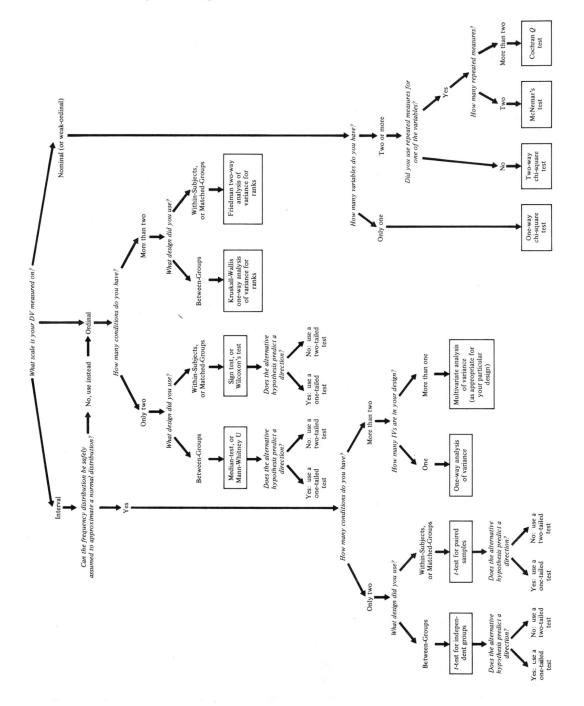

your work. So go back and take a second look at any inferential test results that don't make sense in terms of what a thorough examination of your descriptive statistics led you to expect.

SOME SUGGESTIONS FOR STATISTICS BOOKS

Basic Statistical Texts

Comrey, A. L. *Elementary Statistics*. Homewood, Ill.: Dorsey Press, 1975. Organized around specific statistical problems that may arise in research. If you can match your specific situation with one of his general problems, you will find clear procedures for solving the problem.

Robson, C. *Experimental Design and Statistics in Psychology*. England: Penguin, 1974. A hard-to-find paperback. If you can get a copy, treasure it. Has very clear calculational procedures for both simple parametric and nonparametric tests, as well as sensible discussion of their interpretation.

Weinberg, G. H., and J. A. Schumaker. *Statistics: An Intuitive Approach*. Monterey, Calif.: Brooks/Cole, 1974. A good clear presentation of basic statistics with fewer formulas and a little more explanation than usual.

Nonparametric Statistics

Freeman, L. C. *Elementary Applied Statistics: For Students in Behavioral Science*. New York: Wiley, 1965. A complete consideration of statistics for nominal, ordinal, and interval scales. Procedures are generally very clearly explained with worked examples. Very well organized, but short-changes more complex designs.

Langley, R. *Practical Statistics, Simply Explained*. New York: Dover, 1970. Not as well organized or as complete as Siegel or Freeman, but some of the explanations of tests are clearer.

Siegel, S. *Nonparametric Statistics for the Behavioral Sciences*. New York: McGraw-Hill, 1956. An indispensable book for anyone using nonparametric statistics in research.

Statistical Tables

Burington, R. S., and D. C. May, Jr. *Handbook of Probability and Statistics with Tables*. Sandusky, Ohio: Handbook Publishers. (Reissued by McGraw-Hill), 1958.

Advanced Statistical Texts

Cochran, W. G., and G. Cox. *Experimental Designs*. New York: Wiley, 1957. A very comprehensive but not always well-organized presentation of both complete and partial factorial analyses of variance. If you can match up your situation with one of theirs, you'll find complete formulas and fairly readable calculation procedures.

Lee, W. *Experimental Design and Analysis*. San Francisco: W. H. Freeman, 1975. One of the most sensible and consistent presentations of analyses of variance for the beginner.

Winer, B. J. *Statistical Principles in Experimental Design*. New York: McGraw-Hill, 1971. A very complete and well-organized presentation of analyses of variance, but for the sophisticated reader.

RECAPITULATION

for CHOOSING TESTS

Once you know the scale of measurement of your DV, the characteristics of the distribution of your measures, and the details of your research design, choosing the appropriate statistics to do on your data is cut and dried. Use of the decision tree in Fig. 6.3 will help you find the correct inferential statistic for almost any research situation. Before you do any of the tests recommended in Fig. 6.3, first look at the descriptive statistics for your data so that you have a good idea about how the inferential test will come out. This will help you in detecting errors in your calculations. Even if you don't intend to calculate statistics for yourself, a few reference books will help you in choosing statistics and in interpreting them when you report your research.

BEHAVIORAL OBJECTIVES

for CHOOSING TESTS

1. Given a list of descriptive and inferential statistics, cite for each statistic at least one book you would ask the librarian for if you needed to find calculational procedures. (It doesn't have to be one on the book list in this section if you know about others.)

2. Given a description of a research design and the nature of its DV(s), choose the appropriate descriptive and inferential statistics for analyzing the data and defend your choice.

3. Given a description of an experiment and the analyses performed by the researchers, say whether or not their statistics are appropriate and why.

4. Given the results of both descriptive and inferential analyses of data from a particular experiment, interpret the results and formulate defensible conclusions about the research.

SAMPLE TEST QUESTIONS

for CHOOSING TESTS

1. Sister Joanne Marie Kliebhan (1967): Effects of goal-setting and modeling on job performance of retarded adolescents.

   Forty-eight male retardates from a job training center were randomly divided into three groups. Each of the groups worked in the center's workshop at a different time. Their job was to fix the correct samples of tape to pages in a salesperson's advertising booklet. All subjects were taught verbally how to perform the task during the first week. After this, the control group continued under the same general procedure. For one of the experimental conditions, the foreman counted the number of tapes done in the presence of the workers and then asked each one to specify how much he expected to do the next day. The members of this "expectancy" group were reminded of their prediction at the start of the next day. The other experimental condition had a normal college student model working with the group doing the same task. Subjects in this "imitation" group repeatedly had their attention directed to the model and the way he was doing the job. The number of tapes successfully attached was recorded as an indication of work output. The foreman also evaluated each subject's work as "inferior," "shop average," or "superior."

a. What is the IV in this experiment? How many levels does it have? Is it a Subject or a Non-Subject IV? Is the IV treated Within- or Between-Subjects?

b. Write down the design for this study in shorthand and give it a name.

c. What are the two DVs in this study? On what scale is each one measured?

d. For each DV, describe how you would summarize the results, using the appropriate descriptive statistics.

e. For each DV, state which inferential test you would do on the data.

f. There is an obvious Relevant Variable in this study that could possibly be Confounding. Can you find it?

2. Mahoney, Moore, Wade, and Moura (1973): Effects of continuous and intermittent self-monitoring on academic behavior.

Twenty-seven college students who volunteered for a review session on the verbal and quantitative aptitude portions of the Graduate Record Exam (GRE) were randomly assigned to four conditions: (1) continuous self-monitoring, (2) intermittent self-monitoring, (3) performance feedback, and (4) control. All subjects used a teaching machine programmed with 300 multiple-choice questions, alternating verbal and quantitative. In the continuous self-monitoring group, subjects were given immediate feedback for all answers, and they depressed a counter button after each correct response. The intermittent self-monitoring group were told to press the counter after every third response. The performance feedback students had immediate feedback but did not record their successes. No feedback was given to the control group. The researchers recorded the length of time each subject spent reviewing the material and the number of correct answers separately for the verbal and for the quantitative problems. The data were transformed to ranks and analyzed with the Kruskal-Wallis test because of high within-group variability. Results showed that the two self-monitoring groups reviewed significantly longer than the feedback alone and control groups, and they had significantly more quantitative problems correct. There were no differences for number of verbal problems correct.

a. What was the IV in this experiment? How many levels did it have? Is it a Subject or a Non-Subject IV? Was it treated Within- or Between-Subjects?

b. Write down the design of the experiment in shorthand and give it a name.

c. What three DVs were measured in this study?

d. What type of scale were the DVs originally measured on?

e. What type of scale were the DV measures converted to? Why did the authors perform this conversion?

     f.   What statistical test was used to analyze these data? Explain exactly why the authors chose this test, answering all the necessary questions in the decision tree.

     g.   Why did the authors have such high within-group variability (take a look at the sample size)?

     h.   Can you think of a simple explanation why the two self-monitoring groups took longer to review other than that they studied better? If so, you've found a confounding variable for this research.

3.   Sachs, Bean, and Morrow (1970): Comparison of smoking treatments.

Twenty-four smokers who volunteered for a study on stopping smoking recorded the number of cigarettes they smoked per day for a baseline period of one week. They then were randomly assigned to three treatment groups. The "covert sensitization" group had three weekly sessions in which a therapist had them imagine pleasurable feelings and scenes involving smoking and then pair each pleasurable thought with an aversive scene (like vomiting). They followed this procedure daily on their own as well as in the sessions. The "self-control" group were trained in the three weekly sessions to discontinue smoking in pleasurable situations, starting with the easiest; for example, if they like to read and smoke at the same time, they would do one or the other but not both together. The "placebo-attention" group met for the same number of sessions as the other groups and received attention from and discussed smoking with the therapist. All groups kept records. The mean number of cigarettes smoked per week was analyzed by a test that treated time (the three weeks of the study) as one of the variables. Also analyzed at the end of the study was the number of subjects in each group who had quit smoking altogether.

     a.   What was the main IV in this study? How many levels did it have? Was it a Subject- or a Non-Subject IV? Was it used Within- or Between-Subjects?

     b.   Write down the design of this study in shorthand and give it a name.

     c.   Time was treated in one of the analyses as a second IV, comparing the average measures for each of the three weeks of the study. Was this a Between- or a Within-Subjects comparison?

     d.   What kind of scale was the DV measure "mean number of cigarettes smoked per week?" What kind of analysis could be done on these data using measures from all three weeks. List *all* the information that could be gained from this analysis.

     e.   What kind of scale is the DV measure of whether or not each subject quit smoking? What kind of analysis could be done on these data? Set up to do this analysis for the following results: eight of the covert-sensitization group, six of the self-control group, and two of the placebo group quit smoking.

     f.   One therapist was assigned to the covert-sensitization group, and a different one was assigned to both the self-control and placebo groups. What problem does this cause in interpreting the results?

4.   For each of the tests listed at the bottom of Fig. 6.3 name the authors of a book you would ask the librarian for if you wanted to find the procedures for performing the test.

chapter 7

interpreting the results of research

Doing research doesn't end with collecting and analyzing results. Results must be interpreted to see how they fit into the current body of knowledge and what they imply for the future. Research, after all, is expensive to do. Its value comes only when research results are put to use in increasing available information and in improving decisions.

There are two steps in interpreting research results. First we must ask ourselves whether the results are reliable: Were they obtained in such a way that we can count on getting them again? The answer to this question depends on the way research was conducted and whether appropriate statistics were used. The second step is to decide whether the results can be applied to new situations: Can we use these results to make predictions in new circumstances? The answer to this question depends on judging the similarities and differences between the particular situation in which the research was done and the broader situation to which we wish to generalize the results.

SECTION 1: SAMPLING

When interpreting the results of a research study, you must first decide what population of subjects was actually sampled in the study. Then you need to consider whether this population is sufficiently similar to the one to which you wish to generalize the results.

SAMPLES AND POPULATIONS

Usually, you just don't have the time or resources to observe every possible person you are interested in knowing about. A politician might want to know the community's attitude toward a new program, but there is simply not time or money to ask the opinion of everyone in the voting district. A school administrator may wish to estimate the value of using a new approach to teaching math in the school system, but it isn't feasible to try it out on all elementary school children. A theoretician in learning may want to study visual memory processes in adults as compared with children but can't measure every living adult or every child. The solution to these problems is to measure only a portion, or *sample* of the *population* of interest and hope that what happens in the sample can be generalized to the whole population.

Sometimes the research question will be stated in such a way that it is possible to measure the whole population of interest. If all a teacher wants to know is the IQs of his current third grade class, then it is possible to measure the whole population. If the politician is interested in the opinions of only her staff members on any given matter, she can ask all of them. When the population about which you want information is small and all the members are available, you can achieve complete sampling of the whole population.

Even if you can observe each and every member of a group, however, for each individual you may still be sampling from a wider population of measurements possible for that person. The children in the teacher's class may have slightly different IQ scores if measured again on another day. The opinion of a member of a politician's staff may differ if asked for in another context or by someone other than the boss. Therefore you may need to consider the measures you obtain on any one subject as only a sample of a population of measures that could be taken on that subject.

In interpreting research results you will often find yourself in the position of having to imagine or infer characteristics of a population from measures made on only part of that population. The accuracy of this inference depends on how representative the sample is of the whole population. A **representative sample** is one that reflects the overall characteristics of the population and is of sufficient size to include a variety of population members.

When planning your own research or evaluating research done by others, you must ask yourself three questions about samples. One is whether the samples are large enough to represent the population fairly. Another is whether the samples were drawn so as to let every population member have an equal chance to be in the sample. The final question is whether the population that was sampled is the same as or sufficiently similar to any populations to which you might wish to generalize the results.

SIZE OF SAMPLES IS IMPORTANT FOR INFERENTIAL STATISTICS

Within the limits of time and resources to take the measures, the bigger the sample, the better. The larger the sample size, the closer the sample statistics will approximate population parameters. Also, the more likely it is that you will be able to demonstrate statistical significance between samples from different populations.

Sample Size and Tests on Interval Measures

Sample size occurs in the denominator of the formula for calculating a variance. This means that as sample size increases, the size of the sample variance estimate will decrease. Inferential test statistics for normally distributed, interval measures are calculated as a ratio of differences between sample means (numerator) to within-sample variances (denominator). Therefore, the smaller the size of the sample variance, the larger will be the size of a calculated test statistic. Another way that sample size affects inferential statistical tests for interval measures is that the size of the critical test statistic for any given probability level decreases as the number of degrees of freedom (sample size) increases. Thus increased sample size increases the likelihood of achieving statistical significance. This is especially important when the IV effects you're looking for are relatively small and the subjects you're studying are likely to show a great number of individual differences.

You can find studies in the research literature whose authors have been forced to accept the null hypothesis primarily because their sample sizes were too small to detect anything but extremely large IV effects. There is little point in doing a research study if you predetermine that you'll have to accept the null hypothesis by having too small a sample size.

Another problem introduced by too small sample sizes is the difficulty of knowing whether you are sampling normally distributed measures. If you can't decide whether your interval data are normally distributed, you won't know whether you should use tests based on the normal distribution or whether it would be better to rank the interval measures and treat them as ordinal data.

Sample Size and Nonparametric Tests

For nonparametric statistical tests on ordinal or nominal data, good-sized samples are also desirable. In fact, the Chi-Square test for nominal data cannot be done at all if the sample is too small. For a chi-square with one degree of freedom (either a two-category, one-way chi-square or a four-category, two-way one), all the frequencies expected under the null hypothesis must be greater than 5. For chi-squares with more degrees of freedom, no more than 20 percent of the expected frequencies can be less than 5 and none may be less than 1. Chi-square statistics calculated with too small expected frequencies are not meaningful, and conclusions based on them are misleading. For example, the data on the relationship of toy preferences to sex of 24 normal preschoolers given in Table 5.5 are completely untestable by a two-way chi-square. None of the expected frequencies meet the minimum requirement of 5. For this nominal DV scale, we would need a larger sample of normal preschoolers to come to any statistically defensible conclusions about differing patterns of toy choice in the two sexes. When reading research literature, watch out for Chi-Square tests that are done on samples that are too small. They are published now and then, despite the fact they they are meaningless as inferential tests.

There are limitations on sample size for ordinal tests as well. For example, tables evaluating the results of the Sign test require that you have a minimum of five difference scores with values other than zero to perform the test at all, and even then all five of the data pairs would have to differ in the same direction to declare significance. Similarly, the Wilcoxon Matched-Pairs, Signed-Ranks test requires at least six nonzero difference scores to perform the test. For all ordinal inferential statistical tests, if your sample sizes are small, you must have extremely large differences between the samples to establish statistical significance. Since these nonparametric tests are generally lower in power than the parametric tests, you need to use even larger samples if you intend to use ordinal rather than interval DV measures.

BIASED SAMPLES

Not all your sampling problems can be eliminated by increasing the size of the sample. If your sample is not representative of the population, then any inference you make about the population from the sample will be faulty, even if the sample is enormous. **Biased samples** are a problem in any kind of social science research, causing particular difficulties in attitude or opinion surveying. For example, if you send out questionnaires on some topic, the people who take the trouble to send them back are not a representative sample of the people to whom you sent them. If you ask questions of people in the street, the ones who choose to answer are not a representative sample of all people who go hurrying by. If you go door-to-door in the daytime, you are sampling a different population than if you go door-to-door at night. Even very experienced pollsters can come to grief from sampling errors: the landslide victory headlined for Thomas Dewey in 1948 was a famous polling mistake, to the eternal delight of President Truman!

Biased samples are a problem for laboratory research as well as for attitude surveys of the general population. Much human experimental work is done in universities using the "college student volunteer." Those students who volunteer for research studies are most likely not a true representative sample of all the students in the university. College students, in turn, may not be representative of the entire adult population. For some purposes, these biases may not be important, but it is necessary to be aware of them when generalizing results of university laboratory research. When reporting your own research or interpreting the research of others, it is necessary to pinpoint exactly what population was in fact sampled, so that you are aware of the assumptions you are making when generalizing the results to other populations.

Random Sampling to Avoid Bias

Achieving an unbiased or representative sample from a particular population is not always easy. The most direct method is to sample at random in such a way that every member of the population has an equal chance of being in the sample. Then you have to make sure that you obtain measures on every individual in your **random sample**. In attitude surveys, this means you have to go back and back again until you are able to interview the particular individuals specified by your sample, something that is very costly to achieve in a large-scale study. Sometimes you may want to use a special sampling procedure that allows you to be sure you are sampling all subgroups in a population, like women or certain ethnic groups. In these cases, you may first divide the population into its subgroups and then randomly sample from each subgroup. Sampling approaches such as these, like stratified random sampling or cluster sampling, have their own special set of formulas for estimating population parameters, and use of them will involve looking up the methods in an advanced statistics book.

Typical Cases

Selecting "typical cases" without the aid of random sampling procedures is a sure way to get into trouble. There are many studies indicating that such typical cases are not typical at all but slanted in favor of the selectors' prejudices, no matter how objective they think they are. Yates (1949) reported a study in which a dozen observers were asked to select three samples each of 20 rocks that were "representative" of the sizes of an array of 1200 rocks. Eighty-three percent of the samples selected had means that were larger than the mean of the entire rock collection! Although the observers were trying to create typical samples, they were in fact biased in favor of selecting the larger rocks. Unfortunately, the reporting of "typical cases" is still prevalent in medical, psychotherapeutic, and other kinds of clinical literature. The inferences made from these "typical cases" to the entire clinical population are weakened by the fact that they are almost certainly biased samples.

GENERALIZING RESULTS GATHERED ON ONE POPULATION TO DIFFERENT POPULATIONS

You will usually want to generalize research information to populations that were not sampled in the original study. This is O.K. as long as you keep clearly in mind the possible differences between the populations and estimate the degree to which these differences weaken your conclusions. The more differences between the population on which the research was done and the population you are generalizing to, the less confident you can be about your conclusions. For example, information about the effects of seeing films with aggressive models on the play behavior of university day-care center children may not generalize well to a population of kids from a part of society more directly exposed to violence. Information gathered on verbal learning of college students may not generalize well to a population of elementary school children. Information about the eating habits of horses donated to research centers may not generalize well to the pampered, overfed darlings of top breeding farms. Sometimes, when the discrepancy between population characteristics is large, it may be better to rerun the experiment on a sample from the new population than to make shaky generalizations.

When scientists begin talking in wide-sweeping generalities about their results, look for possible population discrepancies. You will find that even the most sophisticated of thinkers sometimes lose sight of the origins of their information when they start spinning theories. If the research population is very different from the people to whom they are generalizing, scientists should offer their conclusions only with stated reservations. When planning your own research, try to sample a population that is highly similar to the people to whom you wish to apply your results.

RECAPITULATION

for SAMPLING

In any one research study you usually can measure only a limited *sample* of the larger *population* in which you are interested. Such samples must be *representative* of the population. They should not be *biased* toward certain population members; if they are, the inferences you make about the population from the sample will be faulty. The best way to ensure that a sample is representative is to select its members at random from the population. The worst way to pick a representative sample is to rely on your own ability to recognize "typical cases."

For statistical purposes, not only should your sample be unbiased, it should also be of sufficient size. Some statistical tests, like Chi-Square, simply cannot be done at all if the sample is too small. All statistical tests are much less likely to demonstrate IV effects if the samples are small than if they are large. For interval data, moreover, it is difficult to judge whether the frequency distributions are approximately normal when the samples are very small. This in turn makes it difficult to select appropriate statistical tests. For parametric (normal-distribution–based) statistical tests, as the overall variability of the samples increases, the calculated test statistic decreases, and statistical significance is less likely to be found for the results. Since sample variances increase when sample size decreases, the *sample size* is an important determinant of whether or not the null hypothesis can be rejected in any particular study. If you use too small a sample in your research plan, you can literally guarantee beforehand that you will have to accept the null hypothesis.

BEHAVIORAL OBJECTIVES

for SAMPLING

1. Distinguish a sample from a population. Describe how information can be gained about a population, even if it is not possible to measure every member of the population.

2. Given a description of a population and a measure that a researcher wants to take on its members, decide whether it will be possible to measure the whole population or whether it will be necessary to measure only a sample of it.

3. Describe the conditions necessary for a sample to be representative of a population.

4. Describe what is meant by a "biased sample." Explain the errors that are likely when such a sample is used to infer facts about the population from which it was taken.

5. Give an example of a biased sample from a particular population.

6. Given the description of a population, decide how you would take an unbiased sample from it.

7. Describe how the size of a sample influences the following:

    a. The variance of the measures in the sample.

    b. The accuracy of inferring population parameters from sample statistics.

    c. The likelihood of rejecting the null hypothesis when a real difference exists between samples.

    d. The possibility of deciding for interval data whether or not the population can safely be assumed to be normal.

    e. The possibility of using Chi-Square to evaluate nominal data.

SAMPLE TEST QUESTIONS

for SAMPLING

---

1. Jessup and Neufeld (1978): Effects of biofeedback and "autogenic relaxation" techniques on physiological and subjective responses on psychiatric patients: A preliminary analysis.

    Four relaxation techniques were compared for their ability to help hospitalized psychiatric patients to relax. The four treatments used were: autogenic phrases, forehead muscle biofeedback, unaided self-relaxation, and a control. The four treatment groups were assessed before and during four daily 20-minute training periods in a 4×4 independent-groups by repeated-measures analysis of variance design. Forehead muscle tension, heart rate, skin resistance, hand and forehead temperature, and the Nowlis Mood Adjective Check List (MACL) were used to measure baseline and within-treatment effects. Heart rate and MACL "anxiety" decreased significantly with the control treatment. However, except for a decrease in MACL "anxiety" during the autogenic phrases, the three experimental treatments did not significantly affect any of the measures. Twenty psychiatric patients were randomly divided among the experimental conditions.

    a. Using shorthand, indicate the design of this experiment. Was the treatment IV Within- or Between-Subjects?

    b. How many subjects were assigned to each group of the experiment?

   c. What kind of analysis was used to analyze the results?

   d. This study did not get very many significant effects, despite using techniques that have been very effective in other studies. With reference to your answers to (b) and (c), what is a major problem with interpreting this study?

2. Several years ago, an issue of *Life* magazine included a detailed questionnaire on feelings about crime. The editors invited readers to fill it out and return it to the magazine. They subsequently wrote an article on the widespread fear of crime among U.S. citizens. They found not only that people in general considered crime control to be the major national issue, but that this concern increased markedly as people became older.

   a. Describe the sample that the magazine actually obtained.

   b. In what ways were the questionnaires that were returned by the magazine readers a biased sample of all U.S. citizens? (Consider social class, education level, those who send back questionnaires, price of stamps, etc.)

   c. Can you think of any ways that the biases in the selection of the sample might have exaggerated the concern with crime expressed by this sample?

   d. Can you think of how the age effect seen in the data might in part be due to sample biases?

   e. How would you suggest investigating the question of how U.S citizens feel about crime?

3. A teacher of a high school class asked her 38 students to indicate their plans after graduation. The results are given in Table 7.1. From the data in this table she calculated a test statistic that was appropriate for the scale of measurement of the DV. The test statistic she obtained was 10.03 with four degrees of freedom. Checking a statistical table, the teacher found that the critical value of this statistic at the .05 level is 9.49. Accordingly, she concluded that for her class the pattern of postgraduate choices was significantly different between the sexes. At the next meeting of her local educational organization, she reported these results and suggested that they indicate there still is a long way to go in educating women high school students so that they are free to make the same choices as men.

Table 7.1 Observed Frequencies of PostGraduate Choices for 20 Men and 18 Women

	Field of study in college				Not going to college	Total
	Home Economics	Engineering	Liberal Arts	Science		
Men	0 (1.6)*	4 (2.6)	1 (3.7)	6 (4.7)	8 (7.4)	20
Women	3 (1.4)	1 (2.4)	6 (3.3)	3 (4.3)	6 (6.6)	18
Total	3	5	7	9	14	

*Expected frequencies under the null hypothesis are given in parentheses.

    a. What is the DV? What type of scale is it measured on?

    b. What was the "average" or typical choice of the men in the class as to future plans? Of the women?

    c. What kind of statistical test must the teacher have used for these data? (Note that the expected frequencies under the null hypothesis of no difference between the sexes are given in parentheses.)

    d. There are some serious limitations on the conclusions and suggestions she drew from these data.

        1) What is the evidence that her sample size is not adequate? What does this mean for the interpretation of the statistical test results?

        2) In her final interpretation, to what population is she generalizing the results? Is it reasonable that her sample is representative of this population?

SECTION 2: ERRORS IN RESEARCH

Errors that occur in research studies can be categorized into two general types: **random errors** and **constant errors.** Both kinds of errors can mislead you when you interpret research results. The presence of random, or unsystematic, error in DV measurements increases the overall variability of the data. This increased variability makes it more likely that you will have to accept the null hypothesis and conclude that your IV is not having an effect. Constant errors raise even more serious problems for interpretation. Constant errors are produced by the presence of Confounding Relevant Variables, those variables that systematically influence the DV in ways that can be mistaken for IV effects. The existence of constant error in an experiment defeats the purpose of the research, since DV changes that are actually due to the Confounding Variable will be mistakenly attributed to the action of the IV. When you are planning your own research project, the first priority is to eliminate or control all sources of constant error. The next priority is to reduce random error as much as possible. When you are interpreting other people's research, it is important first to ask whether they have left any possible sources of constant error uncontrolled and next to check whether they have held random error to a minimum.

RELEVANT VARIABLES AS SOURCES OF ERROR

In Chapter 2 Relevant Variables were defined as those variables present in a research situation that may cause changes in the DV but that are not intended by the researcher to be IVs. For any DV you want to measure, there may be a large number of Relevant Variables, some of them Subject in type and some of them Non-Subject. For example, if you are studying the effects of a treatment on a person's performance of some task, you need to remember that things other than your treatment will affect that person's score. Is the person nervous? Does he take the task seriously? Did he misunderstand your instructions? Has he done something like this before? Is he not feeling well? Is he sleepy or tired? Does he dislike you? Is he a very bright subject? Is the room uncomfortably cold? Are noises from the hall bothering him? Is the researcher's tight sweater distracting him? Has the experimenter subtly implied that she expects him to do a lousy job? Are his shoes pinching him? Is he thinking about something else? Does he have to go to the bathroom? Does he want a cigarette? Did he skip lunch? Is it his nap time? We could go on endlessly listing possible Relevant Variables. People, and even the animals used in behavioral research are very complicated beings. At any point in time, many variables are affecting their behavior. A researcher needs to be very clever and careful to establish that a particular treatment applied at a particular time is what is really causing DV measures to change.

SOURCES OF CONSTANT ERROR

Relevant Variables become a serious problem for interpretation when they change systematically at different levels of the IV. In this case, their effects on the DV are confounded or confused with IV effects. For example, if you test your experimental (treatment) subjects all in the morning and your control (nontreatment) subjects all in the afternoon, how do you know whether your DV shows a treatment (IV) effect or a confounding time-of-day effect? If your DV measures show the control group doing less well than the experimental group, is it because of the absence of treatment or because subjects tend to be more tired in the afternoon? Every time you have a *con*sistent difference between the time and conditions under which your control and experimental subjects are tested, you run the risk of a *Con*founding Variable introducing *con*stant error into the results. The effects of such Confounding Variables can work either for or against your IV effect. A positive treatment effect on an experimental group might be wiped out, for example, by testing the group at a disadvantageous time.

Non-Subject Confounding Variables

Non-Subject Confounding Variables are variables the experimenter could have directly controlled but did not. For treatment effects to be clearly identified, what happens to an experimental and a control group should differ only as specified by the operational definition of the IV. Both groups need to be measured under exactly the same conditions. Both groups should have the same instructions given in the same way, except where differences are specifically required by the IV. The experimenter should have the same attitude about the likely performance of the two groups. The experimenter should be careful to create the same amount of enthusiasm and expectation of success on DV tasks for both groups. In short, nothing special should happen to the treatment groups other than the treatment specified by the IV.

Subject Confounding Variables

Subject Confounding Variables also cause problems for interpretation. If experimental and control groups vary consistently on some Subject Relevant Variable, then it is hard to say whether a "treatment effect" seen in DV measures is due to the treatment itself or to confounding effects of the unrecognized Subject Variables. Some designs, such as Static-Groups designs, do not provide information about group equivalence. These designs *always* carry the risk of Confounding Subject Variables. Then, too, the possibility of Confounding Subject Variables is always present when one of the IVs in an experiment is a Subject IV. Whenever subjects are categorized according to a Subject IV, it is possible that they also consistently differ in other ways.

Subject attitude toward the experiment is an important Subject Relevant Variable that may be difficult to keep from becoming confounded with IV effects. Whenever subjects realize they are "special," they try harder. When experimental subjects get special attention from the experimenters, they are very likely to have a positive attitude toward their success on any DV tests. On the other hand, if subjects discover that they are the "controls," they often feel they are missing out on something. Subject attitude effects are a special problem in drug research, where the belief in the power of a drug often produces greater effects on subject behavior than the drug itself!

Example of Constant Error

In Chapter 2, we considered the "Spanish textbook case," an applied study done to investigate the effects on student learning of using a new type of Spanish text. We found that this study had so many uncontrolled Relevant Variables that it would be almost impossible to make a responsible interpretation of the results. Several Non-Subject Relevant Variables that were not properly controlled could quite easily have introduced constant errors into the results. For instance, the control classes that used the old book were twice the size of the experimental classes using the new book. We might suspect that students from small classes would do better than those from larger ones, no matter what text they used. Another Non-Subject Relevant Variable that could confound IV effects was the teacher's enthusiasm for the new method, communicated to the experimental classes by a special introduction. There is a good deal of evidence that teacher expectations affect both student attitudes and teacher interactions with the students. The class that had the text the teacher liked better would almost certainly do better, no matter what the text. The most serious problem of all with the design of this study, however, was failure to control a Relevant Subject Variable. The best students of the preceding year were placed in the experimental group! Thus the experimental and control groups were certainly not equivalent at the start of the experiment. They differed not only on previous Spanish performance but probably also on other Relevant Subject Variables, such as grade-point average, type of major, interest in Spanish, and maybe even IQ. Because of all these possible sources of constant error, the results of this study are impossible to interpret unambiguously. (Even so, the college department adopted the new text on the basis of "experimental evidence"!)

CONTROLLING CONSTANT ERROR

So what can be done to remove constant error from your DV measures and eliminate the effects of such Confounding Variables? There are several different techniques you can choose from.

Keeping the Relevant Variable Constant

One way to eliminate constant error from your results is to be sure that all the subjects experiencing different levels of the IV encounter the same value of the Relevant Variable. In the Spanish textbook case, this technique was used with the Non-Subject Relevant Variables of teacher experience and number of hours of class time. Both the experimental and the control subjects met for the same number of hours and had the same teacher. The confounding effects of class size could have been similarly controlled by assigning the same number of students to both the experimental and control classes. The confounding effects of teacher attitude might have been harder to keep constant, but the teacher could have been told of the importance of her attitude and the necessity of making the control subjects feel as hopeful of success with the old book as the experimentals with the new book.

In drug experiments, subject attitude is often held constant by using a **placebo condition.** This is a condition in which the subjects are led to believe they are receiving the experimental drug when in fact they are being administered a neutral substance. By this device, the subject's expectation of a drug effect is held constant between experimental and control groups and is thereby eliminated as a Confounding Variable. Sometimes, however, such a placebo control may not be possible. Experienced marijuana users, for example, can easily detect the physiological effects of marijuana and know whether or not they are receiving a placebo.

The attitude of the experimenter can sometimes be held constant for different IV levels by using a **double-blind** experimental procedure. With this technique, the experimenter is not permitted to know whether a given subject is an experimental or a control subject when administering the treatment or taking the DV measures. In a drug experiment, for example, the experimenter would not be told which subjects had the real drug and which had the placebo. This approach works nicely in some cases, but it's impractical in others. In a drug study, if the real drug produced obvious physiological changes in the subjects, the experimenter might recognize which were experimentals and which were controls without being told. In the Spanish textbook case the teachers certainly would know which classes had the old texts and which had the new.

Changing Constant Error to Random Error

Sometimes it's not possible to control a Relevant Variable by holding it constant. In such a situation, you might try changing the potential source of constant error to a random error. The Relevant Variable is left free to vary in the experiment, but you make sure by randomizing that it can have no consistent effects on the DV.

To conrol for a Subject Relevant Variable, you merely assign the subjects at random to the different conditions of the experiment. This approach, of course, becomes more effective for eliminating constant error as sample size increases. With very small samples, it is possible to create nonequivalent groups even with randomization if by chance one or two extreme individuals are assigned to the same group. In the Spanish textbook case, it would have been difficult to find enough subjects whose previous performance in Spanish was exactly the same in order to hold the Relevant Variable of subject ability constant. However, this variable certainly could have been controlled by random assignment of students to the old and new textbook groups.

Any Non-Subject Relevant Variable that for some reason cannot be held constant for all subjects can also have its effects changed to random error. For example, if it's necessary to continue posttesting for several days, make sure that an equal number of experimental and control subjects, chosen at random, are tested on each day. Or if you have to use more than one experimenter, make sure that each one works with both experimental and control subjects equally. Any time you suspect a confounding order effect when treating an IV Within-Subjects, you can counterbalance IV levels. Counterbalancing does not eliminate the effects of order for any one subject. All it does is spread the order effects equally across the different levels of the IV when the results of all the subjects are added together. Counterbalancing means that overall the order effect no longer confounds the effect of the IV; however, individual order effects add unsystematic or random variability to DV measures.

Although randomization is a useful technique for eliminating constant error, the procedure creates a new problem. Changing a constant error to a random error in most cases will increase the overall variability of DV measures and thereby decrease the possibility of establishing statistical significance. However, since constant error causes much more serious interpretation problems than random error, it is sometimes necessary to pay this price when you can't control the Relevant Variable by holding it constant.

Turning a Confounding Variable into an Additional IV

Sometimes, especially with Subject Relevant Variables, the best strategy may be to treat the variable as another IV in the experimental design. In the drug study of Crancer *et al.* (1969), they found that alcohol affected driving simulator performance whereas marijuana did not. Kalant (1969) speculated that subject attitude in favor of marijuana and against alcohol might have confounded these results, since

Crancer *et al.* used only subjects who were regular marijuana users. If the subjects were striving to do their best in the marijuana condition but prone to "let nature take its course" in the alcohol condition, the experimental results would contain a serious constant error. Subject attitude could be made a second IV through selection of both regular marijuana users and regular alcohol users in a blocked design. If the users are, in fact, biased toward their favorite social crutch, then a significant interaction should appear between the Non-Subject IV of type of drug administered (marijuana, alcohol, none) and the subject IV of type of user (marijuana or alcohol).

As another example of this approach, consider the study described on p. 64 (Sample Test Question 1) in which the researcher used a Static-Groups design to investigate the effects of introducing a new industrial arts curriculum on student self-concepts. Unfortunately, this design left a number of Relevant Variables uncontrolled, and therefore the risk that constant errors would confound the IV effects was high. The two groups in the experiment were composed of students from different schools in different parts of the city. It is quite possible that these students represented different socioeconomic classes, an important Subject Relevant Variable. In addition, the Non-Subject Relevant Variables of size of class, experience of teachers, and teacher attitude were not controlled. A multivariate Randomized-Blocks design would have improved interpretation of the results. Since random assignment of students to the schools was probably impractical, the two schools could have been treated as two levels of a Subject IV, and experimental and control groups could have been randomly created within each school. If the Subject IV of type of school really was important, then the interaction of this IV with the treatment IV would be significant.

Measuring the Relevant Variables

Occasionally it just is not practical to assign subjects at random, and a Static-Groups design will be forced on you. This is especially true for clinical and school settings, in which research has to take a secondary role to education or therapy. Often, in these circumstances, using a Randomized-Blocks design may be difficult. For example, if the proposed industrial arts program involved new machinery or a special teaching technique, it may not have been possible to introduce it into more than one school. It may also not have been possible within a school to run both types of treatment groups. Sometimes the best that can be done in such a situation is to measure each group on a number of Relevant Variables and to demonstrate that, in fact, the values of the Relevant Variables do not consistently differ at the different IV levels. In the industrial arts study it might have been possible to select two schools in equivalent areas of town and to establish by taking various measures that the students in two schools were not very different in socioeconomic status or in IQ. This would not have meant that the static groups were entirely equivalent, but it would have reduced the chance that the measured Relevant Variables were producing constant errors and confounding interpretation of IV effects.

Matching Groups on a Relevant Variable

When possible, instead of just measuring the Relevant Variables for Subject IVs or for Static-Groups designs, we can match the groups on these Relevant Variables. In the industrial arts curriculum study, another strategy might have been to compare matched samples of students from the two schools. A student from one school could have been matched with one from the other for sex, socioeconomic status, IQ, and possibly grade-point average. Then when the comparison was made between schools for the effects of the curriculum, it is unlikely that any of the Relevant Variables for which the two groups were matched would have been contributing constant error to the results.

The matching approach is also useful in improving the interpretation of the effects of a Subject IV. For instance, if in a marijuana-alcohol study we introduced the Subject IV of "type of user," we might have a potential problem with confounding Relevant Subject Variables. It is very likely that a random sample of marijuana users would be younger than a sample of alcohol users. It is also possible that the marijuana-using subjects would represent a different socioeconomic status and would have different occupations. To avoid the problem of all these uncontrolled Relevant Variables' confounding our results, we could decide that the marijuana and alcohol subjects had to be matched for age, socioeconomic status, and occupation. Doing so would reduce the amount of constant error produced by these variables.

Load the Dice against Yourself

In some cases none of the techniques above for eliminating constant error may seem feasible. Especially for experimenter beliefs and subject attitude, holding the Relevant Variables constant may be hard to achieve. Another approach to control for these effects is to try to give the control group all the benefits. For example, if you are interested in seeing whether a new teaching technique is sufficiently effective to justify increased costs of changing instruction, you can weight your experimental design in favor of the control group. Assign your best teachers to the control sections, put the best students in the control groups, and be doubly sure that enthusiasm is encouraged for the old method. Then, if your new method still has superior results in the face of all these variables working against it, you can be sure the effect isn't just due to Confounding Variables.

RANDOM ERROR

The presence of random error in DV measurements means increased variability of your experimental data. Since this increased variability occurs unsystematically at all levels of the IV, random error does not lead to as serious problems for interpretation as does constant error. In fact, one procedure for dealing with constant error is to change it into random error. However, once problems of constant error are solved for a research study, it is important to minimize random error as well to improve your chances of rejecting the null hypothesis.

CONTROLLING RANDOM ERROR

Care in Taking Your Measures

The first step in reducing random error is care in taking your DV measurements. There is no point in increasing the variability of your data by being sloppy.

Increase Sample Size

Since the variance of a sample of normally distributed data decreases with increased sample size, larger samples will mean lower variance estimates. Larger samples also mean, for most statistical tests, that the size of the critical test statistic that must be exceeded for significance will also decrease. Therefore the larger the sample, the better, unless it gets so large that your measurement process becomes sloppy through hurrying to measure all the subjects.

Get Rid of the Relevant Variable When Possible

Holding a Relevant Variable constant as a technique for reducing constant error is preferable to dealing with the variable's possible confounding effects by randomization. Randomization eliminates constant error only at the expense of increased random error. In the Crancer *et al.* (1969) marijuana-alcohol study, the researchers put a long list of restrictions on who would be selected for their 36 subjects. They attempted to reduce the effect of Subject Relevant Variables by limiting the study to subjects who were in good health, had no personality problems, were not taking any medication, and were currently employed or enrolled in school. The subjects also had to be licensed drivers with good driving records, and they had to have the right marijuana smoking habits. Restricting the population this way, by attempting to hold all these possible Relevant Variables constant, would greatly decrease the variability in the measurements and thereby increase the chances of demonstrating significant effects of alcohol or marijuana on driving. However, it would restrict the population to which the results could be safely generalized. Unfortunately, almost every decision you make in research costs you something.

Any Relevant Variable that might distract or annoy the subject should of course be eliminated. Unless it is part of the treatment, there is no point in making your subjects in any way uncomfortable or in subjecting them to outside distractions. This is one of the reasons that, when possible, research is done "under lab conditions," where it is much easier to eliminate such extraneous Relevant Variables than in the natural environment.

Altering the Experimental Design

Depending on the IV being investigated, situations in which there is high variability between subjects often are best handled in a Within-Subjects or a Matched-Subjects design. Since in the statistical analysis of these designs only difference scores are important, the high variability between subjects in their raw scores becomes less important. The fact that one subject is naturally a very high scorer on your DV test and another is a very low scorer becomes irrelevant so long as your treatment causes the same change in both. When there is high variability between subjects, such paired designs will be more sensitive to IV effects than an Independent-Groups design.

Another experimental design that may help to reduce variability is the Randomized-Blocks design. If there is present in the experiment a Subject Relevant Variable that has a large influence on the DV, it may be better to use it as an IV and separate the subjects into homogeneous groups at the different levels of this IV than to swell random error by randomizing. For example, suppose that "test anxiety" is capable of having a large effect on the scores on a test that you are using to compare the effects of two teaching methods. You may want to treat it as an additional IV, blocking your subjects into low, medium, and high anxiety groups and then within each group randomly assigning them to the two teaching methods. This will take the variability due to test anxiety out of your overall variability, and it will also give you a chance of detecting interaction effects between test anxiety and teaching method.

RECAPITULATION

for ERRORS IN RESEARCH

There are two principal types of error in research data that can cause misinterpretation of results. Increased *random error,* produced by anything that increases the variability of DV measures, can greatly decrease the possibility of rejecting the null hypothesis and reduce the sensitivity of the experiment to IV effects. *Constant error,* a far more serious problem for interpretation, is produced when Relevant Variables are allowed to become confounding. When *Confounding Variables* are present in an experiment, DV changes are being produced at least in part by them and not by the IV alone. The presence of such Confounding Variables means that effects interpreted as being due to the IV quite probably are not. The Relevant Variables that produce constant and random error can be either Subject or Non-Subject in type.

Constant error can be eliminated in several ways. One of them is to hold the Relevant Variable constant so that it is the same for every level of the IV. If this is not possible, the constant error may be changed to random error by randomization processes, which make sure that every IV level has a random collection of values of the Relevant Variable. A Relevant Variable may also be important enough to be made an additional IV in the research, with its effects measured separately. If none of these approaches are possible, then the Relevant Variable may itself be measured to establish that it is really not consistently different at different IV levels. Sometimes it may be desirable to go one step further and match groups on the basis of some Relevant Variable to be sure the groups are reasonably equivalent. A final approach is to create an experimental plan in which everything favors the outcome you don't believe will happen and is against the outcome you are hoping for. Then if things come out in your favor, you can feel reasonably secure.

Random error is reduced by taking measures carefully under controlled conditions that eliminate extraneous Relevant Variables. Increasing sample size, which decreases sample variance, is an important technique for decreasing random error. Placing restrictions on the characteristics of your subjects will mean more homogeneous samples with lower variability, although such a specialized subject population will limit the generalizability of your results. Within-Subjects designs that use each subject as its own control and Matched-Subjects designs are also ways of statistically reducing random error. Finally, Randomized-Blocks designs that allow you to isolate the effect of some Subject IV will make it much more likely that you'll be able to see the effects of your treatment IV.

BEHAVIORAL OBJECTIVES

for ERRORS IN RESEARCH

1. Define constant error. Explain how constant error may cause misinterpretation of results. Give an example.
2. Define random error. Explain how random error may lead to misinterpretation of results. Discuss why random error is a less serious problem than constant error.
3. Given a description of an experiment, identify potential instances of constant and random error.
4. Given a description of an experiment, identify Relevant Variables and state which are controlled and which are potentially confounding. For each Confounding Variable you identify, discuss what kind of constant error it could introduce into interpretation of results. Suggest for each one a method for controlling it.
5. Describe at least three different methods for controlling constant errors.
6. Describe at least three different methods for reducing random error.
7. Define: placebo, double-blind, and counterbalancing. Explain what each technique is used to control for.

SAMPLE TEST QUESTIONS

for ERRORS IN RESEARCH

For each of the following brief research descriptions, identify whether the major difficulty in interpreting results will be produced by sources of *random* or *constant* error. Describe the specific effects on interpretation of the research that each error is likely to have. Then suggest an improvement in the experiment that would eliminate the error.

1. Two randomly selected groups of preschoolers were observed while at play. One group had previously watched a film containing a number of violent inci-

dents, and the other had seen a similar but peaceful film. Children from the group who saw the violent film seemed slightly more inclined to aggressive play activities, but the difference between the two groups was not significant. There were four children in each of the groups.

2. In the experiment described in Question 1, the person observing the children's play activities and recording aggressive acts knew which children had seen the violent film.

3. In the experiment described in Question 1, the violent-film children were observed in the morning, and those who had seen the peaceful film were observed in the afternoon.

4. A study on the taste of cola beverages asked subjects to rate each of four colas on a scale of 1 ("totally vile") to 7 ("one of the best tastes ever"). The subjects tasted Pepsi Cola, Coca Cola, Royal Crown, and Diet Pepsi, in that order. All the colas were presented in the same type of cup and at the same temperature, and the subjects were not told which was which. Diet Pepsi got a significantly lower rating than the other three, which did not significantly differ. One hundred subjects were used in the taste test.

5. The results of the study described in Question 4 convinced the experimenter that a different procedure should be used for a repeat of the taste study. In this second study, the researcher randomized the orders of the four colas and saw that equal numbers of subjects used each order. The results of this study, done with 50 subjects, produced no significant differences in ratings for the colas.

6. After showing a film containing violent incidents to a group of ten boys and ten girls, the experimenter observed the children at play. The boys showed significantly more aggressive acts than the girls, and the researcher concluded that seeing such a violent film affected boys more than girls.

7. The rats in the lab colony are fed each morning at 8. At noon, students started running individual rats down a straight alley maze with food as a reward. The time each rat took to run down the maze on its second run was recorded. At random, each rat was injected with either an amphetamine or a saline (neutral) solution after the first run down the alley. Forty rats were run, and the experiment was completed at 6 p.m. The rats injected with amphetamine appeared to run faster than the rats injected with saline, but despite heroic statistical manipulations, the difference between the two groups' average times for the second run didn't quite reach significance at the .05 level.

8. In a study on the effectiveness of training in control of forehead muscle tension through electromyographic biofeedback, an experimental group and a control group were compared for incidence of migraine headaches. Both groups agreed to remain off drugs for the duration of the two-month study. All subjects were initially interviewed as to frequency of migraines. Then 15 were randomly assigned to an experimental group that met three times weekly with the therapist for individual biofeedback sessions. The other 15 control subjects were asked to report back in two months for a final interview and were not seen in the intervening time. At the end of two months, the biofeedback subjects at their final interviews reported at least 50 percent reduction in headache fre-

quency. No similar change was seen for the controls. Five of the controls had to be dropped from the sample because they had resumed using drugs for headache control.

9. Refer again to G. L. Paul's study discussed on pp. 68 ff. Explain exactly why he included his Group 3 in addition to a more conventional control (Group 4).

SECTION 3: LIMITATIONS OF DIFFERENT DESIGNS

Before you even begin to collect your data, the information that your research can yield is limited. At the time you select a research design, you have already determined how far you can go in interpreting any results. Since the circumstances under which you are doing the research sometimes restrict your design choices, you need to be aware of the limitations of the different designs. It is only fair, when reporting your research results, to point out specifically the ways in which design limitations weaken your conclusions.

STATIC-GROUPS DESIGNS

Whenever it is necessary to use preformed groups to represent the different levels of your IV, the possibility of uncontrolled and confounding Subject Relevant Variables has been introduced into your research. It is best to avoid Static-Groups designs, but it is not always practical to do so, especially in educational or clinical settings. In a clinical setting, for example, ethical issues may arise if you want to assign patients randomly to different treatment conditions. Sinclair Lewis's novel *Arrowsmith,* published in 1924, examines the dilemma of a young doctor testing the worth of a new vaccine for prevention of a deadly disease. Can he in good conscience randomly assign people to the control condition and possible death? Usually the situation is not so dramatic, but in some settings you may find yourself not free to make group assignments, and you may be forced to use preformed or self-assigned groups.

A Static-Groups design lacks information about group equivalence. There is always the possibility with this type of design that an apparent treatment effect is actually the result of some preexisting group differences. If you are forced to use such a design, you can strengthen your conclusions somewhat by measuring the preformed groups on as many Subject Relevant Variables as possible. If, as hoped, the two groups show equal values on all these Subject Variables, you have some basis for arguing that the groups are equivalent, even though the design does not in and of itself establish such equivalence. At least, you can state that the variables you have measured are not confounding your results. However, if you do find that the groups differ on one or more of these Subject Variables, then you are obliged to point this out and to discuss in any report how these differences might weaken conclusions from your results.

PRE-POST DESIGNS

One way of establishing group equivalence for Static-Groups designs is to include a pretest. However, pretests, in and of themselves, can affect posttest DV measures. By introducing the pretest into the design, you may have added a Confounding Variable. Not only can the pretest directly affect posttest results, but it can act more subtly by interacting with the effects of the IV. A treatment may have a different effect on subjects just because they were exposed to the pretest. Whenever you use a one- or two-group pre-post design, you must consider these possible pretest effects in your interpretation of posttest results.

If pretest effects are likely to be a serious problem for interpretation, you can use the Solomon Four-Group design, which treats the pretest as a second IV. Of course, this means a more expensive study, but it does remove confounding pretest effects from your interpretation.

SUBJECT IV DESIGNS

One or more of your IVs may be Subject-type and require that your subjects be blocked into groups representing different levels of the IV. A Subject IV always carries with it the risk of other Subject Relevant Variables that may vary systematically with the IV and confound its effects. Consider the effects of "sex of subject" on success in problem solution in the Milton (1959) study described on pp. 235 ff. Milton's research clearly shows his male subjects solving more problems on the average than his female subjects, even when the content of the problems is made more appropriate to the feminine role. But before you interpret this research as demonstrating the superior abilities of the male brain for problem solving, you need to know whether the groups were equivalent on several other Subject Variables. Did both groups have the same IQs? Did both groups have the same concentration of majors, or were more of the men, perhaps, majoring in math and science? Were both of the groups equally practiced at problem solving, or had the men had more course work in which problem solving was demanded? Did the women take the task seriously? Some of these Subject Relevant Variables can be measured. Until they are and until the groups are shown to be equivalent for all of them, you should be careful in interpreting these results as representing primarily a *sex* difference.

CORRELATIONAL DESIGNS

The limitation discussed above for designs with a Subject IV is even more serious for interpretation of the results of correlational studies. A correlation, remember, tells us only the degree of association between two DVs. A correlation simply cannot be used as the basis for a causal statement. You cannot say that changes in one of the DVs cause the changes in the other. The reverse could be just as true. Or some other variable you haven't measured could be simultaneously causing the changes in both DVs. The high positive correlation that exists, for example, between the amount of water in street gutters and the number of umbrellas visible does not mean that if you run water into the gutters from a hose on a sunny day umbrellas will magically appear! Another variable, namely rainfall, is actually responsible both for water in the gutters and for the appearance of umbrellas. Seems like a silly example, but people make silly causal statements every day on the basis of correlational data. Therefore, when you interpret a correlation, don't mistakenly talk about a causal relationship. Remember that all you have in fact established is that two DVs tend to vary together for unknown reasons.

SINGLE-SUBJECT DESIGNS

A Single-Subject design is one in which one or a few subjects are repeatedly measured under different conditions of the experiment. This approach is often used when there are relatively few appropriate subjects available or when the effect being studied requires time-consuming and extensive investigation. The problem in a Single-Subject approach comes in analyzing its results. Statistics necessary for making such analyses are still being developed. Unless each subject duplicates closely the measures taken on the others, you can't be sure whether results for a particular subject are generalizable or whether the subject is unique. A case history on a single subject may make fascinating reading, but it is hardly a basis for wide-sweeping conclusions. Even if an effect for a single subject is made to come and go by repeated reversals of treatment and non-treatment conditions, there still are serious questions of how well any one subject represents any wider population. Unfortunately, Single-Subject studies often report only descriptive statistics and base their conclusions on examination of these alone. Unless some kind of defensible inferential statistics are included in the report of such a study, the research should be regarded as primarily pilot work, which needs to be confirmed by investigation of more subjects.

MULTILEVEL DESIGNS

One of the ways to increase information from an experiment is to use multiple levels of a single IV. However, the way the multiple IV levels are operationally defined can make it very hard to reject the null hypothesis in some circumstances, even if one of the treatments is effective. The Analysis of Variance test statistic for a multilevel comparison measures only whether the variability among the means for *all* the levels is too large to say that *all* the samples were taken from the same population. As the number of IV levels increases, this test statistic becomes less and less sensitive to the possibility that only one of the samples comes from a different population. Some multilevel studies have only one real "experimental" group and a number of "control" groups, each controlling for different things. If a one-way Analysis of Variance is then used, the fact that there are a number of control samples giving approximately the same results ensures that the calculated test statistic will be small and insignificant, even if the single experimental sample does give very different results. The fact that one group in a multilevel experiment is different simply gets lost when all the other groups are the same. For the Analysis of Variance to work right, you should choose your IV levels to produce a range of effects on the DV.

RECAPITULATION

for LIMITATIONS OF DESIGNS

The design you choose for your research limits from the beginning the interpretation of your results. A *Static-Groups* design introduces the possibility that uncontrolled Subject—and sometimes Non-Subject—Relevant Variables are confounding your IV effects. A *design that involves a Subject IV* also runs the risk that Subject Relevant Variables varying systematically with the levels of the IV are what are really producing changes in the DV. In either case, you need to measure as many Subject Relevant Variables as possible to establish that the groups of subjects are not different, at least on the variables you measure. You must be very cautious when interpreting the results of Static-Groups designs or designs involving Subject IVs. The results of *correlational research* can establish only that two DVs covary under the conditions of the study. Such a correlation cannot safely be used to make causal statements, because no IV was manipulated by the experimenter. Some other measured variable may in fact be responsible for simultaneous changes in both of the measured DVs. *Single-Subject designs,* in which one or a few subjects are extensively studied, are difficult to analyze statistically. The results of Single-Subject studies are often overinterpreted without considering whether the single subject is truly representative of any larger population. Finally, *multilevel IV studies* can statistically disguise a treatment effect by introducing a number of "levels" that are really not expected to have much differential effect on the DV. Properly, the IV levels used in such a design should produce a range of different effects. Whenever your design has some such limitation, you are obliged to point it out to your audience and to discuss how the limitation might weaken the interpretation you wish to make of your results.

BEHAVIORAL OBJECTIVES

for LIMITATIONS OF DESIGNS

1. Given the name of a design, describe the limitation that design may place on interpretation of results.
2. Given a description of a research study, identify the design and then suggest how for that particular study, interpretation of its results will be limited.
3. Given a description of a research study and the interpretation the authors have made of their results, identify a design limitation that might weaken their conclusions. Be specific about exactly how and why their conclusions might be in error.

4. Given a description of a study in which Subject Relevant Variables might pose a problem, identify some of these variables, and speculate about what their effects on the results might be.

SAMPLE TEST QUESTIONS

for LIMITATIONS OF DESIGNS

1. From Moore and Smith (1962): A comparison of several types of immediate reinforcement.

   This study compared the effects of five different conditions of "knowledge of results" on student learning in an introductory psychology college course. The class, totaling 220 students, was randomly divided into five groups. All students studied the same programmed materials. These materials consisted of course materials broken into small, usually one-sentence, segments, which required that the student make a written response before proceeding to the next segment. Four of the groups saw these materials on a "teaching machine," a device that exposes the items one at a time, waits for an answer, and then advances to the next item. Group 1 was given no knowledge of the correctness of their answers; the machine merely advanced to the next items. Group 2 saw the actual correct answers after each response. Group 3 didn't see the actual answers but were signaled with a flashing light after each correct response. Group 4 was given the correct answers plus 1¢ for each correct response. Group 5 was the same as Group 3, but read the items from a programmed text rather than using the teaching machine. All subjects were given the same final examination. A one-way Analysis of Variance on the final scores of the five groups yielded a nonsignificant F-ratio. The authors were disappointed that "knowledge of results" didn't seem to make a difference in how their students learned. (P.S.: They reported no descriptive statistics, only the results of the Analysis of Variance. Shame on them!)

   a. What is the IV in this study? How many levels of it did the researchers use? How were these levels operationally defined?

   b. What is the design of this study? Represent it in shorthand and name it.

   c. What is the DV? What kind of scale was it measured on? What is being assumed about the distribution of DV values?

   d. Explain how the way the authors designed their study made it highly likely they would have to accept the null hypothesis, even if "knowledge of results" was an important factor in learning.

   e. Suppose the descriptive statistics were available for these data. What might you expect to see as you looked at the means of the five groups if, in fact, knowledge of results was affecting learning?

2. Below is an excerpt from a newspaper advertisement used in an antiabortion campaign. Whatever your political or moral persuasion, evaluate the information supplied in the ad from the point of view of an experienced researcher.

Do You Care?

Child abuse, VD, and illegitimate births (up 23 percent in 1977 alone!)—all have increased dramatically since we started buying abortions with tax dollars. Has state-financed abortion solved these problems or made them worse? The test of an idea is in its consequences.

a. What kind of "research design" was used as the basis for this information?

b. What are the weaknesses in making a causal interpretation of these results?

3. On p. 64 is a description of a study on the effects of introducing a new industrial arts curriculum into a school. When you first considered this study, you found that there was a Relevant Variable, namely, the difference between schools, which could have confounded the effects of the IV. Suppose that circumstances were such that the researcher could not make random assignment of students to IV levels, and that the expense of the new curriculum prevented introducing it into more than one school. Describe what the researcher should do to decrease the influence of possible Confounding Variables and increase the strength of conclusions from this research within the limitations of the design.

4. From Pagano and Franklin (1977): The effect of Transcendental Meditation on right hemisphere functioning.

Experienced Transcendental Meditators (more than 3 years), subjects who had just begun practicing meditation (less than 1 month), and nonmeditators were compared. All subjects were pre- and posttested on the Seashore Tonal Memory Test (designed as a low-level test of musical ability). A double-blind procedure was used for the experimenters administering the tests. Between the pre- and posttests, the subjects meditated or rested (nonmeditator group) for 20 minutes. No pre-to-posttest differences were found for any of the groups. The experienced meditators were found to be significantly different at both pre- and posttest from other groups.

a. Identify the two IVs in this study. Classify each one as Subject or Non-Subject.

b. Write out the design of this study in shorthand. What is a name for this design?

c. What was the DV in this study? If it is assumed to be a normally distributed, intervally scaled variable, what statistical test would be used to analyze it?

d. Explain what a double-blind procedure is. Why was it used in this study?

e. Although the meditation seemed to have no effect on the subjects' performance within this experiment, the experienced Transcendental Meditators were found to be superior overall on this musical task to nonmeditators or persons just beginning to practice meditation. What reservations would you have if the authors concluded that Transcendental Meditation improves musical abilities (supposedly reflecting improved right-hemisphere brain performance)?

5. O'Leary, Kaufman, Kass, and Drabman (1970): The effects of loud and soft reprimands on the behavior of disruptive students.

Two boys in a second grade classroom who showed high levels of disruptive behavior were studied. Observations were made daily for 20-minute periods, and nine kinds of disruptive behavior were noted. The experiment had four phases, each lasting two weeks. In Phase I the teacher continued reprimanding the children as usual, that is, generally very loud. In Phase II she used only soft reprimands. In Phase III she used loud reprimands, and in Phase IV she returned to soft reprimands. The mean frequency of disruptive behavior was consistently higher when loud reprimands were used.

    a. What is the IV in this study? What were its levels?

    b. What type of design was used for this study?

    c. What was the DV?

    d. What aspects of the design of this study might cause concern about the repeatability of these results?

SECTION 4: EXPERIMENTER EXPECTANCY EFFECTS

In Chapter 1 the tale of "Hans the Clever Horse" was told to demonstrate how tricky it can be to figure out exactly what is going on in a complicated situation. Hans was extensively examined by many knowledgeable and educated people of his day, but the explanation of his impressive "mental powers" was not discovered. Pfungst, a psychologist, concluded that the importance of unintentional cues supplied by Hans's human questioners had been overlooked because the observers of Hans's behavior "sought in the horse what should have been sought in the man." If unintentional nonverbal cues can have such a powerful influence on an animal subject's behavior, it is very likely that such cues from an experimenter can have similar, difficult-to-trace effects on a human subject's behavior. After his work with Hans, Pfungst was so fascinated with the phenomeon that he continued his investigations in the laboratory using human subjects. He found that humans have many unintentional movements and gestures that communicate to other humans, usually without the parties' awareness. In more recent years, Robert Rosenthal and his associates have repeatedly demonstrated in a wide variety of situations that the characteristics and expectations of the experimenter can have powerful effects on the behavior of both animal and human subjects. Such **Experimenter Bias** effects are a potential Confounding Variable in research involving direct contact between experimenters and their subjects.

The beliefs and expectations of experimenters can affect the interpretation of research results in other ways than by directly changing the subjects' behavior. The experimenters may unintentionally choose a design that makes an expected outcome highly likely. The experimenters may let their observations be influenced by knowing which subjects are in the experimental group and which in the control. Improper statistical procedures that favor the experimenters' predictions may be chosen. Finally, in interpreting their research, experimenters may let prejudices creep in, favoring unlikely explanations of results while ignoring more obvious ones.

EXPERIMENTER EXPECTANCY EFFECTS
ON PLANNING RESEARCH

In the planning stages, researchers must be careful to avoid building in their expectations by selection of the design. For example, if you don't really believe the IV will have an effect on your results, it is relatively easy to introduce so much random error that almost no DV differences between experimental conditions could be large enough to be significant. Too-small samples along with collection of data under very variable conditions can predetermine acceptance of the null hypothesis in many cases. More often, however, experimenters believe fervently that the IV will have an effect. In accord with this belief, potentially Confounding Variables may be overlooked in planning the research.

The proper definition of control conditions is essential to prevent the introduction of experimenter expectancy effects at the design stage. Often the appropriate control group for an experiment is not simply a group of subjects to which nothing is done. In the G. L. Paul study (1966) discussed on pp. 68 ff., two control conditions were included in the design. The purpose of the study was to test the effectiveness of alternative therapeutic approaches to reducing distress in public-speaking situations. Reference to Paul's results in Fig. 2.2 shows how essential the "attention-placebo" control group was to interpretation of the results. Without this group, we might conclude that "insight therapy," though not quite as effective as "counterconditioning," nevertheless was an effective therapeutic procedure. After all, it did produce a pre-to-posttest reduction in anxiety measures larger than that seen for no-treatment controls. However, inclusion in the research design of the "attention-placebo" group changes the interpretation of these results. This group was designed to control for attention from the experimenters and for the subjects' belief that they were receiving help—both circumstances common to many different therapeutic procedures. Comparison of the effect of this control procedure and the effects of the "insight therapy" condition lets us see that the latter was not in fact having much special therapeutic effect beyond attention paid to the subjects. When you are creating control groups for your own experiment or evaluating the appropriateness of controls in other people's research, the crucial question you need to ask yourself is whether the experimental and control conditions differ only according to the operational definition of the IV.

Experimenter expectancy effects on research design can be found for a whole field of investigation as well as within single experiments. A study of the designs of nearly 600 social psychology experiments (McKenna and Kessler, 1977) produced evidence of experimenter expectancy effects in selection and operational definition of both IVs and DVs. Studies on interpersonal attraction and on aggression that used either all-male or all-female subject groups were examined. Those studies using female subjects were less likely to have IVs that required active treatment or arousal of the subjects. Also, studies with female subjects were less likely to use DVs that involved measurement of active behaviors. When these studies were designed, the researchers had already made assumptions about what it was permissible to do to female subjects and what behaviors it was permissible to ask them to show.

Given this bias in planning experiments, it would be very hard to compare the results gathered on males and females, since the IVs and DVs are consistently defined differently. Assuming sex differences while planning research will ensure continued sex differences in results. Most likely, investigators never really considered that tacit assumptions about sex roles were a factor in shaping their research plans.

EXPERIMENTER BIAS: EXPERIMENTER EXPECTANCY EFFECTS ON SUBJECT BEHAVIOR

Since the early 1960s a great deal of research has been done confirming that the expectancies and the characteristics of experimenters change subject behavior and therefore need to be controlled. Rosenthal and his associates (Rosenthal, 1966) have done numerous studies in which the bias of the experimenters was manipulated as an IV to determine the effects of this bias on subject performance. In work with animal subjects, student experimenters who were led to believe that their rats were "extremely bright" trained their animals to perform complicated tasks more quickly than did those students who were led to believe that their rats were "dull." In studies of the interaction of experimenters with human subjects, the beliefs of the experimenters were found to have significant effects on their subjects' performance. If the experimenters expected a certain kind of results and/or were motivated to get those results by monetary reward or by praise from their superiors, the data from their subjects were found to be biased toward the experimenters' expectations. The means by which these experimenters unintentionally influenced their subjects appeared to have been both visual and auditory, especially tone of voice and nonverbal sounds of encouragement. The largest biasing effects were seen for experimenters who themselves had a high need for approval from other people, were friendly to the subjects, were inclined to gesture a lot, and impressed their subjects as "high-status" or important people. Interestingly enough, these are about the same qualities that Pfungst reported for persons who could get "clever" answers from Hans the horse.

Rosenthal and others have extended these observations into clinical and educational settings. The beliefs of a teacher about the intelligence of her students, for example, influence the performances of the students, independent of their actual IQs (Rosenthal and Jacobson, 1968). The beliefs of a clinician about the source of a patient's problems influence the way the patient describes those problems to the therapist. The better the student likes the teacher, the more powerful the teacher's influence. The more the patient respects the therapist, the greater the therapist's influence. It is pretty clear that clever Hans was no more sensitive than the average human to slight cues from the experimenter and no less appreciative of signs of social approval. Hans, for that matter, required carrots. We humans seem to need only smiles and satisfied grunts.

Experimenter biasing effects are very difficult to control, and the experimenter must always be alert to the possibility of their existence. Whenever possible, "double-blind" studies should be done in which the experimenter as well as the subject does not know which condition of the experiment the subject represents. Contact between experimenter and subject should be standardized, with instructions to the subject, whenever possible, written or taped. The less direct contact between experimenter and subject, the better. In research designs where interaction between experimenter and subject is necessary, it may be desirable to record the experimenter's behavior as well as the subject's. Even with these precautions, the possibility of Experimenter Bias effects should always be explored when interpreting results.

EXPERIMENTER EXPECTANCY EFFECTS ON THE COLLECTION AND ANALYSIS OF DATA

Chapter 5 began with the story of the physician Morton's measurement of cranial capacities of skulls of different racial groups. Gould's (1978a) reexamination of Morton's data established that the good doctor, probably all unaware, consistently made errors in his measurements in accord with his beliefs of the superiority of one race over another. Gould (1978b) also tells the tale of the posthumous ''growth'' of the brain of the genius mathematician Friedrich Gauss. An early examination of Gauss's brain indicated that it was only ''modestly overaverage'' in size. Comparison of it with the brain of a ''common laborer'' showed no difference in the external appearance of the two brains. Many years later, however, one respected scientist inflated the size of Gauss's brain by ''correcting'' for Gauss's small stature and advanced age. Another praised the brain for the richness of its convolutions and, to prove his point, arranged a sequence of Gauss's brain, a Bushwoman's, and a gorilla's. Ignoring the Bushwoman's sex, probable small stature, and history of poor nourishment, this scientist concluded that ''the brain of a first-class genius like Friedrich Gauss is as far removed from that of the average Bushman as that of the latter is removed from the brain of the nearest related ape'' (Spitzka, 1907, p. 226). Gould concludes that ''data can always be twisted or misused if the expectations are sufficiently powerful.'' (One wonders what future scientists will make of Einstein's carefully preserved brain.)

Don't think such perversion of data is a historical curiosity. Psychologists and others interested in the inheritability of intelligence will be recovering for a long time from the recent disclosures about the published work of Sir Cyril Burt (Dorfman, 1978). Burt's was a very important voice in the debate on the inheritability of intelligence, and his work has been widely recognized both in the United States and in Great Britain. His research results constantly argued against the influence of environment on intelligence and for the overwhelming importance of genetic factors, even when IQ differences found between different social classes were considered. Since the eminent psychologist's death in 1971, reexamination of his published data indicates that they contain not only numerous errors but also extensive and deliberate falsification. Old data, gathered decades before, were republished as collected from new studies that were apparently never done. Numbers that were calculated from theory were presented as research data, which in turn were used to support the theory from which they had been calculated. Unlike Morton's errors, Burt's excesses could hardly have been inadvertent. No one has offered a good explanation for his deception, but quite possibly he was so convinced of the rightness of his theories that he felt it unnecessary to bother with further data collection. Burt knew the rules of the game of science and applied them, sometimes harshly, to others who made statistical or logical errors. What he appears to have forgotten is that when we are doing research, the worst enemy may be our own beliefs and needs.

Any of us can fall into the trap set by our own expectations. Unless the rules by which we are taking our DV observations are very clearly spelled out, it is easy to accept measures that are in accord with our expectations and challenge, redo, or throw out those that don't fit. We are likely to overlook errors which result in measures that meet our expectations while checking again and finding errors in those measures that "look funny." The only way to avoid this kind of bias is either to use measures that are as objective as possible or, if the measurement process requires an observer's subjective judgment, to ensure that the observer does not know which condition of the experiment any given subject represents. When data or calculations are checked for errors, all of them should be checked, not just the "suspect" ones. To guard against our own biases, we have to be sure that all data are collected and analyzed in a consistent fashion.

Statistical analysis of the data may also be influenced by our beliefs. For instance, the literature on extrasensory perception (ESP) abounds with inappropriate application of statistical tests. Very often simple tests are applied to complex situations that do not meet the probability assumptions of the underlying model for the test. For instance, an experimenter may accept close but incorrect guesses as evidence of ESP without realizing that it is necessary to specify *all* acceptable outcomes *before* doing the experiment, or the statistical model for testing the results has no validity. In other cases, the assumption is made that human guessing behavior will be random in the absence of ESP, and the null hypothesis is based on this assumption. Actually, human guessing behavior has been found to be nonrandom. In complex, badly controlled experiments, simple models of chance are not applicable. In some cases reanalysis of a "successful" ESP experiment, when it is possible to construct the appropriate statistical model, has resulted in a disappearance of the "significance" of the effect (Diaconis, 1978). Experiments have to be very carefully designed and conducted to meet the assumptions of available statistical tests. If they are not, we have no way of evaluating the repeatability of the results.

EXPERIMENTER EXPECTANCY EFFECTS ON INTERPRETATION OF RESULTS

Even if you manage to eliminate Experimenter Bias effects on subject behavior, to collect the data in an objective fashion, and to do appropriate statistical analyses, your biases may take over when you interpret your results as support for your pet theory. Many centuries ago, Galen, an early physician, did a marvelous job of interpreting the results of using a favorite medicinal preparation: "All those who drink this remedy recover in a short time, except those whom it does not help, who all die and have no relief from any other medicine. Therefore, it is obvious that it fails only in incurable cases." This may seem funny, until you read some modern-day research interpretations. Consider, for example, research on the effects of amphetamine drugs on decreasing hyperactivity in "minimally brain-damaged" children. When you find researchers classifying children as "minimally brain-damaged" only if their hyperactive symptoms are improved by amphetamine (Wender, 1971) and excluding others as not truly hyperactive, it is no wonder that the drug is found to be effective! The results of any research project usually can support more than one interpretation. The researcher should be aware of alternative interpretations and express good reasons for choosing a particular one over the others.

CONTROLLING FOR EXPERIMENTER EXPECTANCY EFFECTS

Obviously, controlling for experimenter expectancy effects will be difficult, since we are seeking to protect ourselves from ourselves. When doing research, we need to be aware of our beliefs and expectations and to continually examine our choice of experimental procedures to be sure that we are giving alternative beliefs a fair chance. Knowledge of the rules of research design and statistics and proper application of these rules will go a long way toward protecting ourselves from our own biases and set ways of thinking. Reporting our research to a knowledgeable and skeptical audience will often reveal weakness introduced by our biases. Unfortunately, however, this type of feedback usually happens after the research is completed and the damage is done. Good researchers remain ever-skeptical of their own theories and results; impassioned believers are more likely to fall into experimenter expectancy errors.

Experimenter Bias effects on subject behavior are an insidious problem because they change the actual results of the research. Misuse of experimental designs or statistics is likely to be detected sooner or later by others, as happened with Burt and Morton. Experimenter Bias effects on subject behavior, however, often can only be guessed at from published research articles. Many of the subtle differences between experimenter treatment of experimental and control subjects will not be apparent from a published description of a research project. Use of such things as double-blind procedures, placebos, "attention" controls, taped instructions, observers for experimenter behavior, etc., at least establishes that the researchers were aware of Experimenter Bias problems. When planning your own research, the possibility of Experimenter Bias effects should be considered and controlled for. When interpreting your results, you should consider Experimenter Bias effects as a possible alternative explanation.

RECAPITULATION

for EXPERIMENTER EXPECTANCY EFFECTS

The beliefs of the experimenter can influence the design of the research, the results collected in the research, the analysis of results, and the interpretation of the research. Strong experimenter expectancy effects may produce selective errors in the collection and analysis of data that bias the results toward the experimenter's expectations. Designs that ignore important Confounding Variables and statistics that are inappropriate may be used to produce results in accord with the experimenter's beliefs unless the experimenter knows and rigorously follows the rules of scientific method. Since the experimenter can influence subject behavior in many subtle ways, *Experimenter Bias* may become a Confounding Variable in behavioral research and introduce constant error into the results. Experimenter Bias effects are difficult to control. Use of the *double-blind* technique, in which the experimenter does not know which are experimental and which are control subjects, may be possible in some situations. Contact of experimenters with subjects should be standardized and minimized when possible. When not, it may be advisable to measure experimenter behavior to see whether it varies between experimental conditions. Experimenter expectancy effects can also influence interpretation of results. Researchers must be careful to look for explanations of their results alternative to the one their theory suggests.

BEHAVIORAL OBJECTIVES

for EXPERIMENTER EXPECTANCY EFFECTS

1. Describe the different stages at which the beliefs and expectations of a researcher can affect the conclusions reached from the research.
2. Describe what is meant by Experimenter Bias effects on subject behavior. Give a specific example of a situation in which Experimenter Bias could confound results.
3. Given a description of an experiment, recognize possible sources of Experimenter Bias effects and describe exactly what confounding effects they may be having on the results.
4. Given the description of an experiment in which Experimenter Bias effects are likely, suggest a specific way to control for them.
5. Given a description of a research project, identify how either poor choice of design or inappropriate use of statistics may be favoring outcomes expected by the experimenter.
6. Given a description of a researcher's interpretation of results, suggest alternative interpretations of the same results.

SAMPLE TEST QUESTIONS

for EXPERIMENTER EXPECTANCY EFFECTS

1. Based on Jacobson and Koch (1978): Attributed reasons for support of the feminist movement as a function of attractiveness.
    Description of Study. Male and female college students were shown a series of photos of attractive and unattractive women and asked to indicate for each photo the main reason they thought the woman was a feminist. A greater num-

ber of positive reasons were given for the attractive than for the unattractive women. The authors concluded: "The expected main effect of attractiveness is disheartening because it is a put-down of unattractive women. This finding . . . can also be interpreted as a put-down of feminism because it implies that feminism is an ideology that is more appealing to . . . people who are undervalued in society (i.e., the unattractive)." (p. 174)

Details of Procedures. Subjects were run singly or two at a time by a male experimenter. They were told that the study involved person perception on two contemporary issues: hunting and feminism. They were told that people make inferences about other people from what they look like, and that they would be shown photos and asked to pick from a prepared list of reasons the one that most expressed why the woman in the photo was a feminist or the man in the photo hunted. The lists were equally balanced for positive and negative reasons. Each subject was shown twenty photos of attractive and unattractive men for the "filler" hunting task. The order of feminism and hunting tasks was counterbalanced across subjects. Sixteen men and sixteen women participated in the study.

Results of An Analysis of Variance. The male and female subjects showed no significant differences so their data were combined. Subjects attributed more positive reasons to attractive than to unattractive women ($F(1, 30) = 53.99$, $p < .01$). The main effect of order was not significant. The interaction of order of task and attractiveness of photos was reported as significant as well ($F(1, 30) = 3.89$, $p < .10$). The overall average number of positive reasons attributed to the ten attractive women for being feminists was 7.0 while for unattractive women, it was only 4.5.

a. There were three IVs in this study. Identify each and specify whether it was a Subject or a Non-Subject IV. Then decide whether the design treated it as Within- or Between-Subjects.

b. What DV was measured in the study? What is its type of scale?

c. What assumptions did the authors make in choosing their statistical analysis?

d. Can you see any opportunities for Experimenter Bias effects in this study?

e. How would you change the procedures of the study to reduce the possibility of such Experimenter Bias effects?

f. The authors offer as an alternative to their main conclusion that the results could simply represent a "halo effect" in which attractive people have good things attributed to them no matter what is being studied. How might the data for the male photographs used in the hunting task (unreported in the study) help us choose between alternative interpretations of these results?

g. Can you see any limitations in generalizing the results of this study to judgment of feminists by the general public?

2. Review the Boren and Foree (1977) study presented on p. 66. This study compared the effectiveness of a traditional approach to teaching a university nutrition course with a new personalized system of instruction. The "cognitive" DV was measured by objective written tests and showed no difference between

teaching methods. A "psychomotor competency" DV was measured by having the teacher rate the students on their preparation of a meal under set conditions. This DV did show a superiority of the personalized system of intruction.

a. Discuss the possibilities for both Experimenter Bias effects in this research and for experimenter expectancy effects on the assessment of "psychomotor competency."

b. How would you redesign this study to avoid these possible experimenter expectancy effects?

3. Review the Kliebhan (1967) study described on p. 258. Sister Kliebhan found that both setting goals with the foreman and having a model to imitate improved the output of retarded workers. In order to measure the quality of the output, she had the foreman evaluate the products as "inferior," "average," or "superior." A Chi-Square test established that the expectancy (goal-setting) group had significantly more products in the average and superior categories than either of the other groups. The imitation group, in turn, was significantly better than the control group.

a. The control subjects continued under the usual working procedures. The expectancy group had their work evaluated in front of them by the foreman, who discussed it with them and then had them set their goals. The imitation group was periodicallly approached by the foremen to verbally draw attention to the model. Discuss the possibility of Experimenter Bias effects on subject behavior in this research.

b. Describe the possibilities for experimenter expectancy effects in the evaluation of the quality-of-work DV. How would you eliminate this problem?

SECTION 5: HOW DO SUBJECTS RESPOND TO THE DEMANDS OF AN EXPERIMENT?

SUBJECT ATTITUDES AS A POSSIBLE FACTOR IN INTERPRETING RESEARCH

In Section 4 we found that the experimenter's beliefs and expectations might have effects on subject behavior that would lead to misinterpretation of results. However, subjects, especially human ones, cannot be thought of as passive objects being pushed around by the experimenters' biases and by the effects of IVs. Human subjects' thoughts and expectations about an experiment may also affect their behavior. Human subjects must be recognized as active participants in an experiment, seeking their own explanations of the purposes of the research and giving themselves instructions beyond what the experimenters tell them to do. Subject biasing effects on results are even more difficult to detect and deal with than Experimenter Bias effects. When there is a possibility that subject biasing effects may alter interpretation of results, special efforts should be made to control them.

Subject biasing effects can restrict interpretation of research in three different ways. They can introduce constant error, they can increase random error, and they can limit generalization. The first problem is the most serious, since it is the least likely to be recognized. When subject expectations differ consistently for different conditions of the experiment, a Confounding Variable has been introduced, the effects of which may be mistakenly attributed to the IV. If subjects have varied expectations, but these expectations do not differ consistently between conditions, then only random error will be introduced, and the effects on interpretation of results will not be as serious. If the subjects included in the research have different beliefs and expectations from those of the population at large, this factor will have to be taken into account when generalizing, but it does not otherwise change interpretation of results.

The potential harm that subject attitudes, expectations, and self-instructions can do to interpretation of research is partly dependent on what is being studied. Some human behaviors are more likely than others to be affected by these subject factors. The problem is to guess which behaviors are likely to be changed and which are not. Considering that researchers have shown that "involuntary" things as physiological effects of drugs and reactions to a lie-detector task are sensitive to subject expectations, we can't, without evidence, totally exclude the possibility that almost any human response may be affected to some degree by subject beliefs about the experiment.

WARNING SIGNS THAT SUBJECT FACTORS MAY BE IMPORTANT IN A RESEARCH PROJECT

Although subject attitudes are always a factor to be considered, there are a couple of situations that should alert researchers to the possibility of their being a major problem. One occurs when large variations in research procedures elicit unexpectedly similar results. For instance, studies of sensory deprivation produced evidence that subjects experience hallucinatory effects and perceptual changes after prolonged isolation. However, review of the literature in this area (Orne, 1969) indicated that these effects were usually seen about two-thirds of the way through the experiment, whether the experiment ran eight hours or three weeks! Other experiments established that at least some of the "sensory deprivation" effect was attributable to what the subjects expected to happen (Orne and Scheibe, 1964).

Another warning bell is sounded when identical or highly similar procedures carried out in different laboratories yield markedly different results. The research establishing biofeedback as an especially effective technique for inducing relaxation and for relieving various chronic stress reactions may be an example of this problem. Some researchers are reporting it as vastly superior to other relaxation techniques, whereas others are finding that it adds very little if anything to simply getting the subjects to lie down and relax regularly.

WAYS IN WHICH SUBJECT FACTORS CAN AFFECT THE OUTCOME OF RESEARCH

The Volunteer Subject

Who is actually studied in experiments? Except for those studies in which people are observed unawares and without permission, most subjects have volunteered for the experience. Subjects volunteer for a host of reasons. They may be students seeking to fulfill the requirements of a course. They may wish to earn money if participation is paid for. They may be especially interested in the topic being studied. They may have been seduced by a researcher's enthusiasm. They may hope that the research experience will have therapeutic value for them. They may have been curious about an advertisement inviting participation.

Studies indicate that volunteers are special people (Rosenthal and Rosnow, 1969). Volunteers are likely to be of higher educational and occupational status and to have higher IQs than people who do not volunteer. Volunteers are also likely to have a higher need for approval and recognition, factors that make them more easily affected by the experimenters' behavior and by the demands of the experimental situation. The type of person likely to volunteer interacts with the type of research being carried out. In survey-type research, volunteers are more likely to be better adjusted than nonvolunteers, and in medical research, persons with problems are more likely to participate than are those with none. If the task is unusual or threatening, the proportion of female volunteers will drop (sensible of them).

Obviously, the special characteristics of volunteer subjects may limit generalization. When generalizing, the researchers will have to remember that the population actually studied consisted of those persons who *volunteered*. How nonvolunteers would have behaved can only be guessed. Also, the special characteristics of volunteer subjects may on occasion interact with the IV, creating a constant error problem. For instance, if subjects were motivated to volunteer because they expected therapeutic value from the research, those placed in a "control" group and denied the supposed benefits of treatment might perform unusually poorly in their disappointment. This would make the treatment appear especially effective by contrast. Volunteer subject characteristics as a Confounding Variable can also work against your IV. In a survey of the problems of people at different levels of care in a nursing home, it was found that although the people with different degrees of care differed in physical problems, they did not differ as expected in incidence of "mental confusion." However, the fact that the patients had to give informed consent to being surveyed at all eliminated those who were poorly oriented or uncooperative before the study began.

The Hawthorne Effect

An early series of studies in industrial psychology was done in the 1930s (Roethlisberger and Dickson, 1939). The goal of these studies was to establish the effects on productivity of variations in working conditions, such as illumination, temperature, hours of work, rest periods, wage rates, etc. A peculiar thing happened. No matter what manipulation the experimenters tried, productivity increased. For instance, increasing the number or length of rest periods increased productivity, but so did decreasing them! The only interpretation the researchers could find for these puzzling results was that the workers included in the studies felt honored at being chosen to participate and responded favorably to special observation of their production (anything to liven up an assembly line). Every change in factors was regarded by the subjects as a further challenge to excel. Since publication of these studies, the term

Hawthorne effect has been used as a label for the effect on subjects of simply knowing that they are part of a research program. The occurrence of the Hawthorne effect will weaken generalization to real-life situations, where people do not regard themselves as special or challenged. The Hawthorne effect may also introduce a Confounding Variable if subjects in the experimental group perceive themselves as being specially treated but controls do not.

Pretest Sensitization

In Chapter 4 pretesting was suggested as alternative or supplementary to randomization for creating equivalent groups for study. In fact, this procedure can have three design advantages over randomization alone. Without increasing the number of subjects needed, it increases the number of observations by measuring each subject both without (before) and with (after) treatment. It also permits statistical elimination of some between-subject variability by using each subject as its own control. Finally, pretesting can serve as a check that independent groups, whether static or created by randomization, were in fact equivalent on the DV to begin with.

In spite of all these advantages, pretesting may also have some disadvantages. It can introduce a Confounding Variable into the research by alerting experimental subjects to what will be important at posttest time. Also, performance on some DV measures can be changed simply by subjects' becoming more familiar with the measuring process. Unless we use a design that measures the effects of pretesting itself, we can't be completely sure that **pretest sensitization** does not interact with the IV and confound interpretation of results.

The Helpful Subject

Frequently subjects participate in research because they are interested and because they wish to help the researchers. After they have invested their time and energy in the study, they are even more concerned with seeing that their results are meaningful. By and large, volunteer subjects are cooperative beyond all reasonable expectations. If they divine either directly or indirectly how the experimenter wishes things to come out, there is every possibility that they will help the results in that direction. The more subjects like, approve of, or respect the researchers, the greater the possibility of their unconsciously introducing such biases.

The Subject As a Problem Solver

No matter how ambiguous a situation humans find themselves in, they seem to regard it as a problem for which they need to find a solution. Studies of animal behavior report that monkeys will solve problems even if there is no foreseeable reward for doing so. Human subjects usually demand that the experimenter tell them what the "right answer" was, even in studies where there is no right answer and this fact has been explained beforehand. What from the experimenter's point of view is a situation set up simply to observe what the subject does, from the subject's point of view is a situation requiring active seeking of a solution. Depending on the type of experiment, this problem-solving orientation may be more pronounced in experimental subjects than in no-treatment controls, confounding interpretation of results.

Evaluation Apprehension

Humans feel the need to "look good," to receive some sort of positive evaluation, in even the most casual of human interactions. This need can be intensified in an experimental setting, where a person perceived to have special skills and authority is "studying" us. The anxiety of subjects about winning the approval of the researchers has been termed **evaluation apprehension** (Rosenberg, 1965). Subjects try to guess how to perform in such a way as to impress the experimenters with their normalcy, adjustment, maturity, and intelligence. They will do so in spite of assurances from the experimenter that they are just being observed and not evaluated. The evidence of such evaluation apprehension can be seen not only in behaviors but also in physiological measures.

If cues as to "how to behave" are numerous and obscure, then subjects are likely to arrive at a variety of hypotheses about what is "good behavior" and introduce random error into the research. This is bad enough, but if cues about expected behavior are at all obvious, systematically changing behavior in one experimental group or another, then a Confounding Variable may be introduced. When planning an experiment, devising procedures, and wording instructions, remember that your subjects will be actively seeking an explanation of your requests and will be trying to impress you.

Special Demand Characteristics of an Experiment That Can Change DV Measures

Sometimes behavior the researcher may interpret as being caused by an IV is actually a product of what Orne (1969) calls the **demand characteristics** of an experiment. Anything about the experiment that a subject perceives and reacts to may be such a demand characteristic. These demand characteristics can be even harder to isolate and control than are Experimenter Bias effects. The need to identify problems introduced by special demands of a given experiment becomes especially important when investigating the effects of such things as drugs, psychological therapies, hypnosis, sensory deprivation effects of group pressure, etc.

As an example of how effects of demand characteristics might change interpretation of results, consider experiments in which subjects either experience stress or think they are causing distress to others. Subjects knowing that they are "in an experiment" may tolerate more stress and be willing to administer more to others because they know that the situation is ultimately under the control of a powerful figure, namely, the experimenter. The experimental situation carries with it a built-in guarantee that things will not be allowed to go too far. For example, the results of Milgram's (1974) series of experiments on aggression seem to show that people are willing to deliver extremely strong electric shocks and create a good deal of distress simply on the "orders" of a relatively unfamiliar experimenter. However, generalization of these results to everyday behavior must be tempered by the fact that Milgram's experimental subjects implicitly knew that even if they delivered the maximum shock to their supposed victims they wouldn't be allowed to injure permanently or kill them, not to mention that the victims wouldn't retaliate. In real life, people simply don't have the assurance that their aggressive acts will be thus limited in effect and consequences.

Experimenters sometimes forget that subjects believe and act on more than they are told. Instructions intended to deceive them may backfire. The fact that it is an "experiment" insulates subjects from the usual rewards and punishments. The subjects have knowledge from other sources about how to behave. For instance, subjects have some idea how to act "when hypnotized" or "when deprived of sleep," and this knowledge, in addition to the actual experimental maneuvers, may affect their behavior. Interpretation of research on human behavior must allow for the possibility that people will be affected by what they perceive to be the special demands of an experimental situation.

SOME WAYS OF DEALING WITH SUBJECT BELIEFS, THOUGHTS, AND EXPECTATIONS

The techniques described below may be useful in different situations. Of course, they all have their drawbacks. As always in planning research, you'll have to make the compromise that you think will yield the most useful and reliable information.

Full Disclosure

For some research questions it doesn't matter whether subjects know what the experimenters are looking for. As long as you use proper control procedures, such as counterbalancing and double-blind, it may not matter whether the subject knows what your hypothesis is. For instance, if you were investigating the question of whether subjects could identify correctly by taste alone the commercial cola drink they say they prefer, you could be completely candid about your suspicion that they could not. If anything, this approach would act as a challenge to the subjects to prove you wrong, which is just what you want. If the subjects have no physical clues as to what is in each cup, and you, the experimenter, don't know either, then it should make no difference to their behavior if they know the purposes of the study. Whenever the research question and design permit, full disclosure is probably the best policy to keep subjects from making up silly stories of their own (provided they believe you).

Deception

One classical way to control subject biases is to deceive subjects about the true purposes of the experiment. The rationale is that since the subjects don't know which behavior is important and is being measured, they can't bias their results. The clever ruses developed by psychologists over the years could almost be called a science of deception. For many investigators deception has become a habit. However, some social scientists have questioned whether deception is always necessary and whether it works equally well in all research situations.

For one thing, the practice of deception in research seems to have spawned a generation of very suspicious subjects. Just because you tell your subjects something, you don't expect nowadays that they will believe you. Remember that they are intelligent beings who are trying to figure out the situation on their own. Since you are identified as a "researcher," they are likely to be looking for the card up your sleeve, even when it isn't there.

Ethical issues may also be a problem when deception is used as a research technique. Universities, government agencies, grant sources, etc., are increasingly insisting that informed consent be obtained from subjects prior to participation in a research program. If subjects are misled as to the purpose of the research, how can they give informed consent? If deception is used in a research program, subjects must be informed fully about it at the end of the research. When the deception is trivial, repercussions may not be serious. However, subjects won't care for deceptions that tell them something is anonymous and it later turns out not to be so. Nor will they think much of a deception that leads them to act in ways they normally wouldn't care to act. Any deception practiced in a research project should be necessary to the purposes of research and should not upset the subjects when its existence is revealed.

Studying Subjects without Their Knowledge

One way to avoid letting the subjects' knowledge about the research affect their behavior is to study them without their knowing it. This approach pretty much limits you to using a nonlab setting. For example, researchers have conducted many social psychology experiments by staging an event and recording the reactions to it of passersby. A "lost child" asking for directions may reveal differences in readiness of urban and small-town adults to aid a stranger, whereas a questionnaire asking "what would you do if . . ." may not. The drawback to this approach, of course, is that you do not have the consent of the subjects to be participants. Another problem is that if the social scientists keep sending out fake children, staging false heart attacks and the like, the public may become even more suspicious and unhelpful to those in need than it already is!

Postexperiment Inquiry

A relatively inexpensive source of information that is often neglected is **postexperiment inquiry**. After the experiment is completed and all DV measures are gathered, you can ask your subjects, either directly or with a questionnaire, what they thought was going on in the experiment. Information obtained this way must be used judiciously. Subjects may not reveal all they know and may not know everything that is related to their behavior. Subjects who have figured out a deception in an experiment may not be able to tell you exactly when in the course of the experiment they made the discovery. A situation that should cause you concern is one in which subjects in the experimental and control groups reveal consistently different beliefs about the purpose of the research and what they thought they were supposed to be doing. In this case you are very likely to have a Confounding Variable to worry about.

Pampering Control Subjects

Since being a "control" has a derogatory meaning to subjects, you can go out of your way to see that controls feel as special and as valued as your experimentals. Be sure they get equal attention and praise and that their belief in likely improvement in their abilities is the same as for experimentals. G. L. Paul's (1966) research on techniques for reducing anxiety while speaking in public demonstrates that an "attention-placebo" control group showed almost as much improvement as one of his therapy groups. Since any therapy includes attention, therapist contact, and positive expectations of the subjects, a nontreatment, no-contact group simply would not be an adequate control for the effects of therapy per se.

Use of Quasi-Controls

When you suspect that a demand characteristic of an experiment may affect DV measures, you can introduce controls to check this suspicion. One approach is to give a group of subjects exposure to all the instructions, procedures, setting, etc., of the experiment but not actually give them the treatment. The subjects are then post-tested. In some cases you might go one step further and ask the subjects to try to respond on posttest "as if" they had had the treatment—in other words, to try to simulate the responses of an actual subject. The results of such a **quasi-control** (Orne, 1969) are not conclusive, but they can indicate areas where subject beliefs are a possible problem in interpretation. If you find that your quasi-control subjects can produce data very similar to those who actually experience the treatment, you begin to wonder what the treatment can add.

Changes in Design

Sometimes design changes may help control and measure subject beliefs. For example, a Solomon's Four-Group design is an improvement over a randomized-groups, pre-post design when you suspect that pretest sensitization may be an issue. In other cases a Within-Subjects design for an IV may ensure more consistency of subject belief than a Between-Subjects design, since each subject serves as its own control. However, even in a Within-Subjects design, if the implications of experimental and control conditions are different, the subjects may shift their beliefs between conditions.

Reduction of Evaluation Apprehension

There are several ways of making people less apprehensive about being evaluated. You can assure them that a range of different responses is "normal" and there is no one right answer. It may help to have any performance tests administered by someone other than the researchers. There may be less pressure to excel if the examiner is identified as a lowly clerk or technician. Giving the subjects the impression that everyone connected with the research project is warm and supportive rather than judgmental may also help subjects relax. When running a lab experiment, avoid signs that it is a "special" place in any way other than those that are essential for the experiment. For instance, a white coat may unnecessarily intimidate your subjects, and there's no reason why a testing situation can't be as comfortable and cozy as possible. Attention to details like these can help place subjects at ease and reduce some of their apprehension about being studied.

RECAPITULATION

for SUBJECT RESPONSE TO DEMANDS OF AN EXPERIMENT

Subjects are active participants in research. Their thoughts, beliefs, and expectations about an experiment may affect their behavior. Such subject biasing effects may limit generalization of results, may increase random error, and most seriously, may introduce Confounding Variables. The volunteer subject has been found to differ in several ways from nonvolunteers, and the type of person who volunteers changes with the type of research. Simply knowing that one is taking part in a study may change behavior, a phenomenon that has been labeled the *Hawthorne effect*. Pretesting, though a good way to check for group equivalence, may sensitize subjects both to the treatment and to posttesting, introducing a Confounding Variable. Subjects approach an experiment as a problem to be solved. They want to be helpful to the researchers by producing good and usable data. They are apprehensive about finding a correct solution and receiving the experimenters' approval. Although researchers may want only to observe subject behavior passively, they need to keep in mind when planning the research that the subjects will have these active feelings about the research situation. The facets of the experimental situation that cause reactions in the subject have been termed *experimental demand characteristics*. There are several different approaches to controlling subject response to these demands. Deception abut the true purposes of the research is a widely used technique, but increasing concern over both ethical questions and the factor of subject suspiciousness is stimulating a search for alternative techniques. Studying subjects without their knowledge is another approach, but this approach may also raise ethical questions. *Postexperiment inquiry* can be used to check whether experimental and control subjects shared the same beliefs about what was expected of them. Every attempt should be made to give control subjects the same expectations about and satisfaction with their performance as the experimentals receive. *Quasi-controls*, who experience everything about the experiment except the treatment but try to simulate treatment effects, can be introduced to see whether experimental demands in and of themselves are capable of producing changes in posttest behavior. Design changes can sometimes eliminate problems. such as use of a Solomon's Four-Group design to measure *pretest sensitization*. Finally, steps can be taken to reduce *evaluation apprehension*. The fact that such hard-to-control subject factors exist shouldn't result in distrust of scientific information about human behavior. Experimental method has the advantage that it can readily be used to improve itself.

BEHAVIORAL OBJECTIVES

for SUBJECT RESPONSES TO DEMANDS OF AN EXPERIMENT

1. Describe the three ways subject biasing factors may confuse interpretation of results.

2. Give an example of a situation in which special characteristics of volunteer subjects may limit generalization of research results.

3. An experimental situation may result in a variety of different interpretations and expectations by subjects. Explain when this would be a random-error problem and when it would introduce constant error.

4. Describe how a subject's views of an experimental situation can differ from the researcher's view of it simply as an opportunity to observe subject behavior.

5. Describe three different techniques for reducing effects of subject biasing factors, stating a possible limitation of each technique.

6. Define the following terms:
   a. Hawthorne effect
   b. Pretest sensitization
   c. Evaluation apprehension
   d. Demand characteristics of an experiment
   e. Quasi-controls

7. Given a description of an experiment, identify possible effects of subject beliefs and expectations, and suggest a remedy.

SAMPLE TEST QUESTIONS

for SUBJECT RESPONSE TO DEMANDS OF AN EXPERIMENT

1. For a study on the effects on motor performance of relaxation training utilizing electromyographic (EMG) biofeedback, 20 male subjects volunteered from a college living group supervised by the researcher. They were asked to participate in a study on relaxation training being done as part of the researcher's graduate program, and they were not paid for their time. The subjects were ran-

domly divided into two groups, an experimental group who received biofeed-back relaxation training and a control group who did not. Both groups were pre- and posttested on a task measuring eye-hand coordination and another measuring gross motor ability. In the three weeks between pre- and posttest sessions, the experimental subjects received nine half-hour biofeedback sessions each in the researcher's quarters within the living group. Control subjects were seen only for pre-and posttesting. The experimental subjects showed about a 20 percent improvement in motor skills from pre-to-post, whereas the controls showed an insignificant 2 percent. It was concluded that the relaxation training sessions had improved experimental subjects' ability to coordinate their movements during posttest.

a. In what ways do you think the subjects selected for this study might be special?

b. Is there any reason to think a Hawthorne effect might be operating here? Describe the constant error this might introduce into results.

c. If these subjects were concerned with "helping" their living group supervisor complete his research, how might this bias the results?

d. Would you expect to find evaluation apprehension in these subjects? Can you make a case for the amount of evaluation apprehension being different for experimental and control groups? If it were, would this introduce random or constant error?

e. Other research indicates for these motor tasks that pretesting usually greatly improves posttest performance. Yet the control subjects in this study showed little, if any, pre-to-posttest improvement. Consider the control subjects' perceptions of the demands of this experiment, and discuss why they may have failed to show this effect of pretest. If special reactions of control subjects are a factor in this research, how might it change interpretation of results?

f. Suggest ways to improve this research to reduce the effects of subject expectations and perceptions of special demands of the experiment.

2. We have already considered the possibility of Experimenter Bias effects in the Boren and Foree (1977) study described on p. 66. Now discuss how subject expectations and biases might affect results of this study, distinguishing between random and constant error effects.

3. On p. 103 we described a study that tested whether use of a particular machine to teach speed reading is effective. Discuss what additional steps you would recommend for this study to ensure that subject bias factors will not confound results.

4. Following are three types of problems that subject biases can introduce into interpretation of results.

Problem for generalizing research (G)

Random error (RE)

Constant error (CE)

Indicate which of the three problems is most likely to occur in each of the following situations:

a. Subjects are solicited for a study on the processes involved in falling asleep. The subjects in this study will have to sleep for two weeks in a special lab setting. They will not be paid for participation.

b. Within a third grade class, ten children are randomly selected for instruction in reading by a new method. These children meet as a group in a corner of the classroom for one hour each day with a special instructor. At the end of the year, these ten children are found to be far ahead of the rest of the class in reading.

c. Subjects are being used in a study on the effects of different sizes of type and arrangement of test questions on the accuracy of answers. They are told that the test is not intended as an evaluation of either their knowledge or their ability, but few of the subjects accept this. Some think that the important thing is to answer as many questions as possible. Still others think it really is a personality test (after all, it's a psychologist doing the study) and read each question very carefully to determine its hidden meaning.

d. Subjects have volunteered for a study on the effectiveness of meditation as a relaxation technique. Half of the subjects, selected at random, are given meditation instruction for ten sessions, and half are not. Both groups are pre- and posttested in half-hour relaxation sessions, where their abilities to decrease muscle tension, increase hand warmth, and decrease heart rate are measured. Postexperiment inquiry indicates that the meditation subjects felt that they were now very successful at relaxing, and the control subjects did not.

SECTION 6: GENERALIZING RESULTS—INTERNAL AND EXTERNAL VALIDITY

INTERNAL VERSUS EXTERNAL VALIDITY

There are two standards of "truth" against which research is judged. The **internal validity** of a research project estimates the truth of statements concerning the relationship of IVs and DVs used in a particular study. **External validity,** on the other hand, expresses how well the research results **generalize** to new situations. The things you do to increase the internal validity of a research project are not the same as those that are necessary to increase its external validity. An experiment can be designed to have very high internal validity, in the sense that the IV manipulations actually do produce the stated DV changes, but it may still have low external validity if the circumstances of the experiment have little relationship to any situation to which you want to generalize its results.

THREATS TO THE INTERNAL VALIDITY OF RESEARCH

Anything which weakens your statement that changes in one variable do or do not produce changes in another is a threat to the internal validity of your research. Obviously, any source of constant error produced by a Confounding Variable is a serious threat to internal validity. Random error, though regarded as less of a problem than constant error, also reduces the internal validity of research. If too much random error forces you to accept the null hypothesis, someone else may later establish that there really is an effect of your IV, but your work was too messy to demonstrate it.

Lack of Group Equivalence

When we estimate our IV effects by comparing DV measures between groups of subjects, we are depending on the groups being equivalent before treatment. If in fact they are not, we may mistakenly attribute to the IV effects that simply reveal pre-existing group differences.

Loss of Subjects during the Experiment

Sometimes we start out with equal-sized groups that are equivalent on Relevant Variables but lose subjects before the end of the experiment. This is especially true if our treatment is at all lengthy and if we are using human subjects (who are notoriously independent). Loss of subjects can create many problems. Very often the subjects we lose are different from the subjects we keep, so the nature of our sample has changed. For instance, in a year-long study of an elementary school class, the children in families who move are likely to be different from children whose families have a more stable living situation. Also, losing subjects means decreased sample sizes, which will increase our random error. More serious, subject loss rates may differ for different groups of the experiment, introducing a potential Confounding Variable. For example, more no-treatment control subjects than experimental subjects may become discouraged and fail to show for posttest. If this happens, the initial equivalence of experimental and control groups is no longer true at posttest time.

Changes in Subjects during the Course of an Experiment

Subjects may change in some characteristic during the course of an experiment. This is especially true if you are studying young, developing subjects in an experiment that runs for a period of time. Since the processes of **maturation** don't happen at the same rate in different subjects, unequal growth changes can be a source of random error. If for any reason in a Between-Subjects design the experimental and control subjects should mature or change at different rates, then a Confounding Variable has been added to the research. In a Within-Subjects design, such a maturational change would produce pre-to-posttest differences that were not solely a result of an intervening treatment. More subtly, IV and maturational changes can interact. If they do, an IV effect demonstrated for subjects at a particular point in development may not be replicated if subjects at a different stage are used. For example, a "study techniques course" that has a very beneficial effect for entering freshmen may be relatively ineffective with students further along in their college education who have developed resistant patterns of studying and socializing.

Changes That Occur during the Course of an Experiment

Any systematic changes that occur between the beginning and the end of an experiment are potential threats to internal validity. In a Within-Subjects design they create pre-post differences that may be misinterpreted as IV effects. In a Between-Subjects design they can introduce random error or even, if the changes are different for the different groups of the experiment, constant error. A Confounding Variable would be introduced, for example, into a study comparing instructional techniques if one of the classes being compared was exposed to special influences before the end of the study.

Other changes may occur internal to the experiment itself unless special precautions are taken. A piece of apparatus, for instance, may become a progressively less sensitive measuring device as a part fails or a battery weakens. Human observers may shift their criteria as the experiment progresses, categorizing some behaviors differently at the end of the experiment than at the beginning. Changes in instructions given to subjects may creep in, especially if experimenters get tired of saying the same things with the same sincerity over and over. Defects in DV measuring procedures may leave researchers itching to make changes. Pilot testing of experimental procedures should be done to find out what improvements are necessary in instructions and measuring devices before beginning the experiment itself. Repeated checking of equipment and monitoring of human observers can be done to guard against shifts in measurement procedures.

Subject IVs

Operationally defining an IV as a Subject variable always carries the risk that one or more Confounding Variables will be present. Subjects sorted into IV levels according to one characteristic (like intelligence) may also be effectively sorted on other variables (like socioeconomic class, personality characteristics, success in school, etc.). If the DV measures show differences for different IV levels, these differences may be due to the stated IV, or they may, at least in part, be really due to these other related variables. One technique to reduce this problem is to match the subjects on other Relevant Variables. Thus, if you were setting up two groups that differed in intelligence, you might be careful to match them for socioeconomic class. Such matching is an improvement, but there still may be some other important variable for which you did not match.

Other Confounding Variables

Experimenter Bias, subject biases, demand characteristics of experiments, pretest effects, etc., have all been discussed in preceding sections as possible Confounding Variables. The presence of any of these may constitute a threat to the internal validity of an experiment. In addition, other Confounding Variables inadvertently introduced by the researcher, such as systematic testing of experimental and control subjects at different times of day or under different conditions, may also reduce the internal validity of a research project. The actual procedures of any experiment must be very carefully examined to see whether any of these Confounding Variables are present before accepting the idea that a given IV causes changes in a given DV.

FACTORS AFFECTING EXTERNAL VALIDITY

The more differences that exist between the conditions of an experiment and the situation to which you wish to generalize the experiment's results, the weaker the generalization will be. Anything that reduces the generalizability of an experiment is said to reduce its external validity.

Population Studied

Obviously, generalizations will be strongest to populations of subjects like the one you actually sampled. The more differences that exist between the subjects you studied and the people to whom you wish to generalize, the weaker the generalization. If you select subjects particularly susceptible to the effects of your treatment, you may find large IV effects internal to the experiment, but the external validity of the research will be low. This can be a problem when you use volunteers for your study. Volunteers may be specially interested and enthusiastic, expecting beneficial effects of your treatment, and they may give you results that make you feel that your IV is particularly powerful. Use of special subjects may interfere with estimating the effects of any new therapy, educational innovation, or expanded health service. Unusual characteristics of the subjects initially studied may produce encouragingly large treatment effects that are not replicated in later more widespread use of the technique.

Operational Definition of the IV

When generalizing research results, you often go beyond the strict operational definition of the IV. Doing so, of course, weakens your generalization to some degree. Since any experiment has only a finite and usually rather small number of conditions, only a limited range of possible IV values is used. When generalizing, you must take care not to go outside the range of IV values actually studied. The Crancer et al. (1969) study, for example, reported that marijuana consumption had relatively little effect on driving behavior. However, only one low-level dose of marijuana was used. It would be risky to conclude that marijuana use in the general population would have no effect on driving performance unless you were certain that self-prescribed marijuana dosage rarely went beyond what was used in the study.

One researcher's operational definition of an IV may not be the same as another's, and both definitions may differ widely from the situations to which the researchers attempt to generalize results. In a consideration of the effects of stress on levels of corticosteroids released into the bloodstream, for example, the stress experienced in the lab by subjects exposed to a threatening test situation or jolted by an electric shock may be rather different from the stress experienced by a student taking a final or a worker being pressured by a demanding job. Sometimes the operational definition of an IV used in a lab experiment can be so artificial that it bears little relationship to any natural situation. To improve external validity it is necessary to consider the situation to which you wish to generalize when operationally defining the IV and selecting the range of IV values to be studied.

Operational Definition of the DV

Is the DV that was measured one you really care about? When operationally defining a DV so that it can be conveniently and consistently measured, researchers sometimes overlook whether the operational definition is one that will be generalizable to any other situation. For instance, in the literature on techniques to reduce anxiety in human subjects, the usual DV measured is some paper-and-pencil test of "anxiety." It is often questionable how well these tests relate to actual anxiety within an individual, especially since many of the tests do not give the same answer when applied to the same person. In the Paul study (1966), anxiety about public speaking was measured in an actual public-speaking situation. This operational definition should have high generalizability, but the costs of measuring the DV in this way included finding an audience of several experts to observe each speaker individually, and taking time to listen to each speech and to measure physiological indicators. When operationally defining your DV, you have to strike a balance between creating a measure that is easy to use but trivial and creating one that has a very high generalizability but is almost impractical to do.

Special Conditions of the Experiment

Any research study is done in some context. An educational experiment, for example, may be done in the laboratory, in a simulated classroom situation, in an actual classroom under controlled conditions, or in a classroom over which the researchers can exert no control. The results obtained in these different environments may not be exactly the same, since other factors become involved. When generalizing the results of a research project, it is necessary to consider the environment in which the research was done. If it is very different from the environment to which the results are being generalized, then the generalization is weakened. When planning an experiment, you will have to strike a balance between needing an environment over which it is possible to exert control of Relevant Variables and wanting an environment that is sufficiently similar to a real-life situation to permit strong generalization.

IMPROVING INTERNAL VALIDITY

Improving internal validity is largely a matter of *selecting an appropriate design*. Use of Randomized-Groups or Matched-Groups designs will reduce internal validity problems caused by lack of group equivalence. Multivariate designs can be used to investigate the effects of Relevant Variables that you suspect may be interacting with your main IV. Pretesting, although it carries some risks of its own, can give information about before-treatment differences among groups. Matching of subjects in Between-Subjects designs can reduce the number of Relevant Variables that could potentially be confounding.

Care in conducting an experiment will also help increase its internal validity. There is no reason to introduce random error simply through researcher carelessness or looseness of procedures. "Dress rehearsal" pilot experiments can reveal the need for modifications in procedures. Through pilot work you can find out such things as whether your instructions are confusing to your subjects or whether it is really possibe for your experimenters to record information accurately from five different devices every minute. These problems can be corrected before you start collecting data you intend to keep.

Systematic elimination of all possible Confounding Variables is essential to improving the internal validity of an experiment. This means that Experimenter Bias, subject biases, experimental demand characteristics, etc., all have to be searched for and controlled. If eventually someone is going to shoot down your work because of the presence of a Confounding Variable, at least let it be an obscure one.

Monitoring what actually happened in your research is also important in discovering threats to internal validity. The actions of your experimenters should be of as much interest as those of your subjects. If the experiment is of long duration, keep track of what happens to subjects in the intervening time, especially human subjects whom you cannot tuck back in a cage between sessions. Keep checking to see that procedures are carried out and measurements taken according to your original plan. In scientific research, records are kept of many details that are not expected to be involved in the final analysis. If a need for this information arises, however, it is better to have it clearly noted than to try to "resurrect" it from untidy and biasable memories.

IMPROVING EXTERNAL VALIDITY

Increasing external validity of research is largely a matter of *knowing to what situation you are likely to want to generalize results*. Within the limitations imposed by needing to minimize threats to internal validity, you should attempt to design your research to be as close as possible to the conditions to which you wish to generalize.

You can make an experiment more generalizable by *taking care in how the subjects are selected*. Avoid using subjects who are likely to be particularly susceptible to your IV. Homogeneous groups of subjects may decrease random error, but a heterogeneous sample may be generalizable to a broader population. If you suspect that a subject characteristic will interact with your IV effect, then a Randomized-Blocks design, in which you make this subject characteristic another IV, will increase the generalizability of the research.

Increasing external validity of research while maintaining internal validity may be a problem. Carefully and clearly defining the IVs and DVs in an experiment is essential to establishing causal realtionships between variables. On the other hand, such careful operational definitions may create variables that seem artificial and unrelated to real-life situations. *Increasing the number of different ways a given IV or DV is operationally defined* is a technique for increasing generalizability of results. You can increase generalizability of an experiment by operationally defining the DV in several reasonable ways and simultaneously measuring them. For instance, you can make a study on anxiety more meaningful by using physiological and behavioral measures of anxiety in addition to a standardized written test. If all these ways of measuring anxiety lead to the same conclusion, the external validity of the research is increased. Or you may want to repeat an experiment using a different operational definition of the IV. For example, if a general relationship exists between "stressing" an individual and the chemicals released into that person's bloodstream, then this relationship would be demonstrable when the stress IV is operationally defined in a variety of ways.

Research also gains external validity when it is possible to *demonstrate that an IV-DV relationship exists in a number of different environments*. Initially, you may want to use a well-controlled lab situation to ensure high internal validity. Having demonstrated the existence of a phenomenon, you may then repeat the research observations in a less sterile environment. If your IV-DV relationship can be found only in a very exacting situation and any slight change of context destroys the relationship, then you may well suspect that your findings are more a function of experimental context than of any real effect of the IV.

RECAPITULATION

for INTERNAL AND EXTERNAL VALIDITY

Interpretations of research will be judged both for their *internal validity* and for their *external validity*. Internal validity estimates the probability that the variation observed in the DV(s) are in fact caused by the experimenter's stated IV(s). External validity assesses how well the results of an experiment can be generalized to new situations, making accurate predictions beyond the narrow confines of the original experiment. Internal validity is seriously threatened by the existence of uncontrolled Confounding Variables. Internal validity is reduced by such things as lack of group equivalence, loss of subjects during an experiment, changes in subjects during an experiment, other changes occurring throughout the course of the research, unmeasured subject characteristics related to Subject IVs, Experimenter Bias, subject biases, and demand characteristics of an experiment. Internal validity can be improved by selecting an appropriate experimental design, by taking care in conducting research, by monitoring what actually happens in an experiment, and by systematically eliminating all possible Confounding Variables. The external validity of a research project can be improved by selecting more typical and varied subjects, by operationally defining IVs and DVs in more than one way, and by testing IV-DV relationships in a number of different environments. If you are going to do only a single experiment, try, within the restrictions of maintaining internal validity, to increase the research's external validity by making conditions as similar as possible to the situations to which you intend to generalize your results.

BEHAVIORAL OBJECTIVES

for INTERNAL AND EXTERNAL VALIDITY

1. Describe what is meant by the internal validity of research.
2. Describe what is meant by the external validity of research.
3. List three factors that would reduce the internal validity of a research study.
4. List three factors that would reduce the external validity of a research study.
5. Describe three things a researcher could do to increase the internal validity of an experiment, explaining how each one would work.
6. Describe three things a researcher could do to increase the external validity of an experiment, explaining how each one would work.
7. Given a description of an experiment, identify threats to internal and external validity, and suggest how the research might be modified to reduce these weaknesses.

SAMPLE TEST QUESTIONS

for INTERNAL AND EXTERNAL VALIDITY

Read the following brief article. As you do so, examine its procedures and logic carefully for problems with internal and external validity. When you identify a problem, estimate the effect it might have on results or conclusions.

Singh (1968): Effect of urban environment on visual curiosity behavior in rhesus monkeys.*

> In India, rhesus monkeys are found living not only in jungle areas but in villages, towns, and cities as well (Southwick *et al.*, 1961a, 1961b). These habitats provide widely different living environments for these animals. The most obvious difference is that areas inhabited by humans afford the monkeys with more opportunities for varied perceptual and motor experiences; in other words, in comparison with the jungle, conditions in the urban areas are highly stimulating. Our earlier studies have shown that such environmental differences do not influence the learning ability of the animals (Singh, 1966a), but do have marked effects on their social behavior (Singh, 1966c), and also on their responsiveness to novel situations and objects (Singh, 1966b). As reported earlier, in contrast to jungle monkeys, urban ones are highly responsive to novel objects, and will manipulate even highly complex and ordinarily fear-evoking stimuli such as a human skeleton.
>
>   The present experiment was designed to study the effects of urban conditions upon the visual curiosity behavior of rhesus monkeys.

SUBJECTS

Eight adult female rhesus monkeys, three jungle and five urban, served as Ss in this study. The jungle monkeys were caught from interior jungle areas, and the urban

*Reprinted by permission of the Psychonomic Society (copyright © 1968).

monkeys, from bazaar areas of some Indian cities. Prior to their use in the present experiment, they had lived about a month individually in cages measuring $3 \times 3 \times 3$ ft.

APPARATUS

Tests for visual exploration were conducted in a wooden chamber placed in a partially sound-attenuated room . . . The remaining wall of the chamber contained a $3 \times 1\frac{1}{2}$ in. one-way screen to permit observation of the animal by the E. The chamber was equipped with food and water delivery systems which could be operated outside the chamber . . .

Three stimulus displays of different levels of visual complexity were presented. These were: (a) eight simple gray wooden cubes placed on a black wooden board (SWO), (b) a battery of eight empty rat cages (BC), and (c) a toy train with some colored toys moving on a circular track 3 ft. in diameter (MO). These displays were arranged outside the test chamber in a manner such that an animal inside the chamber could get a full view of one of the displays by looking through one of the chamber windows.

PROCEDURE

Each S was housed in the test chamber throughout the experiment. Observations were begun after six days of adaptation. The animal was observed for six successive days, three times a day, at 8 AM, 12 N, and 4 PM, each observation lasting 30 min. An observation session started by opening the three chamber windows. The E recorded the frequency and duration of the animal's responses to each of the three stimulus displays. At the end of each session, the windows were closed. The maintenance procedures, cleaning the metal pan and filling the water and food containers, were completed between 5:30 and 6:30 PM each day.

RESULTS AND DISCUSSION

The cumulative frequency and cumulative duration of each S's responses to each stimulus display during each observation session were determined. Separate analyses of variance were performed on the frequency and duration data, and showed only the following effects to be significant: Effects of time of day observed (Frequency: $F = 6.95$, df $= 2/12$, $p < .05$; Duration: $F = 8.66$, df $= 2/12$, $p < .01$), Jungle vs Urban by Stimulus Displays by Day Effects (Duration: $F = 2.05$, df $= 10/60$, $p < .05$). Further analysis of the observation time effects with t tests revealed a significant ($p < .05$) session-to-session decrease in both measures within a day. Such variations may be attributed to changes in the general activity level of the animals, and also to a visual deprivation phenomenon similar to that described by Butler (1957), as the visual deprivation period preceding morning sessions was relatively longer than those preceding other observation sessions.

The detailed analysis of the Jungle vs Urban by Stimulus display by Day interaction is presented in Fig. 7.1. Compared to the SWO situation both jungle and urban groups spent more time looking at the BC situation ($p < .05$ and $.01$, respectively). This difference was greater for the urban group, but not significantly so. However, the two habitat groups differed markedly (the differences significant at $p = .05$ on the first five days) in response to the MO situation; while the urban monkeys were highly responsive to this display, the responses of the jungle-raised

FIG. 7.1

Mean duration of the visual responses of the jungle- and urban-raised monkeys to the three stimulus displays on six successive days.

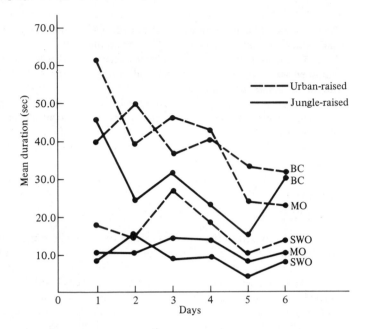

monkeys were as low as their responses to the SWO situation. The highly marked differences between the two habitat groups in response to the MO situation decreased during the course of testing, this being due to a significant (p < .05) decline in the responses of the urban monkeys.

On the whole, these results clearly indicate that in comparison to the jungle monkeys, the urban ones were more responsive to stimulus displays of higher complexity values. These results are meaningful when viewed in terms of the stimulus complexity hypothesis (Dember and Earl, 1957; Sackett, 1965; Vitz, 1966). According to this hypothesis, the manipulatory, exploratory, or curiosity behavior of an individual is to a great extent determined by the complexity level of the individual and of the stimulus situation confronted; an individual with greater perceptual and motor experiences is supposed to interact maximally with stimuli of higher complexity values. Thus, interpreted in terms of this theory, the urban monkeys might be considered as psychologically more complex than the jungle monkeys.

REFERENCES

Dember, N. W., and Earl, R. W. Analysis of exploratory, manipulatory, and curiosity behaviors. *Psychological Review*, 1957, *64*, 91–96.

Sackett, G. P. Manipulatory behavior in rhesus monkeys reared under different levels of early stimulation variation. *Perceptual and Motor Skills*, 1965, *20*, 985–988.

Singh, S. D. Effect of human environment on cognitive behavior in the rhesus monkey. *Journal of Comparative and Physiological Psychology*, 1966a, *61*, 280–283.

Singh, S. D. The effects of human environment upon the reactions to novel situations in the rhesus. *Behaviour*, 1966b, *26*, 243–250

Singh, S. D. The effects of human environment on the social behaviour of rhesus monkeys. *Primates*, 1966c, *7*, 33–39.

Southwick, C. H., Beg, M. A. and Siddigi, M. R. A population survey of rhesus monkeys in villages, towns and temples of northern India. *Ecology*, 1961a, *42*, 538–547.

Southwick, C. H., Beg, M. A. and Siddigi, M. R. A population survey of rhesus monkeys in northern India II. Transportation routes and forest areas. *Ecology*, 1961b, *42*, 689–710.

Vitz, P. C. Preference for different amounts of visual complexity. *Behavioral Science*, 1966, *11*, 105.

1.   Describe the design of this experiment. What is the IV? Is it a Non-Subject or a Subject IV?

2.   What do you think about the sample sizes?

3.   Are there any reasons why either of these samples might not be typical of the population from which it comes? (Consider who gets caught.)

4.   Do you see any opportunity for experimenter expectancy effects on data collection? Describe the effects this might have on the results. Suggest a way to reduce the problem.

5.   Consider the possibility of subject attitude effects. Which type of animal do you think might feel more comfortable with the experimental situation?

6.   Consider the stimulus displays used. They were selected for their "visual complexity." Can you think why these displays might be of more interest to urban than to jungle monkeys for other reasons than their complexity?

7.   Did the experimental conditions produce a significant overall main effect of jungle versus urban monkeys? What aspect of the planning of the experiment might hinder any demonstration of significant differences between the two types of monkeys?

8.   The author concludes, "On the whole, these results clearly indicate that in comparison to the jungle monkeys, the urban monkeys were more responsive to stimulus displays of higher complexity values." He suggests an interpretation as follows: "The urban monkeys might be considered as psychologically more complex than the jungle monkeys." Discuss at least one threat to internal validity and one to external validity that might make you hesitate to accept these conclusions.

SECTION 7: PROBLEMS IN INTERPRETING RESEARCH

The fact that a research study has been published does not mean that it is free of internal or external validity problems. Consumers of research literature have to judge for themselves the worth of the information coming from any particular study. The presence of one or more problems does not necessarily throw out a whole research study, but it does decrease the amount of confidence you can place in conclusions drawn from the research. Some problems in interpreting research are so common that you should be on the lookout for them whenever you read a research report. These problems are ones you should avoid when planning your own research to ensure that the information you produce will be maximally useful.

THE SEVEN DEADLY SINS

Sin 1: Misuse of Statistics

Sometimes, as in the case of Sir Cyril Burt, statistics are consciously misused to support a researcher's pet theory. More often, statistics are misused inadvertently. Few people doing research in the social sciences really have a deep understanding of math and statistics. Statistics is a complex and changing field, and there are many potential research situations for which optimum statistics have not yet been developed. Even if you do not intend to do research, it is important to have enough knowledge of statistics to be able to sense when things "smell bad." If you are going to be impressed by every author who claims that "statistics say that . . . ,"then you are in danger of accepting worthless information as fact.

What are some of the common abuses of statistics? One is the selection of descriptive or inferential statistics that are inappropriate for the scale of measurement of the DV. The most usual example is the treatment of ordinal DV measures as if they were interval. When researchers take this approach, they are making some strong mathematical assumptions and should openly defend them. If they do not, you can suspect that they don't know what they are doing.

Sometimes the statistics selected are inappropriate for the design of the experiment. Most often, this abuse takes the form of multiple t-tests done in a situation where an Analysis of Variance is needed. Multiple t-tests result in declaring more comparisons significant than is actually true.

The statistics chosen may also be inappropriate for the frequency distribution of the data. For example, people often use parametric (normal-distribution–based) statistics on interval (and sometimes even ordinal!) data without examining the assumptions they are making about the shape of their distributions.

Sample sizes that are too small may also lead to abuse of statistics. As discussed before, small sample sizes can predetermine acceptance of the null hypothesis. Small samples of interval data make it difficult to decide whether the data are normally distributed. Also, some inferential test, like Chi-Square, cannot be legitimately done on too-small samples. Unfortunately, some people are not aware of this limitation, and you can find Chi-Square reported and interpreted when, statistically speaking, the test is meaningless.

You have to watch out for reports that interpret "trends" and "tendencies" in descriptive statistics for which the inferential statistical tests have come out nonsignificant. **Nonsignificance** means acceptance of the null hypothesis that the results were due to chance. There is no point in discussing nonsignificant results as if they mean anything, no matter how disappointed the researchers feel.

Some studies avoid the problems of inferential statistics by failing to report any at all. Without this information, you have no way of knowing whether the results described, often in very alluring terms, would be obtained again if the research was repeated.

Sin 2: Ignoring the Lack of Group Equivalence

Whenever a comparison is made between groups to reveal the effect of an IV, you need to take a hard look at what was done in the study to ensure that the groups were equivalent on *all* other variables. The interpretation of results for any research study using a Static-Groups design or a Subject IV should include open discussion of the possible effects of lack of equivalence.

Sin 3: Overlooking Confounding Variables

Sometimes researchers build Confounding Variables into their research without realizing it. If you are lucky, the description of their procedures will be sufficiently complete for you to detect the problem. Effects of Experimenter Bias, subject attitude, and experimental demand characteristics are frequently overlooked. If you identify possible Confounding Variables in a study, you will have to think about how the potential constant error might change interpretation of results.

Sin 4: Interpreting Correlation as Causation

An all-too-common sin is equating correlation and causation. People doing correlational research often forget that they are measuring only relationships among DVs. When you have a large correlation that is statistically significant, it is easy to fall into the trap of talking about the relationship as if it were causal. Without actually doing an experiment and manipulating variables as IVs, you should not make causal statements.

Sin 5: Generalizing Far Beyond the Conditions of the Experiment

Sometimes when researchers begin speculating about the meaning of their results, the sky's the limit. They seem to forget the special conditions under which their research was done. A generalization becomes weaker, the more differences that exist between the research situation and the situation to which it is being generalized. Knowledgeable researchers express reservations when speculating far beyond the conditions of their research.

Sin 6: Ignoring Alternative Explanations

Results are results. If collected properly and analyzed appropriately, the results will stand, no matter how they are interpreted. However, a given set of results can usually be explained in more than one way. Sometimes researchers are so enthusiastic about their own explanation that they don't even see an alternative, simpler one. Just because you trust someone's results, you don't have to accept his or her decision about which theory the results support.

Sin 7: Assuming That Statistical Significance Means Practical Significance

In the intricacies of the research game, people forget that achieving statistical significance is only a minimum requirement for claiming an IV effect. Statistical significance does not mean that an effect is necessarily large or important. You need to look at the descriptive statistics to see the actual size of "significant" effects to decide whether they are large enough to have practical significance for your purposes.

EVALUATING RESEARCH REPORTS

There is a fairly standard set of questions that can be used to evaluate any social science research project. Use of a checklist, such as is given in Table 7.3, can help you spot the weak points and strengths in a published report. You can use the same questions to evaluate your own research efforts and to find areas in which your research could be improved.

RECAPITULATION

for PROBLEMS IN INTERPRETING RESEARCH

There are some problems in interpretation of research results that the alert reader should watch for. *Statistics may be misused*, with the result that conclusions may be in error. Statistics that are inappropriate to the scale of measurement, design of the research, or obtained frequency distributions give an inaccurate summary and analysis of the data. Too-small sample sizes make it difficult to do any meaningful statistics. Sometimes authors illogically discuss "trends" and "tendencies" in the data after their statistics have forced acceptance of the null hypothesis. *Ignoring the lack of group equivalence* and *overlooking Confounding Variables* also undermine conclusions about IV effects. *Interpreting correlation between two variables as indicating that one variable causes the other* is dangerous, since in correlation studies there are no true IVs. The results and their analyses may be all right, but the researchers may then *generalize the results far beyond the conditions of the experiment*, without realizing that doing so greatly decreases the strength of their interpretation. *Ignoring alternative, often simpler, explanations of the results* may obscure the fact that a given set of results has more than one reasonable interpretation. Finally, *statistical significance is only a minimum requirement for declaring that an IV effect exists*. It does not guarantee that the effect is large enough to have any practical application in other situations. The checklist given in Table 7.3 can be used to help readers recognize these problems and weigh accordingly the faith they place in research conclusions.

Table 7.3 Checklist for Evaluating Research

Take a Look at the Researchers' Intentions

_____ 1. Is the problem being investigated an interesting or important one?

_____ 2. Are the IVs operationally defined in a clear and reasonable manner, consistent with the statement of the problem?

_____ 3. Are the DVs operationally defined in a clear and reasonable manner, consistent with the statement of the problem?

_____ 4. Is the design of the study clearly laid out?

_____ 5. Are the samples used in the study of reasonable size?

Take a Look at How the Research Was Carried Out

_____ 6. Is the population sampled clearly described, and are the samples unbiased?

_____ 7. Were Experimenter Bias effects controlled?

_____ 8. Were subject attitude effects controlled?

_____ 9. Were other Relevant Variables controlled to avoid introducing constant error into the results?

_____ 10. Were Relevant Variables controlled to reduce random error (overall variability) in the results?

Take a Look at How the Results Were Evaluated

_____ 11. Are the appropriate descriptive statistics given so that you can see what was actually found in the study?

_____ 12. Were inferential statistics used? If so, were they appropriate for the measurement scale of the DV, the frequency distributions obtained, and the design of the research?

Take a Look at How the Results Were Interpreted

_____ 13. Do the stated conclusions follow logically from the reported descriptive and inferential statistics?

_____ 14. Are the researchers aware of the limitations of the design they used? (This is a particularly important question for Static-Groups designs.)

_____ 15. Do the researchers avoid placing causal interpretations on correlations?

_____ 16. Do the researchers explore the possibility of Confounding Relevant Variables when interpreting the effects of a Subject IV?

_____ 17. Do the researchers consider possible alternative explanations of their results?

_____ 18. Is it clearly stated how the results are like and unlike previous results, with intelligent reasons given for any discrepancies?

_____ 19. When the researchers suggest application of their results, are they aware of how far they are generalizing from their population, from their operational definitions of the IVs and DVs, and from the particular circumstances under which they made their measurements?

BEHAVIORAL OBJECTIVES

for PROBLEMS IN INTERPRETING RESEARCH

1. Give at least three examples of how statistics may be misused in interpreting research.

2. Give an example of a problem in interpretation that might occur if nonequivalent groups were used in a Between-Subjects design.

3. Give at least two examples of Confounding Variables that one might overlook when interpreting research results.

4. Discuss the problem in interpretation that occurs when a correlation is presented as establishing a causal relationship between two variables.

5. Discuss why it is necessary to consider alternative interpretations for a given set of results.

6. Describe the factors that should be similar to strengthen generalization from the results of an experiment to a new situation.

7. Explain the difference between an effect that is "statistically significant" and one that is also "practically significant."

8. Given examples of research interpretations, identify the existence of one or more of the "seven deadly sins," and suggest how they may be affecting the interpretation.

9. Find a recent research article in your area of social science, and evaluate it with the checklist in Table 7.3.

SAMPLE TEST QUESTIONS

for PROBLEMS IN INTERPRETING RESEARCH

1. Each of these brief descriptions of research studies has one or more of the "seven deadly sins." Identify the problem(s), and suggest how it weakens conclusions from the research.

   a. In the study described on page 57 (Question 7), it was found that boys, overall, showed more violent acts in play than did girls. This finding was interpreted as indicating that boys are biologically more prone to aggression than girls.

   b. In the study on the effects of wrongdoing on subsequent helping behavior described on page 61 (Questions 2d and 3), a group of people who had mistakenly fed zoo bears and were reprimanded for doing so were compared with a control group who had not fed the bears and therefore were not reprimanded. The results indicated that having been reprimanded increased the likelihood of a person engaging in subsequent helping behavior.

   c. On page 64 a study was described in which the effects on self-concept of a new way of teaching industrial arts were investigated. The new curriculum was used in one school in Seattle and the old one in another. The new curriculum resulted in a significant increase in mean positive "self-concept" score from 29.2 to 31.1 (on a scale of 50 points). On the basis of this result, it was recommended that the new curriculum be adopted for all the state's schools.

d. The weight-reduction study described on page 67 produced significant decreases in weights of preteen girls whose parents volunteered to participate in the study and were willing to deposit sums of money with the investigators. Fifteen girls were randomly divided into two treatment groups and one control group. At a 31-week no-contact follow-up, there was no significant treatment effect, but there was a trend toward slower weight gain in the "response-cost plus reinforcement" group. It is suggested that this might be a very effective technique for weight control in girls.

e. A college obtained evaluation questionnaires from its students for each course. The students were asked to rate each instructor on a five-point scale on each of five questions. To compare the effectiveness of different instructors, the ratings were averaged. Each instructor's mean ratings were compared to overall means for the whole college.

f. In a study done on more than 1000 adults it was found that alcohol and marijuana use correlated significantly at about $+.23$, and age and amount of marijuana consumption correlated significantly at about $-.75$. This information was interpreted by some as suggesting that dependence on alcohol can lead to abuse of other drugs. It was also concluded that the tensions experienced by young adults who are trying to establish themselves in jobs and in interpersonal relationships result in their more frequently using drugs for escape.

2. Go back to the Singh (1968) study reprinted at the end of Section 6, and use the checklist (Table 7.3) to evaluate it.

3. Apply the checklist (Table 7.3) to a research article. If you haven't found one of your own, here's a suggestion: Pliner, P., Hart, H., Kohl, J., and Saari D. Compliance without pressure: Some further data on the foot-in-the-door technique. *Journal of Experimental Social Psychology,* 1974, *10,* 17–22.

communicating about your research

There's really no point in doing research unless you report your results. Until other people get a chance to review and use the information produced by your work, your experiment, survey, or evaluative study is not complete. To maximize benefits from research, you need to have in mind when you plan your study how you are going to organize and communicate your findings.

Since the overall objective of this chapter is for you to write a research paper or give a talk, there are no behavioral objectives or sample test questions after the sections. Instead, there are some suggested exercises that you can use to check your understanding of the material.

SECTION 1: WHAT ARE SOME DIFFERENT WAYS YOU CAN REPORT YOUR RESULTS?

Unless you have ESP, there are two ways you can communicate your research results: you can talk about them or you can write about them. Talking about them is generally easier and quicker, but it doesn't leave much for others to refer to in the future. If the physician Morton (pp. 148 ff.) had only talked about his measurements of cranial capacity, it would have been impossible for later researchers to discover that there were flaws in the evidence supporting his claim of racial differences in brain size. However, although writing about research does leave a record, the current delays in publication by professional journals may mean that a year or more passes before the report is available to the general public. Most researchers use both routes for communication. Talks inform a limited audience about the research soon after it is completed. An eventual article serves as a more permanent and complete record that is available to a wider audience.

TALKS

Talks are often used to report preliminary or incomplete research, as well as for the prompt communication of completed studies. A talk is particularly useful because it encourages immediate feedback from an audience, allowing stimulation of your thinking about your own research. Sometimes you may find yourself wanting to do things very differently because of pertinent comments from your audience—and sometimes you may want to throw a brick at a dense or hostile listener!

Talks range from relatively informal presentations to colleagues, perhaps as part of a class or colloquium series, to formal presentations before a professional organization. Audiences may range from people totally uninformed in the area of your research to those working on the same problem. For professional societies, usually you will first have to submit a written abstract or brief summary of your research, and then, if your abstract is accepted, you will be scheduled on the program. In this chapter we will develop guidelines for preparing a fifteen-minute talk for an audience that is assumed not to know the intimate details of your research problem.

WRITTEN REPORTS

Written reports can also take a variety of forms. The most common is the research article submitted for publication in a professional journal. Often the same journals accept briefer communications in the form of "letters to the editor," "case histories," "technical notes," or the like, to permit publication of limited findings not needing to be presented in a full-scale article. There are, of course, other forms of written reports. If you are doing an evaluative study for a school, industry, or government agency, you will probably be reporting only to them. Usually research supported under government contract must be reported to the funding agency. Research done as part of a graduate program will be reported in the form of a "thesis," or relatively lengthy document. Since these types of reports are often not generally available, many researchers will in addition write an article for publication in one of the regular journals to maximize communication. This chapter gives guidelines for writing an article for publication in a professional journal.

GENERAL OUTLINE OF A RESEARCH REPORT

Any report about your research will be organized into four general categories: Introduction, Method, Results, and Discussion. In the *Introduction* you state the problem being investigated and give the background on why it is an important or interesting problem. Your *Method* section describes what was done in the study in such a way that it would be possible for others to repeat the research. In *Results* you present both summaries and analyses of your data, pointing out what the statistics suggest. Finally, in the *Discussion,* which is probably the most important section, you summarize your results, interpret them, and discuss their implications. The length, emphasis, and ordering of these general categories may differ for articles and talks, but basically this is the information you need to communicate.

Written articles, in addition, will usually have an abstract section and a list of references. The *Abstract* presents, very briefly, a summary of the information contained in the four main categories of the report. Published works of other investigators that have been specifically referred to in the report are listed in the *References* section. Sometimes in a thesis or a lengthy government report, this references section may be expanded to include works not specifically cited but used instead as background sources. It is then called a *Bibliography* section.

ORGANIZING YOUR MATERIAL FOR A REPORT

The more organizing you do before beginning to write a report or prepare notes for a talk, the easier the actual writing will go. The order of sections in an article is normally: Abstract, Introduction, Method, Results, Discussion, and References. However, it is often easier to organize and write the sections in a different order. A well-organized and logical Results section is the key to a readable research report. It is a good idea to get Results organized and a draft of the section written before turning to the rest of the report. Method is a fairly easy section and can serve as a rest from pulling the Results section together. Introduction and Discussion can be organized and written in tandem. The story begun in Introduction is continued in Discussion, with the added information provided by your own results. Although the Abstract is usually printed first in an article, it is the last section you write, since it must summarize succinctly what you had to say in the rest of the report. Finally, you check back through your whole report to see that your reference list includes all the work of other researchers that you have mentioned.

FALSE ASSUMPTIONS MADE IN PREPARING RESEARCH REPORTS

There are some problems so common to research reports that you should be warned about them before planning a paper or talk. The first is the assumption that *your readers or listeners already know what you are talking about.* If your report is directed only at those with specialized knowledge, you will be severely limiting the audience you can reach. You have to strike a balance, of course, but there is a lot more jargon and obfuscation in the literature than is necessary. Plain English has a lot to recommend it.

A second false assumption is that *your readers or listeners have all the time in the world to puzzle out your report.* Consumers of research information actually have very little time to spend on any one research report. If they are consulting an article, it is usually one of a large number they have to read and make sense of. If they are attending a talk, it may be one of several to which they'll be listening on the same day. Your research results will go relatively unnoticed if they are presented in an unorganized, repetitive, obscure, and lengthy fashion. It takes careful writing to prepare a good, clear scientific report. The needed skills are not exactly the same ones that you use in English literature or journalism classes.

A third false assumption is that *your readers or listeners will see for themselves what your results imply.* Your audience may see implications you have missed, but you are the person closest to the research and responsible for fitting your new information into the general framework. A good research report must go beyond simply summarizing and analyzing data and put the results into some larger context.

RECAPITULATION

for WAYS OF REPORTING RESULTS

Research results may be reported either as talks, generally of 15 minutes or less in length, or as journal articles. Talks have the advantages of avoiding publication delays and of reporting results promptly. Talks are also a good way to communicate preliminary results, permitting feedback from others to help you in further planning and carrying out your research. Articles have the advantage of reaching a larger audience and of being a permanent record. Any research report will contain information in the four general categories of *Introduction, Method, Results,* and *Discussion*. An article, in addition, will have *Abstract* and *Reference* sections. A good research report should not assume that the audience knows a lot of special terminology and should not require that the audience spend a great deal of time puzzling out exactly what was done in the study and what it proves.

SUGGESTED EXERCISES

for WAYS OF REPORTING RESULTS

1. List the four main categories of information necessary in any research report. List the two additional sections that will be included in a research article.

2. For each item in the following list of communication goals, indicate whether it would be better met by an article (A) or a talk (T).

    _____   Reporting preliminary results

    _____   Gaining help from colleagues in planning or interpreting research

    _____   Making a *detailed* presentation of your results

    _____   Making a *detailed* presentation of your methods

    _____   Providing a permanent record

    _____   Avoiding publication lag or delays

    _____   Reaching a larger audience

3. For each of the following pieces of information, indicate the major section of a report to which it belongs: Introduction (I), Methods (M), Results (R), or Discussion (D).

    _____   Table 3 shows that the children in the Reinforcement condition lost significantly ($t = 2.98$, $p < .05$) more weight than those in the No-Reinforcement condition.

    _____   The Reinforcement group received daily points for exercising according to the schedule listed in Table 2. They also received a base rate of 10 points per day for keeping food records and a bonus of 1 point for each 10 calories by which their consumption was below the daily maximum. The No-Reinforcement group was given the same list of exercises, recommended daily calorie goals, and food record books, with instructions as to how these could help them lose weight. Sub-

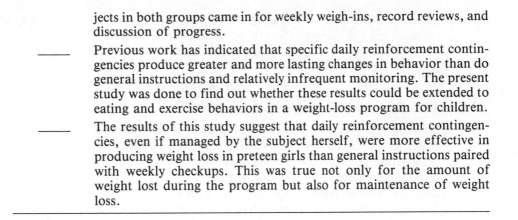

jects in both groups came in for weekly weigh-ins, record reviews, and discussion of progress.

_____ Previous work has indicated that specific daily reinforcement contingencies produce greater and more lasting changes in behavior than do general instructions and relatively infrequent monitoring. The present study was done to find out whether these results could be extended to eating and exercise behaviors in a weight-loss program for children.

_____ The results of this study suggest that daily reinforcement contingencies, even if managed by the subject herself, were more effective in producing weight loss in preteen girls than general instructions paired with weekly checkups. This was true not only for the amount of weight lost during the program but also for maintenance of weight loss.

SECTION 2: GENERAL STYLE OF A SCIENTIFIC ARTICLE

PREPARING AN ARTICLE FOR PUBLICATION

Although all scientific articles have the same general form, different journals have slightly different picky requirements. Some of the professional organizations put out a "publication manual" that summarizes all the requirements for journals approved by the organization. For instance, the American Psychological Association's *Publication Manual* (1974) is a valuable reference for anyone publishing in the social science area.

Selecting a journal for your article is best done by spending some time in the library looking at recent copies of journals in your field. See what kinds of articles they have been interested in publishing. Also consider the audience you want to reach. For example, if you have done a lab experiment that you feel has important implications for counseling practices, you might wish to publish in one of the counseling journals rather than in a straight experimental journal.

Most journals publish a couple of pages of *Notes for the Contributor,* generally in the first or last issue of the year. These notes will give you specific information about the journal's particular requirements, such as how many copies you are to send, whether your figures should be drawings or photographs, etc. It's best to have this information before you start writing your article. If you don't, you may have to rewrite it later.

There are some requirements for manuscript preparation that are standard. Articles must be typed on regular-sized paper ($8\frac{1}{2} \times 11$ in.) with good margins (1 to $1\frac{1}{2}$ in.). Neither erasable bond nor onionskin is acceptable because both smudge. When multiple copies are required by the journal, good xeroxes are preferable to carbons. The typing must be double-spaced to make it easier for reviewers to read and for editors to make corrections. The pages are numbered consecutively in the upper right-hand corner. A neatly and appropriately typed manuscript is a *minimum* requirement for consideration of your article for publication. Even when you are only preparing a report for a class, observing these details will aid your instructor in reading the report.

OVERALL ORGANIZATION OF A MANUSCRIPT

Most journals require that the manuscript be organized in a standard way. The Abstract comes first on a separate page, along with the title, author(s), and author's affiliation. The introduction, usually with title and author information repeated, starts on the next page. Method, Results, and Discussion sections follow the Introduction without interruption. The References section starts on a new page, following the Discussion. After references, there is a page for *Footnotes* (if any) and then the Tables, typed one to a page. If there are any figures, a page of *Figure Captions*, followed by the figures themselves, ends the manuscript.

You have to check the journal's Notes for the Contributor for variations in this general scheme. For instance, if the journal has a "blind review" system for approving articles, you may be instructed to leave the authors' names off at least some of the copies of the manuscript. Some journals worry about pages getting mixed up and require that a short "running head," composed of at least part of the title, be typed with the page number on each page. Some journals request that figures be glossy photographs, and others prefer good xeroxes of drawings. Since the figure captions are typed on a separate page, the Notes will tell you what identifying information to provide on the figures themselves.

GOALS IN WRITING A SCIENTIFIC ARTICLE

Scientific writing has goals that are somewhat different from those of other literary undertakings. The aim of research reporting is to communicate fully, precisely, and rapidly. A good article should leave no question in the reader's mind as to what was done, why it was done, and what was found. The report must be designed in such a way that the reader can get this information quickly without having to look back and forth or to puzzle out the author's meaning. One of the principal reasons for using a standardized format for scientific writing is to make it possible for a reader to find a certain piece of information immediately, without having to plow through the whole article. If you become a consumer of research literature, you will find that you frequently do not want to read an entire article to get the information you need. A poorly constructed article that does not let you find things quickly will be frustrating. Entertainment, mood setting, persuasion, poetic rhythms, stream of consciousness, logic by analogy, and original use of words are not effective techniques for scientific writing. When such devices are mistakenly used in a science article, they get in the way of effective and efficient communication. This doesn't mean that scientific writing requires no technique; it takes a good deal of ingenuity to be clear and precise without being dull and repetitive.

PECULIARITIES OF SCIENTIFIC ARTICLES

Use the Past Tense

A scientific report discusses something that has already taken place. This means that almost all of the article is written in the past tense. In an Introduction you review studies that have already been done and describe a problem you have already investigated. In Method you detail procedures you have already used. In Results you present data you have already gathered. For all of these sections, therefore, the past tense is appropriate. Sometimes in Results you may switch to the present tense when you are discussing the implications of a particular table or figure that is presently before the reader. In Discussion you may want to use the present tense when you are discussing the current state of affairs in the area of your research. Future tense is rarely needed in a scientific article, although it will occasionally be used in Discussion to suggest future research or applications of results. The Abstract, of course, is in the past tense, since it is a brief description of what was done in the research and what the findings were.

Avoid the First Person

Perhaps to underline the objectivity of research, the tradition in scientific writing has been to avoid the first person and to write the article in the third person, using the passive voice. In the interest of livening up the text, there is some shift away from this in social science journals, but it is still better to avoid the use of "I" and "we." Even more impersonal expressions like "the authors" or "the experimenters" are largely avoided. This can be awkward at times, especially when you want to express your own opinions or direct actions. The impersonal passive ("it is thought that" or "it is suggested that") can help you out, but occasionally you may want to blurt out an emphatic "the authors believe that" and, nowadays, you'll get away with it. However, "I" and "we" will probably continue to be looked upon with disfavor, especially if overused.

The Subheadings for Clarity

The main sections of your report will have centered, underlined headings (according to convention, the Introduction main heading is often left out). A short article may need no more than these standard divisions to organize it. Longer articles, however, can be made easier to read and easier to refer back to by judicious use of subheadings. This is especially true for the Method and Results sections.

The first order of subheading under a centered heading is the *flush side heading*. This type of subheading is typed against the left-hand margin on a line of its own and is generally underlined. You may want, for example, to organize a Method section by using flush side headings for such subcategories as *Subjects, Apparatus, Procedures,* etc.

If you wish to further subdivide material, you can introduce *paragraph headings* in addition to the flush side headings and centered headings. A paragraph heading is indented and underlined. The text under this subheading begins on the next line, with the first word also indented.

Subheadings take up more space in the manuscript, but they can be invaluable to the reader for finding specific information. Use of them also helps keep the writer focused on specific issues, discouraging wandering off the topic. Remember, your goal is to make your article as clear and orderly for the reader as possible.

U.A.W.C.: Use Abbreviation with Caution

Abbreviations, especially those that are author-defined, should be used infrequently if at all. True, they do save space, but the resulting alphabet soup can make reading extremely difficult. Suppose you ran across the following.

> The Ss in the NR group showed less WL than those in the R group but improved equally in SC. This suggests that the effects of the R program were not due solely to EB or SA influences.

Unless you have a good memory, you'd have to refer to several earlier pages of the article to find out what all the letters stand for. For a period of time, the use of such self-defined abbreviations in journals was popular, but it is currently being frowned on in the interests of better communication.

Some abbreviations, especially those having to do with time (e.g., sec), distance (e.g., ft), physical measures (e.g., Hz), or statistics (e.g., SD), are standard and can be used without definition. Looking through a journal's articles and reading the Notes to Contributors will tell you which abbreviations are appropriate. There are also several standard Latin abbreviations, which are summarized in most dictionaries. These are frequently used with material in parentheses. Common ones are: etc. (and so forth); et al. (and others); i.e. (that is); e.g. (for example); and vs. (versus or against). As with units of measurements, these abbreviaitons can be used without definition.

A few abbreviations have become so common that they almost have the status of words themselves. The abbreviation IQ, for instance, would be understood by almost everyone. Other abbreviations are extremely common within social science fields. For example, ESP (extrasensory perception), and LSD (lysergic diethylamide) are well known to fairly large groups of people. If one of these common abbreviaitons is entered as a word in the Webster's New Collegiate Dictionary, then it can be used without further explanation. If not, even though its meaning is known to a large group of people, it should be defined when first used in the article. The technique for doing this is to put the abbreviation in parentheses after first using the word itself. Thereafter, the abbreviation can be used:

> One measure of relaxation that has been frequently used is electromyographic (EMG) activity. The most commonly used site for EMG recording is the forehead.

Never start a sentence with an abbreviation or a number. If you find yourself wanting to, either reword the sentence or spell out the initial abbreviation or number. Numbers of ten or less are generally spelled out in text, but larger quantities are expressed as numerals.

Reference Your Sources

Science is an accumulation of knowledge that can be traced back to its sources. Whenever you make a statement of fact, you must give a reference to indicate where that fact comes from. Your reader will not take your pronouncements on faith. Similarly, when you present someone else's theory or speculation, you must be fair and give credit for it by citing your source. Although you can make such specific references anywhere in an article, you are most likely to cite sources in the Introduction and the Discussion, the two sections in which you fit your research study into a broader context. The style of referencing currently used by most social science journals integrates the authors' names and year of publication directly into the narrative wherever information is presented about their work. Techniques for making this kind of citation are given in Section 5 of this chapter.

Condense Information into Tables and Graphs

Most scientific reports present some of the findings in tables, graphs, or other illustrations. Very often details of method or complexities of results can be made clear in this fashion when they would be very confusing and cumbersome if presented solely in text. However, when you decide to use tables or figures, be sure they are necessary. In printed journals, these illustrations require a processing that is different from and more expensive than the processing for straight text. Therefore the journal will discourage their excessive use. When preparing a manuscript for publication, keep the tables and figures separate, and place them at the end. Since tables and figures are unlikely to appear in the printed article exactly where they are referred to, you must number them and refer to them by number in the text. Tables and figures are numbered separately; the first table in the article is referred to as Table 1, and the first figure as Figure 1. All graphs, illustrations, and diagrams of any kind are designated as "figures." The precise format of tables and figures will be discussed in Section 3 of this chapter. Tables and figures are most likely to be used in the Results section, but they may also be helpful in presenting methodology or useful in the Discussion when you are comparing your results with those of previous researchers.

HINTS ON STYLE

Paragraphing

A readable article should carry the reader smoothly from one topic to another without any feeling of sudden change in thought and without the necessity of backtracking to clarify ideas. The author accomplishes this goal primarily by handling paragraphs appropriately.

A paragraph should be, on the average, about 100 words long. Either one-sentence paragraphs or lengthy run-on paragraphs make the article disorganized and reading it difficult. A short, single-sentence paragraph often represents an intrusive idea suddenly dropped on the reader without warning or obvious purpose. On the other hand, a long run-on paragraph is a signal that reorganization is necessary for clarity and logic—and the poor reader would prefer that the author did the reorganizing!

Each paragraph should begin with a topic sentence revealing what is to be discussed. The rest of the paragraph should then bear some recognizable relationship to the topic. If a report is well written, the reader can skim through its paragraphs, reading the first sentence of each to locate specific information. When a paragraph is necessarily long, you might have a summary sentence at the end of it to inform the reader what conclusion can be drawn from the material in the paragraph. Presumably, if you include information in a report, you have a reason; it is better to tell the readers what the reason is than to have them spend time figuring it out.

You also need to provide some logical transition between paragraphs. If you've outlined well, your paragraphs will probably follow naturally in the best logical order. If you reorganize and start moving paragraphs around, be sure you don't end up assuming in one paragraph that your reader knows something you haven't said yet. As you go from paragraph to paragraph, there should be no sudden incomprehensible shifts in topic.

Word Selection and Spelling

Since your goal is clear and precise communication, the words you use should mean exactly what you intend. All of us have idiosyncratic meanings for some words, and with others we are simply sloppy. Sometimes nuances are slight, but they are still important. Consider the difference between "disinterested" party and an "uninterested" party, for example, before you call someone either. A good dictionary is indispensable for any kind of scientific writing. Colloquial expressions and self-manufactured terms, although they were freely used by Shakespeare are not acceptable in scientific publications.

Neither is scientific writing improved by jargon, pompous circumlocutions, or affectations. In the last paragraph, the word "party" is such an affectation. The more common word "person" would do just as well. There is also no reason to use a long word or an obscure one when a simple word would do.

In literary writing, we often make use of synonyms to avoid monotonous, boring repetition of words. In scientific writing, however, repetition of the same term is more acceptable. If you suddenly switch to a synonym or near-synonym, the reader may not know whether you intend to convey the same meaning as the first term or whether you are pointing out a subtle difference.

It is very important in scientific writing to avoid ambiguity. Phrases like "very few," "practically all," or "most of" may have different meanings to different readers. Another source of ambiguity may be the misuse of indefinite terms of reference, such as which, this, that, these, those, their, its, etc. It is often better to repeat a noun or concept than to rely on the correct tracing of one of these terms back to its antecedent. Again, a degree of monotony and repetition is acceptable in scientific writing as the price of clarity.

A new problem in word selection is caused by the lack in the English language of a singular personal pronoun that can mean either a man or a woman. Many journals in the social sciences are prohibiting as a matter of policy the use of "he" and "his" to refer to an abstract person who could be female or male. It is cumbersome to say each time "he or she" or "his or hers" to avoid sex discrimination, and the neuter "it" and "its" are used only to refer to animals, not to humans. Sometimes, however, a sentence can be restructured to avoid personal pronouns altogether. If the subject of the sentence can be made plural, then the correct reference pronouns are the asexual "they" and "their."

A misspelled and poorly punctuated manuscript may be summarily rejected by journal editors and reviewers before they have a chance to become impressed with the significance of your results or the clarity of your logic. A secretarial spelling dictionary is an invaluable aid. It contains correctly spelled and divided words in alphabetical order without definitions. Don't depend on your typist (if you can afford one) to catch spelling errors. Often the typist thinks your imaginary spelling is a special scientific term and types the word in all its asininity.

Handling Quotations

Extensive quoting is not done in scientific articles. Usually the thoughts or findings of others can be more efficiently summarized or paraphrased in the authors' own words. Use of lengthy quotations may make the reader wonder whether the authors really understood the quoted concept or are just passing on words they can't paraphrase. Furthermore, if the quotation is extensive, especially if it represents a substantial portion of the original, you must get written permission from the owner of the copyright.

Short quotations in text are set off by double quotation marks. An omission of some of the material within the quoted sentence is indicated by three ellipsis points (. . .). If the missing material ends a sentence, the three ellipsis points are followed by a period (. . . .). For example: Madsen *et al.* (1968) reported that "Rules alone exerted little effect on . . . behavior" (p. 139). A longer quotation, of several sentences, is set off as an indented block without quotation marks.

> Rules, Ignoring, and Approval conditions were introduced one at a time. . . . The main conclusions were that: (a) Rules alone exhibited little effect on classroom behavior, (b) Ignoring Inappropriate Behavior and showing Approval for Appropriate Behavior (in combination), were very effective . . . , and (c) showing Approval for Appropriate Behaviors is probably the key to effective classroom management (Madsen *et al.,* 1968, p. 139).

Whenever a quotation is used, a full reference, including page number, must be given. The reference can be written into the text, or it can appear in parentheses at the end of the quotation.

But Don't Make It Too Boring

Within the limitations of clear communication, it is still possible to inject some interest and variety into your writing. In the interest of clarity, simple, short sentences are preferable to long, run-on ones, but an article written entirely in short sentences would sound like hail on the roof. Varying sentence length and structure will help to make the paper read smoothly. You should avoid the temptation to make lists. Even though the most precise way, for example, to summarize the findings of a research project may seem to be to list them in a numbered sequence, there is nothing more boring to read. Only the most dedicated reader will stick with you and read a list to the very last item. You may make such a listing as part of your outline, but you'll need to convert it into a readable narrative for your article.

RECAPITULATION

for STYLE OF A SCIENTIFIC ARTICLE

Before preparing a draft of your article, decide in which journal or journals you want to publish, and look at the kind of articles they've recently printed. Most journals have a *Notes for the Contributor* section in the first or last issue of the year. *Publication manuals,* such as that put out by the American Psychological Association, can also be helpful. The overall organization of the manuscript required by most social science journals is: *Abstract, Introduction, Method, Results, Discussion,* and *References.* If tables and figures are used in the article, they are typed or drawn one to a page and are placed after the References in the manuscript. The printer will set them at appropriate locations in the text when the article is prepared for publication. The goals of scientific writing are *clarity, precision, logic,* and *brevity.* There are some writing requirements that are peculiar to scientific reports. Past tense is used for most of the article, and the use of the first person pronouns "I" and "we" is generally avoided. *Subheadings* within the main sections of the report may be valuable for increasing organization and readability. *Abbreviations* are largely avoided; although they save space, they often make reading difficult. The sources for facts and ideas are meticulously referenced in the text, but such information is more commonly summarized or paraphrased than directly quoted. Tables and figures are useful for conveying large amounts of information in a compact space, but they are expensive to print. Proper use of *paragraphing,* attention to the *selection of appropriate words,* care in *transition* between ideas, and *simple but varied sentence structure* all contribute to making a report readable.

SUGGESTED EXERCISES

for STYLE OF A SCIENTIFIC ARTICLE

1. Find a Notes for the Contributor section in a journal in your field.

2. Describe at least three types of heading or subheading that could be used to break up an article. Identify which would be used for major divisions and which for subdivisions.

3. For each of the following, give a brief description of the preferred policy for research articles in the social sciences.

    a. Use of an abbreviation at the start of a sentence

    b. Use of abbreviations in general

    c. Use of first person

    d. Appropriate tense for verbs

    e. Use of "he" and "his" to indicate persons of both sexes

    f. Recommendations for paragraphing

    g. Use of quotations

    h. Referencing previous work

4. For each of the following items, identify the problem with the item and rewrite so that it will be more in accord with present journal policies. (Also, for review, identify the section of a journal article to which each item would probably belong.)

    a. 48 college students served as subjects.

    b. Next, the cups holding the sample colas are placed on a tray out of sight of the subject.

    c. Male ($N = 59$) and female ($N = 60$) college students were given a written protocol describing a competent, achievement-oriented female stimulus person (SP) with either a masculine (M) or a feminine (F) pattern of vocational and avocational interests. Two groups given the M-pattern protocol were also supplied with the SP's supposed responses to items from a "personality" test answered in a predominantly feminine (M-f SP) or masculine (M-m SP) direction. . . . Overall, the results suggested that the M-f SP, in whom femininity was explicitly suggested, received the weakest ratings on a series of achievement-related attributes.

    d. We feel that these results suggest that stereotyping affects short-term memory for information obtained from children's textbook stories.

    e. Previous work [2, 3, 7] has established that group influence can affect supposedly objective judgments of line length. Asch did the classical study in this area. (You will have to make up some imaginary information in revising this.)

    f. The analysis of variance on these data is summarized in the following table. The interaction of the two main IVs, type of instruction, and age of child, is illustrated in the graph below.

    g. Each subject tastes the 3 colas and then indicates which he prefers.

    h. The apparatus used in this experiment consists of the following:

        1) a tray

        2) four paper cups, 3 of them marked, A, B, and C

        3) three brands of cola, served at 40 degrees

        4) water to put in the unmarked cup for rinsing the mouth

        5) a response sheet for him to indicate

            a) which cola he preferred

            b) the identity of each of the 3 colas

    i. Johansson stated that: Stating rules without programming consequences is ineffective in classroom management. . . . Those children who were reinforced for positive behaviors performed more consistently than those who were ignored or those who were punished for rule infractions.

5. Consider the following statements about manuscript preparation. Indicate which of the statements are true (T) for a scientific article and which are false (F).

    _____   Erasable bond is acceptable.

    _____   The typing should be double-spaced.

    _____   If multiple copies are required, use carbons.

    _____   Numbers greater than ten should be spelled out.

    _____   Graphs, diagrams, and other illustrations are called "Figures" and are numbered consecutively.

    _____   It is permissible to start a sentence with a number or an abbreviation.

    _____   Margins should be 1 to 1½ inches.

    _____   It is acceptable to use "I" and "We" when stating the authors' opinions.

    _____   Lists should be avoided.

    _____   Present tense is usually used in the *Method* section.

    _____   The *Introduction* is begun on the same page as the *Abstract* if there is room.

    _____   *References* are started on a new page.

    _____   Abbreviations, other than Latin expressions or standard units of measurement, must be defined the first time they are used.

6. Consider the following headings. Identify which type each one is, and put them in their proper order. Where would each be placed on the manuscript page?

Experiment 1

Method

Apparatus

SECTION 3: RESULTS (WHAT DID YOU FIND OUT?)

Since the Results section is crucial to a good research report, let's get it out of the way first. We'll assume that preliminary descriptive and inferential statistics have been done on the data, and you are ready to start organizing and writing this section. As you do, it is possible that you may see the need for some further statistical analysis.

GOALS FOR A RESULTS SECTION

By the time your readers finish Results, they should know not only your findings but what conclusions can be legitimately drawn from your work. Then they'll be ready to go on to a Discussion section and follow your arguments about the implications of your results. Your first chore in a Results section is to summarize the mass of your data with descriptive statistics and make it comprehensible to your readers. You must describe your results in sufficient detail to justify your conclusions, but rarely do you need to report "raw" data or individual scores. In some cases, the numbers you summarize will be calculated or derived from the observations you actually took, and you must make this process clear. Your readers should always be able to follow the entire chain of evidence from the measures you took to your final conclusions.

Along with descriptive statistics, you report inferential statistics to establish whether or not the results you've described are due to more than chance. You don't just throw all this statistical information at your readers. In the text of Results you discuss the statistics sufficiently so that the readers understand what conclusions you've reached and why you have reached them.

ORGANIZING YOUR RESULTS

If your research has generated a lot of data, organizing Results can be a gargantuan task. One way to approach it is by listing all the questions you think your results can answer. Then you can organize this list in a logical order, being sure that the major questions are given prominence and that more basic questions are answered first. With such a list in mind, you can decide what descriptive and inferential statistics are necessary to support an answer to each of the questions. When more than a few statistics are involved, you can put them into tables or graphs, which will let your readers see the answers for themselves with a little explanation from you.

Suppose, for example, you were reporting the results of a simple experiment comparing the effects of different weight-reduction programs on weight loss over a four-week period. Your design called for two experimental groups, each of which received a different treatment, and a no-treatment control. First, it would be logical to find out what happened to the weights of each group in the experiment. Perhaps you might do this with a table comparing descriptive statistics for before-and-after weights or by a figure graphing the weekly group average weights. You would back up these descriptive statistics with inferential statistics showing that the change in weight was significant for one or more of the groups. Having established that some weight was lost in your experiment, you might next want to compare the amounts of weight lost by the different groups. Perhaps your data could establish that the experimental subjects lost but the controls did not. Perhaps one of your experimental groups lost much more than the other. You would point out these group differences and establish with inferential statistics whether they were significant. If follow-up observations were available, perhaps weights of the three groups taken six weeks after the experiment ended, you might want to use a table or figure to establish that one of your groups maintained weight loss better than the other. With this organization of results, you would provide evidence to answer successively the following questions. Was there any weight loss in the groups in the study? If so, did the experimental groups lose more than the control? Did one of the experimental procedures result in more weight loss than the other? At follow-up, was there still a difference between the groups in weight? With Results arranged in this way, it would be easy to move on to a Discussion section, stating your conclusions and recommendations in an orderly fashion while allowing your audience to easily trace all your speculations back to hard evidence.

With the major questions out of the way, you might want to take up some subsidiary questions raised by your weight-loss data. For example, you may have found that some subject characteristics were associated with weight loss. Perhaps subjects in both experimental groups who indicated at the start of the experiment that they had high expectations of success may have done better at losing weight than those who weren't so hopeful. Or you might find that in one of your experimental conditions it was the heavier people who lost more, whereas in the other it was those with less of an initial weight problem who showed the most benefit. These are both interesting findings, but you would want to present them in such a way that they would not obscure the main thrust of your research. Don't let your Results section get so bogged down in detail that the reader loses track of the study's major findings.

PUTTING TOGETHER TABLES AND FIGURES

Once you've got a tentative idea what information you are going to include in Results and how you'll organize it, you need to decide on the tables and figures around which you are going to construct the section.

When Do You Want a Table or Figure?

Lists of numbers given directly in text are difficult to comprehend and boring. Unless you are asking your readers to compare only a couple of things, the numbers themselves are usually better presented in a table or represented in a graph. Descriptive statistics for an experiment are almost always given in a table or figure. Even when your design has only two groups to compare, complete description would require reporting six numbers representing sample sizes, measures of central tendency, and measures of variability. Inferential statistics may be presented in tables as well, or it may be possible to handle them directly in text, using parentheses to give the exact values of calculated test statistics and probability levels.

Constructing a Table for Descriptive Statistics

Table Format. A clear, concise, explanatory title is centered over the top of each table. This title must make clear which DV measure(s) is being summarized and what the units of the measure are. Sample sizes used in calculating any of the descriptive statistics must be given in the table. This can be done in the title, in a footnote, or if sample sizes differ for different groups, in the body of the table itself. A complete descriptive table includes both measures of central tendency and measures of variability for each group or condition of the experiment. Sometimes, when there is a lot of information, measures of variability may be put into a separate table or summarized in text.

Examples of Tables. Table 8.1 (Romano and Cabianca, 1978, p. 10) summarizes the means and standard deviations of three different DV measures taken in an experiment that had four groups of subjects. Table 8.2 (*Publication Manual* of the American Psychological Association, 1974, p. 47) summarizes two DVs, giving just the averages for a design that consisted of eight groups.

Characteristics of a Good Table. A table or figure used in an article must be able to "stand by itself." This means that an intelligent reader can comprehend the table and its implications without any further explanation. If you study either Table 8.1 or Table 8.2, you can come to some conclusions without knowing anything further about the research projects. From Table 8.1, for example, you can see that programs A, B, and C (all relaxation procedures) decreased posttest scores on a particular test of anxiety (Suinn Test Anxiety Behavior Scale), whereas a control group (D) showed an increase. Examination of Table 8.2 indicates that "pretraining" (what-

Table 8.1

Means and Standard Deviations of the Suinn Test Anxiety Behavior Scale, the Test Anxiety Scale, and the Anagrams Test

| Measure | Program | | | | | | | |
| | A: EMG + SD | | B: EMG | | C: SD | | D: Control | |
	M	SD	M	SD	M	SD	M	SD
STABS								
Pretest	151.6	17.28	156.8	17.54	168.6	21.87	152.0	17.03
Posttest	109.2	30.11	116.2	23.33	127.6	38.40	167.8	27.60
TAS								
Posttest	20.6	7.26	20.7	5.23	24.4	6.96	27.7	5.38
Anagrams								
Posttest	4.2	3.36	2.8	2.25	5.1	3.51	4.6	2.95

Source: Reprinted by permission of the American Psychological Association (copyright © 1978) and J. L. Romano.

Note: STABS = Suinn Test Anxiety Behavior Scale, TAS = Test Anxiety Scale, EMG = electromyograph, and SD = systematic desensitization, $ns = 10$ in each program.

Table 8.2
Mean Number of Correct Responses by Children With and Without Pretraining

Group	n^a	Grade			
		3	4	5	6
Verbal tests					
Girls					
With	20 (18)	280	297	301	319
Without	20 (19)	240	251	260	263
Boys					
With	20 (19)	281	290	306	317
Without	20 (20)	232	264	221	262
Mathematical tests					
Girls					
With	20 (20)	201	214	221	237
Without	20 (17)	189	194	216	135[b]
Boys					
With	20 (19)	210	236	239	250
Without	20 (18)	199	210	213	224

Source: Reprinted by permission of the American Psychological Association (copyright © 1974).
Note: Maximum score = 320.
[a]Numbers in parentheses indicate the number of children who completed all tests.
[b]One girl in this group made only 2 correct responses.

ever that consisted of) seemed to have an effect on both verbal and mathematical measures for both sexes of children and at all grade levels. In both cases, of course, you would need inferential statistics to come to any final conclusion, but the descriptive information in these tables is decipherable without any reference to accompanying text.

A second characteristic of a good table is that it is not too complicated, requiring a great amount of effort on the reader's part to figure it out. If standard deviations had been included in Table 8.2, for instance, it would have made comparisons among the eight group means difficult. There would be just too many numbers cluttering the table. The variability information in this case could better be given in a second table.

Figures

Any supplemental illustration that is not a table is called a **Figure** in research reports. This includes pictures of equipment, diagrams, other illustrations, and graphs of results.

When Might You Want to Use Figures?   There are two situations in which you may want to use figures in Results instead of presenting the same information in a table. When a DV measure changes over time, often a graph can show this fact better than long lists of numbers. In other cases, data that could be deciphered easily from a table are given in graphical form to make a more dramatic and immediate impact on the reader.

Format for Figures.   A figure is captioned at the bottom rather than titled at the top, as for a table. The caption of a figure is often more lengthy and informative than the title of a table. Like tables, figures should stand alone without further explanation. The axes of a graphical figure must be completely labeled with both the names of the variables and the units in which they were measured. If the graph presents a relationship between and IV and a DV, the DV is given on the vertical (y) axis and the IV on the horizontal (x) axis. If the graph represents a frequency distribution, then the DV is scaled on the horizontal axis, and the frequencies or proportions are given on the vertical axis. Like tables, figures should not be cluttered with too much detail. A figure should serve as an immediate visual communication of results.

Examples of Figures.   Figure 8.1 shows the change in a DV measure over a series of trials as subjects learn to respond with a certain numerical answer when pre-

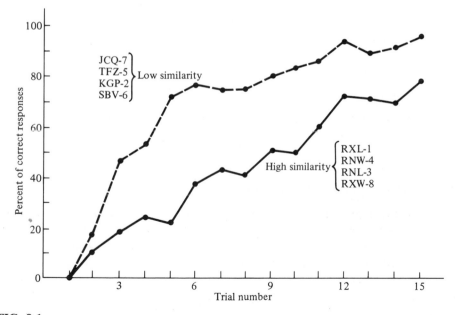

FIG. 8.1

Effect of stimulus similarity on acquisition of a paired-associates list. (Reprinted from The Psychology of Learning and Memory *by Douglas L. Hintzman. W. H. Freeman and Company. Copyright © 1978, p. 222).*

sented with a "nonsense syllable" of three letters. From Fig. 8.1 you can see that a list of nonsense syllables with low similarity is learned much more quickly than a list of syllables with high similarity (which are easily confused). If this same information were given in a table, the reader would have to compare 30 different numbers to come to a conclusion. Figure 8.2 contains a bar chart drawn to dramatize the change in likelihood of mental illness diagnosis with the social class of the patient. This information could as easily be presented in a table, but it makes a more direct visual impact as a graph.

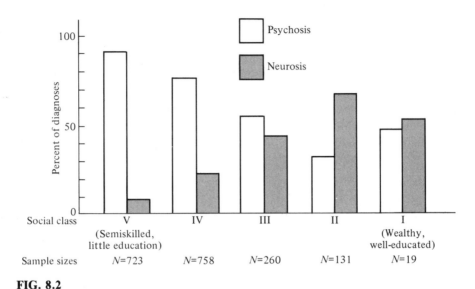

FIG. 8.2

Percent of each social-class sample diagnosed as psychotic (unfilled bars) or neurotic (filled bars). Based on Hollingshead and Redlich, 1958.

WRITING THE TEXT OF RESULTS

Writing the text for Results is a challenge. You have to present a lot of descriptive and inferential statistics, yet the text should be readable. By the end of Results your readers must have a clear verbal impression of all your conclusions and the logic and statistics on which you have based them.

Coordinating the Text with Tables and Figures

Each table and figure must be explicitly referred to by number and discussed at least once in the text. You direct the readers to a specific table or figure and then summarize for them the main things that the table or figure implies. Of course, you don't repeat all the information given in the table or figure, but you do point out to the reader what to look for. For example, in discussing Fig. 8.2 in the text you might say:

> The change in the balance of psychotic and neurotic diagnoses can be seen in Fig. 8.2. Whereas mental patients from the lowest socioeconomic class are almost always diagnosed as "psychotic," those from higher socioeconomic classes are as likely to be labeled "neurotic" as "psychotic."

Back Up Your Descriptive Statements with Inferential Statistics

Whenever you make a statement in Results based on descriptive statistics, you must back up the statement with inferential statistics. In doing so, you specify what inferential tests were done, giving a reference for a test if it is not a common one. In addition to stating the exact probability level at which a test statistic was (or was not) significant, you need to indicate the actual size of the calculated test statistic and its degrees of freedom. These specific numbers can be given in parentheses to keep the text readable. For example, in a discussion of Fig. 8.2, you might go on to say:

> A Chi-Square test of these data indicated that the frequency of diagnosing a patient as psychotic or neurotic was significantly related to the patient's social class ($\chi^2 = 296.45$, $df = 4$, $p < .001$).

It takes practice to give detailed statistical information yet keep text readable and clear. Often, information from Chi-Square, t-test and one-way Analyses of Variance can be incorporated into the text and does not need to be presented in separate tables. For example, in discussing Table 8.1, you might write:

> A one-way Analysis of Variance of the Suinn Test Anxiety Behavior Scale indicated that the groups differed significantly ($F = 19.02$; $df = 3,36$; $p < .001$). A further Neuman-Keuls analysis for multiple comparisons (Lee, 1975) showed that each of the treatment programs differed significantly ($p < .001$) from the no-treatment control, but they did not differ significantly among themselves. The three relaxation programs appeared equally effective in reducing test anxiety.

For more complex analyses, such as a multifactor Analysis of Variance, it is better to give the inferential statistical information in a table. For example, Table 6.6 (p. 233) gives the results of a two-way Analysis of Variance for a study of drug effects on performance. It would be difficult to give all this information directly in the text without confusing a reader. However, you could direct the reader to look at this table and then discuss it briefly in text, as follows:

> The results of a 2×2 analysis of variance are given in Table 6.6. From this analysis it can be seen that consumption of either marijuana or alcohol resulted in deterioration of performance, with alcohol having a somewhat more significant ($p < .01$) effect than marijuana ($p < .05$). Subjects were almost completely unable to solve any anagrams when they took the two drugs together, as is shown by the significant interaction ($p < .01$).

Placement of Tables and Figures in a Manuscript

When you are writing a research report for a class, you'll probably place the tables and figures where they are referred to in text. In a manuscript for publication, the tables and figures are placed on separate pages at the end. This means you must give the printer some directions as to where in the article you would like the table or figure to appear. You do so by breaking the text and inserting instructions to the printer as follows:

```
INSERT TABLE 1 ABOUT HERE
```

You then continue the text as if the interruption had not occurred. Tables are numbered consecutively as they are first referred to in the text. Figures are similarly numbered in sequence as they are first mentioned, and thereafter they are referred to by number.

Keeping Results Organized

It is very easy to lose your reader in a maze of statistics in Results, especially if you are reporting findings from a complex design or have used more than one DV in the research. The list of questions you developed when thinking about how to organize your results can be used as basis for an orderly outline for this section. If the Results section is long, you may want to use subheadings to break it up. For example, if you measured three DVs, you might discuss each one in a different subsection. Each paragraph in Results should be limited to discussion of a single finding or at most a couple of related findings. You should be very explicit in each case in telling the readers what your data and statistics established. Any sudden shift of topic within or between paragraphs in Results will be very confusing to readers trying to keep track of your statistics.

GUIDELINES FOR EVALUATING A RESULTS SECTION

When journal reviewers evaluate or teachers grade a *Results* section for a social science research report, they base their decision on a fairly standard set of questions. To see how you would fare, you can judge your own efforts against these standards.

1. If preliminary processing of raw data was necessary before its analysis, is the procedure clearly described?
2. Is the section well organized, taking up one point at a time in a logical order, not skipping back and forth?
3. Are both descriptive and inferential statistics given to back up each stated finding?
   a. Were the statistics used appropriate?
   b. Are the names of any inferential tests clearly given (and referenced if they are unusual tests)?

    c. Are the calculated test statistic, degrees of freedom, and significance level given for each inferential test?

    d. Is it clear in each case how the reported inferential statistics are related to the conclusion?

4. Are the necessary tables and figures included?

    a. Are they in proper format?

    b. Are they clearly titled or captioned?

    c. Are they optimally set up for easy interpretation?

    d. Can each table or figure be understood apart from explanation in the text?

    e. Is each table or figure specifically referred to by number in the text?

    f. Is the major import of each table or figure made clear in the text?

5. Is the style appropriate for Results?

    a. Has past tense been used throughout except where present tense is appropriate?

    b. Are subheadings used to clarify a lengthy section?

    c. Is the logic behind stated conclusions clearly laid out?

    d. Does each paragraph center on one major finding?

    e. Is it readable?

SUGGESTED EXERCISES

for RESULTS

---

1. Describe the goals of a Results section.

2. Find a research article in your field, and evaluate its Results section.

3. An experiment was done to assess the effects on a rat's performance of its student experimenters' belief that the rat was "bright" or "dull." Below are some questions that could be answered by the data collected in the experiment. Organize these questions into what you think would be the best logical order in which to consider them in a Results section.

    a. Since the student teams were not assigned at random to the five lab days, was there any effect of lab day on the rats' learning?

    b. Did the rats' rate of learning a given exercise correlate with the rate with which they learned the preceding exercise?

    c. Did the rats identified as Skinner-box Bright learn their exercises faster than those identified as Skinner-box Dull?

    d. Did the students who thought their rats were Skinner-box Bright like their rats better than those who thought they were Skinner-box Dull?

    e. Were the effects on learning of identifying a rat as Skinner-box Bright or Skinner-box Dull different for the different exercises in the series?

    f. Were the students who thought their rats were Skinner-box Bright more satisfied with the lab part of the course than those who thought their rats were Skinner-box Dull?

    g. What were the students' responses to an open-ended question about what they thought about the experiment after they had been told that the early instructions were a hoax?

4. Discuss each of the following as if you were writing part of a Results section for which it was a supplemental figure or table.

    a. Figure 8.1

    b. Table 8.2

    c. Figure 5.17 (p. 196)

5. Go back to Question 1 on p. 212.

    a. Make a complete table (with title) giving the descriptive statistics.

    b. Write a part of a Results section discussing this table.

    c. Back up your discussion with inferential statistics.

6. Go back to Question 4 on p. 254.

    a. Make a complete table (with title) giving the requested two-way classification.

    b. Write a part of a Results section discussing this table and including necessary inferential statistics.

7. Mark each of the following statements about Results as true or false.

_____ If it is mentioned in the text, it is not necessary to include sample sizes in a descriptive statistics table.

_____ Most of the Results section is written in the present tense.

_____ When discussing inferential statistics, you must include the name of the test, the calculated test statistic, the degrees of freedom, and the level of significance.

_____ Tables and figures should be referred to by number in the text and then not discussed further.

_____ An unusual statistical test should be referenced to a source describing its procedures.

_____ A figure caption is written above the figure.

_____ Footnotes are permissible in tables.

SECTION 4: METHOD (WHAT EXACTLY DID YOU DO?)

The Method section of a research article is the easiest writing task. It mostly involves straight reporting of what you actually did in your research study. You might as well get it done before attacking the more "literary" parts of your report, namely the Introduction and Discussion.

GOAL FOR A METHOD SECTION

In Method you need to communicate clearly and concisely how you went about investigating your research problem. This section must be sufficiently complete that someone reading your report could repeat your research and, allowing for chance factors, get the same results.

INFORMATION NECESSARY IN METHOD

Information about Design

Both the operational definition of your IV(s) and how you measured your DV(s) must be clearly spelled out. The design itself should be presented in such a way that a reader can see how combinations of your IV levels created the conditions of the experiment and also how you then assigned subjects to these conditions. You may not always directly label them as such, but any knowledgeable reader should be instantly able to pinpoint your IVs, establish how many levels of each were used, decide whether the IVs were Subject or Non-Subject in type, and identify whether they were used in the design in a Between- or Within-Subjects fashion. Unless this information is easily available, it will not be possible for readers to interpret your results, let alone repeat your experiment.

Information about Procedure

In addition to overall design information, you need to specify exactly what procedures you used in each of the different conditions of the experiment. Sometimes, even though the intention of the design may be good, the actual procedures introduce potential Confounding Variables that you may not see yourself. For instance, little things, such as whether you put instructions to the subjects on tape or present them in person, may make a difference in results. Your description of procedures should be complete enough so that readers can detect these problems even if you don't. If you have introduced special controls, like a double-blind procedure or a placebo condition, you need to advertise the fact. This information is important for your audience to have when evaluating and interpreting your study.

Information about Subjects

The characteristics of your subjects place limitations on the generalizability of your results. When interpreting a research study, the strongest generalization can be made to the population actually sampled for the study. As your readers attempt to apply the results to different populations, generalization is weakened. In your report you must give enough information about your research subjects so that your readers can figure out exactly what population was sampled and how it was sampled. In addition, since the strength of inference from a sample to a population rests on sample size, you always need to include information on the number of subjects and the number of observations taken on each subject.

Information about Apparatus and Materials

In order to replicate your research, other people may need to duplicate your apparatus and materials. For example, if you used a questionnaire or test as your DV measure, the readers need to know more than its name, especially if it is of the "home-grown" variety. Although it's not always feasible to print the whole test or questionnaire as part of your report, you should describe it enough, perhaps giving a sample item or two, to allow your audience to see its general nature. Then, in addition, you must make it possible for readers to get copies for themselves. For widely used tests, like the MMPI (Minnesota Multiphasic Personality Inventory) or WAIS (Wechsler Adult Intelligence Scale), just the name may be sufficient. For other commercially available tests, you may want to write a footnote with the company's address. For home-grown tests or tests borrowed from other researchers, you have to give enough information so that interested persons can obtain copies.

When special apparatus is used, in addition to describing its general nature, you must give the company name and any other relevant information (e.g., model number) that would permit someone else to obtain the same piece of equipment. If you built your own apparatus, then you need to provide a description, picture, circuit diagram, etc., that would allow any reasonably knowledgeable person to construct a similar piece of apparatus. In some cases equipment is so standard (e.g., a typewriter or a projector) that you need not go into detail since any reasonable facsimile will do.

But Don't Go Overboard

Although you want to make your Method complete, you don't want to muddy the waters with trivial detail, knowledge of which is not vital to repeating the research. For example, if your subjects "wrote down their responses," it's not really necessary in most cases to go on to specify that they used "paper and pencil" (or to specify the brand of paper or the make of pencil). Nor is it likely to be relevant who later ran the data analyses. A *t*-test is a *t*-test, whether it was calculated by yourself, the computer, or your reluctant spouse. When you are deciding what constitutes trivial detail, the guiding principle is whether that piece of information is essential to repeating the research and getting the same results. If it is not, then it is trivial. Admittedly, there are some instances when it will be unclear whether a piece of information is essential or trivial. Then the safest course is to include the information in the report. Elimination of trivial details saves space, makes the Method section more readable, and simplifies the reader's task of discovering important aspects of the method necessary to replicate the research.

WRITING YOUR METHOD SECTION

Subheadings

Use of subheadings greatly improves the organization of a Method section for any but the simplest of experiments. If Method is long, subheadings make it much easier for a reader to check back for particular methodological details.

A Useful Scheme of Organization

A very common organization is to divide the Method section into *Subjects, Materials and Apparatus, Design, Procedures,* and perhaps *Preliminary Data Analysis.* This organization works well for most experiments. Sometimes, however, especially when work with the subjects is prolonged, you may wish to emphasize different phases of the experiment and, accordingly, have subsections such as *Pretesting, Training, Posttesting,* etc. There are no hard-and-fast rules about exactly what subsections to use, but you should select your categories to make reference back to the section easier. You've done your job well if the reader wanting a particular piece of information can immediately identify the subsection in which to seek it.

Don't Use a Chronological Organization

It might seem that the most accurate way of reporting what you did in your research is to give a blow-by-blow description of everything in order, from start to finish. This approach might indeed mean that you would get in all the information, but such a piecemeal organization would make it difficult for the reader to comprehend the overall design of your research and to separate important from unimportant details. Consider, for example, how annoying it would be for a reader to have to sift a whole chronologically organized Method section in order to determine what apparatus and materials would be needed to replicate your experiment. Similarly, suppose that someone just wanted to know the design of your study but had to plod through the whole Method section to find out that each subject experienced three different conditions in counterbalanced order. Whether you actually use subheadings or not, it is much better to sort and organize information about your Method appropriately.

GUIDELINES FOR EVALUATING A METHOD SECTION

When a journal reviewer evaluates your manuscript or your teacher grades your research report, each will be judging your *Method* section by the following guidelines.

1. Is it clear who were the subjects and how many of them were used?
2. Are the materials and equipment used in the research described sufficiently so they could be reproduced?
   a. Are manufacturer names given for purchased equipment?
   b. Is sufficient information given for construction of home-built equipment?
   c. Are the sources of any special tests, questionnaires, etc., given?
   d. Are figures used when appropriate to illustrate details of apparatus or lab setup?
3. Is the design of the project clearly described?
   a. Are IV and DV operational definitions clear?
   b. Is it clear how subjects were assigned to the different groups in the experiment?

    c. If any special controls were used, are they identified by name and described?

4. Are the specific procedures used with the subjects described in enough detail so that they could be duplicated?

    a. If verbal instructions are important, are they given verbatim or sufficiently summarized?

    b. Is it clear when and under what conditions the subjects were observed on the DVs?

    c. If the timing of the procedures is complex and hard to follow, have they been diagrammed in a figure to clarify them?

    d. Is there enough information to let the reader determine the possible roles of Experimenter Bias and Subject Attitude effects?

5. Is the style used appropriate for Method?

    a. Has past tense been used throughout?

    b. Is the section well organized, permitting a reader to go back and locate a specific piece of information?

    c. Has all the information absolutely necessary to replicate the research been included?

    d. Has trivial and repetitive information been left out?

    e. Has a chronological reporting style been avoided?

SUGGESTED EXERCISES

for METHOD

1. Find an article in your social science area and evaluate its Method section according to the guidelines given above.

2. Here are some sentences (some of them modified) from a Method section of a report by Rosenthal and Lawson (1964). Place each one in a Method subcategory according to the type of information it is principally conveying. Note that for some of them there is more than one possible answer; you should be able to defend the answer you chose. (Key: S—Subjects, M—Materials or apparatus, D—Design, P—Procedures)

    _____ Each laboratory team (of two or three students) performed three different functions during each of the exercises: experimenter, timer, and recorder.

    _____ The 30 male and 9 female students enrolled in a laboratory course in experimental psychology participated in the experiment.

    _____ The 39 students were divided into 16 laboratory teams, each composed of two or three students.

    _____ The 16 laboratory teams were each assigned a rat. At random, half of the teams were told their rats were "Skinner-box Bright," and half were told their rats were "Skinner-box Dull."

_____ The basic equipment employed in the studies was commercially made demonstration Skinner boxes with feeders.

_____ Each rat was run through a total of seven "exercises" as follows:

_____ The students used Homme and Klaus's laboratory manual, substituting food pellets for water reinforcement.

_____ A questionnaire that was used consisted of 30 (20-point) rating scales on which the students could rate their satisfaction with the lab and their feelings about their rat.

_____ The students were expected to complete each of the seven "exercises" with their rat in one two-hour period per week. If they did not complete within the scheduled time, they had to return to the lab and continue working until the rat was ready to go on to the next scheduled "exercise."

3. Explain why each of the following statements might be considered inappropriate for a Method section.

    a. The tape recorder was switched on by a graduate student so that subjects could listen to taped instructions.

    b. The stimulus cards were typed with a Smith-Colora Electra 120.

    c. First the subjects came into the room and sat down. Next they took a pretest, writing their answers in pencil.

    d. The data were analyzed by an Analysis of Variance done by the university's computer.

SECTION 5: INTRODUCTION (WHAT DID YOU DO AND WHY DID YOU DO IT?)

The Introduction and Discussion sections of a report are the hardest to organize since they are not as cut-and-dried as Method or Results and they require some original thinking on your part. To some extent, there is a trade-off between the two sections. For example, if there is a particular earlier research study you wish to mention, you may need to decide whether it is better to present it in the Introduction, where you are building a case for doing your research, or in the Discussion, where you are interpreting the results of your research in the context of previous work. There are no rules to help you here; you'll just have to see where the information best fits without interrupting the flow of your argument.

GOAL FOR AN INTRODUCTION SECTION

By the end of the Introduction, you want your readers to understand what research problem you investigated, why you chose to investigate it, and why you decided to take the particular approach that you will present in the Method section. Building the case for doing your research will rely heavily on your evaluation of what was known in the area before you carried out your project. Therefore, for writing an Introduction section, you'll have to learn how to reference the work of other researchers and thinkers properly. Everything you say in a research article must be traceable back to its source.

SUGGESTED ORGANIZATION FOR INTRODUCTION

Introductions vary a lot from paper to paper. Although no one organization is standard, you could organize a good Introduction by answering the following series of questions in succession.

What is the general area of your research problem?

Why is this an important or interesting area to study?

What previous work has been done in this area that is directly related to your problem?

What research does this earlier work suggest needs to be done next?

What is the specific problem that you investigated in your research?

What answers did you expect to get and why?

The first two questions, the general nature of the problem and why it is of interest, usually can be taken care of in the same paragraph. The next paragraph or two can then be devoted to the examination of relevant earlier work. This examination is not an exhaustive historical review but a brief presentation of studies that are directly related to the present research study and may even actually be the basis for it. You summarize these studies briefly, giving major conclusions, findings, relevant methodological features—and, perhaps, flaws—only as they are needed to develop the reasons that your own research seemed necessary. When controversies exist, they should be presented simply and fairly.

The continuity between earlier work and your specific research problem must be emphasized. If your research stems from a theory, you should explain the theory and give the logic as to how your research will be a test of that theory. You can't expect the reader to supply continuity or logical connections. After all, you are the expert who decided to do the research, and presumably, you know your reasons best.

Finally, an Introduction should end with a paragraph that clearly states the specific problem the study was designed to investigate. This is usually not done as a formal statement of research hypotheses such as you would write for an inferential statistical test, but such hypotheses should be clearly in mind when you write it. The IV(s) and DV(s) should be presented in this paragraph, although they are often not directly labeled as such. You may indicate what results you expect to get and, logically, why you expect to get them. This last paragraph is important. It gives your reader a context in which to judge both your methodological choices and your obtained results. Without this final paragraph detailing the specific research problem, the reader can only guess at the direction in which your paper is heading.

SPECIAL STYLE REQUIREMENTS OF AN INTRODUCTION

Avoid Statements Requiring Special Knowledge

You want your research to reach as many people as might be able to make use of its information. This means that you may have to do a little explaining in Introduction. If you use technical terms, you should briefly define them; otherwise you will greatly decrease the number of people who'll be able to follow your logic. If you refer to previous work, you should briefly summarize its relevant portions. If you don't, only readers who happen to be familiar with that research will be able to understand you. The explanations needn't be long-winded; often a few carefully chosen words will do.

Continuity Is Essential

Since an Introduction is what convinces the reader to wade through the rest of the paper, it should be readable. Good narrative style, attention to paragraphing, provision for continuity of ideas, avoidance of statements intelligible only to a limited audience, etc., are all basic requirements for writing a good Introduction. This section should read smoothly from start to finish. If the reader has to skip back and forth to follow your logic or needs to make wild guesses as to why there has been a sudden shift of topic, then the overall style of your Introduction is poor.

All Sources Must Be Referenced

In the Introduction you must give credit for ideas that are not your own and for results achieved by previous researchers. When you state "facts," they should be based on referenced sources rather than your "personal experience." When you offer speculations, it should be clear whose they are. Thus Introduction, more than any other section of your report, will be peppered with **citations.** It's hard to do this gracefully while continuing to make a narrative readable. An older citation system, which is still in use in some journals, consisted of numbered footnotes. This system had the advantage of not intruding on the narrative, but it forced the reader to flip to the References section repeatedly to check who said what when. Most journals in the social sciences now use a system that integrates the author's last name and the publication date of each work cited directly into the text.

FORMAT FOR MAKING CITATIONS

Single-Author Articles for Books

If the author is referred to by name in the text, then the year of publication follows in parentheses: "C. Little (1789) suggested that the sky is falling." Or if you prefer, you can simply give both author and year in parentheses after making a general statement based on that person's work or ideas: "Some researchers have suggested that the sky is falling (Little, 1789)." Switching back and forth between these two methods of referencing will give some variety to your narrative. When a book is referenced, you may want to follow the year of publication with a page reference to make it easier for your reader to find the specific source of your remarks.

Multiple Authors

If there are only two authors, you always give both names. If there are more than two, you list all the names the first time you cite the study, and then, in additional citations, you give only the senior (first) author's name followed by "*et al.*" For example:

First occurrence: "Mark, Ranke, and Todd (1921) found that. . . ."
Second occurrence and thereafter: "Mark *et al.* (1921) suggested that. . . ."

Citing Secondary Sources

In scientific writing you usually trace each idea to its original source. Sometimes, however, this may not be practical. Some historical sources may be available only in later works that refer to them. In other cases, you may have to rely on translations. It is risky to reference a primary source you haven't seen. The way out of this dilemma is to use the originator's name in text and follow in parentheses with the name and date of the **secondary source** you actually consulted. For example, you might write: "A long time ago, Chicken Little said the sky was falling (Palazzo, 1960)."

Multiple Citations

Sometimes you really want to clobber the reader with evidence and back up your statements with several sources. In this case, you list different studies by the same author in chronological order and different studies by different authors in alphabetical order. Such multiple referencing is usually done parenthetically and not as a part of a sentence. For example: "Recent studies (Abel, 1971; Baker and Charley, 1970, 1973) have shown. . . ."

No Author

Some works you may want to reference will not have an author. These are usually referenced by title. When citing them in the body of your article, you should give at least the first two or three words of the title so that your reader can easily find the entry in your reference list (*American Psychological Association Publication Manual,* 1974, p. 58).

Not Published

Try to make your references only to published sources; otherwise your readers will have a hard time checking up on you. If you must cite unpublished manuscripts, talks, personal communications, etc., as sources, they may be listed separately from your more legitimate references. One system uses "Reference Notes," which follow the Reference section itself. Such "notes" are cited in the text in the same way as references, except that the word "Note" and a sequence number replace the date. Thus, if you wanted to reference a talk given by Rogers, you would cite it as "Rogers (Note 1)" or "(Rogers, Note 1)". In your Reference Notes you would explain exactly where this unpublished information came from.

GUIDELINES FOR EVALUATING AN INTRODUCTION

Since the *Introduction* is the first section that your reviewer (or teacher) is likely to read, it's important that it make a good impression. The standards by which the section will be judged are as follows:

1. Is the general area of the research clearly introduced and a case made for why more knowledge is needed in the area?
2. Is information given from previous work summarizing the present state of knowledge in the area?
3. Has a case been built for why the particular approach to be used in the present research study is a reasonable one?
4. Are the sources of any facts, ideas, and speculations clearly given?
5. Is the specific problem the present research study is designed to investigate clearly stated before going on to the Method section?
6. Is the style appropriate for an Introduction?
   a. Is past tense used throughout?
   b. Are citations of work by other researchers done in proper format?
   c. Is it possible to read the section smoothly from beginning to end, following the author's logic without sudden transitions or skipping back and forth?

SUGGESTED EXERCISES

for INTRODUCTION

1. Describe the goals for an Introduction.
2. Describe the suggested organization for the Introduction presented in this section.
3. Read an Introduction from an article in your social science area and do the following:

a. Figure out what the author's organization scheme was.

b. Evaluate it according to the Guidelines.

(If you can't find an article on your own, hunt up: Doob, A. N. and Macdonald, G. E. Television viewing and the fear of victimization: Is the relationship causal? *Journal of Personality and Social Psychology,* 1979, **37,** 170–177.)

4. Identify the following statements as True (T) or False (F) for an Introduction.

_____ It is written mostly in present tense.

_____ It is limited to 100 to 175 words.

_____ It should contain a detailed description of the methods of the present study.

_____ The literature review should be in considerable historical depth.

_____ The final paragraph should state the specific research problem investigated in the study.

SECTION 6: DISCUSSION (WHAT DID YOU PROVE?)

GOALS FOR THE DISCUSSION SECTION

When you get to the Discussion, you at last have a chance to hold forth on what your research proves. Since Discussion is the last section of your article, it leaves the strongest impression of the meaning of your research. You want your readers, when they finish this section, to have a firm idea both of your major findings and of any implications of these findings for practical application, future research planning, or theoretical controversy.

WHAT GOES INTO DISCUSSION?

You should begin the Discussion with a *clear statement of your answers to the questions posed in the Introduction.* Since you have already established the evidential base for these answers in Results, your presentation of them in Discussion needn't be burdened with a lot of statistical detail. However, you must summarize the important points established in Results for those readers who may have lost track of them while wading through all the statistics.

The content of the rest of Discussion is variable from paper to paper, and there isn't a standard outline for this section. What you should discuss depends both on the nature of your research problem and on what you got in the way of results.

To give weight to your findings, you should *examine the similarities and differences between your results and those of others.* Whenever you find apparent disagreement with previous work, you should spend some words discussing why. Of course, any earlier work you cite must be carefully referenced, just as in the Introduction.

There may be some *limitations that either the design or procedures of your study place on interpretation of results.* For instance, if you have a Subject IV, you may want to consider the possibility of other relevant variables causing the observed results. However, you shouldn't dwell compulsively on every possible flaw in the study. You just need to bring up those problems you feel may have affected the DVs and tell how they could change interpretation of results. This self-criticism both assures your audience that you were aware of these factors when making interpretations and helps future researchers avoid these problems.

When you interpret your results, you may want to include *alternative interpretations* and say why you prefer a particular one. Then you should *specifically point out the implications of your research.* The answers you have found to your research questions may have practical applications. Or your results may be consistent or inconsistent with some broader theoretical position. Perhaps your results suggest to you that there is need for a new theory, which could be tested in future research. Maybe your experiences suggest some ways this type of research could be improved. The readers may see still other applications and implications, but don't depend on them to discover the ones you've thought of.

If you wish, the evidential base established in your research may invite *speculation* about matters that you have not directly investigated. A little of this is fine, as long as it is clear that it is speculation. However, don't let wild speculations dominate your Discussion.

ORGANIZATION OF DISCUSSION

A Discussion must be readable, having good continuity of thought throughout. As mentioned above, it is the section that leaves your readers with the final impression of the whole study. Beyond the suggestion that the section should begin with a reminder of the major findings of the study, there isn't really a standard order for the types of information that can be included in Discussion. You might have, for example, a paragraph reviewing findings and comparing them with earlier work. This could be followed by a paragraph on limitations of the study and another paragraph on implications. Or if your research is answering more than one question, you might devote a paragraph to each finding, discussing all the relevant information, and then close with a paragraph that ties everything together. Either organization is fine, just so long as it is an easy one for the reader to follow. Since subheadings are rarely used in the Discussion, you have to pay attention to transition of thought between paragraphs and clue your readers in to what you are discussing from moment to moment.

RELATION OF DISCUSSION AND RESULTS SECTIONS

If you did a thorough job of presenting your data and analyses in Results, all you need in Discussion is a very brief statement about your findings. Then you can move on to discussing interpretations and implications. Some authors prefer to say less about their data in Results and take them up in more detail in Discussion. However, you can't refer to any DV measures in Discussion that have not been previously presented and analyzed in Results. Although you may want to emphasize in the Discussion particular observations or statistics to highlight the more important or interesting findings, it is not usual to include a lot of numbers or make direct references to tables or figures. The better the job you do of making the Results comprehensible, the easier it is to write the Discussion.

RELATION OF DISCUSSION AND INTRODUCTION SECTIONS

A good starting point for the Discussion is answering the questions you used to close the Introduction. Discussion is a continuation of Introduction, with the new information provided by your research now being available. Often you will find information that could logically be presented either in Introduction or Discussion. For instance, if your research stems from a theory, you might present that theory in Introduction. Then all you would have to do in Discussion is say whether or not your data fit the predictions of the theory. On the other hand, you may feel that your results have implications for an existing theory although your research wasn't specifically designed to test that theory. In this case, you might prefer to save presentation of the theory for the Discussion. How much you talk about something in the Discussion depends on how much you said about it in the Introduction.

Introduction and Discussion are similar in their heavy use of references. In Introduction you cite previous work that led directly to your research problem, and in Discussion you see whether your results agree or disagree with this previous work. How much information you present about earlier studies in Discussion depends on whether you described them in Introduction. You can cite the same study in both sections, but it is not necessary to repeat lengthy descriptions. As for the Introduction, in Discussion you must carefully distinguish between those remarks that are based on evidence, your own and others', and those that are pure speculation. Paranoid as it may seem, all information in a scientific article must be traceable to a specific source.

GUIDELINES FOR EVALUATING A DISCUSSION SECTION

When a Discussion section is reviewed or graded, the evaluator doesn't have as specific a set of guidelines in mind as for the other sections. However, the Discussion section leaves the final impression of the worth of the research and will strongly color evaluation of the whole article. Here are some of the questions an evaluator might ask.

1. Are the major results of the research clearly summarized and emphasized?
2. When these results differ from what the author indicated in the Introduction might be logically expected, are reasons for these differences considered?

3. Are similarities and differences between these results and those of other researchers discussed?

4. If the design had limitations and/or there were procedural problems, are the possible effects of these on the results considered?

5. Is the author's interpretation of the results made clear?

6. Are alternative interpretations also considered?

7. Does the author make suggestions for future research or application of the results?

8. Is the style appropriate for Discussion?

   a. Is past tense used to discuss the research being reported and any other work cited?

   b. Is statistical detail kept to a minimum?

   c. Is the author careful not to present any new methodological or results information that should have been given in earlier sections?

   d. Is the section well organized so that the reader can follow the logic behind the author's interpretations?

   e. Are all statements of fact traceable to their sources?

   f. Does the section come to a definite conclusion rather than just stop?

SUGGESTED EXERCISES

for DISCUSSION

1. Explain the special relationship of the Discussion and Introduction sections.

2. Find an article in your social science area and read its Discussion; then do the following.

   a. Categorize the information in it as

      1) summarizing results,
      2) exploring similarities with and differences from other work,
      3) discussing limitations of the study,
      4) interpreting the results,
      5) presenting alternative interpretations,
      6) discussing implications of the results,
      7) speculation.

   b. Evaluate it according to the guidelines for Discussion.

   c. Suggest improvements in content and organization to increase reader comprehension.

3. Decide whether the following statements are more likely to be taken from a Results or a Discussion section. For those belonging to Discussion, decide what kind of information is being given.

a. "Of the 4000 passing vehicles, 93 stopped. With the model car absent, 35 vehicles stopped; with the model present, 58 halted" (Bryan and Test, 1967).

b. "The findings then are quite consistent: the presence of helping models significantly increases subsequent altruistic behavior" (Bryan and Test, 1967).

c. "The relative frequency and duration for each category of expressive behavior are given in Table 4.1. Subjects varied in the amount of time they took to walk from one room to another. Therefore, the absolute frequency and duration of nonverbal gestures were transformed to a proportion for each subject . . ."(Efran and Cheyne, 1974).

d. "The results of this analysis indicate a very significant overall heart rate increase ($F = 312$, $df = 2/24$, $p < .001$)" (Efran and Cheyne, 1974).

e. "As one would expect, the results of the four areas differed significantly in their overall fear of crime. The average factor scores are shown in Table 1. Analysis of variance on factor scores revealed a main effect for high/low crime area that was highly significant, $F(1,296) = 17.79$, $p < .01$" (Doob and McDonald, 1979).

f. "The second general point that should be made about the data is that although the correlation between TV viewing and fear dropped off when neighborhood was used as a controlling factor, this same factor did not eliminate the relationship between TV viewing and other factors" (Doob and MacDonald, 1979).

g. "Since progesterone brings about readiness to incubate without increased crop weights, the finding of Riddle and Lahr (1944) that crop weights were increased after several days of progesterone-induced incubation does not show that progesterone stimulated prolactin secretion. Rather, it confirms Patel's (1936) report that . . ."(Lehrman, 1958).

SECTION 7: FINISHING YOUR ARTICLE WITH A TITLE, ABSTRACT, AND REFERENCES

With the four main sections of your article written, all you have left to do is compose a title, write a brief abstract, and put your reference list in order.

TITLE

Goal for the Title

Somehow you need to attract people to read your research report. As the amount of scientific information increases, it gets harder to match a particular reader with a particular article. People locate articles by leafing through journals and looking at titles, by seeing an article referenced in another article, and by searching published indexes, such as *Psychological Abstracts, Sociological Abstracts, Education Index,*

Index Medicus, Mental Retardation Abstracts, Child Development Abstracts and Bibliography, etc. They may also find your article through a library computer search. The indexing and abstracting services, as well as computer searches, rely on key words in the title to sort articles into special areas of interest. The way you write your title has a lot to do with your article's being properly classified. Once the reference is found by a reader, the wording of your title will determine whether the reader hunts up your article.

Form of a Title

The maximum length for a title is 12 to 15 words. If you are clever about it, within these few words you can convey your study's IV and DV and even something about the subjects. Sometimes the nature of the subjects can be guessed from the rest of the title, and there is no need to waste more words. For example, the words "verbal learning" would indicate to most readers that animals had not been used for the study. However, a title like "Motivational effects of rewarding intracranial stimulation" (Bindra and Campbell, 1967) leaves something to be desired. A select in-group who knew about the work being done in this area in the sixties would accurately guess what kind of animal had been studied, but for the rest of us "in rats" at the end of the title would be a help. You should avoid jargon words and abbreviations because they limit your potential audience, but vague terms (like "motivational effects") may result in your article's being passed over by a reader in a hurry. For instance, the title "Response by the calf to stimulus change" (Beauchamp, Chapman, and Grebing, 1967) could be improved by indicating that the "response" was maze-learning and the "stimulus change" was change in brightness of a visual stimulus.

A good title should be explanatory by itself. It may seem contradictory both to urge specificity and to require that the title be short. However, you can fit a good deal of specific information into a title if you avoid padding it with words that serve no explanatory purpose. Such expressions as "a study of" or "an experimental investigation of" don't really add anything.

IDENTIFYING THE AUTHORS

Under the title, you list the author(s) of the article. In addition to your name(s), you have to give enough information so that readers can contact you, send you hate mail, etc. The full name of each author is given, with the "senior author," or person who has taken major responsibility for the study, listed first. Persons listed as authors should be only those who have made substantial contributions to the research. Other persons who have assisted in some way but were not directly involved with the planning and interpretation of the research should be listed in footnotes. The trend to multiple authorship can sometimes get extreme. There is a study in the literature with four authors and only one rat as a subject (Laties, Weiss, Clark, and Reynolds, 1965)!

The affiliation (place of work, academic institution, or course identification) is listed below the authors' names. Both authors' names and the title itself may be footnoted to give the reader additional information, such as the source of funding, acknowledgments for special help, and sources from which readers may get additional information about the research. These footnotes may be numbered in sequence or just asterisked, depending on the journal's style requirements.

ABSTRACT

Goal for the Abstract

A busy reader will go through the **abstract** first to see whether the rest of the article is worth reading. Like the title, the abstract can serve as a way of attracting readers. In addition, the abstract is a reminder of what was in the article and, if well done, can save readers the task of making notes on your study for their files. Some journals even print abstracts on file cards that can be torn out. Some library search services give you abstracts as well as titles of articles.

Format for an Abstract

Although the abstract comes first in the manuscript, it is usually the last section written. It is a condensed version of the entire research project, including a statement of the problem, a description of the method, a summary of the major results, and an indication of the most important conclusions. Since the abstract may be reprinted without the article, it must be completely self-contained; in fact, it is a brief report in its own right. Abbreviations used in the article must be redefined in the abstract. It is rare for an outside study to be specifically referenced, since an abstract may be reprinted without the article's reference list. The abstract is written as a single paragraph and is generally limited to between 100 and 175 words (the exact length limit varies with different journals).

A knowledgeable consumer of scientific articles expects to find some specific information in abstracts. The type and number of subjects is very important. For example, readers might not feel it worth their while to look up a study on taste preferences done with five persons but would be very interested in one done with 50. The specific research design utilized should be named if it is a familiar one, or else it should be briefly described. Test instruments, research apparatus, or special data-gathering procedures that might be interesting in and of themselves can be mentioned if it is possible to do so without a lot of explanation. Any drugs used in the study must be identified, and their generic names must be given. The summary of results should give levels of statistical significance if inferential tests were done. A closing sentence should emphasize the major conclusion of the research. To fit in all this specific information, you have to become skillful at writing compressed sentences and avoiding meaningless words and phrases.

REFERENCES

Goal for References Section

All sources referenced in your article must be traceable. If your readers wish to check a source you cite, they must be able to find it without having to contact you first.

What Goes into References?

All the articles, books, etc., that you have cited must appear in your reference list. However, do not include any sources to which you have not specifically referred, even if you feel they provide "background" material.

Organization of References

Start the section on a separate page with "References" centered at the top. Then list the references alphabetically by surname (last name) of the senior (first) author. If the same person is senior author for more than one reference in your list, then the references are ordered chronologically for that person. If the same person supplies more than one reference for the same year, then the different references are labeled "a," "b," etc., in parentheses after the reference, and when such a reference is cited in text, the letter is given in addition to the year. The purpose of this organization is to make it easy for the reader to match up any citation in text with its full reference in References.

Style of References

The exact style of a given reference depends on what kind of source is being referenced. To write a reference correctly, you have to be very picky about word order, capitalization, and punctuation. There are some general rules, but the best guide is a sample of the type of reference you want to make.

Journal Articles.   Most of your references will be to journal articles. The two examples given below show how to reference single-author and multiple-author articles. In writing your reference, follow these examples, paying close attention to capitalization and punctuation. Note that only the first word of an article title is capitalized, whereas for the journal name all important words are capitalized. Author(s), title, and journal information are separated from one another by periods. The name of the journal and the volume are underlined. At the end of each reference, the page numbers for the whole article are given. An older referencing system abbreviated journal names to save space, but most journals are giving up on that because there seemed to be no agreement on what abbreviations to use.

```
Doob, A. N., and MacDonald, E. G. Television view-
    ing and the fear of victimization: Is the rela-
    tionship causal? Journal of Personality and
    Social Psychology, 1979, 37, 170-179.
Haas, K. Verbal conditioning of affective
    responses. Journal of General Psychology,
    1962, 67, 319-322.
```

Popular Magazines. You usually won't be referencing articles in popular magazines since they are not a verifiable source of scientific information. If you do need to reference a popular source, you will often find that there is no volume number and that the magazine does not follow the convenient journal policies of numbering pages in order throughout an entire year and of keeping all the pages in an article consecutive. Therefore references to popular magazines must also indicate which issue of a given year of publication is being cited. The following is an example of referencing a popular source.

```
Gerbner, G., and Gross, L. The scary world of TV's
    heavy viewer. Psychology Today, April, 1976,
    pp. 41-45 (& 89).
```

Books. Books are identified by author, title, publisher, and year. As for a journal article, only the first word of the book title is capitalized. Unlike the title of a journal article, the book title itself is underlined. The necessary publisher information includes the city of publication, the name of the publisher, and the year of publication. If the city of publication is not a major one (like New York, London, or San Francisco) then its location must be further identified, as in the following example.

```
Nagel, S. S. The legal process from a behavioral
    perspective. Homewood, Ill.: Dorsey Press,
    1969.
```

A Chapter in a Book. Some books are collections of works by different authors. In this case you want both to reference the person who actually wrote the information you cite and to tell in what book to locate it. The form of reference you need is about what you would expect from the combination of a journal reference and a book reference.

```
Latané, B., and Darley, J. M. Some determinants of
    bystander intervention in emergencies. In J.
    Macaulay and L. Berkowitz (eds.), Altruism and
    helping behavior: Social psychological
    studies of some antecedents and consequences.
    New York: Academic Press, 1970, pp. 13-27.
```

Technical Reports. There are some reports that have "semipublished" status. They are issued by organizations, such as a university or government agency, and have limited circulation. Enough information must be given about them so that a reader can contact the organization and learn the whereabouts of a copy. If a report comes from a government agency, it will often have an identifying number, which must be included in the reference. The following are a couple of examples of references to technical reports.

```
Byrne, D., and Lamberth, J. The effects of erotic
    stimuli on arousal, emotional responses, and
    subsequent behavior (Technical Report of the
    Commission on Obscenity and Pornography, Vol.
    8). Washington, D.C.: U.S. Government Printing
    Office, 1971.
Timmons, W. M. Decisions and attitudes as out-
    comes of the discussion of a social problem
    (Teachers College, Contributions to Educa-
    tion, No. 777). New York: Bureau of Publica-
    tion, Columbia University, 1939.
```

No Personal Author. Constructing a clear reference without a personal author to cite can be inconvenient, if not an outright mess. If the "author" is an agency or association, then the reference will be alphabetized according to the first significant word of the association's name. As mentioned earlier in this chapter, the following authorless book is a good one to have when preparing articles in the social science area.

> American Psychological Association. Publication
> Manual, 2nd ed. Washington: American Psy-
> chological Association, 1974.

If no person or organization is willing to be blamed for the work, then the title moves into "author position," and the reference is alphabetized by the first significant word of the title.

Theses. Doctoral and masters theses are usually unpublished, but the universities for which they were written have bound copies. Also, most doctoral theses are available through University Microfilms in Ann Arbor, Michigan, but they are very expensive. It is better not to refer to theses unless absolutely necessary since your readers will have difficulty obtaining the material. The form of the reference is simple.

> Haas, K. The conditioning of affective verbal
> responses. Unpublished masters thesis,
> Pennsylvania State University, 1955.

Unpublished Sources

It is unfair to the reader to refer important points to sources that can't be traced. Many journals, if they allow such references at all, will insist that they be separated from the reference list proper and appear as numbered "Reference Notes." It is more acceptable to reference such a source when you wish to give someone credit for an idea than to use it as a source of "hard facts." Such "evidence" becomes a lot less convincing for the readers when they find they can't trace it. In the following paragraphs are some examples of unpublished sources you may wish to reference.

To reference a *book in preparation,* you simply follow the author and title with "Book in preparation" and the year. For example, the current book in manuscript form would be referenced as follows (Saslow, Note 1):

> 1. Saslow, C. A. Basic research methods in the
> social sciences. Book in preparation, 1979.

In addition to identifying the speakers and the title of a *talk,* you have to specify the association at which the paper was presented, the location of the meeting, and the month and year (Russell *et al.,* Note 2).

> 2. Russell, C., Waller, A., James, A., and Ames, E.Maternal influence on infants' play with sex-stereotyped toys. Paper presented at the annual meeting of the Western Psychological Association, San Francisco, April, 1978.

When citing a *personal communication,* you must give as exact a date as possible. Such citations should be very rare (Saslow, Note 3).

> 3. Saslow, C. A. Personal communication, Aug. 1, 1979.

Check Your References Section Carefully

Journal editors won't rewrite your References for you. If your article is accepted, they'll simply write you a brusque note telling you to correct your references. Even more serious, no one is going to check the accuracy of your references. If your article is published with an incorrect reference, it won't be possible for readers to trace your citations even if your original intentions were honest. At a future date an inaccuracy may cause serious problems for someone trying to locate a particular piece of information.

GUIDELINES FOR EVALUATING THE OVERALL FORM OF AN ARTICLE

Before delving into the article itself, your reviewer or grader will check it over to see that it has the proper overall organization and that the title, abstract, and references are appropriate. The following are some of the guidelines they'll use when doing an evaluation.

1. Is the title informative and of proper length?
   a. Is the major IV mentioned?
   b. Is the major DV mentioned?
   c. Is the type of subject mentioned or implied?
   d. Is there enough information so that a reader could decide whether or not to look further at the article?
   e. Is it 12 to 15 words in length?
2. Are the authors' names, affiliations, and other relevant information given with the title?

3. Does the abstract contain sufficient information about the research to interest potential readers and to serve as a brief record?

   a. Is the abstract a single paragraph 150 to 175 words in length?

   b. Is the major research problem clearly stated?

   c. Is enough said about the method so that a reader can guess how the experiment was done?

   d. Is enough said about the analysis of results so that a reader knows what the significant findings were?

   e. Is the major conclusion of the research clear?

   f. Are the type and number of subjects stated?

4. Do the Introduction, Method, Results, and Discussion sections follow in that order, each section marked off with a centered heading?

5. Is the Reference section complete?

   a. Does it start on a new page with a centered heading?

   b. Does it include an entry for every source mentioned in the article?

   c. Is it alphabetized by the last name of the senior author?

   d. Are the citations in proper format?

   e. Are any citations listed that are not specifically referenced at some point in the article?

SUGGESTED EXERCISES

for FINISHING YOUR ARTICLE

1. Put as much as is appropriate of the following information into proper format for a title page for a manuscript.

   A study was done using an IV consisting of four different types of Relaxation Training Therapy. The DVs measured were both general test anxiety and performance under stress. College students were used as subjects. The authors were John Michael Stromm and Roger T. Tiddle; Tiddle was the person who supervised the project. At the time they did the study they were both at Ohio State University, but since that time Tiddle has moved to Western Reserve. Marianne Simms, a student, helped significantly with the running of the study. A grant for doing the research came from Alto Medical Foundation.

2. Here are some titles of published articles. Rank them from most to least informative. Then critique each of them for information content.

   The effect of rearing conditions on behavior (Harlow and Harlow, 1962).

   Breed differences in the dog's emotional behavior (Mahut, 1958).

   An experimental study of early childhood memory (Burtt, 1930).

   Sex differences in problem solving as a function of role appropriateness of the problem content (Milton, 1959).

   Postdecision dissonance at post time (Knox and Inkster, 1968).

3. Here is an abstract of an article. Evaluate it in terms of how well it communicates the research to you and whether any vital information has been left out.

(Williams, J. E. and Bennett, S. M. The definition of sex stereotypes via the Adjective Check List. *Sex Roles: A Journal of Research,* 1975, **1**, 327.)

The Adjective Check List (ACL) was employed in the empirical definition of male and female stereotypes by 50 male and 50 female college student subjects. Judgments by male and female subjects correlated highly. There were 33 male adjectives and 30 female adjectives on which at least 75% of both sexes agreed. With a 60% agreement criterion, there were 98 male and 83 female adjectives. Both male and female stereotypes were treated as hypothetical persons and were shown to be highly deviant on standard ACL norms, with the male stereotype being more deviant and perhaps more "disturbed" than the female stereotype. It was concluded that the ACL is a promising method for the definition and study of sex stereotypes.*

4. For each of the following statements, indicate whether it is true for titles (T), abstracts (A), both (B), or neither (N).

_____ Maximum length is 12–15 words.

_____ The section is broken into several paragraphs.

_____ Past tense is preferable.

_____ Abbreviations defined in other sections of the paper can be used without redefinition.

_____ IV, DV, and type of subject should be given.

_____ The number of subjects must be mentioned.

_____ The length is between 200 and 250 words.

_____ Should be able to stand by itself without the rest of the article.

5. Correct all the errors in the following reference list.

REFERENCES

Berkowitz, L., and Daniels, Leroy R., Responsibility and Dependency. Journal of abnormal and social psychology. 1963, 66, 429-436.

Wispé, L. G. Positive forms of social behavior: An overview, <u>Journal of Social Issues</u>, 28, 1972, pp. 1-19.

Freedman, J. L., Carlsmith, J. M., and D. O. Sears. <u>Social psychology</u>. Englewood Cliffs, N.J., Prentice-Hall, 1970.

Turner, R. G. <u>Self-Monitoring and the Generation of Humor</u>. Paper presented at the annual W.P.A. meeting, San Francisco, 1978.

---

*Reprinted by permission of Plenum Press (copyright © 1975) and John Williams.

6. Indicate whether the following statements about References are true or false.

_____ A References section includes background material in addition to studies specifically cited in text.

_____ The list of references is organized alphabetically by the surnames of the senior authors.

_____ A period is used between the authors' names and the title of the article, but a comma separates the title from the journal name.

_____ Article titles are underlined; book titles are not.

_____ References to talks and to personal communications are commonly accepted in reference lists.

_____ Only the first letter in a title is capitalized (unless the title has a colon.)

SECTION 8: GIVING A TALK

WHAT CAN YOU ACCOMPLISH IN TEN TO FIFTEEN MINUTES?

Unless your study is very simple and your results straightforward, you won't be able to give as complete a presentation of your research in a talk as you can in an article. Not only is your time limited, but a talk does not allow individual members of the audience to slow down the rate of information presentation or to back up for another look at something that confuses them. Three to five major points are about all your listeners will be able to retain from a short talk. You need to decide what your most important points are and to emphasize them and repeat them. Your audience should leave the talk with an impression of the nature of your major findings and their importance or usefulness. Details of methodology and statistical analysis should be played down; only enough information need be given to convince your listeners that the research was carried out in a competent manner and that the results are believable. And remember, it never hurts to make your talk interesting.

ORGANIZING A TALK

In contrast to a journal article, a talk follows no set format. Many speakers do use the same ordering of information as for an article, but this can create problems. A journal article, for instance, leaves Results and Discussion to the end. If you start to run out of time, as happens to many speakers, the most important things about your research will get short-changed. One way to avoid this difficulty is to state your major findings at the beginning of your talk and follow them with the evidence backing up your conclusions. Your listeners then will have some framework into which to fit the information you subsequently give them about methodology, results, and statistical analysis. If you just start spouting a lot of details without your listeners' knowing where you are heading, you may lose your audience before you get to the punch line. At the end of the talk, you can again state your major findings, thereby increasing the chances that your listeners will remember the implications of your study.

One possible organization for a talk is given in Table 8.3. Deciding exactly what specific information to include in such an outline for your talk is like getting ready for a back-packing trip. You lay out everything that is "essential" and then throw half of it away; otherwise, your pack will be too heavy to carry. If you leave too much "baggage" in your talk, you'll have to race through it. The worth of a talk is measured in what the audience carries away, not what the speaker puts out.

Table 8.3 Suggested Outline for a Talk

---

1. What problem were you investigating?
2. Why is this problem of interest?
3. What overall answer do you think you found to the problem?
4. How did you go about finding an answer?
5. What is your evidence that your answer to the problem is the best one?
6. What, again, do you think is the best answer to the problem?
7. What implications for the future does your answer suggest?

PREPARING YOUR VISUAL AIDS

Characteristics of Good Visual Aids

Most scientific talks are accompanied either by slides or by handouts. These visual aids usually present the results in tables or graphs. Sometimes they may be used to illustrate some special detail of equipment or experimental setting. They have to be planned well ahead of time so that you can build your talk around them. If you use handouts, you'll have to estimate audience size to be sure you'll have enough. Somewhere on the handout should be the title of the talk, the speaker's name, and the speaker's affiliation. Handouts are often saved, and this information will make them more useful. If you use slides, you'll need to be sure that appropriate projection equipment will be available.

When you are preparing a table or a graph to accompany a talk, two things are important: (1) *keep it simple,* and (2) *be sure it can stand by itself* without a lot of explanation. A complicated table of numbers with several rows and columns, an incomplete title, and undecipherable abbreviations is more trouble for the audience to figure out than it is worth. When the speaker spends five seconds on the table and then changes the slide to something else, little information of any use has been conveyed. A graph with many lines and symbols, axes labeled in abbreviations (if labeled at all), a long caption, and no key to the symbols becomes an exercise in understanding abstract art. Even when the table or graph is printed in a handout, it should be kept simple. After all, you probably are not going to give your listeners very long to puzzle over it before you move on.

TABLES

Tables and figures appropriate for an article may not work for a talk without some revision. For example, Table 8.1 (p. 339) contains means and standard deviations for three DVs measured on four groups. There is too much information in this table to make a dramatic presentation in a talk of the finding that three different relaxation procedures all produced the same amount of reduction of anxiety test scores. In Table 8.4, only the means for the two anxiety DVs are reported. These means are rounded back to three places to further reduce numbers in the table. The investigator has calculated the pre-to-post change in mean score for one of the DVs instead of forcing the audience to do the calculation in their heads. Some of the abbreviations are spelled out. This simplified table is much more suited to presentation in a talk.

Table 8.4 Means of Anxiety Test Scores for Four Groups

| | | *Group (N = 10)* | | |
Test		*EMG and Systematic Desensitization*	*EMG Feedback*	*Systematic Desensitization*	*No Treatment*
Suinn Anxiety Behavior Scale	pre	152	157	169	152
	post	109	116	128	168
	change	− 43	− 41	− 41	+ 16
Test Anxiety Scale (posttest only)		20.6	20.7	24.4	27.7

About Your Art Work

Since tables and graphs contain verbal information, the letters you use on your slides must be large enough to be read even at a considerable distance from the screen. This is another reason for not cramming too many numbers into a table or too many lines onto a graph. If your table is typed, be sure the ribbon in the typewriter is fresh and the numbers are well spaced on the table. Decide whether you want your audience to read the numbers in the table across or down, and space your rows and columns of numbers accordingly. Lettering on graphs is often too small, especially if the graph is drawn large and the verbal information typed in regular-sized type. Use extra-large type (¼ inch), or if large-sized type is not available and you have limited skill at hand lettering, get some of the rub-on letters that come in large sheets. Be sure the symbols on the graph are large and distinct. It is embarrassing to be talking about the difference between the results represented by "filled dots" and those represented by "open dots" when your audience can't distinguish which is which.

DELIVERY OF YOUR TALK

Don't Read It

If you are not familiar with giving talks, the temptation may be to write it out ahead of time and then read it. This approach has many disadvantages. Unless the speaker is an actor skilled at reading from a script, listening to a talk that is read is particularly boring. Too much information is given monotonously at too rapid a rate, since the speaker is not letting the reactions of the audience set the pace. Try making a tape of a short speech and compare the result with giving it in person to an audience. You'll find that on the tape you'll "save" one-third to one-half the time. A talk should be more like conversation. You have to look at your audience now and then for the nonverbal cues that mean they are following your reasoning.

Talk from a Good Set of Notes

If you are fearful of "drying up," you can write out some key sentences to read verbatim at the appropriate places in the talk. You may feel more comfortable writing out your opening and closing statements. Then you can be sure they will come out exactly as you want them. At other places in the talk, when you have a particularly important point to make, you may also want to have it written out.

Though not written out in full, all the details you want to bring up in the order you want to mention them should be in your notes. Work out this order ahead of time and stick to it. When a speaker starts skipping back and forth or "remembers" stray bits of information left out of the original notes, the talk begins to sound very disorganized, and the audience may stop trying to follow such a grasshopper presentation. Seeing your audience's reaction, you may want to spend more or less time on a particular point, but don't mess around with your organization.

If you are using visual aids, reference them at the appropriate places in your notes. Circle each reference or put it in a different color so you won't forget to direct your audience to look at a particular graph or table before you begin talking about it.

Control Your Timing

To be sure that you don't run overtime, at several points in your notes write the time at which you should reach that part of your talk. Then you can see the need to speed up or slow down before they start pushing you off the stage.

An aid to controlling your timing is to include removable sections in your notes. Such sections contain information you can include if you have time or skip if time is running short. Mark them so that they are distinct, and be sure that if they are skipped the continuity of the talk won't be destroyed. An "expendable," for example, might be an expanded description of your subjects. Beyond pointing out that they were "college students," you might describe the class from which they were selected and the general type of college—all relevant information, provided there is time. You may even have some of your visual aids marked in your notes as expendables.

Relax and Talk to Your Audience

There is something about talking to a mass of people that can daunt even the most confirmed chatterbox. Really, the only way to get over nervousness about public speaking is to do a lot of it. The scientific reporting situation is not threatening, provided you've done your organization and preparation ahead of time. No one expects a polished performance from you; after all, those in your audience are more interested in your information than your act. And most of them have been or will be in the same boat. You can expect a good deal of sympathy from your listeners for any awkwardness in delivery. As a rule, researchers are not among the world's most dynamic speakers, and your audience will not expect to be entertained. Your goal is to tell a coherent story and to convey a reasonable amount of information.

It often helps in your delivery if you pick one or two persons in the audience to look at occasionally while giving your talk. Human speech, even when in the form of a monologue, is very dependent on feedback from listeners. You literally need your audience if you are to keep going. Looking at a couple of responsive audience members located in different parts of the room will greatly improve the delivery of a talk. Like Hans the horse, we humans need all the nonverbal encouragement we can get to go on talking. Looking at audience members will also help control pacing, slowing you down to a more reasonable rate of presentation.

Try Your Talk Out Beforehand

Find a friend who is intelligent but not particularly knowledgeable about your research, and who is willing to listen when you try out your talk. Then ask your friend to summarize for you what you have said, to tell you what he or she now understands about your research. From this kind of feedback you can discover what points you meant to make that aren't being given sufficient emphasis and what confusions your presentation may leave in the minds of your audience. Trying a talk out in this way also gives you an idea of the actual length of your presentation. If a friend isn't available, try recording your talk and then listening to it, but remember that in doing so you are likely to underestimate the real length of the talk.

Explaining your research to a friend can also be useful at an earlier stage of planning a talk. Try to explain your research in conversation. When you answer your friend's questions as she or he attempts to understand your research, you can get a feel for what ideas must be included and what is an optimal organization.

Don't Distract Your Audience

All of us have mannerisms that may become more pronounced when we are nervous. Some of them can be very distracting to an audience. Verbal "tics" like "you know" and undecipherable grunting can make a talk hard to follow. Pacing around, rocking back and forth, and making frequent mysterious gestures may also be distracting. Often a speaker is unaware of these automatic behaviors. Practicing beforehand and placing a confederate in the audience are ways of obtaining feedback about which of your personal mannerisms are getting out of hand and need to be worked on. The goal is not to turn you into a professional orator but to modify anything that may be in the way of getting your message across.

One distraction that is easy to control is your appearance. If your audience can remember what you looked like, they may not be able to remember what you said. A speaker with thong sandals that make an audible "slap" as he paces back and forth may impress the audience more with his rhythm than with his logic. A lady whose every gesture at a slide of her results exposes several inches of black lace slip may have a hard time getting the audience to pay attention to her data. (Save the clothes that express your individuality for the cocktail hour.)

Speak Up

If you can't be heard, all your organization and practice will go to waste. Your voice sounds different to you than to anyone else. To you it sounds both louder in volume and lower in pitch than it actually is. In addition, acoustical problems in a room or interfering noises may mask different voices differently. Audience behaviors (yawning, scratching, squirming, cupping ears) serve as cues to how well your voice is carrying. A confederate seated in the back row of the room ready to signal you to increase volume is a more reliable guide. If you are doubtful, you can always stop and ask the people in the back row if they can hear you.

DEALING WITH QUESTIONS AND INTERRUPTIONS

You may feel you can handle the talk O.K. but are concerned about "thinking on your feet" in response to questions. Most questions will be simple inquiries for clarification, which are easily dealt with. Be sure, however, that you understand the question before answering. If there is any doubt, paraphrase or repeat the question and get the person's agreement that that *is* what he is asking before proceeding.

Paraphrasing is also a way to gain yourself a little bit of time while organizing your answer. You do sometimes encounter hostile and persistent questioners, but don't let them fluster you. When you keep your cool, they will quickly lose audience sympathy. If there is a question you can't or don't wish to answer at the moment, simply say you want to think about it and will talk to the person after the meeting. It's better to say you don't know or want to think about something than to get yourself into a debate. Handle interruptions in your talk similarly. Tell the person that the answer is coming later in the talk or that you'll answer the question at the end. Since your presentation was allotted a certain amount of time on the program, you are as responsible as the person running the meeting for cutting off questions. It's only fair to let the next speaker start on time.

GIVING AN IMPRESSION OF COMPETENCE

There are several pieces of information that will be looked for in any research talk. Their absence will suggest to the audience that the speaker is unaware of their importance or has ignored them completely in the research. The species of the subjects and any relevant subject characteristics are necessary for the audience to know how far the results can be generalized. The number of subjects studied and the way they were assigned to experimental conditions is also important. If the design of the study is at all complicated, you should be entirely clear about what was done with each experimental group. A diagram of the design may be necessary. If the study had only a few subjects, the duration of their training and the number of times they were observed should be emphasized so that your audience has an idea of the amount of data actually collected. If the procedures of testing are at all complicated, in either their ordering or their timing, they should be clearly spelled out. The audience should have no doubt about how the DV measures were obtained. Finally, the type of inferential statistics used and the statistical significance of the results should be explicitly mentioned. Any methodological problem that might affect interpretation of your results should be brought up in order to assure your audience that you are intelligently self-critical about your work. If these points are not adequately covered in your talk, don't be surprised if you get questions.

GUIDELINES FOR EVALUATING A TALK

One way to get ideas for your own presentation is to listen critically to other people's talks. You'll soon learn what pitfalls to avoid. A common problem is that the speaker uses incomplete explanations or unfamiliar expressions, apparently assuming that the audience already knows a great deal about the research. Another frequent difficulty is that the speaker crams too much information into the talk. These and other problems interfere with effective communication. Here is a list of questions you could use for evaluating a talk.

1. What was (were) the speaker's major finding(s) or conclusion(s)? (They should have been mentioned at least twice.)

2. Were you given enough evidence to have faith in the conclusions?

   a. Did the speaker present enough of the method so that you understand approximately what was done?

   b. Were the results presented in a form you could readily grasp?

   c. Did the speaker report the statistical analyses necessary to establish that the results weren't due to chance factors?

   d. Did the speaker make a clear, logical argument as to why the results supported the conclusions?

3. Did the speaker give you the information that would allow you to generalize from the results? Some examples follow.

   a. Type and number of subjects and other subject characteristics relevant to the research.

   b. Duration of training of the subjects.

   c. Any peculiar conditions of the setting of the experiment that might not be easily reproducible elsewhere.

   d. Information about potential Experimenter Bias or Subject Attitude effects.

4. Did the speaker relate the findings to any wider field of research or application?

5. Did the speaker lose you at some point by any of the following?

   a. Using jargon or self-defined terms

   b. Drowning you in detail

   c. Presenting information too rapidly

   d. Failing to emphasize the important points and distinguish them clearly from less important information

   e. Distracting you with personal mannerisms

6. Was the talk interesting?

SUGGESTED EXERCISES

for GIVING A TALK

1. Here are some sample audience questions. For each one, discuss how you would answer it.

   a. "Isn't it true that studies on sex differences are inherently discriminatory and should not be done at all?" (You have just finished your paper on "Sex Differences in College Students on a Verbal Learning Task," there are 39 seconds left before the next speaker's turn, and three other audience hands are raised.)

   b. "What was the sample size of your control group?" (You did mention this. You are afraid that a questioner who missed this information may also have missed your design, which required that the experimental and control groups have equal sample sizes.)

c. "Wouldn't the Whosis and Whatsis study completely disprove your results?" (You've never heard of the blasted study. Where was it published? In the Journal of Irreproducible Results?)

d. "Doesn't your work suggest that young children would develop better if separated from their mothers at birth and placed in a child-care center?" (You've just finished a paper on "Comparison of Mother versus Peer Group Influences on the Social Behavior of Infant Squirrel Monkeys.")

e. "Why didn't you do an Analysis of Covariance on these results?" (You don't know why; you aren't familiar with this statistical procedure.)

f. "Why didn't you do an Analysis of Variance on these data?" (Your DV measures were ordinal.)

g. "What kind of animal did you do this study on anyway?" (You forgot to mention this. Yipe!)

2. Table 8.5 contains data from a cross-cultural survey of sex differences in child-rearing practices. How might you modify this table or change it into a graph in order to make it a good visual aid for a talk? Explain the changes you would make.

Table 8.5 Ratings of Cultures for Sex Differences on Five Variables of Childhood Socialization Pressure

Variable	Number of Cultures	Both Judges Agree in Rating the Variable Higher in		One Judge Rates No Difference; One Rates the Variable Higher in		Percentage of Cultures with Evidence of Sex Difference in Direction of		
		Girls	Boys	Girls	Boys	Girls	Boys	Neither
Nurturance	33	17	0	10	0	82	0	18
Obedience	69	6	0	18	2	35	3	62
Responsibility	84	25	2	26	7	61	11	28
Achievement	31	0	17	1	10	3	87	10
Self-reliance	82	0	64	0	6	0	85	15

From Barry, Bacon, and Child (1957): A cross-cultural survey of some sex differences in socialization. Reprinted by permission of the American Psychological Association (copyright © 1957) and H. Barry, III.

3. Consider the study on the effects of preschool education and nutrition on the IQs of children in Columbia, as described on p. 165. Make notes for a short talk on this study. Decide what visual aids you would want.

chapter 9

planning your own research project

This chapter is intended for people who have little or no experience doing research. It is aimed at those of you who want to attempt a first, relatively small-scale, social science research project. You may already be a professional, such as a businessman, social worker, therapist, or teacher, and feel that you need more valid information on which to base a decision. Or you may be a student, either an undergraduate who is ready to carry out independent research or a graduate student needing to plan research for a thesis. Or you just may be insatiably curious.

Since the main objective of this chapter is production of an actual research proposal, there are no behavioral objectives or sample test questions listed after the sections. When appropriate, there will be some suggested exercises to help you check whether you understand the new information. By this point in the book, however, you have mastered the basic skills necessary to design research. The purpose of this chapter is to suggest a series of steps that will help you in planning your own study.

SECTION 1: FINDING A RESEARCH QUESTION

FIRST APPROXIMATION

Thinking of a researchable question is usually the hardest step. For those who have been doing research, new questions often arise out of previous work. But where does a beginner start? This problem can be especially irksome if some external force, such as a course requirement or a graduate program, is what is galvanizing you into action as a fledgling researcher.

Your starting point might be a definite question that arises from your professional interests or stems from something you've heard in a class or run across in your studies. More likely, you will start from a general area of interest. For example, in an undergraduate class in research methods, one student project began with several students' deciding they were "interested in investigating care of the aged." Another group of students were intrigued with "the factors determining how people perceive one another," something that had been discussed in their Social Psychology class. Still other students decided they were interested in the possibility that training and practice in one of the verbal relaxation techniques could be used to reduce anxiety while taking a test. All rather vague ideas to begin with, they nonetheless represent a place to start.

GO TO THE LIBRARY

When you have identified a general question or an area of interest, the next step is to read current research in that area. You can use one of the abstracting services mentioned in Chapter 8, Section 7, to help locate articles. Or if you know the journals that are publishing the kind of research you are interested in, going through the last few years of titles may turn up studies that are relevant. Even "facts" in your textbooks may serve as points of departure. Tracing facts to their original source may reveal that the evidence they rest on is weaker than you would like and may suggest new experiments to do. Not only can library research help you formulate a researchable question; it also keeps you from unnecessarily repeating work that has already been done. The more reading you do, the more likely your research question will be a good one and its answer will contribute information useful to you and to others.

DECIDING ON A RESEARCH QUESTION

Correcting Errors

Suppose that in your reading you find an experiment relevant to your initial interest, but you feel the research was not well done. Perhaps a Confounding Variable was overlooked. Perhaps the research study had unreasonable amounts of random error. The students interested in effects of relaxation techniques, for example, became bothered by the realization that researchers in the area paid little attention to the possibility of Experimenter Bias and Subject Attitude effects on results. This started them thinking about doing an experiment where these factors were adequately controlled. Detecting errors in earlier research studies is one source of ideas for new research.

Replicating Unusual Findings

Sometimes when doing background reading in your area of interest, you may come across an experiment whose results are unusual or surprising. Perhaps you have other information that makes you feel the results are unlikely or, at least, indicative of a special case. In this situation, you might want to replicate the original experiment to see whether you can confirm its results. After all, rejection of the null hypothesis in research is probabilistic rather than absolute. Results "significant at the

.05 level'' still might represent a chance occurrence. Or if you feel the results are real, you still may wonder whether they are limited to a specific context. For instance, the Crancer *et al.* (1969) study showed little effect of marijuana on driving. However, if you thought that this drug affected judgment rather than skill, you might wonder about limiting the testing to a driving simulator. Concerns such as these could lead you to repeat an experiment in a different situation or with different subjects to test generalizability of the results.

Seeing Whether a Correlation Represents a Cause-Effect Relationship

Another origin of an experimental research question may be the existence of a correlation between two variables. The researchers discovering a correlation may feel (and may sometimes be so injudicious as to say) that one of the variables is causing the changes seen in the other. However, you as a knowledgeable research consumer realize that a correlation cannot safely be interpreted this way. You might decide to set up an experiment in which you manipulate one of the variables as an IV to see if the relationship is really causal. Or you may think of another variable that is possibly responsible for the changes seen in both correlated variables. For example, Doob and MacDonald (1979) felt that a correlation that had been reported between amount of TV watching and degree of fear of violence might represent the action of yet another variable and not, as earlier researchers had concluded, a harmful effect of TV watching itself. Accordingly, they planned a study that compared neighborhoods with high and low rates of crime. They found that people in the low-crime neighborhoods both watch TV less and fear violence less than do people in the high-crime neighborhoods. However, within each type of neighborhood there was relatively little correlation between amount of TV viewing and fear of violence. From their research it appears that the people who are more likely to experience violence fear it more, no matter what their TV viewing habits. The report of a correlation between two variables is often the starting point for a number of further observational and experimental studies trying to pin down the reason for the correlation.

Testing a Theory (Basic Research)

If you are a novice researcher, it's unlikely that you have a full-fledged theory of your own. However, there are a lot of proposed theories about human behavior in the literature that may lead you to hypotheses of your own. For instance, the group of students interested in ''how people perceive one another'' decided to base their research on ''attribution theory,'' a theory stating that behavioral acts that are not in agreement with the stereotype of a person are likely to be attributed to that person's ''personality,'' whereas those acts that *are* in accord with a stereotype are seen as being caused by the situation the person is in. Combining this attribution theory with an interest in male/female roles, the students arrived at their specific research question. They speculated that since males are expected to be aggressive and assertive and females are not, subjects viewing a situation in which a person responds with anger will attribute the anger to the irritations of the situation if the person is male but to an "aggressive personality" if the person is female. Furthermore, the students suspected that the female's anger would be judged as of greater magnitude. Any good theory is capable of giving rise to many such testable research questions or hypotheses.

Checking Out a Practical Application (Applied Research)

In applied research the origin of the research question is a practical concern; the researchers want to test in a real situation whether something works or not. For example, an applied research project conceived by some undergraduate men investigated the arrangement of rear brake lights on a car that would result in the fastest foot-braking response. (The motivation for this research question was their own interest in cars combined with the demand of their professor that they design and carry out independent research.) Similar kinds of research are carried out regularly in industrial laboratories to improve machines that are used by humans.

FORMULATING YOUR RESEARCH HYPOTHESIS

Having decided on a research question, you need to reword it into a specific, testable hypothesis. This hypothesis must be stated in such a way that it is capable of being disproved if it is wrong. Furthermore, it should be specific enough to give you guidance in your operational definition of variables. The students interested in relaxation techniques hypothesized that when care was taken to create positive subject attitudes about success at relaxing, relatively unguided practice at relaxing would be as effective in reducing test anxiety as use of a specific verbal relaxation technique. Researchers interested in the effects on driving of drugs might hypothesize that marijuana effects, absent in the driving simulator, would show up when driving was assessed by performance in a "driving rodeo" in which an actual car is piloted around a difficult course under time pressure. Doob and MacDonald (1979) hypothesized that the correlation reported between the amount of TV viewing time and fear of violence would not be found if the factor of actual rates of violence occurring in a neighborhood were controlled. The students investigating attribution theory hypothesized that both male and female subjects would be inclined to attribute an outburst of anger to "personality" if the angry person were female and to "demands of the situation" if the person were male. The students interested in brake-light design hypothesized that an arrangement in which the brake light and taillight were side by side would result in faster response than when braking was signaled by a change in the intensity for a single taillight. These different hypotheses all share the common feature, necessary to scientific research, that they can be disproved if they are not accurate statements of how things really work.

RECAPITULATION

for FINDING A RESEARCH QUESTION

For a beginning researcher the starting point for developing a research question may be simply identifying a general area of interest. Reading the current research literature in this general area and talking, when possible, to others doing research in the area is the first step in arriving at a researchable question that has not yet been answered by other investigators. There are many sources of ideas for social science research. Sometimes an investigation may be sparked by discovering an obvious error in a previous study. In other cases results may be so unusual or contrary to other findings that the research needs replication. A correlation that has been reported between two variables may suggest further observational or experimental research to determine whether there is an underlying causal relationship between the variables. Theories about human behavior proposed by others may suggest a hypothesis that you can test. Such basic research is often fascinating, because there is usually a larger body of research results into which you can fit your own. Your professional or personal interests may be the source of a practical question that you can answer through applied research. Whatever you decide on for a research question, you will then have to word it as a specific research hypothesis that is capable of being confirmed or disproved by your research.

SUGGESTED EXERCISES

for FINDING A RESEARCH QUESTION

1. Read a research article in your area of interest. Given the results of this study, decide what research question it would next be of interest to answer. From this question derive a specific testable hypothesis.

2. From your everyday experience with your fellow humans, think of an applied or basic research question one might ask about human behavior. Then try to come up with a testable hypothesis based on this question.

SECTION 2: INITIAL PLANNING FOR YOUR RESEARCH

QUESTIONS TO ANSWER IN PRELIMINARY PLANNING

What Kind of Study Do You Want to Do?

Once you have formed your research question, the next decision you make concerns the kind of study that will give you the best answer. Is your question one that can be answered by *observational research*, or do you want to establish a cause-effect relationship through an *experimental study?* Are you going to manipulate variables, or are you going to be able only to observe variables without exerting any control over them? In the latter case, you may want to do a *correlational study,* measuring a number of things about your subjects to see what variables tend to change together. Along with picking the kind of study, you need to decide whether your research question is best studied under controlled laboratory conditions or in a natural setting, where control of some Relevant Variables may be more difficult.

Whom Do You Want to Study?

Whom you study determines the population to which you can most safely generalize results. However, there may be practical reasons why you can't actually sample the desired population. For instance, a good deal of animal research is done to answer questions really posed about human functioning when the research on humans would involve risky or time-consuming procedures. Also, some kinds of human subjects are more readily available than others. The wealth of research with college student subjects has more to do with their availability than their representativeness of humans in general. For some research questions, the use of these specialized populations probably does not interfere much with generalizing results.

What DVs Do You Want to Study?

In developing your research question, you have specified in general terms what you want to observe about your subjects. However, now you need to think about how you are going to make the observations and what kind of measurement scale you will use. Furthermore, there may be some additional DVs you can measure that will greatly increase the information obtained from your research with relatively little increase in the time it takes you to do the study.

For example, the students studying "person perception" needed to find some way of having their subjects describe an individual's personality. They could just ask each subject for a verbal description, but that might produce such a variety of answers that it would be impossible to compare them. These students decided to go back to the research literature and see how other investigators in the same area had measured this DV.

At this point in the planning of most research projects, DV measures may not yet be completely operationally defined. However, you should have enough of an idea about what you are going to measure so that you can begin to think about research design and even consider the eventual statistical analyses you will need to do.

What IVs Do You Want to Use?

Your major IV, of course, is stated in general terms in your research question. Now you have to think about exactly how you are going to define that IV—in particular, about how many levels you are going to investigate and how you intend to create each level. To specify how you are going to create the IV levels, you have to decide whether you are going to treat your IV as a Non-Subject or a Subject IV. There may also be some additional IVs you would be interested in including in the research, and you need to define these as well.

For example, the major IV contemplated for the "person perception" study was the sex of an "angry person" in a group debate viewed by the subjects. It was defined as a Non-Subject IV with two levels. The student researchers decided that the Subject IV of sex of the subjects judging the angry person's personality should also be studied. Other possible IVs were discussed, such as whether the group debate should be presented live or on video tape and whether the sex ratios of the people in the group debate should be varied. It was decided to hold these variables constant in order to avoid having too complicated an experiment.

After you have tentatively identified the number of IVs, specified the probable number of levels of each you want to investigate, and decided whether you will be operationally defining the IVs as Subject or Non-Subject, you can start thinking about the design of your research project.

What Design Do You Want to Use?

With your IVs and DVs tentatively identified, you can begin constructing your design. Since it is often possible to use more than one design to answer a given research question, you have to make some choices. Do you want to use your Non-Subject IV(s) Between- or Within-Subjects? Do you want to study more than one IV and gain interaction information? If the conditions of your experiment require different groups, on what basis are you going to assign subjects? Do you want to use random assignment, or do you want to match subjects on some basis? For situations in which you are forced to use static groups or to block subjects into groups according to a Subject IV, is there some basis on which you can match subjects to ensure some equivalence of the groups? Do you want a pretest, or will pretesting create problems? Are you going to be able to round up enough subjects to fill the groups required by a complex design? If you are doing a correlational study, what sample size will you need to be likely to demonstrate relationships? If your DVs are nominal or ordinal, do inferential statistics exist that will allow you to analyze the results of a complex, multivariate design? The major factor influencing design choice, of course, is whether the design will yield the information you need. However, the final choice of a design will be partly influenced by the resources available for doing the research.

The students in the "person perception" project decided on a simple 2×2 design, which would combine the Subject IV of sex of the person viewing the debate with the Non-Subject IV of the sex of the "angry" person whose personality was to be judged. They could see no way of making the Non-Subject IV a Within-Subjects one since they planned to use the same script for the debate with an angry male as for the debate in which a female has the angry part. Anyway, they thought there would be no particular problem in achieving the group sizes they wanted since they could have a number of subjects view a video tape at the same time.

You have now made a preliminary decision about research design, and you are in a position to estimate whether the available resources will permit you to complete the research. Can you find sufficient subjects? Do you have the time and manpower to carry out the entire project as you have tentatively designed it? Is the apparatus available that you need for producing your IVs or measuring your DVs? Is it reasonable to expect your subjects to suffer through a lengthy Within-Subjects design? Practical considerations like these may lead you to modify your final decisions about design.

What Resources Will You Need?

With your tentative design in hand, you can estimate the resources that will be necessary to complete the research. If some of these are not available, it may simply not be possible to use your original design.

Can You Find Enough Subjects?

Are subjects of the type you are interested in studying willing to be studied? Are they available in adequate numbers for your design? Some multivariate experiments, especially if they involve DVs that are likely to have high levels of variability, require very large numbers of subjects to demonstrate any IV effects. Correlational designs with which the researcher hopes to establish the presence of relatively weak relationships (small correlations) also need large numbers of subjects. And observational studies whose results are to be generalized to large populations require large, unbiased samples. If your research is lengthy or requires a lot of subject time and energy, you may find it hard to acquire and keep track of subjects. The students doing the relaxation training project, for example, needed dependable subjects who would agree to come in for several training sessions, possibly over a period of weeks. Such subjects aren't easy to find. If the right kinds of subjects aren't likely to be available in sufficient numbers or are uncooperative, you will have to redesign your study or decide to do something else.

Where Are You Going to Do Your Research?

You need to specify the environment in which you wish to do the research and see whether an adequate location will be available. How much of a problem this will be depends on the particular study. The "person perception" group, for instance, could probably make do with any room large enough to allow several subjects to view a videotape and write down responses outside the visual range of one another. The project investigating optimal brakelight design, however, would have more stringent requirements. It would need a distraction-free place where equipment could be set up for however long it would take to run the individual subjects. Since the circumstances in which research is done can introduce factors that will affect the outcome of the study, your preliminary research plans must include specifying and locating the appropriate environment.

How Long Will It Take to Do the Study?

The length of time it will take to carry out a research project is often underestimated. You have to allow time for preparing the research, for finding subjects, for pretesting and orienting the subjects, for having each subject experience the treatment(s), and for observing the subjects. The "person perception" researchers, for example, would probably find that most of their time was spent in preparing acceptable videotapes. The actual running of their experiment should be relatively brief, since a whole group of subjects could be observed at the same time. However, projects in which the subjects are tested individually, such as in the brakelight experiment, or have to receive several training sessions, as in the relaxation study, would have to allow much more time for collecting data.

What Personnel Is Needed?

To estimate your personnel needs accurately, you have to start thinking about your research procedures. Since the human factor in research is often the weakest link, it is a good idea to duplicate experimenters when possible. For instance, the "person perception" sessions could be run by a single experimenter, but it would probably be better to have two persons present, one to run the equipment and the other to organize and instruct the subjects. Experiments that require individual contact with each subject, like the brakelight project or the relaxation investigation, consume great amounts of experimenter time. An accurate estimate of the time and personnel necessary to do the research may reveal that the demands of your research design greatly exceed available resources. It's better to figure this out before you begin than to find it out partway through the project.

What Equipment Will You Need?

Early in the planning stage you should start a list of needed equipment and supplies. You may have to borrow some of it; you may need to find funds to buy some of it; you may need to order some of it; and you may need to build some of it. Often waiting for orders to come or building equipment yourself can add weeks to the amount of time estimated for a research project. The "person perception" investigators, for example, would have to arrange to make their videotapes and to borrow equipment to show the tapes to their subjects. The brakelight researchers would have to design and build their own apparatus, complete with reliable timing devices. If the relaxation study used questionnaires, standardized tests, or written response sheets, arrangements would have to be made for their purchase or duplication. Before arriving at your final research plan, you have to find out whether needed supplies and equipment will be obtainable.

Are Any Special Skills Required of the Researchers?

To carry out your intended research project, you may find that you must acquire some new skills. Certainly you have to become competent at operating any equipment and understand enough about its functioning to spot problems before you lose data or alter the experiment. In any research with human subjects you must be able to put people at their ease, to explain instructions clearly, and to carry out any deceptions with a straight face. In addition, researchers often have to develop habits of orderly note-taking and accurate data-recording that may not be natural for them. Any skills such as these must be acquired before the research project begins. "Learning on the job" introduces too much error into research.

How Are You Going to Analyze the Data?

Even in preliminary stages of planning research, the eventual analysis of data has to be considered. You should be able to estimate how many measures will be taken per subject and what the scale of measurement will be. Knowing the volume and type of data your study is likely to produce should tell you whether you will be able to process the data by hand or should have access to a computer. Sometimes researchers get snowed under by masses of data that a little foresight could easily have warned them about.

THE VALUE OF PILOT WORK

Some of the questions raised in the preliminary-design and resources-inventory stages of planning research may best be answered through pilot work. At the very least any proposed research procedure should be given a dry run with subjects whose data you don't intend to use in the final analysis in order to ensure that everything is running smoothly. Such pilot testing can avoid later errors in research that may greatly weaken interpretation of your research results.

RECAPITULATION

for INITIAL PLANNING FOR YOUR RESEARCH

In arriving at a final research plan, you have to consider both how to answer your research question and how to obtain resources for your research. First you need to decide what kind of study you wish to do, whether experimental, observational, or correlational. Who you study and where you are going to do the study are also specified early in planning. Next you need to settle on what DVs and IVs are to be included in your study. In order to design an experiment, you must specify the number of IVs and decide the type and probable number of levels of each. With this information, it is possible to construct a tentative design that will yield an answer to your research question. Once you have thought of a possible design, you can begin to inventory the resources that will be necessary for carrying out the research. The kinds of resources you need to consider are the type and availability of subjects, characteristics of an optimal location for your study, the length of time necessary to complete the research, the personnel required to do the study, any equipment or supplies that may be needed, special skills necessary on the part of the researcher, and provisions for collecting and analyzing the data. If your proposed research design greatly exceeds available resources, you may have to alter your plans. On occasion, the results of pilot studies may help you make some of the final decisions about your proposed research.

SUGGESTED EXERCISES

for INITIAL PLANNING FOR YOUR RESEARCH

1. Go through preliminary planning for one of the research questions you posed in doing the exercises for Section 1.
2. Find a research article in your area of interest, and do a resource inventory for that study. As well as you can, list all the resources that you can think of that were necessary for completing that study.

SECTION 3: EVALUATING YOUR PROPOSED RESEARCH, ESPECIALLY FOR ITS ETHICS

Once you've tentatively designed your research, it's time to sit back and take a critical look at what you are proposing to do. Doing research takes time and costs money. Most research studies involve imposing on someone, usually your subjects. There are three important standpoints from which to examine your proposed research: ethics, significance of the research question, and quality of the proposed design. If your research involves the possibility of any risk, embarrassment, discomfort, or inconvenience to your subjects, you'll have to either modify these aspects or make a very strong case for the worth of your research question. You can hardly justify inconveniencing or risking your subjects, even if they agree to it, for a poorly designed study about a trivial question. Therefore, along with considering the ethics of your research, you need to look at the significance of the research question you are asking and the likelihood that your particular approach will in fact yield repeatable and usable information. If your proposed research passes these tests or can be modified so that it will pass, you're ready to put together your final research plan.

ETHICS OF DOING RESEARCH WITH HUMAN SUBJECTS

The ethical use of other human beings by social science researchers has always been an issue of concern, but it wasn't until the late 1960s that professional organizations began to publish extensive guidelines for their members and institutions began to require that researchers submit their plans to special committees for ethical evaluation. Before then, ethics was pretty much left to the individual researchers, occasionally with disastrous results. A few spectacular cases, mostly from medical research, of the clear abuse of human beings sensitized the public and disgusted many scientists. Government agencies that support medical, biological, and social science research began to insist that ethical standards be stated and followed in order for individuals and institutions to continue to receive funds. This development reinforced the growing concern of many researchers themselves about inadequate attention to the rights of subjects. No longer was the individual researcher's "need to know" considered adequate justification for any and all research practices. Nor was the argument of "benefit to humanity" sufficient to overrule the rights of individual subjects. Sometimes ethical considerations come into conflict with research procedures that are necessary to yield a clear answer to your research question. You have an obligation as a scientist to do the best possible study, but you also have obligations to your fellow humans. Balancing these obligations is not always easy, and the solution of ethical dilemmas is not always clear. Let's take a look at some of the ethical issues you may have to face when evaluating your own proposed research.

Informed Consent

One ethical principle widely accepted among social science researchers is that people should consent, usually in writing, to their inclusion in a research project. Furthermore, this consent should be obtained only after prospective subjects have adequate and accurate information about all features of the research that might be expected to influence their willingness to participate.

There may be some problems with obtaining *informed* consent. The mere fact that a subject agrees to be studied doesn't give you carte blanche to do whatever you please. Not only must you provide information about what's going to happen, but you must make certain that the subject understands. Subjects may be so impressed by your knowledge and expertise that they agree to something they wouldn't tolerate at all if it were explained in simple terms by someone less impressive. Also, some subjects, such as children or the mentally ill, may still not understand after explanation and may not be legally able to give their consent anyway.

A methodological problem with obtaining informed consent may arise in studies in which you do not want the subjects to know they are being observed. One way to reduce reactivity of measurement is to hide or disguise the observer. In many observational studies of public human behavior, the researchers don't even personally know the individuals they are studying. For example, in Chapter 1 (p. 28) we read about a study on how passing motorists reacted to a (decoy) disabled car, and in Chapter 2 (p. 61) we considered research on the effects of public reprimands on subsequent helping behavior of persons who had ignored zoo signs about feeding the bears. In these studies the subjects never consented to being observed. In other social science studies, researchers have disguised themselves as "participant observers" recording behavior in political or industrial situations, again without obtaining prior consent of the persons observed. Similarly, people receiving educational instruction or clinical therapy have sometimes been studied unawares. If you intend to conduct a research study without your subjects' knowing they are being observed, you must realize that you are taking a great deal of responsibility on yourself. In defense, you might argue that the observations will be innocuous and not apparent to your subjects. In the zoo study, however, the people observed were subjected to a certain amount of public embarrassment when reprimanded. Even in the decoy car study, the persons who stopped in busy traffic to help the supposedly disabled car ran some risk of accident when doing so. Saying that your subjects "will never know" isn't in and of itself an adequate defense for lack of their informed consent.

Invasion of Privacy

If your proposed research requires covert (hidden) observation or the obtaining of information from third parties, you need to worry about the issue of invasion of privacy. Secret filming, phone taps, hidden tape recorders, opening of mail, and examination of personal records may be illegal as well as unethical. Even the time-honored one-way mirror is being looked at askance, and many researchers feel that for ethical reasons subjects must be informed about its existence and use. Increasingly, certain records that researchers in the past considered casually available for examination, such as school and health records, are being released only with individual consent. Examine your proposed research to see whether you will be compromising your subjects' rights to privacy in any way.

Deception

Deception is a frequently used technique in social science research. Some research questions are not answerable if the subject knows beforehand exactly what is being sought. Control of experimental demand characteristics, especially those affecting subject attitude, may require a certain amount of deception. Deception is not always bad. It depends on what you deceive your subjects about. If you hold back information that might make your subjects unwilling to participate if they knew it, then your research is ethically questionable. Sometimes you can play fair with your subjects by getting their consent to a research program of a general type without exposing specifically what you are trying to find out. Of course, when you take this approach, you must make clear all possible risks, discomforts, etc.

Full Disclosure

Researchers have the responsibility of clarifying for their subjects after completion of the research the exact nature and intent of the study, especially if deception was involved. Any misconceptions should be corrected, and the subjects should be informed of the value of their participation. If with full disclosure you are afraid of angering or disillusioning your subjects, then you probably shouldn't do the research. Such a response would indicate that if the subjects had been fully informed, they might not have given their consent to participate.

Full disclosure may not be possible when you observe subjects without their knowing it and have no way to contact them later. Also, in some studies full disclosure to some subjects may jeopardize finding future unsuspecting subjects. In the zoo study, for instance, it would have been possible to inform subjects as they exited that the ''reprimand'' was fake and that the lady who dropped her purse was bogus. However, the researcher might have received a (possibly deserved) punch in the nose, and the word might have spread that visitors should avoid the bears until the lunatic scientists went home. As an alternative solution, the researchers might have used a subsequent ruse to obtain names and addresses of subjects so that a later report could be mailed to them. However, such a report might disillusion people about ''accidents'' like purse dropping and make them less helpful in the future. If your research design won't permit full disclosure, you'd better take a hard look at ethical implications and be ready to justify yourself.

Coercion to Participate

Another important principle to consider is that your subjects should have the freedom to choose not to participate or to withdraw from participation. A great deal of social science research in the past has been done in college, business, hospital, military, and prison settings, in which individuals could hardly refuse to participate even if they objected to the methods or purposes of the research. The need for freedom from coercion becomes more important as the risks or costs to the subjects increase. Examine your own proposed research to see if there is any direct or implied coercion of subjects, and if so, see if you can redesign your study to remove it. In addition to not forcing subjects to participate, you should make some allowance for your subjects to withdraw from participation if they find the experiment objectionable.

Anonymity and Confidentiality

Whenever possible, but especially when you are collecting information about personal or sensitive topics, your subjects should be anonymous. After all, they may have given you permission to obtain information for your purposes, but that doesn't mean they have given permission to anyone else. It is generally accepted that researchers do not publish information traceable to a particular individual or, in some cases, even to a particular group of individuals. Complete anonymity, however, may create methodological problems. For instance, you may need some kind of identification to avoid observing the same person more than once. Or if you want to do follow-up observations, you may need to be able to connect future information about an individual with information you have already have. Code numbers are often used as a solution to this problem, and the code list is destroyed as soon as all the data is collected. If the subjects' responses are not anonymous, the subjects should not be misled into believing that they are. For instance, in the early 1960s an extensive intimate survey of "sexual behavior of college women" was mailed out to numerous female college students. In the cover letter with the questionnaire, the prospective subject was assured that her response was "completely anonymous." If so, then why was there a small code number printed obscurely on the back of the last page? Tricks such as these are not ethically acceptable. You must let your subjects know exactly what you are doing to preserve confidentiality of their responses.

If you obtain information about illegal behavior, you need to be aware and to make your subjects aware that your status as a "researcher" does not make the communication privileged in a legal sense. Social science researchers have been subpoenaed into court to testify about information gathered in their research and have not been able legally to refuse to reveal sources. Don't assure your subjects of protection you can't provide (unless you are willing to go to jail to protect your sources).

Protection from Physical and Mental Stress

It's your responsibility as a researcher to make sure that your subjects will not be subjected to physical or mental stress that will yield any effects outlasting the research, even if the subjects consent. If there is any such risk or stress present in the experiment itself, even if it is not likely to cause enduring effects, the subjects must be fully informed about it before consenting to be studied. If there are any stressful aspects of your research, first see whether they can be eliminated, and then be sure you've presented them fairly to your subjects.

Special Permission

Before you wade happily into your research, you must determine whether you need special permission. If you are a member of an institution—for instance, a student at a university—you may need to submit your research proposal to a "Committee for the Protection of Human Subjects" for permission. Even if you think you are working alone, any objection to your research may be visited on the institution with which you are identified. If your proposed subjects are connected with some institution, such as school children or patients of a mental health clinic, permission to study them will need to be sought from that institution. If your proposed research raises no serious questions in regard to any of the ethical issues presented above, it's likely that permission will be granted.

EVALUATING THE WORTH OF YOUR RESEARCH

When people look at the ethical issues involved in your research, they are to some extent going to be influenced by the importance of the research question you are asking. It's up to you to point out the theoretical and practical implications of likely results from your research. The set of research projects that would be possible to do is much larger than the number of studies that actually can be carried out. Therefore you must present some logical reason why the information you seek in your particular study will be of value. Not only do you need to make a case for your research, but you have to do it in such a way that persons not as familiar with your area as you are can see the importance of what you propose to do.

EVALUATING THE QUALITY OF YOUR RESEARCH DESIGN

You may have a good research question, but your study is too poorly designed to yield a clear answer. You can't ask people to approve possible ethical risks or to support costly research if the design of the study is unlikely to yield reliable information. All the criticisms we have launched at other people's research should now be directed at your own. Independent and Dependent Variables must be operationally defined in ways relevant to your research question. Confounding Variables that might compromise your interpretation of results should be looked for. If there are Confounding Variables that you cannot see any way to control, it will be a waste of time to do the study. The same is true if you can't figure out how to reduce random error, to obtain samples of sufficient size, or to find subjects from the population to which you wish to generalize.

RECAPITULATION

for EVALUATING YOUR PROPOSED RESEARCH

Before making your final research plan, you need to evaluate your proposed research from several standpoints. You must decide whether you are treating your human subjects ethically. Issues of informed consent, invasion of privacy, deception, coercion to participate, lack of anonymity, confidentiality of data, protection from physical and mental stress, and full disclosure must be considered. If any of these ethical issues arise about the proposed research, you should redesign the study to avoid or reduce them. The researcher must be prepared to take responsibility for anything that is ethically questionable. The importance of the research should also be considered. A trivial study yielding information of little use to anyone justifies neither the subjects' time nor the expense of running the study. You also need to look critically at your research design and procedures to see if they are likely to yield the information you are seeking. Subjects shouldn't be asked to inconvenience themselves, nor should resources be wasted, for a study that is unlikely to yield interpretable results because of anticipatable problems of inadequate operational definitions, existence of Confounding Variables, excessive random error, too-small samples, or lack of access to the desired subject population.

SUGGESTED EXERCISES

for EVALUATING YOUR PROPOSED RESEARCH

1. Find a study in your social science area or select one from the list below. Read the study and point out any ethical problems that might be involved in carrying out the research. Discuss whether the importance of doing the research balances the ethical issues.

   Doob, A. N., and MacDonald, G. E. Televison viewing and fear of victimization: Is the relationship causal? *Journal of Personality and Social Psychology,* 1979, **37,** 170–179.

   Efran, M. G., and Cheyne, J. A. Affective concomitants of the invasion of shared space: Behavioral, physiological and verbal indicators. *Journal of Personality and Social Psychology,* 1974, **29,** 219–226.

   Hass, K. Verbal conditioning of affective responses. *Journal of General Psychology,* 1962, **67,** 319–322.

   Madsen, C. H., Jr., Becker, W. C., and Thomas, D. R. Rules, praise, and ignoring: Elements of Elementary Classroom Control. *Journal of Applied Behavior Analysis,* 1968, **1,** 139–150.

   Pliner, P., Hart, H., Kohl, J., and Saari, D. Compliance without pressure: Some further data on the foot-in-the-door technique. *Journal of Experimental Social Psychology,* 1974, **10,** 17–22.

2. A study was done on public reactions to a suicide threat. The researcher placed a classified ad in a widely circulated newspaper stating that he was a young man contemplating suicide and asking people who thought he shouldn't to write to a box number. He then collected and organized the responses and published his summary of them. A couple of years later, an undergraduate college student decided to repeat this study by inserting a similar ad in four college newspapers. This resulted in repercussions not anticipated by the student. At one of the colleges, for example, psychologists from the college counseling center spent a good deal of time trying to track down the supposedly suicidal college student. When the truth of the research was exposed, the student found himself facing accusations of being unethical, which he could counter only by pointing out that he was repeating already published research.

   a. Discuss the ethical issues of this kind of study.

   b. Discuss the importance of the research question.

   c. Discuss the "design" of this research study as one likely to yield usable information.

   d. If this research proposal had been examined by the criteria given in this section, would you have recommended that the research be carried out?

   e. Does the fact that someone else has done a study and had it published make it ethical?

   f. If this study had *not* raised an outcry, would it have been more ethical? Does the fact that there *was* an outcry make it less ethical?

SECTION 4: OUTLINE FOR A FINAL RESEARCH PLAN

Before you start any research project, there are a host of things to work out in detail to ensure that the research will run smoothly and that useful results will be obtained. You've examined your initial plan for its worth, practicability, ethics, and quality of research procedures. After making modifications in one or more of these areas, you are ready to write down your final plan. There are certain elements you need to include in this plan, no matter what type of research you are doing. The following questions can be used to outline your final plan.

1. *What is your specific research question?* Write down the hypothesis or hypotheses you are going to test.

2. *What kind of study are you doing?* Describe it briefly as an observational or experimental study being done under natural or laboratory conditions.

3. *What are your DVs?* Operationally define each one by specifying its measurement categories, the rules by which you will assign measures, the type of scale, the person(s) doing the observing, and the way observations are to be recorded.

4. *What are your IVs (for an experimental study)?* Operationally define each IV by specifying whether it is Subject or Non-Subject and listing all its levels.

5. *What design will you be using?* Decide for each IV in an experimental study whether it is to be treated Between- or Within-Subjects. Then lay out the design of the study, noting what treatments are to be given to what groups and exactly when observations are to be taken. You can use the design shorthand.

6. *How will you assign subjects?* Decide whether subject assignment to the conditions of your design will be on the basis of static groups, will involve blocking, will be at random, will be on some matched basis, or will necessitate repeated measures on the same subjects.

7. *How many subjects will you want?* Decide how many observations you want for each condition of the study, and then calculate the total number of subjects necessary. Remember to allow for some loss of subjects.

8. *How will you find your subjects?* Decide what subject population(s) you wish to sample. Then lay out the procedures you are going to use to attract appropriate subjects. Draft a consent form (or obtain one from your institution) for your subjects to sign.

9. *What apparatus and supplies do you need?* Make a list, noting sources for each item. Design any special forms that may be needed for collecting background information on subjects and for recording data.

10. *Where are you going to do the research?* List any special conditions you need, and make arrangements for facilities.

11. *What specific procedures will you use with each subject?* Describe everything you intend to do with the subjects from first greeting them until the end of the session(s). Write out any specific instructions you'll be giving them.

12. *How are you going to schedule things?* Subjects need to be scheduled for specific times. Have a schedule sheet ready, and give subjects written reminders of when you'll need them.

13. *What Confounding Variables are you controlling?* Specifically list everything you are doing to control constant error, such as counterbalancing, placebos, etc.

14. *What are you doing to reduce random error?* List specific things you are doing to decrease random error, and see if you can think of more.

15. *How are you going to analyze your data?* List the specific statistical procedures you intend to use, even though these may be modified by the actual frequency distributions you obtain.

16. *Have you obtained the necessary permission to do the research?*

17. *Have you provided for full disclosure to your subjects?*

18. *Have you thought of everything?* If you've written detailed answers to all the other questions, you've thought of pretty near everything, and you're ready to begin.

SECTION 5: WRITING A RESEARCH PROPOSAL

THE NEED FOR A WRITTEN RESEARCH PROPOSAL

Formal, written research proposals are required for a variety of purposes. If you are seeking grant funds, the agency you are applying to will certainly require one before it decides to shell out. Graduate students are usually required to submit formal research proposals to their supervising committee before starting their doctoral research. Students in an advanced research-methods course may be required to do one before starting on a small-scale, independent research project. If your institution has a "Protection of Human Subjects Committee" or something similar, they'll want to see a written proposal before giving permission to do the study. If you are trying to get an institution to agree to your using their facilities or people, a written research proposal is a good idea.

FORMAT FOR A RESEARCH PROPOSAL

The format for a proposal may vary, depending on whom you are preparing it for. A graduate thesis committee or a granting agency is likely to want very complete proposals. An ethics committee will be most interested in details of procedure that will affect subjects. In some other cases, a brief summary of proposed research may be all that is wanted. Find out if the agency or committee for which you are writing the proposal has a set of guidelines or even a specific form. In the case of grant agencies, you may find that the form has to be filed by a certain deadline for review in competition with other proposals.

CONSIDER YOUR AUDIENCE

Often the audience for a research proposal is less likely to be well informed in your particular area of research than the audience for a research article. In a proposal you should be very careful to explain things clearly and to avoid jargon. Furthermore, you can't assume that the people reviewing your research proposal will be as enthusiastic about the information you are seeking as you are. You'll need to communicate not only what you want to find out but also the possible importance of your findings to the world at large and to any particular concerns of the agency to which you are applying.

LENGTH OF A RESEARCH PROPOSAL

The length of a written proposal will vary with the purpose for which you are writing it, but in general you should try to keep it short and well organized. If the proposal is lengthy, a summary or abstract paragraph will be necessary to leave your audience with a clear final impression of what you are proposing to do.

CONTENTS OF A RESEARCH PROPOSAL

A complete research proposal consists of Abstract, Introduction, and Method sections similar to those you would prepare for a research article. The Introduction is usually not as lengthy as that of an article, but the Method section should be as complete as you can make it without actually running the research. In addition, you need to describe how you intend to analyze the results statistically. You can write such a description as a brief subsection at the end of your Method section. You may also want to write a brief section describing the different possible ways the research might come out, or you may include this information in your Introduction. If you are applying for a grant, you'll have to include a Budget section and an estimate of how long the research will take.

INTRODUCTION FOR A RESEARCH PROPOSAL

For a graduate thesis proposal, the Introduction section may consist of a complete literature review, intended to serve later as the first part of the final thesis. For other kinds of proposals, a somewhat abbreviated research-article Introduction will be adequate. The research question and the importance of getting an answer to it needs to be emphasized. Relevant earlier research that led to your research question and/or the approach to be taken in your study needs to be cited and reviewed. For a research proposal, clearly presenting the logic of your research approach is more important than dragging in every possible reference. The format for an Introduction to a proposal is the same as that for a research article, except that you may have to include answers to some specific questions posed by the agency to which you are applying. At the end of your Introduction the reviewer should understand both what you are proposing to do and why you are proposing to do it.

METHOD SECTION FOR A RESEARCH PROPOSAL

The Method section of your proposal should be substantially as it would appear in a final research article (pp. 346 ff.). In addition, you may include some explanation of why you want to do things a particular way, which would not be likely to appear in a final article. If your proposal is for financial support, you may want to emphasize the need for certain kinds of equipment or expensive procedures. If your proposal is for an ethics committee, you will want to emphasize what is being done to each subject and what safeguards you are including. If the proposal is for your thesis committee or a research-methods course instructor, you may need to emphasize the controls you've introduced into your research procedures. In some cases, you may be more explanatory about procedures in a proposal than in a final research article since you have to convince people outside your area of the necessity of doing things in a particular way.

PROPOSED STATISTICAL ANALYSES

You should discuss both the descriptive and the inferential procedures you intend to use with the different DVs. You also need to explain the logic for selection of these procedures, especially when they are not common ones. If this information is not lengthy, it may fit best as a subsection at the end of your Method section. Your discussion of statistical analyses, as well as your Method section itself, must leave your audience with the impression that you are competent to do the proposed study.

BUDGET SECTION

Most grant agencies will have specific formats for budgeting. Some private agencies may not, especially if their grant awards are small lump sums.

What Is Included in a Research Budget?

Equipment Costs.   Large items of equipment will have to be specifically identified with their purchase price. The cost of components for equipment you plan to construct will also need to be listed. Don't forget to allow for shipping costs and possible price increases before the equipment is actually purchased.

Supplies.   Supplies range from those necessary for the lab to secretarial supplies that may be needed for keeping records or writing up results. Usually these are estimated rather than itemized. You need to go carefully through your procedures to see what supplies you are using for each subject, and you then multiply by the total number of subjects. For some items, you need to allow for a certain amount of wastage—for example, a purchased standardized test that is spoiled by a subject's not quite understanding how to do it and has to be replaced. Certain supplies are likely to be needed for repair and maintenance of equipment. Planning a supplies budget is similar to buying all the food you need for a year on a remote island in the South Seas.

Computer Costs. If you are planning to do any data analysis using your institution's computer services, you are very likely to find that those services have a price tag as soon as you get "outside support." Consult the computer center for an estimate of charges. If they are to give you a good estimate, you'll have to tell them about the design, data collection procedures, and planned analyses for your research.

Salaries. If you are paying people to carry out or participate in the research, you'll need to estimate their salaries, including in most cases any extra benefits that may be provided by the institution that will actually be doing the hiring for you. Your own salary or part of it may be part of the proposal. You also have to consider the salaries for research workers, secretarial and clerical aides, and any special-skills employees (programmers, electrical technicians, etc.). If you are paying your subjects for participation, this cost must also be estimated. If there is a possibility of an increase in the rate of pay of any of your workers in the period before money is granted and research begun, you'll have to allow for it.

Publication and Report-Preparation Costs. If your procedures include issuing final written reports to all subjects and other interested parties, you'll have to allow for the expense of preparation and distribution. Also, an increasing number of journals are requiring "page charges" on articles they accept for publication, especially if the research had financial support.

Travel. Depending on the granting agency, travel may be part of a budget. Such travel may include attending programs to acquire research skills and going to professional meetings to present research results. A travel budget needs to include transportation costs, hotel expenses, meals, and registration costs for meetings.

Overhead. If you are a member of an academic or research institution, there is most likely to be an "overhead" charge that will be added to your grant request. This charge is a fixed percentage of the total amount of money you are requesting. The logic is that by doing the research at the institution you will be occupying space and using facilities that could be used for other purposes.

Will You Need a Budget? Even an undergraduate student contemplating research may find that there is money available for independent projects from such sources as honors programs, special awards, or, on occasion, student government. It pays to ask around; you may find there are some resources you never considered. In applying for these funds, you probably will need to make out at least an informal budget to justify the amount you are seeking. Even if you yourself are going to absorb all the costs of doing your research, a budget will tell you what you have to face before you get in too deep.

REFERENCES

If any point in the research proposal you reference another source of information, as you most certainly will do when writing the Introduction, you will need to include a reference section. This section will have the same format as that for a research article (pp. 363 ff.).

ABSTRACT OR SUMMARY PARAGRAPH

You should summarize your proposed research and its methods in a single readable paragraph. This abstract should be intelligible, even without the accompanying official proposal. It can be useful when you go to talk to people whose help you need. Attached to a longer research proposal, such an abstract can leave a clear impression of your research in the minds of reviewers who are probably reading many other proposals at the same time.

RECAPITULATION

for WRITING A RESEARCH PROPOSAL

Before beginning research you may need to seek permission from one or more groups and may also want to get financial support or other aid. A full research proposal consists of Abstract, Introduction, Method, and Reference sections. These follow the same format as for a research article. In addition, if funds are being sought, the proposal will need a Budget section. The length and emphasis of a research proposal may change with the requirements of the committee or agency to which you submit it. Find out if there are specific guidelines or a form that you should be using. Research proposals are often read by people less involved in your specialized area than are the readers of a research article. It is particularly important in a proposal to be clear, logical, and well organized, and to avoid or explain any special terms. A one-paragraph written Abstract will be useful for communicating about the research to people who don't require a full-scale proposal.

SUGGESTED EXERCISE

for WRITING A RESEARCH PROPOSAL

There's no need here to give you a fabricated exercise. By now you are qualified to plan and carry out your own research project if there is some information you are interested in seeking. Although good social science research involves a lot of planning and work, it's also intellectually satisfying and can be a lot of fun. After all, it is the accumulated results of both informal and formal research efforts that make up a good part of the body of knowledge that Adam and Eve were so actively seeking in Mark Twain's version of the Garden of Eden. We all hope social science research will continue to supply information that can improve the decisions we make that affect the lives of other people.

glossary

ABSOLUTE VALUE The numerical value of a signed number, disregarding the sign.

ABSTRACT A short summary statement of the purpose, procedures, and results of a study that appears at the beginning of a research article.

ALTERNATIVE (or research) HYPOTHESIS The hypothesis in a statistical test that is accepted when the null hypothesis is rejected.

ANAGRAM TASK Each word in a list has its letters scrambled. The subject unscrambles as many words as possible in a fixed amount of time.

ANALYSIS OF VARIANCE An inferential statistical test used for normally distributed, interval data when the design has more than two conditions and/or more than one IV.

APPLIED RESEARCH Research whose purpose is to answer a specific question about a practical problem.

ASYMMETRICAL DISTRIBUTION A frequency distribution that is not the same shape on both sides of the median DV value.

AVERAGE RANK The rank calculated for subjects that have the same DV value. It is the average of the ranks that would be assigned to these subjects if they could be ordered.

B In the design shorthand, the process of blocking subjects into a group according to their classification on a Subject IV.

BAR CHART (or graph) Pictorial representation of a frequency distribution for ordinal or nominal DV measures. The height of each separate bar represents the number or proportion of subjects with that particular DV value.

BASELINE Measure of some aspect of a subject's behavior taken over a period of time before a treatment is introduced.

BASIC RESEARCH Research done to test a theory and produce results generalizable to a large number of situations.

BETWEEN-SUBJECTS DESIGN An experimental design in which different subjects are assigned to the different levels on an IV. Either a Subject IV or a Non-Subject IV can be treated between-subjects.

BIASED SAMPLE A sample that does not fairly represent all members of the population from which it was drawn.

BIASED VARIANCE (or standard deviation) Measure of variability of a sample calculated by using N (sample size) in the denominator of the variance formula. Although it is an accurate description of the sample, it gives too small an estimate of population variability.

BIMODAL DISTRIBUTION A distribution with two peaks rather than a single one.

BLOCKING Selection of subjects to represent different levels of a Subject IV according to characteristics the subjects already possess.

CASE STUDY (or history)   A narrative description of an individual's history, symptoms, behavior, and response to treatment.

CAUSE-EFFECT RELATIONSHIP   A relationship in which changes in one variable produce changes in another.

CHI-SQUARE (χ^2)   An inferential statistic calculated to determine whether or not the frequencies of nominal measures produced in a particular experiment are the same as would be expected according to a null (chance) hypothesis.

CITATION   A specific reference to earlier published work appearing in the text of a research article.

CLASSES   Equal-sized intervals defined along an interval scale of measurement for the purpose of making a frequency distribution.

CLASS LIMITS   The exact upper and lower boundaries of each class defined along an interval scale of measurement.

CLASS SIZE   The width of each class defined along an interval scale of measurement.

COMPARISON INFORMATION   Information that is available from an experiment when the design has at least two different conditions whose effects can be compared.

COMPLETELY RANDOMIZED DESIGN   A design in which all IVs are treated Between-Subjects, and assignment of subjects to the different conditions of the design is made at random.

CONDITION   A combination of treatments representing different levels of IVs in a multivariate design. Two IVs, each of which has three levels, will produce nine conditions.

CONFOUNDING VARIABLES   Uncontrolled variables in an experiment that alter the DV in ways that can be mistaken for effects of an IV. Any Relevant Variable that changes consistently for different IV levels, produces constant error in an experiment.

CONSTANT ERROR   Error introduced into DV measurements by a Confounding Variable. Since systematically different amounts of constant error may be introduced at different IV levels, it can result in misinterpretation of IV effects.

CONTROL GROUP   A group of subjects that differs from the experimental group only in the way specified by the IV. Often it is a group that does not receive any experimental treatment.

CORRECTION FOR TIES   Nonparametric, inferential statistical tests for ordinal data often involve ranking subjects. If several subjects are tied for the same rank, the test may require that a special correction factor be calculated.

CORRELATION   A descriptive statistic that indicates the degree of association between two different DV measures taken on the same subject.

CORRELATIONAL RESEARCH   Research in which there are multiple DVs. The researcher wants to determine which DVs tend to vary together rather than to establish cause-effect relationships.

COUNTERBALANCING   In a Within-Subjects design, the assignment at random of an equal number of subjects to each and every possible order of conditions. This technique controls for the constant error introduced into the results by order effects.

CRITICAL VALUE OF A TEST STATISTIC   The size a test statistic has to be for the researcher to reject the null hypothesis in a particular test. It is found by use of an appropriate table.

CROSS-SECTIONAL SURVEY   Simultaneous surveying of a number of different groups to see whether they differ at the time of the survey.

DECILE RANGE   The difference between the 90th and the 10th percentiles. It is a nonparametric measure of variability.

DEGREES OF FREEDOM   Most test statistics need an accompanying value related to the size and/or number of samples being tested. The same book that gives the formulas for calculating a particular test statistic will tell how to figure this term.

DEMAND CHARACTERISTICS   Anything about the experience of being in an experiment that the subject reacts to, other than the IV.

DEPENDENT VARIABLE (DV)   A variable observed and measured as the outcome of research. It is operationally defined by specifying the measurement scale and the conditions of measurement.

DESCRIPTIVE STATISTICS   Measures that summarize and describe a sample of DV values. They include sample size and measures of central tendency, variability, and correlation.

DESCRIPTIVE VARIANCE (or standard deviation)   A value calculated to describe the variability of a sample of normally distributed, interval data. The variance equals the sum of squared deviations from the mean divided by the sample size. The standard deviation is the positive square root of the variance $(\text{Var} = \Sigma(X - \bar{X})^2/N;$ $\text{S.D.} = \sqrt{\text{Var}}).$

DESIGN   A plan for an experiment that specifies what IVs will be used, how many levels there are of each IV, how subjects are to be split into groups, and when and how often DV measures are to be taken.

DEVIATION (or difference) SCORE   The difference between each individual interval score and the mean of all the scores.

DISTRIBUTION   See Frequency distributions.

DISTRIBUTION-FREE TESTS (or statistics)   Statistics that do not require any assumptions about the shape of the frequency distribution (also called "nonparametric").

DOUBLE-BLIND   Describing a procedure in which neither the experimenter nor the subject knows which condition of the experiment the subject represents.

EQUIVALENCE OF GROUPS   The degree to which groups to be compared in an experiment are the same with respect to all Relevant Variables.

ERROR TERM   A measure of all the unexplained (random) variability in a set of DV measurement. This measure, also called the "mean square for error" in an Analysis of Variance, forms the denominator of the F-ratio.

EVALUATION   A set of procedures for gathering information about the effects of social, clinical, or educational processes on human welfare. The evaluator seeks to establish whether the process yields any product and whether the product is worthwhile.

EVALUATION APPREHENSION   Anxiety of a subject to win the approval of the researcher.

EXPECTED FREQUENCY   In a Chi-Square test, the frequency of times a given outcome would be expected if the null hypothesis were true.

EXPERIMENTAL GROUP (or subjects)   The group that receives an experimental treatment and is to be compared with a second (control) group which does not.

EXPERIMENTAL RESEARCH   Research in which the experimenter makes changes in one or more variables to observe the effects on the subjects' behavior.

EXPERIMENTER BIAS   The effects of the experimenter's attitude, expectancies, and behavior on the behavior of the subject. It may be an unrecognized Relevant Variable in any research involving direct experimenter-subject interaction.

EXTERNAL VALIDITY   The degree to which the results of a particular experiment can be generalized to new situations.

EXTREME VALUE   A value that is at or near the very bottom or very top of a set of DV values.

FACTOR   In statistics, a synonym for "variable."

FACTORIAL DESIGN   A design with two or more IVs that are combined to produce a number of conditions equal to the product of the number of levels of each IV.

FACTORIAL TABLE   A table in which the rows represent the levels of one IV and the columns represent the levels of another. Useful for figuring out all the conditions of a multivariate experiment.

FIGURE   Any graph, picture, diagram, or illustration in a research article.

FOLLOW-UP COMPARISON INFORMATION   Information obtained some time after the end of an experiment when subjects are again observed on the DV to see whether there have been any changes over time.

F-RATIO   The inferential test statistic calculated in an Analysis of Variance. It compares the variability in the data produced by a given factor (numerator) to the overall variability produced by error (denominator).

FREQUENCY   The number of times a particular DV value is assigned to a subject in a group being observed.

FREQUENCY DISTRIBUTION   A tabular or graphical representation of the number of subjects assigned to each DV value on a scale of measurement.

FREQUENCY HISTOGRAM   A graphical representation of a frequency distribution of interval data in which the number of subjects falling into each DV class is indicated by the height of a bar.

FREQUENCY POLYGON   A graphical representation of a frequency distribution of interval data in which the number of subjects falling into each DV class is represented by a dot over the midpoint of the class. The dots are then connected.

FRIEDMAN TWO-WAY ANALYSIS OF VARIANCE BY RANKS   A nonparametric inferential test of ordinal data used when there are more than two conditions and the design is either within-subjects or matched-subjects.

G   In the design shorthand, the assignment of subjects to a group.

GENERALIZING   Using the results of research done in one particular situation to predict what will happen in a new set of circumstances.

GOODMAN AND KRUSKAL'S COEFFICIENT OF ASSOCIATION   A correlation statistic expressing association between two ordinal DV scales. Useful when one or both scales have a large number of tied ranks.

GROUP   A set of subjects formed to receive similar treatment in an experiment.

H_A Abbreviation for the alternative or research hypothesis in an inferential statistical test.

H_O Abbreviation for the null hypothesis in an inferential statistical test.

HAWTHORNE EFFECT   The effect on subjects of knowing that they have been designated a special or experimental group and are being observed.

HYPOTHESIS   A specific prediction stemming from a broader theory about what will happen in a particular set of circumstances.

INDEPENDENT-GROUPS DESIGNS   Designs in which the subjects in the groups being compared are not the same or matched in any way. They include such Between-Subjects designs as Blocked, Static-Groups, and Randomized-Groups designs.

INDEPENDENT VARIABLE (IV)   A variable that the experimenter creates or manipulates as input to an experiment. It is operationally defined by specifying all its levels, and it can be either Subject or Non-Subject in type.

INFERENTIAL STATISTICS   Statistics calculated to determine the probability that a particular set of results happened by chance and do not represent repeatable effects.

INFERENTIAL VARIANCE (or standard deviation)   A value calculated from a sample of interval data to estimate the variance of the normally distributed population from which the sample was drawn. The inferential variance equals the sum of squared deviations from the mean divided by one less than the sample size. The standard deviation is the positive square root of the variance ($\text{Var} = \Sigma(X - \bar{X})^2/(N - 1)$; $\text{S.D.} = \sqrt{\text{Var}}$).

INTERACTION   When the effects of one IV on a DV are altered by the presence of a second IV, the IV effects are said to interact. This type of information is available only from designs that have more than one IV.

INTERNAL VALIDITY   The degree to which the changes observed in a DV were in fact caused by the IV(s) in a particular experimental situation.

INTERQUARTILE RANGE   The difference between the 75th and 25th percentiles. It is a nonparametric measure of variability.

INTERVAL SCALE   A measurement scale with ordered categories that are equidistant from one another.

KRUSKAL-WALLIS ONE-WAY ANALYSIS OF VARIANCE BY RANKS   A nonparametric inferential test of ordinal data used for a Single IV, Between-Subjects design with more than two conditions.

LATIN-SQUARE DESIGN   An incomplete factorial, Within-Subjects design used when complete counterbalancing of conditions is not practical.

LEVEL (OF A VARIABLE)   Any single value that can be taken by a variable.

LEVEL OF SIGNIFICANCE   The largest probability of error acceptable for rejection of the null hypothesis. Usually $p = .05$ is used, although in some cases $p = .10$ may be acceptable.

LITTERMATE   An animal from the same litter as the experimental subject. Often used as a basis for matching in animal research.

LONGITUDINAL SURVEY   The surveying of the same group of people at successive times to see how they change.

M   In design shorthand, the process of matching a subject in one group with one and only one subject in the other group(s).

MAIN EFFECT   An Analysis of Variance term. Each IV in a multivariate design has an effect that is tested separately from all the other effects in the experiment.

MANN-WHITNEY U TEST   An inferential test for ordinal data when an Independent-Groups, Between-Subjects design with no more than two conditions has been used.

MATCHED-GROUPS DESIGN   Between-Subjects design in which each subject in one group has been paired on some basis with one and only one subject in another group.

MATCHED RANDOMIZED-GROUPS DESIGN   A design in which subjects are first matched on some basis into pairs and then within each pair the members are randomly assigned to groups.

MATURATION   The changes in a developing organism that occur with the passage of time.

MEAN   Measure of central tendency for a distribution of interval data. It is the sum of all DV values divided by the total number of values.

MEAN SQUARE   A stage in the process of calculating F-ratios in an Analysis of Variance. A mean square is calculated for each main effect and each interaction. The ratios of each of these to the mean square for error give the F-statistics.

MEASUREMENT   Assigning a subject to a category on a scale.

MEASURE OF CENTRAL TENDENCY   A descriptive statistic that summarizes a whole distribution by a single typical value. The mean, median, and mode are measures of central tendency.

MEASURE OF VARIABILITY   A descriptive statistic that summarizes in a single number the amount of spread of a distribution along the DV scale. The variance, standard deviation, decile range, interquartile range, and variation ratio are all measures of variability.

MEDIAN   The DV value that divides the area of a frequency distribution in half. It is equal to the 50th percentile and is an appropriate descriptive statistic for interval or ordinal DVs.

MEDIAN TEST   A nonparametric, inferential statistical test for ordinal data from a two-condition, Independent-Groups design.

MIDPOINT (OF A CLASS)   Half the sum of the upper and lower real class limits. Used in graphing a frequency polygon.

MIXED DESIGN   A multivariate design in which one of the IVs is treated Between-Subjects and the other Within-Subjects.

MODE   The DV value in a distribution that occurs most frequently. For interval data it is the midpoint of the most frequently occurring class. An appropriate descriptive statistic for nominal, ordinal, or interval data.

MULTI-LEVEL COMPARISON INFORMATION   Information available from designs that have more than two levels of an IV.

MULTI-LEVEL DESIGN   A design that has a single IV with more than two levels.

MULTIPLE BASELINE   A single-subject procedure in which baseline data are collected simultaneously on several different behaviors. Then the same experimental treatment is introduced for each behavior at a different time.

MULTIPLE-COMPARISONS TEST   If a main effect is significant for an Analysis of Variance of a multi-level design, it may be desirable to establish specific significances between any and all pairs of levels. To do so, an additional statistical test is necessary.

MULTIPLE t-TESTS   The practice of doing *t*-tests on all possible pairs of means yielded by a multi-level design. The procedure is inadvisable because it yields some spurious significances.

MULTIVARIATE DESIGN   A design that has more than one IV.

NATURALISTIC OBSERVATION   Studying people or animals in their natural setting without the subjects' being aware that they are being observed.

NEGATIVE CORRELATION   Relationship between two DVs such that a person who scores high on one tends to score low on the other.

NOMINAL SCALE   A measurement scale consisting only of two or more unordered categories.

NONPARAMETRIC STATISTICS OR TESTS   Statistics that do not make any assumptions about the shape of the frequency distribution. Useful for nominal and ordinal data as well as for interval data with badly skewed distributions.

NONREACTIVE MEASURE   A measure that does not change the thing being measured during the process of measurement.

NON-SUBJECT IV   An IV whose different levels are produced by the experimenter's direct manipulation of the subjects.

NORMAL DISTRIBUTION   A frequency distribution of intervally scaled data that is bell-shaped, symmetrical, and unimodal and has its highest frequency in the middle. It can be specified by a particular mathematical equation for which the mean and the standard deviation are parameters. Also known as the Gaussian distribution

NULL HYPOTHESIS   The hypothesis that chance is responsible for any differences found in an experiment. Inferential statistical tests are designed around the assumption that the null hypothesis is true.

O   In the design shorthand, the time at which DV observations are taken on the subjects.

OBSERVATION   The act of taking a measure on a subject. In statistics, this term represents a single DV measure taken on a single subject.

OBSERVED FREQUENCY   The frequency of times an event actually occurs in a particular experiment. In a Chi-Square analysis, this frequency is compared with a frequency expected for the same event if the null hypothesis were true.

ONE-GROUP, PRE-POST DESIGN   A Within-Subjects design in which a single group is pretested, given a treatment, and then posttested.

ONE-SHOT DESIGN   A design in which a single group is given a treatment and then tested.

ONE-TAILED TEST   An inferential test on a two-condition design in which the alternative or research hypothesis predicts a particular direction of effect. In such a test, the null hypothesis then includes the possibility of the opposite direction as well as the possibility of no difference.

ONE-WAY MIRROR (or window)   An arrangement that permits the researcher to observe a subject without being seen.

OPEN-ENDED QUESTIONNAIRE   A collection of questions to which people can respond in any way they want and at any length.

OPERATIONAL DEFINITION   Complete specification of a variable in a particular research study so that any other researcher will define it the same way. Operationally defining an IV requires stating its levels and describing exactly how each level was created. Operationally defining a DV requires stating the measurement scale and describing the rules by which subjects were assigned to measurement categories.

ORDER EFFECT   In a Within-Subjects design, the possibility that the order in which conditions occur alters the effects the conditions would have by themselves.

ORDINAL SCALE   A measurement scale consisting of two or more ordered categories. The distance between categories cannot be assumed to be equidistant.

OVERALL EFFECT   For a multivariate experiment, the effect of a particular IV, ignoring (averaging across) any other IVs in the design. *See* Main effect.

PARAMETERS OF A DISTRIBUTION   A frequency distribution that follows a curve according to a particular mathematical equation can be described by giving the values of the constants, or parameters, of the equation. The parameters for any normal distribution are its mean and standard deviation.

PARAMETRIC STATISTICS OR TESTS   Statistics or tests which assume that the frequency distribution of the data is normal.

PEAK (of a distribution)   The highest point of a frequency distribution.

PEARSON'S PRODUCT-MOMENT CORRELATION   Correlation coefficient calculated between two intervally scaled DVs. It is assumed that the frequency distribution for each of the DVs is approximately normal.

PERCENTILE   The DV value that has a certain percent or proportion of a frequency distribution falling below it. For example, the 10th percentile is the DV value that is greater than or equal to the lower 10 percent of the distribution and less than the upper 90 percent.

PILOT STUDY   A simple study done to test research procedures. Its results are usually not published, because it has insufficient comparison information and poor control over Relevant Variables.

PLACEBO CONDITION   A condition in which subjects are led to believe they are receiving a drug or experimental treatment when in fact they are given a neutral substance or treatment.

POPULATION   The entire set of subjects about which the researcher wants information.

POSITIVE CORRELATION   A relationship between two DVs such that persons who score high on one tend to score high on the other.

POSTEXPERIMENT INQUIRY   After an experiment is over, the subjects are asked what they thought was going on in the experiment.

POSTTEST   Observations on the DV taken immediately after the subject has experienced the treatment.

POSTTREATMENT INFORMATION   Information about how subjects behave immediately after they have experienced the treatment.

POWER (of a test)   The likelihood that an inferential test will reject the null hypothesis when it should be rejected.

PRETEST   Observations on the DV taken just before a subject experiences a treatment.

PRETEST SENSITIZATION   The fact that subjects have taken a pretest may change how they react to the treatment or may directly alter the posttest score.

PRETREATMENT INFORMATION   Information about how subjects behave just before they experience a treatment.

PROPORTION   The fraction of the total group that falls in a particular category or class.

PURSUIT-ROTOR TASK   An eye-hand coordination task in which subjects attempt to follow a rapidly moving light on a screen with a hand-held pointer.

QUALITATIVE MEASURES   Measures that categorize subjects according to which qualities or characteristics they possess.

QUANTITATIVE MEASURES   Measures that categorize subjects according to how much of a characteristic they possess.

QUASI-CONTROL   A procedure in which the subjects are exposed to all the instructions, procedures, setting, etc., of an experiment but are not actually given the treatment. In addition, they may be asked to pretend they have had the treatment.

R   In the design shorthand, the process of assigning subjects randomly to groups.

r   The symbol used for Pearson's product-moment correlation coefficient. Sometimes used to represent other types of correlations.

RANDOM   Not systematic; by chance.

RANDOM ERROR   Anything that increases the overall variability of DV measures and does not change systematically with different IV levels.

RANDOMIZED-BLOCKS DESIGN   A multivariate design with one or more Subject IVs and one or more Non-Subject IVs. Subjects are blocked according to the Subject IV(s) and then assigned at random to levels of the Non-Subject IV(s).

RANDOMIZED-GROUPS DESIGN   An Independent-Groups design in which subjects are assigned to the groups at random.

RANDOMIZED-GROUPS, PRE-POST DESIGN   A Randomized-Groups design in which a pretest is given after random assignment to groups but before treatment.

RANDOM SAMPLE   A sample selected so that every member of the population has an equal chance of being included.

RANKING OR RANK-ORDERING   A process by which subjects measured with either an interval or an ordinal DV scale are ordered in relation to each other from highest to lowest scorer. Each DV value is then replaced by a number indicating its position or rank. This process changes intervally scaled data to ordinal.

RATING SCALE   An ordinal scale with verbally or numerically labeled, ordered categories. Widely used in questionnaires and in observational studies.

RAW SCORE   The actual DV value assigned to a subject. This value may be replaced by the results of statistical manipulations, such as ranking or conversion to a *z*-score.

REACTION-TIME TASK   A task in which the subject is asked to make a simple response each time a stimulus is given. The time between the start of the stimulus and the beginning of the response is measured.

REACTIVE MEASURE   A DV measure that is altered by the process of making the measurement.

RELEVANT VARIABLE   A variable in an experiment, other than the IV(s) that can alter DV values. If uncontrolled, it may be either a Confounding Variable or a source of random error.

RELIABILITY   The extent to which a process of measurement produces the same results if used repeatedly.

REPEATED MEASURES   Measures taken of the same subjects on the same DV scale at more than one point in time in a research study.

REPEATED-MEASURES DESIGN   A design in which one or more of the IVs are treated Within-Subjects.

REPRESENTATIVE SAMPLE   A sample whose overall characteristics are the same as the population from which it was drawn.

REVERSAL DESIGN   A single-subject design in which a subject serves as his or her own control by being returned to baseline between subsequent administrations of a treatment.

S   An abbreviation for subject.

SAMPLE   A part of a population, from which the researcher hopes to be able to infer the characteristics of the entire population.

SAMPLE SIZE (N)   The number of individuals included in a particular sample.

SAMPLING ERROR   Chance variation between descriptive statistics for random samples taken from the same population.

SCALE OF MEASUREMENT   A set of at least two mutually exclusive categories to which subjects can be assigned.

SCATTERPLOT   A graph that gives a visual impression of the degree of association or correlation between two DV measures taken on the same subjects.

SECONDARY SOURCE   A citation of a person's ideas or results as reported by someone other than the originator.

SEMI-INTERQUARTILE RANGE   A nonparametric measure of variability equal to half the difference between the 75th percentile DV measure and the 25th.

SIGN TEST   A nonparametric, inferential statistical test for a two-condition, Within-Subjects or Matched-Subjects design.

SINGLE-SUBJECT DESIGNS   Designs in which each subject is intensively studied, either by being repeatedly exposed to the same treatment or progressively exposed to different treatments.

SINGLE VALUE OF A VARIABLE   One of the categories on the scale of a variable.

SKEWED DISTRIBUTION   A distribution that is not symmetrical, having either the upper or lower tail extended.

SOLOMON'S FOUR-GROUP DESIGN   A Randomized-Groups design that treats pretesting as a second IV. Two groups are pretested and two are not. One of the pretest groups and one of the no-pretest groups are given the experimental treatment.

SPEARMAN'S RHO (RANK-ORDER CORRELATION)   A correlation coefficient calculated between the rankings of two DVs measured on ordered scales. Can be used for either ordinal or interval data.

STANDARD DEVIATION   The parameter of a normal distribution that summarizes its degree of spread. It is the appropriate descriptive statistic of variability for normally distributed, interval measures.

STANDARD SCORE   A derived score based on z-scores, which has an arbitrary mean and an arbitrary standard deviation. Used principally in educational testing, it facilitates comparison of test results.

STATIC-GROUPS DESIGN   A design in which the groups destined to receive different treatments were formed by processes not under the researcher's control.

STATIC-GROUPS DESIGN WITH MATCHING   A Static-Groups design in which the researcher attempts to improve group equivalence by matching each subject in one preexisting group with a similar subject in another.

STATIC-GROUPS, PRE-POST DESIGN   A Static-Groups design in which pretests are given before treatment. The researcher wants information as to whether the pre-existing groups in the study are initially similar on the DV measure.

STATISTICAL SIGNIFICANCE   The conclusion reached when an inferential statistical test on the results indicates that the null hypothesis can be rejected with a low probability of error (usually less than .05). The same or similar results are likely to be obtained again if the study is repeated.

SUBJECT   A person or animal that is being studied.

SUBJECT IV   An IV whose levels represent characteristics the subjects already possess at the start of the experiment.

SUBSCRIPT   A label used to indicate a particular subject or group (e.g., S_1, S_2, S_3, . . .).

SURVEY STUDY   A large-scale observational study done on groups of humans, often using written questionnaires or individual interviews.

SYSTEMATIC OBSERVATION   Observation of behavior according to a standard set of rules specifying what is being observed, who is doing the observing, who is being observed, what the conditions of observation are, and how the observations are recorded.

T   In the design shorthand, the administration of a treatment. It may be subscripted to indicate different treatments.

T In inferential statistics, the symbol for the test statistic calculated in Wilcoxon's Matched-Pairs, Signed-Ranks test.

t Symbol for the test statistic calculated in the t-test.

TAIL OF A DISTRIBUTION   The upper or lower end of a frequency distribution. Usually applied to graphical distributions of interval data.

TEST STATISTIC   A value calculated in an inferential statistical test to determine whether the null hypothesis should be accepted.

THEORY   An explanation of why an observed event is happening.

TIED RANKS   In the ranking of a set of DV measures, two or more subjects that have the same DV value are said to be tied. All tied subjects are given the same average rank.

TREATMENT   What is done to a group of subjects according to the requirements of a Non-Subject IV.

t-TEST   An inferential test for normally distributed interval data collected in a two-condition design.

t-TEST FOR A CORRELATION   A variant of the t-test that determines whether a correlation between two DVs is different from zero and is likely to be found again.

t-TEST FOR AN EXPECTED MEAN VALUE   A variant of the t-test which tests the idea that the mean of a single sample is or is not some stated value.

t-TEST FOR INDEPENDENT SAMPLES   A *t*-test appropriate for a two-condition, Between-Subjects, Independent-Groups design.

t-TEST FOR PAIRED (CORRELATED) SAMPLES   A *t*-test appropriate for a two-condition, Within-Subjects or Matched-Subjects design.

TWO-TAILED TEST   An inferential statistical test for a two-condition design set up to reject the null hypothesis for either a positive effect or a negative effect.

TWO-WAY CLASSIFICATION   Classification of subjects in accord with two variables at the same time.

U   Symbol for the test statistic calculated in the Mann-Whitney test.

UNBIASED VARIANCE (or standard deviation)   Sample variance calculated by the *N*-1 formula, intended to be used to infer population variance.

UNCONTROLLED VARIABLE   A Relevant Variable that is not eliminated or otherwise controlled by the experimenter and that may distort interpretation of results.

UNIMODAL   Characteristic of a frequency distribution that has only one hump.

UNOBTRUSIVE MEASURE   A nonreactive measure taken by observation not of the behavior of the subjects but of the by-products of that behavior.

VALIDITY   An estimate of how well a DV measures what it claims to measure.

VALUE   A level of a variable or a category on a scale of measurement of a variable.

VARIABLE   Anything that can vary along some dimension by taking two or more different values.

VARIANCE   A measure of variability for normally distributed, interval data. It is the sum of all squared deviations from the mean divided by either sample size (descriptive variance) or by one less than the sample size (inferential variance).

VARIATION RATIO   Measure of variability for nominally scaled data. Gives the proportion of subjects who did not fall in the modal category.

WEAK-ORDINAL SCALE OF MEASUREMENT   An ordinal scale with very few categories. Statistically it may be treated as if it were a nominal scale.

WILCOXON'S MATCHED-PAIRS, SIGNED-RANKS TEST   A nonparametric test for a two-condition, Within-subjects or Matched-Subjects design. Used for ordinal and skewed interval data.

WITHIN-SUBJECTS DESIGN   A design that uses the same subjects for different levels of a Non-Subject IV.

YATES'S CORRECTION   A correction factor necessary in a Chi-Square test when the design has only one degree of freedom. Also called a "correction for continuity."

z-SCORE   A value calculated for normally distributed, interval measures that tells how many standard deviations each raw score is above or below the mean.

references

Alpert, R., and Haber, R. Anxiety in academic achievement situations. *Journal of Abnormal and Social Psychology,* 1960, **61,** 207–215.

American Psychological Association Publication Manual. Washington, D.C.: American Psychological Association, 1974.

Aragona, J., Cassady, J., and Drabman, R. S. Teaching overweight children through parental training and contingency contracting. *Journal of Applied Behavior Analysis,* 1975, **8,** 269–278.

Bandura, A. Influence of models' reinforcement contingencies on the acquisition of imitative responses. *Journal of Personality and Social Psychology,* 1965, **1,** 589–595.

Barry, H., III, Bacon, M. K., and Child, I. L. A cross-cultural survey of some sex differences in socialization. *Journal of Abnormal and Social Psychology,* 1957, **55,** 327–332.

Baruch, D. W. *One little boy.* New York: Julian Press, 1952.

Beauchamp, K. L., Chapman, A., and Grebing, C. Response by the calf to stimulus change. *Psychonomic Science,* 1967, **9,** 125–126.

Bindra, D., and Campbell, J. F. Motivational effects of rewarding intracranial stimulation. *Nature,* 1967, **215,** 375–376.

Boren, A. R., and Foree, S. B. Personalized instruction applied to food and nutrition in higher education. *Journal of Personalized Instruction,* 1977, **2,** 39–42.

Bryan, J. H., and Test, M. A. Models and helping: Naturalistic studies in aiding behavior. *Journal of Personality and Social Psychology,* 1967, **6,** 400–407.

Burington, R. S., and May, D. C., Jr. *Handbook of probability and statistics.* Sandusky, Ohio: Handbook Publishers, 1953.

Burtt, H. E. An experimental study of early childhood memory. *Journal of Genetic Psychology,* 1930, **40,** 287–295.

Campbell, D. T., and Stanley, J. C. Experimental and quasi-experimental designs for research. In N. L. Gage (ed.), *Handbook of research on teaching.* Chicago: Rand McNally, 1963.

Canady, H. G. The effect of "rapport" on the IQ: A new approach to the problem of racial psychology. *Journal of Negro Education,* 1936, **5,** 209–219.

Chow, K. L., Riesen, A. H., and Newell, F. W. Degeneration of retinal ganglion cells in infant chimpanzees and raised in darkness. *Journal Comparative Neurology,* 1957, **107,** 27–42.

Cochran, W. G., and Cox, G. M. *Experimental designs.* New York: Wiley, 1957.

Comrey, A., and Newmeyer, J. Measurement of Radical-Conservatism. *Journal of Social Psychology,* 1965, **67,** 357–369.

415

Crancer, A., Jr., Dille, J. M., Delay, J. C., Wallace, J. E., and Haykin, M. D. Comparison of effects of marihuana and alcohol on simulated driving performance. *Science,* 1969, **164,** 851–854.

Crawford, D. G., Friesen, D. D., and Tomlinson-Keasey, C. Effects of cognitively induced anxiety on hand temperature. *Biofeedback and Self-Regulation,* 1977, **2,** 139–146.

Crawford, J., and Kielsmeier, C. *The prudent peapicker's guide to experimental design.* Albany, Ore.: Albany Printing, 1970.

Darling, E. F. *A herd of red deer.* Oxford University Press, 1937.

Diaconis, P. Statistical problems in ESP research. *Science,* 1978, **201,** 131–136.

Doob, A. N., and MacDonald, E. G. Television viewing and the fear of victimization: Is the relationship causal? *Journal of Personality and Social Psychology,* 1979, **37,** 170–179.

Dorfman, D. D. The Cyril Burt question: New findings. *Science,* 1978, **201,** 1177–1186.

Efran, M. G., and Cheyne, J. A. Affective concomitants of the invasion of shared space: Behavioral, physiological, and verbal indicators. *Journal of Personality and Social Psychology,* 1974, **29,** 219–226.

Fables of Aesop according to Sir Roger L'Estrange. New York: Dover, 1967.

Freeman, L. C. *Elementary applied statistics.* New York: Wiley, 1965.

Galanter, M., Wyatt, R. J., Lemberger, L., Weingartner, H., Vaughn, T. B., and Roth, W. T. Effects on humans of Δ^9-Tetrahydrocannabinol administered by smoking. *Science,* 1972, **176,** 934–936.

Goodall, J. My life among wild chimpanzees. *National Geographic,* 1963 (Aug.), **124,** 272–308.

Gould, S. J. Morton's ranking of races by cranial capacity. *Science,* 1978a, **200,** 503–509.

Gould, S. J. The brains of geniuses. *Science,* 1978b, **202,** 372–374.

Harlow, H. F., and Harlow, M. K. The effect of rearing conditions on behavior. *Bulletin of the Menninger Clinic,* 1962, **26,** 213–224.

Harlow, H. F., and Suomi, S. J. Induced depression in monkeys. *Behavioral Biology,* 1974, **12,** 273–296.

Hebb, D. O. *The organization of behavior.* New York: Wiley, 1949.

Hintzman, D. L. *The psychology of learning and memory.* San Francisco: W. H. Freeman, 1978.

Hollingshead, A. B., and Redlich, F. C. *Social class and mental illness.* New York: Wiley, 1958.

Jacobson, M. B., and Koch, W. Attributed reasons for support of the feminist movement as a function of attractiveness. *Sex Roles,* 1978, **4,** 169–174.

James, W. *The principles of psychology.* New York: Holt, 1890.

Jessup, B. A., and Neufeld, R. W. J. Effects of biofeedback and "autogenic relaxation" techniques on physiological and subjective responses in psychiatric patients: A preliminary analysis. *Behavior Therapy,* 1978, **8,** 160–167.

Kalant, H. Marihuana and simulated driving. *Science,* 1969, **166,** 640.

Katzev, R., Edelsack, L., Steinmetz, G., Walker, T., and Wright, R. The effect of reprimanding transgressions on subsequent helping behavior: Two field experiments. *Personality and Social Psychology Bulletin,* 1978, **4,** 326–329.

Klieban, Sister Joanne Marie. Effects of goal-setting and modeling on job performance of retarded adolescents. *American Journal of Mental Deficiency,* 1967, **72,** 220–226.

Knox, R. E., and Inkster, J. A. Postdecision dissonance at post time. *Journal of Personality and Social Psychology,* 1968, **8,** 319–323.

Langley, R. *Practical statistics.* New York: Dover, 1971.

Laties, V. G., Weiss, B., Clark, R. L., and Reynolds, M. D. Overt "meditating" behavior during temporally spaced responding. *Journal of the Experimental Analysis of Behavior,* 1965, **8,** 107–116.

Lee, W. *Experimental design and analysis.* San Francisco: W. H. Freeman, 1975.

Lehrman, D. S. Effects of female sex hormones on incubation behavior in the ring dove. *Journal Comparative and Physiological Psychology,* 1958, **51,** 142–145.

Lewis, O. *Pedro Martínez.* New York: Random House, 1967.

Lewis, S. *Arrowsmith.* New York: Harcourt, Brace, 1924.

Lipscomb, D. M. *Noise: The unwanted sounds.* Chicago: Nelson-Hall, 1974.

Madsen, C. H., Jr., Becker, W. C., and Thomas, D. R. Rules, praise, and ignoring: Elements of elementary classroom control. *Journal of Applied Behavior Analysis,* 1968, **1,** 139–150.

Mahoney, M., Moore, B., Wade, T., and Moura, N. Effects of continuous and intermittent self-monitoring on academic behavior. *Journal of Consulting and Clinical Psychology,* 1973, **41,** 65–69.

Mahut, H. Breed differences in the dog's emotional behavior. *Canadian Journal of Psychology,* 1958, **12,** 35–44.

Manheimer, D. I., Mellinger, G. D., and Balter, M. B. Marihuana use among urban adults. *Science,* 1969, **166,** 1544–1545.

McKay, H., Sinisterra, L., McKay, A., Gomez, H., and Lloreda, P. Improving cognitive ability in chronically deprived children. *Science,* 1978, **200,** 270–278.

McKenna, W., and Kessler, S. J. Experimental design as a source of sex bias in social psychology. *Sex Roles,* 1977, **3,** 117–128.

Mead, M. *Coming of age in Samoa.* New York: Morrow, 1928.

Milgram, S. *Obedience to authority.* New York: Harper and Row, 1974.

Milton, G. A. Sex differences in problem solving as a function of role appropriateness of the problem content. *Psychological Reports,* 1959, **5,** 705–708.

Moore, J. W., and Smith, W. L. A comparison of several types of immediate reinforcement. In W. L. Smith and J. W. Moore (eds.), *Programmed Learning.* New Jersey: Van Nostrand, 1962.

Myers, J. K., and Bean, L. L. *A decade later.* New York: Wiley, 1968.

O'Leary, L. D., Kaufman, K., Kass, R., and Drabman, R. The effects of loud and soft reprimands on the behavior of disruptive students. *Exceptional Children,* 1970, **36,** 145–155.

Orne, M. T. Demand characteristics and the concept of quasi-controls. In R. Rosenthal and R. L. Rosnow (eds.), *Artifact in behavioral research.* New York: Academic Press, 1969, 147–181.

Orne, M. T., and Scheibe, K. E. The contribution of nondeprivation factors in the production of sensory deprivation effects: The psychology of the "panic button." *Journal of Abnormal and Social Psychology,* 1964, **68,** 3–12.

Pagano, R. R., and Franklin, L. R. The effect of Transcendental Meditation on right hemisphere functioning. *Biofeedback and Self-Regulation,* 1977, **2**, 407–415.

Palazzo, T. *Henny-Penny and Chicken Little.* New York: H. R. Wilson, 1960.

Parlee, M. B. The friendship bond. *Psychology Today,* 1979 (Oct.), 43–54.

Paul, G. L. *Insight vs. desensitization in psychotherapy.* Stanford, Cal.: Stanford University Press, 1966.

Pfungst, O. *Clever Hans (the horse of Mr. von Osten): A contribution to experimental, animal, and human psychology.* (Translated by C. L. Rahn.) New York: Holt, 1911.

Pliner, P., Hart, H., Kohl, J., and Saari, D. Compliance without pressure: Some further data on the foot-in-the-door technique. *Journal of Experimental Social Psychology,* 1974, **10**, 17–22.

Pronko, N. H., and Bowles, J. W., Jr. Identification of cola beverages. III. A final study. *Journal of Applied Psychology,* 1949, **33**, 605–608.

Riesen, A. H. Arrested vision. *Scientific American,* 1950 (July), **183**, 16–19.

Robinson, J. P., and Shaver, P. R. *Measures of social psychological attitudes.* Ann Arbor, Mich.: Survey Research Center, Institute for Social Research, 1973.

Roethlisberger, F. J., and Dickson, W. J. *Management and the worker.* Cambridge, Mass.: Harvard University Press, 1939.

Rohrer, J. H., and Edmonson, M. S. (eds.). *The eighth generation: Cultures and personalities of New Orleans Negroes.* New York: Harper, 1960.

Romano, J. L., and Cabianca, W. A. EMG biofeedback training versus systematic desensitization for test anxiety reduction. *Journal of Counseling Psychology,* 1978, **25**, 8–13.

Rosenberg, M. J. When dissonance fails: on eliminating evaluation apprehension from measurement. *Journal of Personality and Social Psychology,* 1965, **1**, 18–42.

Rosenthal, R. *Experimenter effects in behavioral research.* New York: Appleton-Century-Crofts, 1966.

Rosenthal, R., and Jacobson, L. *Pygmalion in the classroom.* New York: Holt, Rinehart and Winston, 1968.

Rosenthal, R., and Lawson, R. A longitudinal study of the effects of experimenter bias on the operant learning of laboratory rats. *Journal of Psychiatric Research,* 1964, **2**, 61–72.

Rosenthal, R., and Rosnow, R. L. *Artifact in behavioral research.* New York: Academic Press, 1969.

Sachs, L., Bean, H., and Morrow, J. Comparison of smoking treatments. *Behavior Therapy,* 1970, **1**, 465–472.

Santschi, F. Le mécanisme d'orientation chez les fourmis. *Revue suisse Zoologie,* 1911, **19**, 117–134.

Shaw, M. E., and Wright, J. M. *Scales for the measurement of attitudes.* New York: McGraw-Hill, 1967.

Siegel, S. *Nonparametric statistics for the behavioral sciences.* New York: McGraw-Hill, 1956.

Singh, S. D. Effect of urban environment on visual curiosity behavior in rhesus monkeys. *Psychonomic Science,* 1968, **11**, 83–84.

Spielberger, D., Gorsuch, R., and Luchene, R. *The STAI manual.* Palo Alto, Cal.: Consulting Psychologists Press, 1970.

Spitzka, E. A. A study of the brains of six eminent scientists and scholars belonging to the American Anthropometric Society. *Transactions American Philosophical Society,* 1907, **21,** 175–308.

Stanton, W. *The leopard's spots: Scientific attitudes towards race in America.* Chicago: University of Chicago Press, 1960.

Terrace, H. S., Petitto, L. A., Sanders, R. J., and Bever, T. G. Can an ape create a sentence? *Science,* 1979, **206,** 891–902.

Tervsky, A., and Kahneman, D. Judgment under uncertainty: Heuristics and biases. *Science,* 1974, **185,** 1124–1131.

Tinbergen, N. The curious behavior of the stickleback. *Scientific American,* 1952 (Dec.), **187,** 22–26.

Twain, M. *Letters from the earth.* B. DeVoto (ed.), Greenwich, Conn.: Fawcett Publications (Crest), 1938.

Wade, N. Does man alone have language? Apes reply in riddles, and a horse says neigh. *Science,* 1980, **208,** 1349–1351.

Webb, E. J., Campbell, D. T., Schwartz, R. D., and Sechrest, L. *Unobtrusive measures: Nonreactive research in the social science.* Chicago: Rand McNally, 1966.

Wender, P. H. *Minimal brain dysfunction in children.* New York: Wiley, 1971.

Werner, J., Minkin, N., Minkin, B., Fixsen, D., Phillips, E., and Wolf, M. Intervention package: An analysis to prepare juvenile delinquents for encounters with police officers. *Criminal Justice and Behavior,* 1975, **2,** 55–84.

Wiesel, T. N., and Hubel, D. H. Effects of visual deprivation on morphology and physiology of cells in the cat's lateral geniculate body. *Journal of Neurophysiology,* 1963, **26,** 978–993.

Wiesel, T. N., and Hubel, D. H. Extent of recovery from the effects of visual deprivation in kittens. *Journal of Neurophysiology,* 1965, **28,** 1060–1072.

Williams, J. E., and Bennett, S. M. The definition of sex stereotypes via the Adjective Check List. *Sex Roles: A Journal of Research,* 1975, **1,** 327.

Winer, B. J. *Statistical principles in experimental design.* New York: McGraw-Hill, 1971.

Woolf, C. M., and Dukepoo, F. C. Hopi Indians, inbreeding and albinism. *Science,* 1969, **164,** 30–37.

Yates, F. *Sampling methods for censuses and surveys.* London: Charles Griffin, 1949.

index

Primary discussion of terms can be found on pages indicated by boldface type.